RUMI AND HIS FRIENDS

RUMI AND HIS FRIENDS

Stories of the Lovers of God

Excerpts from the *Manaqib al-'Arifin*

Selected and Translated
by Camille Adams Helminski
with Susan Blaylock

FONS VITAE

First published in 2013 by
Fons Vitae
49 Mockingbird Valley Drive
Louisville, KY 40207
http://www.fonsvitae.com
Email: fonsvitaeky@aol.com

Library of Congress Control Number: 2013939290
ISBN 978-1887752-88-6

Printed in Canada

Cover image: copyright© The Metropolitan Museum of Art. Image source: Art Resource, NY. Detail section of "Zahhak Is Told His Fate": From the *Shahnama* (*Book of Kings*), ca. 1523–24, Attributed to Sultan Muhammad (Iranian), Iran, Tabriz. Colors, ink, silver, and gold on paper (1970.301.4) The "garden detail" depicted is painted in the Turkman style practiced in Tabriz.

Contents

Preface

The Seeds That Keep Blooming

Sultan Bahauddin Walad told us one day:

> My father (Mevlana Rumi) said, "O Bahauddin, when the seed of my teaching has taken root in your heart, you will understand—reflect deeply on my teaching and really try to absorb it and if you do, felicity will be yours. Know that the body of the prophets, the saints, and their friends will never perish. A seed thrown into the earth may appear to die and disappear, however, at the end of a few days it comes to life and grows into a flourishing tree. In a similar way the body of the prophets and the saints will also come to life again."
>
> He was absorbed in the mystery described in the Qur'an [51:21]: *Have you not looked within?*
>
> There is nothing in the world that exists outside yourself;
> look into the depths of your being for that which you desire.[1]

*****

Shamsuddin Ahmad, otherwise known as Aflaki, was the author of the collection of stories of the founders of the Mevlevi order of dervishes—the followers of the mystic path opened by the example and being of Mevlana Jalaluddin Rumi who have become better known around the world as the "whirling dervishes" due to their majestic "whirling ceremony," the "sema" or *mukabele* (the "meeting face to Face" with the Divine). Frequently within the anecdotes recorded by Aflaki he notes semas spontaneously taking place, some lasting for many days in exaltation. Awareness of the Divine in each human being and within all of creation is a part of the practice of those who follow this mystic path—as it is said in the Holy Qur'an: *Wherever you turn, there is the Face of God* [*Surah al-Baqarah* 2:115]. And as Rumi's father, the Great Master Bahauddin Walad once said, "One can see the Creator in every created object

1. See Selection #251 of this volume.

and contemplate the Light of Truth in every particle." Within the sema ceremony, as it was established by the son of Mevlana[2] and his descendents and representatives of the order, the dervishes continually bow, as they move around the traditionally circular sema hall, each time that they step across the invisible equator line, the "*hatti istifa*," which signifies the threshold between the seen and the Unseen world. In traversing these stories recorded by Aflaki, we come to recognize how for Mevlana and his companions the Mysteries of the Unseen are continually being revealed *on the farthest horizons and within ourselves* [41:53]—may our eyes and hearts become capable of seeing more fully.

Aflaki wrote in Persian, and his work is called *Manaqib al-'Arifin*, or "The deeds or 'feats' of the Mystic Knowers, the 'knowers (*arifin*) of God'." The title of *Kashef al-asrar wa-matla' al-anwar*, "the unveiler of mysteries and ascent of lights" is attributed to him by the manuscript which served as a guide to the present translation. It was long ago that a dear friend first made us aware of the *Manaqib* and shared a copy with us. We wish to extend our sincere thanks to Susan Kovner for that introduction and also to Susan Blaylock who, many years ago, worked with the translation with us. Most of all, we wish to express our gratitude to our shaikh, Suleyman Dede, whose example and being elucidated for us many of the qualities we discovered in this volume of stories of Mevlana, and, also, all the elders of the tradition throughout the centuries who have carried the teachings of the beautiful *adab* (courtesy) of Mevlana and those around him.

The *Manaqib al-'Arifin* was begun in 718 A.H. (1318 C.E.) and finished in 754. It was written at the request of the then Master of the Order, Chelebi Jalaluddin Amir 'Arif, Afalki's spiritual guide, and

---

2. "Mevlana" means "our master," "our protector." It was used as a title of respect and appreciation in the world in which Jalaluddin Rumi lived. After Mevlana Jalaluddin Rumi became the tremendous light among humanity that he became, now when it is spoken, most people would understand it to be referring to the renowned Master of the Heart, "Mevlana" Jalaluddin Rumi. Throughout this text, when the term "Mevlana" is used, it refers to him; sometimes it is also used in translation as "our Master" in the text. "The Great Master" refers to his father, Bahauddin Walad of Balkh. It was Mevlana's son, Sultan Walad (also named "Bahauddin Walad," after Mevlana's father, who formally established the "Mevlevi order" after the passing of Mevlana.

grandson of Mevlana Jalaluddin Rumi,[3] who, after his father Sultan Walad, assisted in further formulating the practices of the order. The *Manaqib* was based on oral accounts given by those who were associated with the order during the early years of its formation, and is divided into ten chapters devoted to the biographies of the following:

1) Bahauddin Walad (d. 1231 C.E.), the father of Jalaluddin Rumi and his first teacher;

2) Burhanuddin at-Tirmidhi (d. 1244 C.E.), disciple of Bahauddin Walad and early teacher of "Mevlana" before the connection with Shams of Tabriz;

3) "Mevlana" Jalaluddin Rumi (b. September 30, 1207–d. December 17, 1273 C.E.) (This section comprises more than half of the manuscript);

4) Shams (the Sun) of Tabriz (d. 1247 C.E.), beloved spiritual friend and mentor of Mevlana;

5) Salahuddin Feridun (d. 1258 C.E.) otherwise known as Zarkub, "the Goldsmith," also trained by Burhanuddin and attendant at gatherings with Shams of Tabriz, the closest disciple and companion of Mevlana after the disappearance of Shams;

6) Husamuddin bin Akhi Turk (d. 1284 C.E.), the devoted disciple of Mevlana who transcribed his masterwork, the *Mathnawi* and the first "Shaikh" of the order after Mevlana's passing;

---

3. Whenever one is attempting to render into English names and words from Arabic, Persian, or Turkish, all of which languages were in currency at the time of Rumi and were used by him (the daily language of the era was Turkish, the scientific language and that of the religious scholars was Arabic, while Persian was the literary language), one must make choices as to the most appropriate way to render the spelling. We have chosen to keep the more Turkish manner of spelling "Mevlana" rather than the more Persian transliteration of "Mowlana/ Mowlawi" or the more Arabic of "Mawlana/Mawlawi," since Rumi rests in Konya in what is now Turkey and our awareness of the Mevlevi tradition has been predominantly through spiritual masters of Turkey. He was born in Balkh in what is now Afghanistan, wrote in classical Persian with an Afghani inflection of meaning, and also in Arabic, the language of the Qur'an and the *hadith* (sayings of the Prophet Muhammad) in which he was so well-versed, and also the vernacular Turkish of the community where he eventually settled in Konya, the land of the Seljuk Turks, known as Rum (Anatolia or "Asia Minor"), since it had been under the rule of the Romans. From this place his name emerged: Mevlana (our Master) Jalaluddin (Majesty of the Religion) Rumi (of the land of Rum). In general, we have attempted to simplify the transliteration for the ease of the reader.

7) Sultan Bahauddin Walad (b. 1226; d. 11-11, 1312 C.E.), the beloved son of Jalaluddin Rumi, who married Fatima, the daughter of Salahuddin Zarkub, and further established the Mevlevi Order;

8) Jalaluddin 'Arif (d. 1320 C.E.), also known as Chelebi Amir 'Arif, eldest son of Fatima and Sultan Walad and first successor, the spiritual guide of Aflaki who encouraged him to compile the *Manaqib*;

9) Shamsuddin Amir 'Abid (d. 1338), another son[4] and successor of Sultan Bahauddin Walad after Jalaluddin 'Arif;

10) Descendants of the above.

The text upon which this work is based was a three hundred and one page manuscript in Persian script. It was transcribed at the end of the month of Rabi' in 1017 A.H. (July, 1608 C.E.) by the dervish 'Othman. The Bibliothèque Nationale of France has several manuscripts of the work, the oldest of which was copied in 964 (1556) in old Persian script; two examples are found in the British Museum, and one in the library in Vienna.

Within the sections of the *Manaqib*, the anecdotes include stories of various mystic phenomena—the foretelling of the future, dreams, second sight, divination of the hidden, thought transmission, lights surrounding a human being or a monument, doors opening by themselves, bilocation, or the gift of being in several places at the same time, indifference to physical cold or heat, healing of the sick, control of events from a distance, alchemical transformations, communication from the Beyond, theophanies—many include bursts of related poetry of Rumi, some added by Aflaki. We have chosen samplings of each, some of which we have shortened to include the essential pith of the anecdote. Approximately one half of the original manuscript material is included here—we have especially chosen anecdotes that illuminate for us some of the family history and provide a context for the unfolding of the teachings of Mevlana ("Our Master") Jalaluddin Rumi.

4. Shamsuddin Amir 'Abid was the son of Sultan Walad and Nusrat Khatun (whose union, according to Aflaki, Fatima had foretold during a life-threatening illness Sultan Walad endured), 'Arif Chelebi's half-brother, who became the Chelebi (holder of the lineage) after him.

A Brief Family History

We learn from the noble Friends of the Way (May God increase their numbers until Resurrection Day) that Bahauddin Walad, the Sultan ul-Ulama, father of Mevlana Jalaluddin Rumi, had two sons and a daughter. The older of the boys was named 'Alauddin Muhammad. Muhammad Jalaluddin, who was to become known as "Mevlana," was the youngest.

It was his grandmother, the princess of Khorasan, Malika-i Jihan Amatullah Sultan, who first lit the spark of inquiry in Rumi's father, Bahauddin Walad. It was under her care (Bahauddin's father died when he was two years old) that he grew to be the "Sultan of the learned" and a great spiritual light for his world. Mevlana's mother, Mu'mine Khatun, a devout and saintly lady, was very dear to him. Mu'mine Khatun was the beautiful daughter of Rukhnuddin, the governor of Balkh in what is now Afghanistan.

As the threat of the Mongol hordes approached, when Mevlana was about five years old, his father and mother and he and his older brother together with loyal students of his father and extended households all set out together to emigrate from Balkh. His sister, Fatima Khatun, having already married, chose instead to settle with her husband in her native country. She came to be known as one of the wisest women of her time and was often consulted on legal matters.

The caravan of family and friends journeyed to Mecca and Damascus and then after some years passed, heading north, came to rest in Laranda (Karaman) where they remained for almost seven years. Just as Bahauddin Walad was about to move his family to Konya where he had been invited to teach by Sultan 'Alauddin Kaykubad, Mu'mine Khatun passed away. Her tomb remains in Karaman as a place of pilgrimage for many of the women of Anatolia.

Aflaki notes that according to Sayyid Burhanuddin, Bahauddin said of his son, Jalaluddin:

> My son, the great master, is of noble lineage, and his sanctity is accompanied by nobility. His grandmother was the daughter of Shams al-A'imme Sarakhsi, who was a *sharif* (descendent of the Prophet Muhammad). On his mother's side he was descended from the Commander of the Faithful, 'Ali, (May God bless his countenance) and on his father's side from Abu Bakr i-Siddiq (May God be pleased with him). My mother was the daughter

> of the Kharazm-shah, the sovereign of Balkh; and the mother of my grandfather, Ahmad Khatibi,[5] was also the daughter of a King of Balkh, Ibrahim Adham.[6] Our intention in citing this genealogy is not to boast, but to inform the genealogists that this lineage consists of monarchs of the world of appearances as well as of the spiritual world.[7]

Mevlana Jalaluddin (May God sanctify his secret) was married in Karaman to Gevher Khatun, "Mistress of the Life Beyond," daughter of Khwaja Sharifuddin Lala of Samarkand, whose family had traveled from Balkh with the Sultan ul-Ulama. Mevlana and Gevher Khatun had two sons. The oldest was called Bahauddin Muhammad Walad, after his grandfather, and the younger, 'Alauddin Muhammad. Not long thereafter, Gevher Khatun passed away, shortly after the passing of Mevlana's own mother, Mumine Khatun. Bahauddin Walad then moved the family to Konya at the invitation of Sultan 'Alauddin Kaykubad, arriving there on May 3, 1228.

Some time after Gevher Khatun's death and the family's relocation to Konya in "Rum" (Anatolia), Mevlana married Kira Khatun of Konya, who gave birth to Meleke Khatun and Chelebi Amir 'Alim

5. See section #1-3 of this volume.

6. The story of Ibrahim Adham [d. 777] is told in the *Mathnawi* as well as in the *Maqalat* of Shams; see *Rumi's Sun, the Teachings of Shams of Tabriz,* translated by Refik Algan and Camille Adams Helminski, Morning Light Press, 2008, p. 18:

> Before he gave up the kingdom of Balkh, the king, Ibrahim Adham, was continually giving away his possessions and tiring his body through ascetic practices and vigils. "What must I do?" he would ask, "so that I might find an openness of heart within myself?"
>
> ... On this way, God has granted new life to those who have sacrificed themselves until their livers were torn to shreds. Some people's stomachs have filled with blood; when God kills them in this world, they give up all their possessions, properties, and all attachments to self or others, and just like Ibrahim Adham they reach another life.
>
> Mevlana was looking for the path of Truth. After all, someone who falls in love with a woman or a man turns away from his or her shop or business. And if someone were to say, "They're going to hang you," to such a person, "So what, hang me," he or she would answer. The lover has no fear for his life; possessions and properties no longer have value for him either. He or she would willingly die for such an ephemeral darling—they will both be buried beneath the earth. Instead, be the lover of the Pure One who has no beginning nor end, and who is pure of any kind of incompleteness—love Him, because it is He who is Everliving.

7. *Menaqib al-Arifin*, #81.

(also known as Muzaffaruddin Amir 'Alim). Mevlana's daughter, whose formal name was Meleke Khatun, was better known as *Efendi-poulo* or "Daughter of the Master." Mevlana's eldest son, Sultan Walad, was deeply devoted to his father and almost inseparable from him, sitting beside him at most gatherings. Upon seeing them together, many people thought that they were brothers.

When Sultan Walad was eighteen, Mevlana arranged for him to marry Fatima Khatun, the refined and deeply spiritual daughter of Shaikh Salahuddin who had grown up at the feet of Mevlana and whom he, himself, had taught to read and write. Together, she and Sultan Walad had three children: one son, Chelebi Jalaluddin Amir 'Arif, and two daughters. The oldest of the daughters was named Mutahhara Khatun and the younger, Sharaf Khatun. Mevlana called the elder "'Abida" (the Adoring Devoted One), and the younger, "'Arifa" (the Knowing, Wise One). Both were holy women who could perform miracles, and the majority of women in Asia Minor looked to them for guidance and became their disciples.[8]

Even in the 1200's there were premonitions as to the world-wide dissemination of Mevlana's verses and teachings through his descendents and companions and followers, lovers of the Way, as you will witness as you make the journey through this volume. His masterwork, the *Mathnawi*, six volumes of 26,000 verses filled with teaching stories and flights of mystical inspiration that illuminate the Oneness of the Divine; his *Divan-e Shams-i Tabrizi*, a collection of 2000 quatrains and about 3250 *ghazals* (longer lyric poems, which though composed by Mevlana he completed as though written by Shams of Tabriz—hence the title of the work); and his *Fihi ma Fihi* (a transcription of some of Mevlana's discourses) continue to be read and studied by countless people today. As Aflaki relates in anecdote number 305 of the *Manaqib*:

> One day, Shamsuddin, the professor's son, was sleeping in his dervish cell and, out of forgetfulness or negligence, had placed the *Mathnawi* behind his back.
>
> Suddenly, Mevlana entered and saw the book there: "Our words—have they come only to end up behind your back? By God, by God, from the place where the sun rises to where it sets this meaning will take hold and will become known in all

8. For further descendents, please see http://www.mevlana.net/family_tree.html.

> regions. There will be no gathering where it will not be recited, even in the churches and temples; all the nations of the world will don the garments of these words and will delight in them."

The words of Rumi have indeed been translated into the languages of every continent, and countless people world-wide continue to delight in his words. More and more find spiritual sustenance in his words and his example as to how to live a truly human life as a spiritual being inspired by Divine Love.

We hope this selection from the *Manaqib* will assist in illuminating hearts, providing a more substantial glimpse into the environment and atmosphere in which Mevlana lived and taught. May God forgive us for any errors. Numerous accounts included here mention the power of Mevlana's glance (*nazar*); it is often through just such a glance from a beneficent one that the seeker is transformed.

Many of the accounts shared by Aflaki, which are not always presented in chronological order, end with notation of numerous people present in the cited incident becoming disciples of Mevlana. Yet Mevlana was not calling people to his side to join a spiritual club, but rather calling them into the experience of the Divine Abundance and Beauty such that the rough edges of selfhood might soften and the luminous inner Spirit of each being might shine, illuminating the enveloping Oneness of God. His life was as he said of his *Mathnawi*, "a shop of Oneness"; anything you find within it is just in service to the elucidation of that Supreme Oneness by which we are held and through which we breathe.

From an early age, Rumi was deeply devoted to God and throughout his life shared the nourishing inspiration that he received, as it says in the Qur'an: *Spend on others of the sustenance provided to you by God.* [2:3] *And God grants sustenance to whom He wills, beyond all reckoning* [3:37].

As Aflaki relates in section 82 of this volume, "A Grateful Servant":

> One day, when Mevlana was seven years old, during the early morning prayer, he was absorbed in reciting the chapter in the Qur'an that begins: *Truly, we have bestowed upon you the source of abundance (kawthar)* [108:1].
>
> "I was calling to God," said Jalaluddin, "when all of a sud-

den, in His Infinite Mercy, He revealed Himself to me and I lost consciousness. When I came to, I heard a mysterious voice that said, 'O Jalaluddin, in Our Infinite Majesty, I order you to cease your striving, because from now on you will be immersed in contemplation.'

"To show my gratitude, I have made every effort possible on the spiritual path and hope that it might be said of me, *Behold, he was a most grateful servant of Ours!* [17:3]. I strive, burning, so that I might enable my companions to reach a beauty and perfection in ecstasy.

> My heart and my soul, in the world of witnessing
> have become as thin as a thread,
> so that the end of the thread reveals itself to me.
> We have traveled difficult roads to their very end,
> and so made the road easier for others."

As Aflaki reflects at the end of his preface to the *Manaqib al-Arifin*:

> *And praise be to God who has guided us to this. Had God not guided us, we would surely not have been guided* [7:43]. And it is God who gives success to complete it by exercising His universal generosity and beneficence.

Camille Adams Helminski
al-faqira al Mevlevi

PART ONE

The Early Days

Stories of Mevlana's father, Sultan ul-Ulama Bahauddin Walad, and Sayyid Burhanuddin as told by Sultan Walad (Mevlana's eldest son), and others.

Chapter I
Bahauddin Walad

The deeds of our Great Master, Bahauddin Muhammad, the son of Al-Husayn, son of Ahmad, Al-Khatibi, Al-Balkhi, Al Bakri (May God be pleased with him and with his ancestors and descendents in this beautiful lineage).

Dreams of Union [1-3]

The transmitters of the tradition related:

'Alauddin Muhammad Kharazm-shah, the sovereign of Khorasan and the paternal uncle of Jalaluddin Muhammad Kharazm-shah, was a renowned and respected monarch. He had a daughter whose beauty was without equal.

"In your capital of Balkh," his minister told him, "lives a man called Jalaluddin Husayn Khatibi who is a descendant of Abu Bakr, the Sincere."

That same night, this saint, Husayn Khatibi, saw our Prophet (Peace and blessings upon him) in a dream—he said, "Marry the daughter of the Sovereign of Khorasan."

And, as Divine fate would have it, also on the same night, the sultan, the vizier, and the princess all saw the Prophet (Peace and blessings upon him) in their dreams, and he told them: "Give the Princess to Husayn Khatibi in marriage, because we have saved him for her, and from now on she is his."

Sultan of the Wise [4-8]

Nine months after their marriage, Bahauddin Walad was born. When he was two years old, his father, that great mystic, passed into the Unseen. His mother introduced him to the library of his father and began his education.

In Balkh one night, three hundred religious leaders each beheld the Prophet Muhammad in a dream, and he told them to address Bahauddin Walad as the Sultan of the Scholars (*Sultan ul-ulama*). From then on in Khorasan, this was his title, and they all became his disciples. However, jealousies arose among the other spiritual leaders and jurists, Fakhruddin Razi in particular, who pushed the sultan to challenge him.

Listening to the Call [9]

Bahauddin said, "Send my greetings to the Sultan. Tell him that the power and glory of this world belongs to rulers such as he. I am just a poor and simple dervish. What use could I make of his empire? It is we who, with contented hearts, should go into exile and leave the Sultan in peace.

> Someone whose soul beats the drum of 'Poverty is my pride,'[1]
> what concern could he have for a crown, a throne, and a flag?"

Then he told his followers and companions, "Friends, the time has come to leave. Let us prepare."

Traveling to God [14]

The night before Bahauddin and his entourage would arrive in a town, the inhabitants would see the Prophet (May peace and blessings be upon him) in their dreams, telling them, "Go and welcome this renowned person with full honor and open hearts." As the Friend of God drew near, the people would go out to meet him, even as far as a day's march, and would greet him with great enthusiasm.

After many adventures, they finally arrived in Baghdad. "Who are you and where do you come from?" the guards of the city asked.

Bahauddin leaned out of the palanquin and answered, "We are travelling from God to God; and *there is no power and strength but with God.* We have come from the Placeless and are returning to the Placeless."

The guards were astonished and ran to report to the caliph that a large company of wise men and religious scholars had arrived from Khorasan. He was very surprised and immediately sent

---

1. "Poverty is my pride" is a saying (*hadith*) of the Prophet Muhammad, who followed the way of poverty, always ready to give away whatever came to him, and found in that his sustenance. Hence dervishes are called "*faqir*" (poor one) as those who emulate the Prophet's habit and trust (*tawwakul*) in the provision from Heaven [51:22].

for the great Shaikh, Shihabuddin Suhrawardi (May the Mercy of God be with him).

The Shaikh told the Caliph, "No one else but Bahauddin Walad al-Balkhi could express himself with such reverence, so eloquently."

A Royal Welcome for the Devoted [25]

Fakhruddin of Erzinjan (May the Mercy of God be upon him) was a monarch of illumined heart and one of the devoted. He had faith in and great respect for the Friends of God.[2] His gentle and virtuous wife, Asmati Khatun, whose holiness was renowned, knew through communication with the Unseen Realms that the blessed *Qutb* was approaching their city. She immediately mounted her horse and set off in search of him.

When Fakhruddin's servants informed him of his wife's departure, he decided to follow her and set off, accompanied by several horsemen. They caught up with Bahauddin Walad near Aqshehir, which is near Erzinjan, dismounted, and prostrated themselves in front of him. The saint greeted them with great affection and received both of them as disciples.

King Fakhruddin begged Bahauddin to return to Erzinjan with them.

Bahauddin said, "If you are my disciples and my friends, build a *medresse* (school) for me in this village, so that I can reside there a while."

They built a medresse for him in the village of Aqshehir near Erzinjan, and for four years the saint taught publicly under the protection of that Queen of the World.

The Joining of Beauties [26]

When Fakhruddin and Asmati Khatun passed into the Mercy of God Most High, Bahauddin Walad made his way to Laranda, one of the dependencies of Konya, where Amir Musa was the prefect and

2. *Awliya* (Friends of God) may also be translated occasionally in this volume as simply "saints." The dervish companions are referred to as "Friends." Similarly, the word *'arif* (knower) may be sometimes translated as 'knower of God' or as 'mystic' as that is what is implied, acknowledging that the true knowledge is knowledge of Divine Reality (*al-Haqq*), and that those who come into intimacy with God, the Ultmate Reality, and become "Friends of God" are the saints and protectors of this earthly realm.

governor. Amir Musa was a Turk, a courageous and sincere man with a pure heart. When he discovered that such an eminent and saintly person was arriving from Khorasan, he set out on foot to welcome him, along with his soldiers and the people of Laranda. He invited the saint to stay at his palace, but Bahauddin refused and asked instead to be lodged in a medresse. The governor ordered a medresse to be built in the center of the town, where the Friend of God lived for about seven years.

When our Master Jalaluddin reached the age of maturity, it was arranged that he would marry the daughter of Khwaja Sharifuddin Lala of Samarkand, a well-respected man of noble origin and an influential merchant. His daughter, Gevher Khatun, was extremely beautiful and gracious, without equal in beauty or perfection. They had a magnificent wedding in 623 (1226 C.E.). Sultan Walad and 'Alauddin Chelebi were their sons, born from this marriage.

When Sultan Walad (May God sanctify his tomb) came with his father to gatherings, most of the people present thought that they were brothers. At the time of his marriage, Mevlana had been eighteen years old. At gatherings Sultan Walad always sat beside his father.

Power from Beyond [29]

When Amir Musa conveyed the message of invitation to Konya from Sultan 'Alauddin, Bahauddin set off with his children and companions. When news of the Saint's arrival reached the Sultan, he gathered the scholars and inhabitants of the city and went out to meet him.

He got off his horse long before he could see the shaikh and waited to kiss his knee, to demonstrate his respect. He wanted to take our Great Master's hand, but he extended his staff instead. When the Sultan felt the power of Bahauddin's awesome presence, he began to tremble:

> "It's awe of God, not of his creatures,
> not awe of the man in this rough robe.
> It's the partridge's awe of the falcon,
> a horsefly could never cause such awe."

Lodging with the Infinite [30]

The Sultan wanted to invite him to the palace, but our Great Master declined the invitation and answered that a medresse would be more appropriate for him, since he was an imam. He went on to say that dervishes were to be found in dergahs, amirs in palaces, merchants in caravanserais, the debauched in lodges, and foreigners in tents. He accepted quarters in the Altunpa Medresse, which was the only one then in Konya. The walls of the city had not yet been built. As was the custom of that time, the nobility sent him all sorts of gifts of welcome, but he refused to accept anything.

The Knowledge of Love [39]

One day, when Mevlana's father, Bahauddin, the Sultan of the Learned, was teaching, Jamaluddin Hasiri began arguing about theology. . . . The Sultan of the Learned spoke strongly to him: "What a difference there is between a pebble and a pearl! What would you do if nothing remained of these heavy tomes of which you are enamored? Where would you turn if there were no medresse, no scholarly pulpit? What text would you use and what lessons would you give?

"Strive with every effort possible to commit to memory one page of the heart's subtle text, and remember that until the end of time. This is the knowledge of Love that will sustain you.

O master of jurisprudence, for the love of God,
gain the knowledge of the heart,
for what will remain of your laws and decrees when you die?"

Contemplating the Light of Truth [40]

Our master, Mevlana Jalaluddin (May God preserve his power) paid homage to his father at a gathering of devoted friends with these words:

One Friday, at a gathering in Balkh, Bahauddin Walad was speaking about Resurrection Day, and how on that day God will reward good works and good character and shower blessings on the faithful by the presence of *houris*[3] in the golden pavilions of Paradise. Just then, an old man, who had been seated, bent over, in a corner of the mosque, jumped up and said, "O Imam of Muslims, let us concentrate on the traditions today in this world. Let us leave for tomorrow the contemplation of the faces of the *houris*. What good would it do to see them?"

Our Master answered, "Dear one, if I have spoken of *houris* and golden pavilions, it is because of the weakness of the intelligence of the average person; the goal is to behold the Beloved, and that vision has all sorts of names. One can see the Creator in every created object and contemplate the Light of Truth in every particle."

Communing with the Beloved [49]

One day, Sultan Walad (May God Bless his Tomb) said, "My grandfather, Bahauddin, lived to be eighty-five years old. He would often walk in the cemeteries and pray in this way: 'O God, make us content and enable us to bear burdens.' . . . He would tell us, 'During the day, visit the graves of the dead and at night, contemplate the brilliant stars in the heavens, following the custom and counsel of the Prophet, peace and blessings upon him, so that you might behold wonders.' "

The Splendor of God's Light [50]

As a result of his intense asceticism Bahauddin had very few teeth left. He continued to perform vigils at night and to live an exemplary life of study and service during the day. When his disciples questioned him about the rigors of his life he answered, "I do this for my Friends and my children."

One night, an initiate saw Bahauddin in a dream. He had been raised to a very high station—the top of his head touched the foot of God's Throne. The disciple asked, "How have you attained this? How have you reached this rank?"

Bahauddin answered, "The profound inner life and exemplary behavior of my son, Jalaluddin Muhammad, inspires me and fills

3. *Houris,* the radiant pure companions of Paradise, are mentioned in several places in the Qur'an, for instance: *And [with them will be their] companions pure, most beautiful of eye, like unto pearls still hidden in their shells.* [56:22-23]. As the "eye" is "the gateway to the soul," a *'houri'* might be understood as being particularly of "soulful" companionship.

me with great joy. The assembly of prophets, illuminated beings, and Friends of God guide and encourage him on the Path. My soul leaps with joy because of this! He is growing older, and if Divine Will permits he will attain heights far beyond the manifest world.

> This is the lesson learned by our students.
> But where does the fruit of all our struggles go?
> To a place beyond the idea of place,
> where only the radiant splendor of God's Moon exists—
> a place far from all hypotheses and imaginings—
> Light upon light upon light upon light upon light upon light!"
> [*Mathnawi* VI: 2144-2146]

Merging and Expanding Light [55]

Sultan Walad said, "When I look at the tombs of my grandfather and my father, I see two huge lights which intertwine above them and then, after a few moments, join. This is a sign, as though to say, 'We are united and form only one light.'

> When you see two Friends meet,
> they are at the same time one and six hundred thousand."[4]

In the Shade of the Beloved Friend [56, 57]

[Sultan Walad related the following:]

---

4. See *Mathnawi* II:186-189, *Rumi Daylight*, translated by Camille and Kabir Helminski, Threshold Books, 1994, p.98:

> When you see two Friends meet,
> they are at the same time one and six hundred-thousand.
> Their numbers are like waves
> which the wind has brought into multiplicity.
> The Sun, which is spirit,
> became separated into rays through the windows
> which are bodies.
> When you gaze on the Sun's disk, it is one,
> but one who is screened by his perception
> of bodies is in some doubt.
> Plurality is in the animal spirit;
> the human spirit is one essence.
> Inasmuch as *God sprinkled His light upon them,*
> they are essentially one.
> In Reality, His light never becomes separated.

At the moment of his death, my father said, "O Bahauddin, know that we will all be under the shade of the Great Master on the Day of Resurrection and that, thanks to his intercessions and his grace, we will be in God's presence and He will be merciful to us."

When his father, Bahauddin,[5] left this world, our Master Jalal-uddin Rumi was twenty-four years old. . . . Upon many occasions, in the meetings with the Friends of God, he said, "Our Great Master spent a long while on this earth. For me, the meeting with Shams of Tabriz is essential. Every prophet needs an Abu Bakr, and Jesus also had disciples."

> Every prophet traveling the straight path
> performed miracles and sought companions.

Radiating Light [58]

The Sayyid [Burhanuddin] (May God be Pleased with him) said:

Last night, I saw in a dream that one of the doors of my shaikh Bahauddin's tomb was open. A bright light shone forth out of it, and since there was no obstacle that could block the way, it reached our house. The light shone inside, and I woke up suddenly within it. I cried out in joy and awe, "*La illaha il Allah* (There is no god but God)!" The light grew stronger until it embraced the whole town, and then the entire world. I lost consciousness and no longer knew who I was. The explanation of this dream is that the mysterious light radiated by this family will shine over the whole world and attract Friends of God and disciples from everywhere.

> The light of the human being has covered the East and the West;
> in their astonishment, the heavens bow low.

A Citadel of Charity [59b]

During the days before the walls of Konya had been constructed, the site of Bahauddin's tomb had not yet been chosen. One day, when the Friend of God was out riding on his mule, he arrived at a certain spot, dismounted, and meditated there a while. Then he said, "This will be the place where my tomb will be built, as well as that of my children, my grandchildren, and my successors."

---

5. The father of Mevlana, Bahauddin Walad, after whom Sultan Walad was named, was often referred to as the "Great Master."

When Sultan 'Alauddin had finished the construction of the wall surrounding the city, he asked Bahauddin to tour the walls and inspect his work. Our Great Master said, "This is indeed a fine construction and will protect the city very well against enemy sieges, but how can you protect yourself against the arrows of the prayers of the oppressed which are able to penetrate a hundred thousand towers and can bring down empires? Ask God for help in striving to construct a citadel of charity and justice and to protect yourself with the sincere prayers of well-wishers. That is worth more than a thousand impenetrable fortresses. On this depends the security of the world and the safety of the people."

The Sultan took the guidance of the Shaikh to heart in complete sincerity, and until the end of his days he attempted to act with justice and good-will towards all and thereby attained felicity.

The Return [37]

On a Friday, in the morning, the 18th of Rabi' al-Akhir, in the year 628 (February 23, 1231 C.E.), Bahauddin, the Sultan ul-Ulama, went to be in the presence of Allah, the Almighty, and to take his place in the Kingdom of Divine Mercy and Truth.

> He has left for Paradise and Eternal Life,
> to forever live near God in perfect Truth.
>
> This heavenly peacock who embellishes God's Throne has returned,
> summoned by Heavenly voices and the scent of the Divine.

Chapter II
Sayyid Burhanuddin

The deeds of Burhan-al-Haqq-uddin Al-Husayn at-Tirmidhi, the Master of Mysteries (May God bless his tomb).

Swimming in the Sea of Becoming [61]

Burhanuddin at-Tirmidhi was known in Khorasan, Tirmidh, Bokhara, and other places as the All-knowing Master of Secrets (*Sayyid-i Sirr-dan*); he spoke continuously about the subtle mysteries of this world and the Beyond. When Bahauddin Walad left Balkh, the Sayyid went to Tirmidh and withdrew from the world.

One day, in the morning, on Friday, the 18th of Rabi' al-Akhir, 628 A.H. (February 23, 1231 C.E.), when he had been speaking of the knowledge of God for several days, he cried out and wept copiously, saying, "Alas, my shaikh has left this world for the World of Purity." Those who were present recorded the date and the time, and later when he arrived in the kingdom of Rum,[6] it was verified that this moment was the moment of Bahauddin Walad's passing.

Sayyid Burhanuddin offered the funeral prayers and began the period of mourning, and all the prominent people of Tirmidh joined him in observing the mourning period of forty days. After forty days, he said, "The son of my shaikh, my Jalaluddin Muhammad, is alone and is calling me; it is my duty to go to the land of Rum and to honor him by rubbing my face on the dust of his feet and to enter his service, honoring the sacred trust that has been given to me."

The people of Tirmidh wept at the idea of being abandoned by the Sayyid, who, nevertheless, set out for Konya accompanied by several faithful companions.

A year had passed since the death of the Shaikh when he reached Konya. Mevlana had gone to Laranda. The Sayyid went into

6. The region of Anatolia, or "Asia Minor," was referred to as "Rum," because it had been a part of Roman territory, hence the name of "Rumi (pronounced somewhat like 'roomy' and meaning 'from Rum') became Mevlana's appelation. During Mevlana's time the region was under the rule of the Seljuk Turks.

retreat in the Sanjari mosque for several months and sent a message by two dervishes to Mevlana containing various words of wisdom, and asking him to return right away and to meet him at his father's tomb. . . . When Mevlana read the Sayyid's letter he was overjoyed and, rubbing the letter across his eyes, kissed it, and said:

> "It takes a thousand years for a flower like you
> to bloom on fortune's branch in the garden of certainty.
> Not every era, every alignment of stars, sees one like you.
> Only rarely, at God's command, does one like you appear!"

He returned to Konya immediately and went directly to the Sayyid, who ran out of the mosque to embrace him:

> "We have both learned to swim in the sea of becoming;
> two souls have been sewn together without a seam."

They both fainted, and the companions who were there cried out. Then the Sayyid questioned Jalaluddin on various aspects of knowledge, to which he replied in manifold ways.

The Sayyid praised him, kissed his feet, and said, "You have surpassed your father in theology and religious thought a hundred-fold. He was gifted in the science of words (*qal*) and in the science of states (*hal*). From now on, I advise you to follow in his footsteps in the science of 'hal,' or mystical states, in which he was so adept. This is the transcendent Way of the Prophets and Saints, as the Qur'an says: *We imparted knowledge issuing from Ourselves* [18:65]. I was taught this knowledge by my Shaikh; you are to learn it from me, so that you might be your father's successor in every way, both in the inner and the manifest world, and become like him."

Our Master Jalaluddin Rumi obeyed all of the Sayyid's commands. He took the Sayyid to his own medresse where he was then the Sayyid's devoted servant for nine years. Some say he became his disciple there, while others say that it was in Balkh that the Sayyid took him on as a student, while Bahauddin was still alive. It is also said that the Sayyid had been Jalaluddin's tutor when he was young, often carrying him on his shoulders and walking about with him.

Between Student and Shaikh There Is a Hidden Way [63]

Faithful Friends and pure brethren report that, after having been by his side for a long time, the Sayyid asked Mevlana's permission to go to Kayseri. Mevlana did not want him to leave Konya. The Sayyid's heart was occupied with going, and yet he could not find the opportunity to do so.

One day, a group of dervishes put the Sayyid on a mule and led him off to visit the gardens. As he was riding along, the Sayyid was overwhelmed by the thought of Kayseri, which he saw clearly in the mirror of his mind. Just at that moment, the mule reared up and threw the Sayyid to the ground, and his blessed foot was broken. He cried out and lost consciousness. The Friends transported the Sayyid to the garden of Homamuddin, Sipehsalar. The Sayyid remained silent about the circumstances of the accident, but when his boot was removed, it was clear that his toes had been crushed into small pieces. Mevlana and the Friends broke into tears and were distraught.

"What a bold student, who breaks his shaikh's toes!" said the Sayyid.

Mevlana put his blessed hand on the wounded foot, blew on it gently, and it was immediately healed. He then gave the Sayyid permission to go to Kayseri because he loved that place so much. The Sayyid went to the mountain of 'Ali (May God be pleased with him) and called upon God day and night.

The Grand Minister, Shamsuddin Isfahani, who was the governor of that town, was full of good will for the Sayyid; he rendered him many services, then became his disciple and servant, and received his glance (*nazar*)[7] and loving attention.

Carried by the Wave of Prayer [64]

Sayyid Burhanuddin was asked to perform the duties of imam in the mosque in Kayseri. He would become so lost in contemplation that he could spend the entire day standing up in prayer, then kneeling, and prostrating. Some people could not accompany him through this intensive practice.

7. Numerous accounts included in this volume mention the power of the glance (*nazar*); it is often through just such a glance from a beneficent one that the seeker is transformed. In Turkish there is a phrase: "*söz, göz, öz (word, glance, essence)*"—one may be brought close first through words, then through the glance, and finally through shared essence. This is similar to *'ilm al-yaqin, 'ayn al-yaqin, haqq al-yaqin* (knowledge of certainty, or closeness; vision of certainty; truth of certainty, when the seeker is brought near the Beloved, enfolded in intimacy.)

One day, the Sayyid apologized: "I am overcome by madness, please forgive me. I'm not suited to be an imam—look for an imam who is more reasonable."

The people cried out, "One cycle of prayer (*rakat*) led by you is better than a thousand led by another. We accept your madness."

Eventually though, he gave up his duties as an imam.

Emptying [65]

After the Sayyid had become a disciple of Bahauddin Walad, he acted like a madman living in the desert. He was disturbed by the manifestation of lights, and mortified himself to the point that he wandered with bare feet and head through the forests and mountains for twelve years. He had a little goatskin filled with barley flour. He would make a soup with a few of these grains and subsist only on that. He fasted so much his teeth fell out.

One morning, at dawn, a mysterious voice that came from the Unseen world cried, "From now on, don't torture yourself with such excessive mortifications."

"By Allah," answered the Sayyid, "who sent our Prophet Muhammad (Peace and blessings upon him) to both black and white, to all of humankind, I cannot give up my practices just yet."

God helped him in his efforts, and he attained all that which he had been seeking from the Divine Presence. After attaining intimate Friendship with God (*vilayat*), and the highest degrees of holiness, he was absorbed in inner peace until the end of his dear life.

Medicine from the World Beyond [66]

When he wanted pickles for the gatherings, he would say, "Turnip pickle is beneficial and is the best of all the pickles—one's vision is strengthened by eating raw turnips." The Sayyid was knowledgeable in medicine and the healing arts—he received his wisdom and direction from the World Beyond.

One day, Sahib Isfahani came to pay a visit on the Sayyid. The attendant called out: "The *vizir* has come to visit the *Pir*."[8] The Sayyid came out of his retreat cell and sat at the entrance, and the

8. *Pir* (elder) has the meaning within sufism of "elderly mature one," no matter what one's actual age might be. The one through whose example and being a Way has opened as a mystical path becomes known as the *Pir* of the spiritual order (*tariqah*). While the *vizir* is the representative of the King within this mate-

vizir and the amirs arranged themselves on the ground nearby. The Sayyid revealed such knowledge of the Divine and mysteries of the World Beyond that the vizir fainted, and a great crowd gathered.

He concluded his talk by saying, "*Today, May God forgive you your sins; for He is the Most Merciful of the merciful*! [12:92]." Then he returned to his cell and shut the door firmly. The vizir, Sahib Shamsuddin, thanking him for the great joy he had received, distributed gold to the poor and left weeping and sighing.

A Sacrifice for God [68b]

A noble lady, an Asiya[9] of the age, became a disciple of the Sayyid. One day, teasing him, she asked, "When you were young, you were very strict in your practices and mortifications: why is it that now at the end of your life you no longer fast and miss most of the daily prayers?"

"My child," answered the Sayyid, "I've carried heavy burdens just as a camel does, experienced hardships of one kind and another, and traveled long and difficult roads, and passed through many stations. I've seen the hairs and the skin of my existence fall away; I have become thin, and now it is time to gain a little weight. Now they are feeding us barley in order to fatten us up, so that we might be sacrificed on the day of reunion with God. One never sacrifices thin animals in a sultan's kitchen, only plump ones.

> Understand that I am like the cow of Moses, bestowing life.
> Every part of me brings the resurrection of a free man.
> If a cow rests and is fed,
> it's to fatten it for the sacrifice and the feast."

The noble lady began to cry. She threw herself at the Sayyid's feet and asked his forgiveness.

A Key to Wisdom [70]

Shaikh Salahuddin (May God illuminate his tomb) was one of the Sayyid's disciples. He reports that the Sayyid was continuously

---

rial realm, the *Pir* is acknowledged as the representative of God supported from the Divine realm.

9. Asiya was the wife of pharaoh who adopted the infant Moses, standing firm for Truth and Love in opposition to the command of her husband and king. She is revered in the Qur'an as an exemplar to those who have faith. See *Surah* 66:11.

telling his Friends the following:

"Fasting is the most important of the acts of devotion. Keep yourself hungry, because an empty stomach is a source of wisdom. Prophets and saints have always gained their strength from fasting; it opens the springs of insight, but it must be undertaken by degrees. Nothing helps an ascetic reach his goal faster than fasting, nor wins greater favor in the eye of God. It is one of the keys to the treasures of wisdom."

Mysterious Devotees [71]

Chelebi Amir 'Arif (May God bless him) told us that one day, in Kayseri, the Sayyid was plunged into Divine ecstasy and was drunk with joy. The Mongol army was in the process of pillaging the city, and suddenly a fierce Mongol appeared at the door of the Sayyid's cell with a drawn sword and shouted, "Hey! Who are you?"

The Sayyid replied, "Don't say, 'Hey'! You may have the appearance of a Mongol, but I can see beyond that. I know who you are!"

Immediately, the soldier got down off his horse and bowed to the Sayyid. The mysterious visitor sat for a moment, and then he was gone.

The Companions of states (*hal*) asked the Master about this, and he replied, "He is one of the Elect of God, hidden beneath His domes, concealed in this coat."[10]

Some time later, the soldier came back, put some gold coins in the Sayyid's shoes, bared his head, became his disciple, and departed.

States of Being [72]

The saintly Fatima Khatun,[11] daughter of Shaikh Salahuddin (May the mercy of God be upon her, and on her husband, and her father) related the following:

One day the Sayyid was visiting us, and he said, "I have made

10. This refers to a *Hadith Qudsi*: God says, "My saints are hidden beneath my domes, and no one knows them but Me." (See Section #138 of this volume.)

11. Fatima Khatun, was the daughter of Salahuddin Zarkubi, the goldsmith, close friend of Mevlana and his closest companion after the passing of Shams of Tabriz. She became the wife of Mevlana's son, Sultan Walad and is sometimes referred to as "Kiraga."

a gift of my state (*hal*) to Shaikh Salahuddin and of my words (*qal*) to Mevlana."

He also said, "A human being has three needs in his external conditions to want more than which is excessive. First, an amount of food that is sufficient; second, clothing enough to protect one against the cold and the heat; and third, a position in society that is not slavery."

On the Land and Within the Sea [75]

According to Sultan Walad (May God bless his innermost secret), at a meeting one day, the question was raised: "Does the path to God have an end?"

The Sayyid answered, "The way has an end, but the stations do not. There are two stages in our journey: one stage involves traveling towards God, and the second, within God. The first stage has an end, since it involves passing beyond existence and this lowly world. We are then delivered from our personality and our ego self (*nafs*)—all this has an end and a limit. But when the seeker has reached God, then he is journeying within the knowledge of the Supreme Being, and this has no limits.

> There are traces of footprints in the sand,
> until the footprints become lost in the Sea of nothingness.
> The stations on the fixed earth are the villages,
> the houses, and caravanserais.
> The stations of the ocean, suspended in the waves,
> are held in an infinite space
> and are invisible, unmarked, and nameless."

Sultan Walad told us that Sayyid Burhanuddin, with the enthusiasm of his youth, would stay seated by our Great Master [Bahauddin]'s side, absorbed in his holy presence, and that it was during such a period of forty days that this occurred.

Words from Beyond [75b]

Upon learning of the death of Mevlana's father, Bahauddin, the Sayyid went into mourning for a long while and was overcome with sorrow at the separation. Then one night, he saw the Shaikh in a dream looking at him angrily and saying, "O Burhanuddin, how is it that you aren't paying attention to Mevlana, how can you leave him alone? This isn't appropriate behavior for a tutor and a guardian. What excuse do you have?"

The Sayyid woke up, stunned, and left immediately for Rum to be with Mevlana and to serve him.

Silent Channels from Sea to Sea [77]

The following anecdote was told by Sahib Shamsuddin:

When Shaikh Shihabuddin 'Omar Suhrawardi (May God have mercy upon him) came from Baghdad, the seat of the Caliphate, to the service of the Sultan of Asia Minor (Rum), he went to pay a visit on the Sayyid. When he arrived, the Sayyid was sitting on the ground, completely motionless. The shaikh bowed and sat down at a distance. Not a word was said. Then, after a while, the shaikh got up, weeping, and left.

"You didn't exchange a single word," remarked his disciples. "What does this mean?"

The shaikh replied, "Between mystics who are in a state of ecstasy (*hal*) communication takes place by means of that state, not through words (*qal*).

In the presence of one who sees, silence is golden;
Listen in silence, so that you might be graced with God's mercy [7:204].

Words alone, if they are not linked to ecstasy, have no power to resolve the difficulties of the heart." Sahib Shamsuddin and his Friends continued to question the shaikh: "Tell us more about the Sayyid."

"He is like a foaming ocean," said the shaikh. "His thoughts are like pearls resplendent in the crown of the secrets of the Way of Muhammad. He is both obvious and clear, and at the same time subtle and mysterious, and it is difficult for me to imagine a greater adept, with the possible exception of Mevlana Jalal al-Haqq wa'l Din (May God sanctify his innermost secret)."

Going Home [73]

When the Sayyid's life was drawing to a close, he asked his servant to bring him a jug of hot water. The servant recounts the following story:

When I had heated the water, my Master told me to bolt the

door when I left and to announce in the streets, "The Sayyid, a stranger, has left this world."

I watched to see what the Master would do. He completed his ablutions and prepared to leave this world. He bowed his head and cried out, "How pure the heavens are! Celestial beings are approaching in all their purity—O Lord Most High, You who have entrusted me with a loan, with Your kindness come and receive it back; *You will find me, if God so wills, among those who are patient in adversity* [37:102]." He readied himself to depart and recited these verses:

"O Beloved Friend, receive me, and take my soul;
intoxicate me, and take me beyond the two worlds.
Set my soul on fire, and take everything I might think I own."

He then delivered his soul up to God.

[The Sayyid passed into Truth in Kayseri in 1244 C.E.]

PART TWO

Mevlana Jalaluddin Rumi and Shams of Tabriz

Chapter III
Mevlana Jalaluddin Rumi

Our Master, Mevlana Muhammad Jalaluddin Balkhi ar-Rumi (May God bless us by means of his precious innermost secret), was born in Balkh, on the 6th of Rabi' al-Awwal 604 A.H. (September 30, 1207 C.E.).

Visitors from the Unseen [78]

It is recounted by the collectors of the mysteries who were versed in the Truth that at the age of five, Mevlana was so agitated at times that the disciples of the Sultan of the Wise[12] would take him to sit in their midst. He was seeing the spiritual beings of the Unseen world who acted as messengers, from among the angels, the pious jinns and holy men—the veiled ones of the heavenly mansions concealed by the domes of God. Just as the Prophet (Peace and blessings upon him) saw the archangels at the beginning of his mission, as Mary saw the Angel Gabriel, as Lot and Abraham saw the four angels, Mevlana would see these holy messengers.

The Sultan ul-Ulama was aware of his son's gift and to reassure him said, "These are beings from the mysterious World of the Beyond, and they come with grace to you. They bring messages and gifts from the Unseen, and it is in accordance with the tradition."

Journeys to Heaven [79-80]

Shaikh Badruddin Yawash Naqqash al-Mevlevi told us the following:

Sultan Walad said he found in Bahauddin's blessed writing an account of how Jalaluddin Muhammad, at the age of six, used to recite the Qur'an on the terraced roof of the house. The sons of the notables of Balkh would come every Friday and stay until it was time for the prayers. Upon one occasion, one of the little boys said to another, "Watch while I jump from this terrace to that roof over

12. "Sultan of the Wise" (*Sultan ul-Ulama*) refers to Mevlana's father, Bahauddin Walad.

there—I bet I can do it."

Mevlana, smiling, answered gently, "O my brothers, it's a shame that a human being, who is so honored by the Qur'an, should occupy himself with such tricks worthy of a dog, a cat, or some other animal. Instead, look inside yourself for the spiritual strength necessary, and we will fly to Heaven and visit Eternity."

In that moment, Jalaluddin vanished from the group. The children became afraid and began to cry out. But then in an instant, he was back again, and his blessed body had been transformed. The children fell to his feet and became his disciples.

He said, "As I was talking to you, beings dressed in green transported me to Heaven and showed me the marvels of the spiritual world. When your cries reached my ears, they brought me back."

At the time, he would only break his fast once every three or four days or, at times, every seven days.

A Grateful Servant [82]

One day, when Mevlana was seven years old, during the early morning prayer, he was absorbed in reciting the chapter in the Qur'an that begins: *Truly, we have bestowed upon you the source of abundance (kawthar)* [108:1].

"I was calling to God," said Jalaluddin, "when all of a sudden, in His Infinite Mercy, He revealed Himself to me and I lost consciousness. When I came to, I heard a mysterious voice that said, 'O Jalaluddin, in Our Infinite Majesty, I order you to cease your striving, because from now on you will be immersed in contemplation.'

"To show my gratitude, I have made every effort possible on the spiritual path and hope that it might be said of me, '*Behold, he was a most grateful servant of Ours!* [17:3].' I strive, burning, so that I might enable my companions to reach a beauty and perfection in ecstasy.

My heart and my soul, in the world of witnessing
have become as thin as a thread,
so that the end of the thread reveals itself to me.
We have traveled difficult roads to their very end,
and so made the road easier for others."

Witnessing the Ocean of Eternity [83; 89-90]

The second year after the death of his father, Bahauddin, Mevlana left for Syria in order to continue his studies and perfect himself in the religious sciences; he went to Aleppo, then to Damascus. . . .

One day, Mevlana was walking in the grand bazaar in Damascus. He suddenly saw a strange individual dressed in black felt, wearing a black hat on his head. He approached our Master, kissed his hand, and said, "You who are as skilled in the trade of ideas as a money-changer is with coins, catch me!"

It was Shamsuddin Tabrizi. Our Master tried to engage this stranger in conversation, but he vanished into the crowd.

Shortly after, our Master left for Rum. When he arrived in Kayseri, the wise men and mystics welcomed him warmly and with great honor. Sahib-i Isfahani would have liked him to stay at his palace, but Sayyid Burhanuddin objected, saying that our Great Master (Mevlana's father) usually stayed at a medresse.

When Mevlana had retreated from the crowds, in friendship, the Sayyid said, "Praise be to God. You have surpassed your father in the exoteric sciences; now, it is my wish that you immerse yourself in the esoteric sciences, so that you will one day find the pearl of transcendence. I hope that you might go into retreat under my supervision." When Mevlana accepted, he encouraged him to make a retreat for seven days.

Mevlana responded, "That's not long enough—let it be forty days."

The Sayyid found a suitable place for the retreat, and once our Master was installed, plastered up the door. He had nothing but a jug of water with which to perform his ablutions and a few slices of barley bread.

When the forty days was up, the Sayyid opened the door of the cell. When he entered, he saw our Master in a state of perfect peaceful presence (*huzur*), lost in contemplation of the World Beyond and the wonders of Heaven, beyond space and time. He was absorbed in the mystery described in the Qur'an, *Have you not looked within*? [51:21].

There is nothing in the world that exists outside yourself;
look into the depths of your being for that which you desire.

Jalaluddin stopped his meditation for a moment but did not look at the Sayyid, who quietly closed the door again and left him for another forty-day period. When the Sayyid returned, he saw that our Master was standing in prayer and supplication, and that tears were flowing from his blessed eyes like two springs (55:50).[13] Once again, he paid no attention to the Sayyid, who left, closing the door firmly. At the end of the third forty-day period, the Sayyid broke open the door of the cell, and Mevlana emerged from his retreat. The look in his eyes was that of a saint drunk with Divine Love from the Ocean of Eternity, and on his lips was a beatific smile.

In the depth of his eyes, we can see the Beloved Face of the Friend.

The Sayyid prostrated himself in gratitude and respect. He wept and took our Master in his arms, kissing him, and saying, "In all the traditional and rational sciences, you were unequalled, but now you are renowned among the prophets and Friends of God as an adept versed in the esoteric mysteries as well, and in the unveilings of spirit, and in the vision of hidden things. All the shaikhs and wise men who have gone before have endured bewildering sorrow so that they might be blessed by meeting such a one as you and learn the Way to the Divine assembly. *Praise be to God in this world and in the next* that I, poor creature that I am, have had the sublime good fortune to meet you. Now, *in the Name of God*, set out, and awaken human souls to a new life and to infinite mercy. Lead those poor unfortunates who are lost in the world of appearances in the direction of Truth and Love."

It was shortly after Mevlana's return to Konya, after the passing of Sayyid Burhanuddin, that our Master Shamsuddin Tabrizi (May God preserve his innermost secret) appeared for the second time on the 26th Jumada al-Akhar 642 A.H. (November 29, 1244 C.E.).

Shams, the Flyer [91]

Our Master Shamsuddin Tabrizi (May God glorify his remembrance) was the disciple of Shaikh Abu Bakr, otherwise known as *Zanbil-baf* (the basket-weaver), a spiritual teacher of a high degree of sanctity and clarity of heart. Shamsuddin was not satisfied with the station he had reached in his journey, and yearned to surpass his teacher, pass through further degrees, and reach a degree of complete perfection. He set off to journey throughout the world and wandered, distraught, so far and wide that he was given the name of "the Flying Shams." One night in his prayers and supplications, plunged in

13. This refers to the two springs of Paradise granted to those who stand in awe of their Sustainer, mentioned in *Surah ar-Rahman* (the Infinitely Compassionate), *surah* 55 which has the refrain, "*Which of your Sustainer's favors can you deny?*"

adoration of the Divine, he cried out, "O Lord, show me one of Your hidden ones, one of Your beloveds."

The answer came, "This veiled beauty that you are looking for, this generous being, is the beloved son of Bahauddin Walad of Balkh, the Sultan of the Wise."

"O my Lord, show me his blessed face!" cried Shamsuddin.

"What will you give in return?" was the question from Heaven.

"My head," Shams answered. "I made the promise in Tabriz to offer up my head, since that is all I have."

Following Instructions [92]

The revelation came to Shams: "Go to Rum (Anatolia) to achieve your goal." Since his soul was attached to his Lord's by the belt of sincerity, he immediately set out for that region, full of love.

Some say that he came to Konya from Damascus, others that he went from Tabriz to Konya. He went directly to the caravanserai of the sugar merchants and took a room there. He locked the door with a weighty iron padlock and tied the key into the corner of his handkerchief to give people the impression that he was an important merchant. Yet in this room there was only an old mat, a broken jug, and a brick for a pillow. Every ten to fifteen days he would crumble some dried biscuits into a broth from sheeps' trotters, and so would break his fast.

A Deep Thirst [93]

One day, this Sovereign of the Kingdom of the Spirit was seated at the door of the caravanserai, when Mevlana (May God sanctify his secret) left the medresse in the cotton trader's market. He was riding on a mule, while some of his students and various Friends walked beside him. Suddenly, Shamsuddin jumped out of the doorway and ran in front of him as he passed. He seized the bridle of the mule and declared, "O you who are as knowledgeable in meanings as a money-changer is with coins, tell me who was greater, Muhammad, the Elect of God, or Bayazid?"[14]

"Muhammad is the Prince and the Commander of all the prophets and all the Friends of God (*awliya*); all power and greatness is his."

The leader of our caravan is the Elect of God, Glory of the world.

14. Bayazid Bastami (d. 874), also known as Abu Yazid, was one of the early sufi masters of Islam, known for his intoxication with God.

We are happy to sacrifice our lives for him.

Shamsuddin asked, "In that case, what does it mean that the Prophet said, 'Glory be to You! We have not known You as You ought to be known,' while Bayazid said, 'How great is my glory. How exalted am I, the sultan of sultans.'"

Mevlana answered, "Bayazid's thirst was quenched and the container of his comprehension filled by a single sip, and he appeared to have been satisfied. The light entered in proportion to the opening of his heart. The Chosen one of God (Peace and blessings upon him) had a profound desire that had yet to be satisfied. For the Prophet it was thirst upon thirst; his blessed chest had become God's vast dominion, opened wide by the passage from the Qur'an, *Have we not expanded your heart?* [94:1], so he seemed to be always thirsty. Every day, he came closer to God. The aspiration of the Chosen one was immense; he did not consider his journey to God to be like that of other people, since he was chosen (May God praise and bless him), and every day he drew closer to God and saw the Light of His Majesty and Power grow. For that reason he said, 'I have not known You as You ought to be known.'"

Then Mevlana let out a cry and fainted; he remained unconscious for an hour. When he came to his senses, he took Shams-uddin's hand, and they returned to the medresse on foot where they remained in total seclusion for forty days. Some say that they withdrew from the world for three months.

Drunk with Joy [94]

Mevlana told me, "When Shamsuddin asked me that question, I saw a window open at the top of my head, and smoke emerged that reached to the Heavenly Throne."

Having abandoned teaching and the medresse, together with Shams, he became absorbed in contemplation of the mysteries of the Spirit. As he said:

"Like the planet Mercury, I was a lover of language
and took my place in the forefront of the world of letters.
But when I saw the Heavenly tablet offered by the Cupbearer,
I became drunk with joy and threw away my pen."

If You Have an Ear, Listen [95]

It seemed to the inhabitants of Konya that the spiritual conversation and withdrawal from the world of the two Friends was excessive. Mevlana's disciples and followers were troubled as well, since no one knew where Shamsuddin had come from, nor what sort of a person he was, and they were suspicious of him.

Then full of zeal, together, they attacked him, and caused a great calamity among the Friends. . . . Mevlana Shamsuddin disappeared without a trace.[15] They searched for him for a month, but could not find the slightest trace of him.

Our Master then ordered a cloak (*faraji*) for himself in hindibari material, and he put on a hat made out of wool the color of honey. In this country it was a sign of mourning to wear hindibari clothing—it had been the custom since ancient times, in the same way that one would wear a horseblanket (*ghashiya*). He also put on a shirt open at the chest, and on his feet, slippers that were known as Mevlevi boots. He unwound his turban in the manner known as shakaraviz,[16] with the end hanging down to his heart, and gave the order that from then on the *rebab*[17] would be made in a hexagonal shape, even though it had always previously been square.

He said, "The six corners of the *rebab* will symbolize the secret of the six directions of the world.[18] And the 'alif'[19] that is the straight

---

15. See also sections #545 and #555-556 of this volume.

16. See section #375 of this volume.

17. The *rebab* is a stringed instrument beloved of Mevlana, and also his son Sultan Walad, which became one of the essential instruments of the sema, in addition to the the *ney* (reed flute), and the *qudum* (drums).

18. As Mevlana said, "I asked for one kiss and you gave me six." . . . See "The Six-Faced Mirror," *Jewels of Remembrance*, selected and translated by Camille and Kabir Helminski, Threshold Books, 1996, p.98:

The Prophet said, "God doesn't pay attention to your outer form:
so in your improvising, seek the owner of the Heart."
God says, "I regard you through the owner of the Heart,
not because of prostrations in prayer
nor the giving of wealth in charity."
The owner of the Heart becomes a six-faced mirror:
through him God looks out upon all the six directions.
[*Mathnawi* V: 869-870; 874]

19. The 'alif' (similar to the letter "a") is the first letter of the Arabic alphabet, indicated with a straight line in Arabic script, symbolic of the human being standing in witness to the Oneness of Divinity.

string of the *rebab* will represent the intimacy of the spirits as the 'alif' within the word, 'Allah.'

If you have an ear, listen; if you have an eye, see."

And so, the sema began! The flame of mystic love and the tumult of the lovers spread across the world, as all heads turned towards Mevlana. Everyone began to recite poetry, and occupied themselves with music, and immersed in a mutual love and ecstasy that did not ebb for a single instant. . . .

Flowers from the Hand of the Friend [96]

Kira Khatun (May God have mercy on her), Mevlana's wife, who was the purest woman of the era, like a second Mary, recounts the following:

It was winter. Our Master was in retreat with Shamsuddin of Tabriz. He was deep in contemplation, leaning against Shams of Tabriz's knee, and I was listening through an opening in the door to try to understand what they were saying. All of a sudden, the wall of the house split open and six awesome-looking individuals came in and greeted him, placing a bouquet of roses before him. They sat there absorbed together, without saying a word, until the noon prayer. Mevlana made a sign to Shamsuddin and said, "Let us offer the *salaah*; you be the imam."

"When you are present, no one else should fill this role," responded Shamsuddin.

After Mevlana had led the prayer, the strange individuals bowed in respect and vanished through the same wall through which they had come. In awe, I fainted, and when I came back to consciousness, Mevlana came out and gave me the bouquet of roses, saying, "Keep these well."

I sent several petals to the shop of the attar-maker, asking, "We have never seen this type of rose—where do they come from, and what is their name?"

All the druggists were amazed at the freshness, color, and fragrance of these flowers and wondered where they could possibly have come from in the middle of winter. A well-known merchant named Sharifuddin Hindi, who had made many trips to India on business, and who had often brought back marvelous and strange merchandise, was shown these flowers. He cried out in astonishment, "It is an Indian rose; it grows especially in Serendib (Ceylon).

What is such a rose doing here? I must find out how they got here!"

Kira Khatun's maidservant brought the flowers back and reported what he had said. The amazement of her mistress increased a thousandfold. Suddenly Mevlana entered and said to her, "Take special care of this bouquet, and don't show it to any of the deniers, because it was brought to us by blessed beings from the Sanctuary of Generosity, by the guardians of the garden of Irem.[20] The *qutbs*[21] of India brought this for you, to serve as nourishment for the palace of your soul, and to give your eyes and your body strength. By God! Guard it well so that the evil eye does not fall upon it."

It is said that Kira Khatun kept these flowers until her last breath. With our Master's permission she gave a few petals to Gurji-Khatun, the sultan's wife. When someone had an eye ailment, she would rub the afflicted area with a petal, and it would be immediately healed. The color and the fragrance of these flowers remained forever fresh.

Travel in Search of a Friend [98b]

A rich and noble merchant, anxious to receive spiritual guidance, arrived from Tabriz; he went to the caravanserai of the sugar merchants and asked about the shaikhs and the wise men who could be found in the town, in order to visit them, learn from them, and profit from their knowledge.

"The goal of a world traveller is to discover wise human beings and pious shaikhs, not just to do business and make money. It is the spiritual journey that makes the discomforts of travel worth putting up with," he said.

> God has said: "Wherever you go on a journey
> you should first seek out a real human being."

The other merchants told him, "In this city, there are a number of great and noble spiritual teachers, but the Shaikh of Islam, the traditionalist of the era, is Shaikh Sadruddin,[22] who is without equal

---

20. The ancient garden of Irem is a legendary garden that was built as a model of the Garden of Paradise by Shaddad b. 'Ad in Southern Arabia.

21. *Qutbs*, often not publicly known, are the spiritual "poles," divinely inspired beings around whom others turn in their devotion. It is taught that it is through their spiritual presence and connection with the Unseen that the world is maintained in being and blessing. (See note #56 of this volume.)

22. Shaikh Sadruddin al-Qunawi (also transliterated, "Konevi") (d. 1274 C.E.) was a renowned mystic of the era, the son-in-law and successor of Ibn al-Arabi (d.

in the religious sciences and within the mystic path of the shaikhs of certainty." Then they took him to see Sadruddin, bringing with them strange and marvellous gifts worth almost two hundred dinars. When they got to the shaikh's door, the merchant from Tabriz saw many servants, young slaves, chamberlains, porters, eunuchs, and various other servants. Bewildered and upset, he asked, "Have I come to visit a prince or a *faqir?*"[23]

They answered, "This display does not reflect on the character of the shaikh—he is a perfect being. It's like halvah which does no harm to the doctor but can be harmful for the one who is ill."

He entered hesitantly and had the honor of being admitted into the shaikh's presence. He spoke with him and asked for his blessing; he mentioned various financial hardships that had fallen upon him recently and asked for these to be relieved. He said, "At the end of the year I give alms, and I never refuse money to those in need, as far as I am able. Why have these hardships come upon me?" Despite his requests and supplications, the shaikh paid no attention to him, and the merchant left disappointed and disgusted.

The next day, he asked his fellow merchants, "Is there no other dervish or revered person with whom I might speak and find joy in his company and relief?"

They answered, "Jalaluddin Rumi is such a man. He has renounced all pleasures other than God. He has overturned the shop of the two worlds, and night and day he is occupied in worshipping God. With encouragements and divine insights, he is an ocean of meaning."

The merchant from Tabriz, filled with a burning desire to see our Master, asked to be taken to him: "Even just hearing about him fills me with joy." After he had knotted fifty dinars into the corner of his handkerchief, a few of the merchants guided him to our master's medresse.

They came upon Mevlana sitting alone in the meeting hall, engrossed in his books. They greeted him and immediately felt transported beyond themselves. The merchant of Tabriz lost his senses with one glance from Mevlana and began weeping copiously.

Mevlana said, "The fifty dinars are accepted; they are worth more than the two hundred that you lost. It was God's wish to send you a calamity and disaster, but because of this meeting, the calamity is over. Don't be in despair, from now on there will be no more

---

1221 C.E.) and a friend of Mevlana's.

23. A *faqir* is a man of "poverty," one who occupies himself with polishing of the heart, devoted to the Divine, rather than worldy means and acquisitions.

misfortunes; your past deeds are forgiven."

The poor merchant was stupified by these gentle words and filled with joy.

"The reason for your misfortune," continued Mevlana, "is perhaps the lack of generosity that you displayed in the land of the western Franks. You passed through a district of the city where a Frankish dervish, a great saint, was sleeping near the bazaar. You spat on him and turned away at the sight of him. The blessed heart of this saintly man became hardened towards you. This is the reason that you have had such bad luck and financial losses lately. Return and ask his forgiveness, that you might be released; and send him our greetings, as well."

The unfortunate merchant was very troubled by this advice.

"Do you wish to see him?" asked the Master, "Look!"

He placed his blessed hand on the wall, in which a door opened. The merchant saw the man asleep at a crossroads in the land of the Franks. Immediately he lowered his head and tore his clothes, and, overcome with chagrin, he set out to find him.

When he had arrived in that country and had gone to the same neighborhood looking for the dervish, he saw him asleep in the exact spot that Mevlana had revealed. He prostrated himself in front of him.

"What could I do? Mevlana stopped me," said the dervish. "Otherwise, I would have revealed myself to you, and shown you the great Power and Glory of God. Now, come closer."

He embraced the merchant and kissed him on both cheeks.

"Now," he said, "You will see my shaikh and my Lord."

The merchant was enabled to see Mevlana drunk with ecstatic joy, dancing in his medresse, reciting these verses:

"The Kingdom of our Lord holds the rough and the pure;
for Him, all kinds are desired.
Be a carnelian or a ruby,
or even a brick or a stone.
If you are truly of the faithful, He will find you;
if you are a denier, He will refresh you;
On this road, be an Abu Bakr;[24]
on that road, be a Frank."

24. Abu Bakr (d. 634 C.E.) was the close companion of the Prophet Muhammad and became the first of the four "Rightly-guided Imams" of the Muslim community after his passing. He was one of the first to witness to the truth of Muhammad's prophethood, and became known as *as-Siddiq* (the truthful), for his deep faith and truthful sincerity.

The merchant of Tabriz returned to Konya, carrying with him the blessings and greetings of the Frankish dervish. He distributed many gifts among the companions, settled in Konya, and became one of the sincere lovers.

The Power of a Glance *[99-100]*

One night there was a concert in the palace of the Parvana Mo'inuddin. All the shaikhs and eminent people were there. Mevlana was so overcome he cried out with one deep cry after another; at last he went into a corner of the room and stood there. After a short while, he told the reciters to be quiet. Those gathered were bewildered. Then he lifted his head, and they saw that his two eyes had become pools filled with blood. He cried out, "O Friends, come closer, and see within the depths of my eyes the grandeur of the Divine lights."

No one was capable of such a glance (*nazar*); those who tried found their eyes overwhelmed, powerless. The Friends cried out and lowered their heads.

Then our Master turned his gaze to Chelebi Husamuddin and said to him, "Come to me, O my religion! Come, O my faith! Come, O my soul! Come, O my sovereign." The Chelebi cried out and wept.

Then the Parvana whispered to Tadjuddin Mo'tazz Khorasani, "Listen to what Mevlana has said about Chelebi Husamuddin! Does he really possess such qualities? Does he deserve such praise, or is Mevlana just exaggerating his affection?"

Immediately, the Chelebi came forward, firmly took hold of the Parvana, and said, "O Amir Mo'inuddin, even if it had not been so, the moment that our Master commanded it, immediately he conveyed those qualities to my soul and bestowed them on me: *Truly, His command is such that when He wills a thing to be, He but says to it, 'Be' and it is* [36:82].

> His action is described by these words: *'Be!' and it is*;
> it doesn't depend on any secondary cause.
> It's known that by alchemy copper can become gold;
> by this rare alchemy, a bit of copper
> has become a transforming philosopher's stone.

Considering Mevlana's kindness and friendship to all, these things should not seem strange."

At these words, the Parvana was humbled and broke out in a

sweat. He prostrated, asked for forgiveness, and then sent, as a token of his gratitude, considerable gifts.

Among Mevlana's many miracles was this: no one was able to look into his blessed eyes because of the penetrating brilliance of the light emanating from them. Because of this brilliance, people who came into his presence would cover their eyes and gaze at the ground.

Dancing to the Music [102]

In the beginning of his career, Judge (*Qadi*) 'Izzuddin disapproved of music. One day, Mevlana had an inspiration. He left the medresse, whirling, and went to the judge's chamber, grabbed him by the collar, and shouted, "Get up and come to the celebration of your Lord!"

Mevlana then dragged him to the gathering of the lovers and showed him how to participate to the best of his ability. The Qadi tore his clothes and joined the whirling, crying out. Eventually, after demonstrating his good will and devotion, he became a sincere disciple.

The Way of Conscious Insight [103]

One day, three qadis, 'Izzuddin of Amasia, 'Izzuddin of Sivas and 'Izzuddin of Konya (May God Most High have mercy on them) asked Mevlana, "What path do you follow?"

He replied, "*Say, 'This is my way: Resting upon conscious insight accessible to reason ('ala basirah), I am calling to God—I and they who follow me.'*" [*Surah Yusuf* (Joseph) 12:108].[25]

In that moment, all three bowed and became devout disciples.

Making Peace [104]

One day, our Master was passing through a certain district in the city when he came upon two men who were arguing and hurling insults at each other. He observed them from a distance and heard one of them say to the other: "Do you realize who you're talking to? By God, if you say another word, you'll hear a thousand from me!"

Our Master approached them and said, "No, no, come! Say to me whatever you need to say. Even if you say a thousand things, you won't hear me say a single word."

25. This Qur'anic verse continues to be part of the initiation ceremony of a Mevlevi dervish.

The two adversaries fell at his feet in shame and immediately made peace with each other.

Remember, Spacious Is God's Earth [105]

Our Master Shamsuddin Malati (May God have mercy on him) told us how one day a religious scholar came with his students to visit Mevlana. They asked him to ask them difficult questions in order to test him—secretly, they said to each other, "Now, let's see to what extent Mevlana knows Arabic."

When they were seated in his presence, Mevlana began sharing numerous subtle points and then began to relate the story of a jurist and a grammarian:

"They were out walking together. Suddenly, they came upon an abandoned well. The jurist, who was a simple man, made a comment in Arabic, saying, 'And many an abandoned well (*Wa bir un mu'attalatin* [22:45])!' However, he forgot to put the *hamza* inflection in the word *bi'r*. The grammarian, who was lauded as being extremely intelligent, was offended: 'Don't say "*bir*," but "*bi'r*"—it's more elegant.'

"A furious debate broke out between the two about the presence or the absence of a *hamza*. They quoted book after book of grammar and quite exhausted themselves, each attempting to prove his point. Finally, the discussion drew to a close, since night had fallen and they found themselves in total darkness.

"On the road home, they came upon an abandoned well, and as fate would have it, the grammarian fell in.

"The jurist could hear him crying out, 'O dear companion! O compassionate jurist! For the love of God Most High, rescue me from this dark place.'

"'I will save you, but only on one condition,' said the jurist, 'and that is that you remove the *hamza* from the word, *bi'r*.'

"The unfortunate grammarian had no choice but to remove the *hamza*." Mevlana continued, "In the same way, until you remove from your self the *hamza* of doubt and preoccupation with your own existence, you will never be delivered from *the dark depths of the well* [12:10] of the *nafs*[26] and its desires. You will never reach the vast

26. According to the Sufi path there are seven stages of the soul and its subtilization as we move through the process of polishing the heart: *nafs al ammarah*—the commanding self (commanding to follow its desires), *nafs al-lawammah*—the repentant self (the self that repents of its waywardness), *nafs al mulhimah*—the inspired self (the stage of the self when one recognizes more fully one's connection

plain of delightful fragrances of: *And remember, spacious is God's earth* [39:10]."

With this, the professor and his students who were visiting removed their turbans, tore up the belt of denial, and demonstrating their sincere goodwill, became devoted disciples.

> We caught the grammarian in his own net,
> and so taught you the grammar of detachment.
> Know that self-effacement is what you need here, not grammar.
> If you have died to self, you can dive safely into the Sea.
> Jurisprudence, syntax, and morphology will only drown you,
> dear friend.

Manners of the Way [107]

One day at a gathering, Mevlana was teaching when a young man from a distinguished family came in and sat in a spot that was more elevated than one occupied by an elderly man.

Mevlana said, "In the past, the Divine command was that a young man who sat higher than an old man would immediately be knocked to the ground; that was the law of the community. But now we see young people, just out of school, pushing old people around, with no fear of retribution.

"One day, the Victorious Lion of God, Commander of the Faithful, 'Ali[27] (May God ennoble his face), the son of Abu Talib, was on his way to the Mosque of the Prophet to offer the morning prayers. Halfway there, he came upon an elderly Jewish man walking ahead of him. The Commander of the Faithful, who had a considerate, chivalrous, and generous nature, did not barge ahead of the old man but walked gently in his footsteps. When he got to the mosque, he saw the Prophet (Peace and blessings upon him) already bowed down performing the first prostration. Immediately, from a majestic com-

---

with the Divine Reality), *nafs al-mutmainnah*—the contented or tranquil self (the one who begins to be content with God's Presence); *nafs ar-radiyah*—the pleased self (the one who is pleased with all that God gives); *nafs al mardiyah*—the self that has become pleasing (to God); *nafs as-safiyyah*—the purified self of vast heart.

27. 'Ali ibn Abi Talib (d. 661 C.E.), cousin of the Prophet Muhammad (d. 632 C.E.) and husband of his daughter, Fatima (d. 633 C.E.), from whom his offspring are descended, became the fourth of the four rightly guided Imams (leaders)—the close companions who became caliph and guide of the early Muslim community after the passing of the Prophet. The first caliph was the Prophet's close friend, Abu Bakr as-Siddiq, then 'Omar, followed by 'Othman, and then 'Ali.

mand on high, Gabriel appeared and gently put his hand on the blessed back of the Messenger of God, causing him to pause, so that the Commander of the Faithful would not miss the benefit of being at the first prostration of the dawn prayer. For truly, the reward of it is worth more than a hundred years of devotion, and the Prophet (Peace and blessings upon him), himself, has said, 'The first prostration is worth more than the world and all it contains.'

"After the Prophet (Peace and blessings upon him) had finished his prayer and his supplications, he asked Gabriel, 'What is the secret of this?'

"Gabriel replied, 'The reason for it is that the Commander of the Faithful, on his way to the mosque, encountered an elderly Jew, and out of politeness did not want to go in front of him. God, the Sublime and Exalted, did not think it just that 'Ali should be deprived of the merit of attending the dawn prayer, and so He bestowed this grace.'

"See to what extent God rewarded the Commander of the Faithful's consideration for an elderly Jew.... Should not an old man who has spent his life in the service of God, and whose beard has grown white in the community of Islam, receive great consideration? God Most High, in exchange for respect shown to one of His servants, will bestow many favors and has said, '*All honor belongs to God, and to His Messenger, and to the faithful* [63:8].'

"If you would like good fortune that is always fresh, hold fast to the edge of the robe of an elderly mystic. A young man will never become a wise elder without the guidance of a truly mature one (*pir*), nor will he ever be able to accomplish wise miracles.

Choose a *Pir*,
for without a *pir* this journey
will be full of disasters, fears, and dangers.
It is not the passage of days that brings wisdom,
but the grace of God.
I don't seek heaven, but the *Pir*;
seek the *Pir*, seek the *Pir*!
Not the ancient sky,
but an elder of worth in this world,
of good guidance, and *God knows best*."

Taking Rightful Care of Your Donkey [107b]

One day our Master was giving a discourse at his school and said,

"God, in the glorious Qur'an said, *And so, be modest in your bearing, and lower your voice, for, behold, the ugliest of all voices is the loud braying of the donkey* [31:19]." . . .

His students asked him to elaborate.

"All animals have their own particular cry, by which they manifest their created essence and glorify their Creator," our Master replied. "The camel has its grumbling; the lion, its roaring; the stag, its moaning; the fly, its buzzing; the bee, its humming, and so on. In heaven, the angels and the spirit beings have their songs of thanksgiving and their hymns of praise. The human being has his prayers, professions of faith, and the many ways he can worship with his voice and his body. The poor donkey brays upon only two occasions—when he is hungry and when he wishes to mate, as it is said in the arab verse:

Consider the wayward donkey:
if you feed him too much, he kicks;
if you don't feed him enough, he brays.

"The donkey is a slave to its sexual organs and its belly. In the same way, a person who has no longing for God in his soul, no lament of mystical love in his heart, and without a passion, with no secret in his head, is in the eyes of the Divine even less than a donkey: *They are like cattle—no, they are even less conscious of the right way* [7:179].

Know that this lower self (*nafs*) is like a donkey—
to be its slave is a great shame.
If you are not sure of the way,
do the opposite of what this donkey wants,
and discover the straight path."

. . . One day, the Master, mounted on a donkey, went to Chelebi Husamuddin's garden, accompanied by all the Friends.

"The donkey is the mount of worthy men," he said. "Many prophets have ridden on donkeys: Seth, Idris, Jesus, as well as our own beloved Prophet (Peace and blessings upon them).

Mount a donkey without a saddle, O you who talk too much!
The donkey was no longer naked
    when the Prophet rode upon him!"

That man of God, Shihabuddin, the reciter, who was one of the Friends, was also riding a donkey. Suddenly his mount began to bray very loudly, and Shihabuddin got very angry and began to hit it on the head.

"Why are you beating that poor animal?" our Master asked. "Are you not aware that he is carrying you, that you are above and that he is below? How would you behave if the reverse were true?[28] Actually, his complaint can only come from one of two reasons, either he is hungry or he has sexual desires; in both those areas, all creatures are similar, so it would follow that all creatures, including man, should be hit on the head and treated like that."

Shihabuddin, seeing that he was at fault, dismounted, kissed the feet of his donkey, and was then kind to him.

Welcoming Adversity [108]

Someone was complaining about his lack of money. Mevlana said, "Go, and from now on don't consider yourself to be a friend of mine, since the world possesses you." And then he recited these verses:

> "Come, be like me, as tranquil and pure as the moon!
> Don't run after money or any of life's luxuries—
> that is the realm of Satan, of kings and flags."

---

28. In his *Mathnawi*, Mevlana also tells us: "Let your donkey (your ego-bodily self) carry your Jesus, don't make your Jesus carry your donkey [*Mathnawi* II: 450]." See also *Mathnawi* II: 1857-1862, "This Lower Mind Is Like a Donkey," *The Rumi Daybook*, Translated by Kabir and Camille Helminski, Shambhala Publications, 2011, p.168:

> This lower mind is just like a donkey:
> it can't stop thinking of how to get its fodder.
> But Jesus' donkey acquired a soul:
> it made a home in intelligence.
> In Jesus reason was strong;
> his donkey was made lean by a strong rider,
> but from the weakness of reason,
> this worn-out ass becomes a dragon.
>
> But if you have a guide like Jesus
> and he has made you heart-sick,
> don't forget that your health, too, is from him.
> Do not run away from him.
> How do you deal with affliction,
> you who have the healing breath of Jesus inside?
> For in this world there's always a snake
> guarding the treasure.

And he added, "One day, one of the companions of the Prophet (Peace and blessings upon him) said to him, 'I love you.'

" 'Then why are you not prostrating in awe?' asked the Prophet. 'Put away your sword, and be prepared to welcome adversity, since misfortune is the gift made to those who love their Lord.'

And Mevlana concluded with these words:

"And He asked, '*Am I not* [your Lord],' and you answered, '*Yes!*'[29]
What is the secret contained in this '*Yes*'?
It is to welcome adversity."

Which do You Love Best? [109]

Once a mystic asked a rich man, "Which do you love best, money or sin?"

"Money," he answered.

"That's not true," said the Friend. "It is sin and perdition that you prefer. Don't you see that one day when you die you will leave your fortune behind. However, you will take your perdition and sin with you, and you will be judged accordingly by God. Your goal should be to take a fortune with you without committing sin—if you love God, you will find the means to send Him the payment before going there yourself. He has said: *Whatever good deed you may offer up on your own behalf, you shall truly find it with God—even better, and richer in reward* [73:20]."

The True Place of Honor [109b]

One day, the Parvana Mo'inuddin (May God elevate his rank) was holding a gathering in his palace. All the wise, the shaikhs, the masters of chivalry (*futuwwah*), contemplatives, and travelers from afar

29. See *Surah* 7:172. This refers to what is known as the "Day of *Alast*," when in pre-eternity all the spirits were gathered and asked this question: "Am I not your Lord (*Alastu bi Rabbikum*)?" To which the faithful answered "Yes," and are continually called to remember this trust and their promised faithfulness.

"According to the Qur'an, the ability to perceive the existence of the Supreme Power is inborn in human nature (*fitrah*); and it is this instinctive cognition—which may or may not be subsequently blurred by self-indulgence or adverse environmental influences—that makes every sane human being 'bear witness about himself (or herself)' before God. As so often in the Qur'an, [in this verse, also] God's 'speaking' and the human being's 'answering' is a metonym for the creative act of God and of the human being's existential response to it." ~Muhammad Asad, *The Message of the Qur'an*, The Book Foundation, p.198.

were there. The important dignitaries were seated in places of honor. Then the Parvana thought, "What if Mevlana were to grace our gathering—since he is the pride of our epoch?"

Majduddin-i Atabak, the Parvana's son-in-law, was one of Mevlana's disciples; he was also a man of great merit and one of the faithful. He arose to go to invite Mevlana. There was a murmur of agitation among the dignitaries and the important people of rank, who were overcome by inner whisperings—they said, "We are all already seated appropriately according to our rank. If Mevlana comes, let him sit wherever he will."

When Madjduddin eloquently conveyed the invitation to Mevlana, he then gathered Chelebi Husamuddin and the Friends, and they all set off. The Friends walked ahead, and Mevlana followed them. When Chelebi Husamuddin entered the palace of the Parvana, out of respect, all the dignitaries arose and gave up to him a place of honor. When Mevlana arrived, the Parvana and the noble ones ran to greet him. The Pervana kissed his blessed hand, and asked forgiveness, "We have caused our master pain, but it is a mercy for your servants."

When he entered the palace, Mevlana saw how all the dignitaries were already seated high and low; he greeted them and then went to sit in the courtyard of the palace. Chelebi Husamuddin got up and rushed to sit at Mevlana's side. The majority of the dignitaries there then did the same, except for those who in hypocrisy had come to an agreement among themselevs, like Shaikh Najiruddin, Shaikh Sharafuddin Hariwe, Sayyid Sharafuddin, and other fools who followed their example. Each one of them was a walking library of all sorts of knowledge; it was said that Sayyid Sharafuddin was a natural-born philosopher, a scholastic theologian, but he was also ugly and rude. When he observed this situation in which many of the important people had left their honored seats, and a great person such as our Master had gone to sit where the shoes were kept, he asked, "Where is the place of honor, now? And where is the place of honor for a mystic on the path?"

The Qadi Sirajuddin responded, "In the medresse of the religious scholars, the place of honor is the middle of the sofa, where the teacher sits."

"For those who practice pious retreat (*i'tikaf*)," said Sharafuddin Hariwa, "and according to the *pirs* of Khorasan, the place of honor is in the corner of the lodge (*zawiya*)."

"According to the mystics," answered Shaikh Sadruddin, "it is the end of the sofa, which in reality is the place where one removes one's shoes."

After this, as a test, they asked Mevlana, "According to your custom, where is the seat of honor?"

He replied:

"In reality, where is the threshold and the seat of honor?
You and I, where are we? Wherever the Friend is."

"Where is that?" asked Sayyid Sharafuddin.

"Are you blind? Don't you see?" asked our Master:

"Don't you have eyes, to see Him?
From your head to your foot, it is all He."

He rose; the whirling began and quickly gained in intensity. All those great people present tore their clothing in ecstacy.

Sitting with the Beloved [109c]

Some chroniclers say that the former incident took place at the large celebration that Jalaluddin Qarata'i gave when he had completed the construction of his medresse. On that day as well, dignitaries and religious scholars were debating about the location of the place of honor. Then Shamsuddin Tabrizi appeared and went to sit in the place where the shoes were left. Of a common accord, they asked Mevlana, "What do you consider to be the place of honor?"

He answered, "For the religious scholars, it is the middle of the sofa; for the mystic knowers, it's the corner of the room; for the sufis, it's the end of the sofa; for lovers, it's beside the Friend."

Unable to contain himself, Mevlana went to sit beside Shamsuddin Tabrizi. It was said that this was the day this Friend became famous among the people of Konya.

Come Closer [111b]

"One day," recounts Shamsuddin Malati, "I went to Mevlana's house. I found him sitting alone in the assembly hall of the medresse. I bowed and sat down.

"'Come closer,' he said. I approached, and he kept saying, 'Come closer.' Soon, I was kneeling so close that my knee was just next to his, and I trembled in fear.

"Again he said, 'Come, sit so that your knee touches mine.'

"Then he described, so vividly, the virtues of Sayyid Burhanuddin and the miracles of Shamsuddin Tabrizi (May God bless their innermost secrets) that I fainted.

"Then after that he said, 'Our Sultan [Muhammad] said, "Whenever one mentions the righteous, mercy descends." This means that whenever one speaks of the righteous within this community, the rain of mercy pours down; whenever one speaks of us, God Himself pours.'"

Being Ever Watchful of the Nafs [111c]

When Mevlana would go to the bathhouse, his wife, Kira Khatun (May God be pleased with her), would ask the Friends to watch over him, because he would not pay any attention to himself. The Friends would carry with them a rug and a towel, which they would spread out for him in the cooling room, where he would sometimes rest and the Friends would massage him.

One night, in the middle of winter, he set out for the bathhouse and the Friends, according to their custom, spread out a rug for him, and the cloth they had brought, in the cooling chamber. When he had taken off his coat and entered the chamber, he took one look at the things gathered there and quickly left. Some time passed; the Friends went out after him and saw him standing on a piece of ice and holding another piece of ice on his head. The Friends cried out in concern.

He told them, "My ego desires were directing me towards ill and becoming unruly. Praise be to God, we are dervishes, not people of the house of Pharoah! We are of the house of that king who was the Sultan of the Poor [Prophet Muhammad]." And putting his turban and cloak back on, he left.

Guiding Those Who Have Lost the Way [114]

One day, Amir Parvana said, "Mevlana is an exceptional teacher, but his students are terrible and don't know how to mind their own business." One of the Friends overheard this and, deeply hurt, went to tell Mevlana.

Mevlana then sent the Parvana a note, saying, "If my students were perfect, it is they who would teach me, and I would be their disciple. It is because they have faults that I have accepted them as students and given them a chance to improve and become mature human beings.

I am not blind, but I have the philosopher's stone;
that is why I can buy counterfeit coin.

I swear by the pure soul of my father, God has not yet become their stronghold so that He might grant them Mercy, nor have they yet been accepted within the pure heart of the servants of God.

Those who are chosen are saved, and the sinners cursed—
I have come to seek mercy for those who have lost their way."

When the Parvana read the note, his faith increased a thousandfold. He went on foot to visit Mevlana, asked for forgiveness, and bestowed many gifts of gratitude.

Awakening to Gratitude [115c]

One day, a few Friends were talking among themselves: "The amirs, and the important people of this city go to visit other shaikhs and are coming less often to visit our Master. What could be the problem? Perhaps they don't realize how wise he is and don't understand his teaching?"

Mevlana responded, "You see that they don't come, not how they are driven away—if they were allowed to come, there would be no place left for those who are really thirsty and for our Friends."

The next morning all the amirs of the city, including Sahib Fakhruddin, the governor of the coast, Nuruddin, the son of Jija, the Parvana Mo'inuddin, Jalaluddin, the minister of finance, the Atabak Majduddin, and others (May God perfume their tombs), all came to pay a visit; the meeting room of the medresse was so full that all the Friends had to leave.

Mevlana spoke so profoundly and with such subtlety, and with such inspiration beyond description, that everyone was drunk with divine joy. That day, he paid no attention at all to the Friends, who were hurt beyond words.

When the amirs had left, the Friends cried out and fell prostrate at Mevlana's feet, "We were denied our portion of the Divine truths today!" they lamented.

Full of compassion, he calmed them, "*Alms are only for the poor and the needy* [9:61]—our mystical conversations, our secrets, are for our Friends, however, through the blessing that comes for them, it may also spill over into the souls of others—it is thus that one drinks the ewe's milk at the expense of the lambs. This situation has come about because of the reproach and complaint among the Friends. When the amirs come and pay us a visit, the Friends are displeased. So prayers are needed that in future the amirs will be kept occupied taking care of their own business and that of the people and might not disturb the 'moments' of the Friends, so that this spiritual food, this splendid light might be saved for our Friends."

Climbing out of the Well [115d]

Mevlana also told the following story to the Friends:

"A grammarian had fallen into a well. A dervish of enlightened heart came to the opening of the well and cried: 'Bring a rope (*risman*) and a pail (*dul*), so that I might pull the grammarian out of the well!'

"The grammarian, in his usual presumptuous way, objected: 'Say *rasan* and *dalv*, not *risman* and *dul*,' he called out.

"'In that case, just stay in the well while I learn grammar,' said the dervish, as he stopped his efforts to help.

"Now, those who are stuck in the well of self-absorption and pride themselves on their spiritual progress will not be delivered until they have set aside their vanity and pride and bow before the Friends of God. They will not walk on the wide plain of *and spacious is God's earth* [39:10], nor will they attain their goal. Enough said!"

Be as You Appear, Appear as You Are [115e]

Shaikh Salahuddin (May God glorify his memory) had a disciple, a rich merchant, who wanted to go on a trip to Constantinople. Accompanied by the shaikh, he came to find Mevlana, whom he loved sincerely, to ask his permission and blessings for the journey.

After being given the honor of kissing Mevlana's hand, he was told by our Master, "Near Constantinople there is a flourishing village, where you will find a monk who lives in seclusion in his monastery. Convey to him our greetings and love and inquire how he is."

The merchant bowed and left. When he arrived in that territory, he inquired about the monk. He found the village and entered the monastery respectfully. He saw a figure in a corner like a treasure, with his head embraced in darkness, but bathed in light like a jewel. As it is said: "The light is within the darkness."

The merchant was overcome at this sight and could barely convey our Master's greeting. The monk jumped up and cried, "*And peace be with you and with the chosen servants of God* [27:59]." Then he lowered his head again, and remained bowed in prayer for a long while.

When the merchant looked into another corner he saw Mevlana, in the same clothes and turban as he had been when he was with him, sitting in contemplation. He cried out and fell senseless to the ground.

After some time, when he came to himself, the monk said to him, "If you become initiated into the secrets of the free, you will become one of the good men of piety." Then he wrote a letter addressed to the Emperor of Constantinople in which he said, "Protect this man since he has important business to conduct in this region. Make sure he has safe passage, and tell the guards of the roads and officers in the city not to cause him any trouble."

When the merchant arrived in the city, he delivered the monk's letter to the Emperor, who received him well—he gave the merchant gifts of welcome and ordered that it be as the monk requested. They helped him complete his business and to leave in security with his profit.

On his return, he stopped to see the monk, who said, "Take my greetings and humble respect to Mevlana and ask him, in his infinite grace, not to forget this poor needy monk, so full of longing."

When the merchant arrived back in Konya and spoke with Shaikh Salahuddin, the shaikh told him, "Everything said about the Friends of God is true and comes to pass without doubt or supposition.

O Lord, bestow upon me
all the qualities attributed to the saints.
Everything that is said about the prophets
We believe, and we witness to be true.

But don't discuss this with anyone who is unworthy—keep it to yourself."

The shaikh then got up and took him to see Mevlana. The merchant entered, bowed, and conveyed greetings from the monk.

"Look," said Mevlana, "you will see wonders."

When he looked into the corner of the meeting room, he saw Mevlana just as he had appeared in the monk's cell, bowed in contemplation, wearing the same clothes and turban. Bewildered, the merchant tore his clothes and cried out in astonishment, whereupon our Master embraced him.

"From now on," he said, "you are privy to our secrets, but you must guard them, and especially that of the people of vision, from mean and inconsiderate strangers.

> Don't tell the Sultan's secrets to just anyone;
> don't pour sugar in the presence of flies.
> Only he who, like the lily, has a hundred tongues but is silent
> can hear the Divine secrets of Splendor."

For the Friends, the merchant sacrificed his entire fortune, hosted semas, put on the dervish robe, and withdrew from the world.

Follow the Trail of the Prophets [118]

Ikhtiyaruddin, the jurist (May God bless his spirit), was one of Mevlana's disciples. One Friday, he stayed very late at the mosque, and Mevlana called for him several times before he finally came.

When at last he returned from the mosque, Mevlana asked, "What was the obstacle that made the brothers of purity so late?"

He answered, "A preacher from Khojand had mounted the pulpit and was giving advice. I suddenly felt overwhelmed by the terror of the people and was not able to leave."

"What did the preacher say, what was his point?" asked our Master.

"In his sermon, he was promoting this idea: 'Praise and thanks to God! *Praise be to God who has guided us to this* [7:42], and has not created us to be among the unbelievers, but in every way has made us superior to them.' Everyone in the mosque abandoned themselves to supplication and lament."

Our Master smiled sweetly and said, "What a malicious one! Witness the blind leading the blind! This man looks down on the unfaithful saying: 'I am better than they are by a *danek*.' He gloats over this, but if he were any kind of a man he would instead be measuring himself by the prophets and Friends of God—then he would see his proper worth and understand what constitutes real perfection in a man.

> There are men far above him who are on the trail of angels
> and prophets—God is their prey."

Alchemy of the Spirit [118b]

Husamuddin, that illustrious man of letters, otherwise known as Ibn Ayinadar of Siwas (May God have mercy on him), told the following story, as it was recounted to him by 'Alauddin of Amasia, one of the great *khalifas*[30] and his spiritual director:

Badruddin Tabrizi, the architect of the blessed tomb of Mevlana, was known for his many accomplishments and for his knowledge of astrology, mathematics, geometry, alchemy, and unknotting magic.

One day, at a gathering of the Friends, he said, "Once I was in the company of Mevlana in the garden at Chelebi Husamuddin's house—that night there was a large sema going on until the moment when they call '*Hayya* . . . .'[31]

"After that, Mevlana, out of compassion, gave a sign to stop the sema in order to allow the Friends to rest a bit. They each settled into a nook or hollow and fell asleep. I also settled on a little hill and was dozing off to sleep, while watching our Master below. I could see that he was immersed in contemplation of holy visions.

"I thought to myself, 'Moses, Jesus, Idris, Solomon, Luqman, Khidr,[32] and other prophets (Peace be upon them) had a hundred

30. *Khalifa* has the meaning of "representative"; one who is the spiritual leader acting on behalf of the shaikh of an order, a spiritual elder (of any age) in training closely at his side until he (or she) takes on the role of shaikh upon the passing of his (or her) teacher or when he (or she) is appointed as a shaikh (or still as a *khalifa*) for another district where one is needed.

31. *Hayya 'ala-s-Salah* ("Go quickly to the prayer!") is part of the beginning of the call to the ritual prayer (*adhan*) that would echo from the minarets five times a day, here before the dawn light for the first prayer of the day.

32. These are some of the prophets who manifested many miracles. Moses, Jesus, and Solomon may be quite familiar.

Idris: see *Surah al-Anbiya* 21:85-86; also: *And call to mind (dhikr), through this divine writ, Idris. Behold, he was a man of truth, a prophet, whom We exalted to a lofty station* [19:56-57].

"The majority of the classical commentators identify the Prophet Idris—who is mentioned in the Qur'an once again, namely in 21:85—with the Biblical Enoch (Genesis v. 18-19 and 21-24), without, however, being able to adduce any authority for this purely conjectural identification. Some modern Qur'an-commentators suggest that the name Idris may be the Arabicized form of Osiris (which, in its turn, was the ancient Greek version of the Egyptian name As-ar or Us-ar), said to have been a wise king and/or prophet whom the Egyptians subsequently deified (cf. Maraghi XVI, 64, and Sayyid Qutb, *Fi Zilal al-Qur'an*, Cairo, n.d., vol. XVI, 44); but this assumption is too far-fetched to deserve any serious consideration.

thousand talents besides their manifest miracles.' I reflected on the fact that Moses was skilled in alchemy, Jesus in the craft of dyeing, David in making coat-of-mail, and because so many perfect Friends of God manifested miraculous and extraordinary works that defied reason, I wondered if a divine wise master like Mevlana also had a special talent or not: 'God protect me from thinking that he does not! On the contrary, he probably just doesn't want to display it and wishes to take refuge in obscurity from the calamity of fame.'

"I was still lost in these reflections when our Master suddenly leaped towards me like a raging lion: 'O Badruddin,' he shouted, 'Get up and come with me!' Then he picked up a stone with his right hand, said a prayer, passed it over into his left hand and gave it to me, saying, '*Take that which God has given to you and be grateful* [7:144].'[33]

"In the moonlight, I could see that the stone was, in fact, a ruby, very transparent and brilliant, such as I had never seen, even in the treasury of a king. Terrified, I screamed loudly and awoke all the Friends.

"They complained, 'What is this terrible racket—we were just getting to sleep!' "

When Badruddin would cry out during the sema, they would say it was a cry as loud as that of ten men.

Finally, some of the earliest Qur'an-commentators ('Abd Allah ibn Mas'ud, Qatadah, 'Ikrimah and Ad-Dahhak) assert—with, to my mind, great plausibility—that "Idris" is but another name for Ilyas, the Biblical Elijah." ~ Muhammad Asad, *The Message of the Qur'an*, p. 402-403.

Luqman (see *Surah Luqman* 31:12:19) was a prophet known for his healing capacities, one who in ancient Arabian tradition is the prototype of the wise one who turns away from worldly honours to strive for inner perfection.

Khidr: see *Surah al Kahf* 18:60-82 and sections #168, 169, 170, 251b, 388, 526 VIII, 537, 546, and 557 of this volume.

33. This refers to a moment when Moses wanted to see God: See *Surah* 7:143-144:

And when Moses came [to Mount Sinai] at the time set by Us, and his Sustainer spoke to him, he said: "O my Sustainer! Show [Yourself] to me, so that I might behold You!"

Said [God]: "Never can you see Me. However, behold this mountain: if it remains firm in its place, then—only then—will you see Me."

And as soon as his Sustainer revealed His glory to the mountain, He caused it to crumble to dust; and Moses fell down in a swoon. And when he came to himself, he said: "Limitless are You in Your glory! Unto You do I turn in repentance; and I shall [always] be the first to have faith in You!"

Said [God]: "O Moses! Behold, I have raised you above all people by virtue of the messages which I have entrusted to you, and by virtue of My speaking [to you]: hold fast, therefore, unto what I have given you, and be among the grateful!" [7:143-144].

"I wept and told them what had happened, and they lowered their heads and apologized. I also apologized for my impudent thoughts; Mevlana was compassionate towards me.

"I took the ruby to Gurji Khatun as a gift and told her how it had come to me. Its value was estimated at one hundred and eighty thousand dirhems soltani—she gave me this sum and clothed me with robes of honor. In addition, she gave countless gifts and robes of honor to the other Friends, as well.

"Mevlana said to me, 'Have you read in our *Mathnawi* the story of the dervish who transformed the new twigs of a tree into gold? All these tales told about others are a description of the work of our Friends. The great adepts of the past have accomplished great alchemy with bodies—that is not so amazing. What is amazing is the work of transformation of the mind and the spirit.

It is amazing to see alchemy transform copper into gold;
but what about copper that, with every blink of an eye,
creates a transformer!'"

This Time Is That Time [121]

Shaikh Mahmoud Najjar (May the Mercy of God be upon him) recounted:

One day, the Sultan of Mystics was sharing divine insights. All the Friends were present. Suddenly Shamsuddin of Mardin (May God have mercy on him) entered.

"Come, come," said Mevlana. "Welcome! Though people have spoken of God, and you have listened to many discussions about Him, from now on, listen to Him directly, without an intermediary."

Then he added, "There will come a time when the Most High will be the spiritual director of His servants, without intermediaries. Actually, in every way, He already is, and even more astonishing is that He is at the same time, teacher and disciple. I know that, in reality, this time is already that time."

And he recited this verse:

"This magnificent Sovereign had firmly closed the door.
He has put on Adam's coat again,
and today, come from on High."

What Is Your Real Work? [122]

One day the Amir Parvana organized a gathering at the lodge (*zawiya*) of Shaikh Sadruddin, and Mevlana was also present. When the sema began, because of Mevlana's enthusiasm and intensity quite a tumult arose, as Mevlana immersed deep into the realms of vision.

Kamaluddin, the amir for the gathering, was standing beside Amir Parvana and was speaking ill of the Friends, saying, "For the most part, Mevlana's disciples are artisans and common people. Scholars and the distinguished don't often mix with them. Wherever there is a tailor, a cotton merchant, a grocer—he accepts them readily as students."

All of a sudden, Mevlana let out such a loud cry in the middle of the sema that everyone took leave of their senses. Then he said to Kamaluddin, "O accursed one, our Mansur was a cotton-carder (*hallaj*) and Shaikh Abu Bakr of Bukhara, was he not a weaver (*nassaj*)? And that other perfect being, was he not a glassmaker (*zajjaj*)? Did their professions in any way harm their inner knowing and insight?"

The Parvana was speechless, and both he and Kamaluddin bowed and asked for forgiveness.

Waiting for the Beloved [124]

One day, our Master was passing through a neighborhood where little children were playing in the streets. When they saw him coming from afar, they ran to greet him and bowed before him, and he bowed to them. One child, who was left behind, cried, "Wait! Wait for me!" Mevlana stopped and waited, until the little child could catch up and be consoled.

That was the period during which there was so much opposition to him, *fatwas* against him, and the people were citing various passages from the Qur'an against sema and the *rebab*. He bore all this, thanks to his open-hearted generosity, kindness, and compassion, and didn't say a word. After a while, the furor died away, and it was as though all of that had never existed. Meanwhile, the Way that he created and the unfolding of his family line will endure, increasing, until the Day of Resurrection.

Opening the Door [125]

One day, Mevlana was invited to the Amir Parvana's house. When he arrived, he stopped and waited outside a long while, saying, "Let all the Friends enter."

Finally when all the Friends had gone inside, Mevlana did as well.

Later, when they were leaving, Chelebi Husamuddin asked Mevlana why he had waited outside so long.

"If we had gone in first," he answered, "the porter might have prevented some of our Friends from coming in, and they would have missed the gathering. If, in this world, we cannot bring all our friends into the palace of an amir, how, on the day of Resurrection, will we be able to bring them into the palace of the Hereafter and the presence of our Sustainer?"

The Friends, humbled in the presence of such consideration, gave thanks to God for his thoughtfulness.

Look to See Who Has Sugar in His Shop [125b]

Shamsuddin Malati told us that one day in his medresse, our Master was reflecting aloud. "Among other things, he said, 'I love Shamsuddin very much, but he has one fault. Let us hope that the Most High will cause it to disappear from him and will remove from him this desire.'

"Right away, I bowed in all humility and begged him to tell me immediately what this fault was.

"Mevlana answered, 'It is that you think that God can be found in everyone in existence and you run in pursuit of this illusion:

Many a devil has the face of a human being—
don't put your hand in the hand of just anyone.
Since you don't have an eye that see's within someone,
you imagine there's a treasure within everyone.'

"I asked in all sincerity to be forgiven for this, and then God bestowed on me a vast discernment, so that I became one of the truthful (*saddiq*). Before Mevlana pointed out my fault, I used to pursue all the important people, shaikhs, ascetics, and dervishes, and ask for their help and support. Being a loyal student, I would return from them without success.

"When Mevlana showed me what was needed and opened my eyes, I gave up their company; I saw the true nature of God and the secret of His Truth (*Haqiqat*) was revealed to my eyes. That day, our

Master repeated the following verse over and over, until the Friends knew it by heart:

> In this market-place of attar-sellers, don't idly wander around;
> sit down with the one who has sugar in his shop."

Drink the Wine of Paradise [125c]

Once at a gathering, Mevlana was sharing insights and said:

"That sovereign of the knowers of God (*arifin*), Abu Yazid (Bastami) (May the Mercy of God be upon Him) said something very beautiful and marvellous: 'I don't have faith in Muhammad the Messenger of God (Blessings and Peace be upon him) because he split the moon in two, shattered the rock, brought the trees together, and heard plants and rocks speak, but because, in his perfect wisdom, he forbade the Companions and his community to drink wine and made it unlawful.'"

Then Mevlana added, "Yes, by God, whoever does so will weep more and be more filled with remorse, because if there were in it a taste, a pleasure or benefit, Muhammad would have drunk it and encouraged his followers to, also. Since he was God's pure messenger, what he heard from God is what he did and said.

> If you go without this wine for a day or two,
> you might taste the wine of Paradise.
> Since most men are rough and unworthy,
> he forbade wine to everyone."

The Blessings of Gratitude [125d]

One day at the Parvana's house, Mevlana was sharing profound ideas and unusual insights.

Among them, he said, "The Commander of the Faithful, 'Othman ibn 'Affan (May God be pleased with him), complained to the Prophet about his wealth and the abundance of his fortune, and that he was disgusted by it: 'I've distributed alms (*zakat*), tried to give extra (*sadaqa*), but the more I give away, the more my wealth increases. My soul would be at peace, if I could only get rid of this embarrassment of riches. I know that the repose of the soul and the ornament of the religion is poverty and that well-being is attached to it for *God wants to lighten your burdens* [4:28]. What remedy, what advice does the Prophet recommend?'

"'O 'Othman,' answered Muhammad, 'Go and stop being grateful to God for all His blessings; practice ingratitude for a while—your fortune will diminish and you will become poor more quickly, until no blessing remains for you.'

"'O Prophet of God,' replied 'Othman, 'How can I not praise the Unique One and thank Him for His infinite blessings—this praise is a part of my being, and I am accustomed to it.'

"Muhammad responded, 'Haven't you read the passage in the Qur'an: *If you are grateful, I will give you increase* [14:7]? That is to say, God, in His Eternal Word, has promised increase to those who are grateful. I have also said, "Gratitude is a hunt for increase and a duty of friendship for His servants."'

Thankfulness increases good fortune,
ingratitude removes it.
Increase is God's promise to the grateful,
just as nearness to God
is the recompense for prostrations.

"Muhammad continued, 'O 'Othman, you must accept these riches and this wealth, for there will never be a loss or decrease in your fortune.'"

Witnessing the Opening of the Heart [125e]

The religious scholar known as Shamsuddin Mo'allim (the professor), one of the close Friends, related:

One day, Mevlana looked at his friends and said, "Our Prophet Muhammad (Peace and blessings be upon him) said, 'When the light of God enters the heart of the faithful one, his heart opens and expands and becomes like a beautiful countryside, pleasing and soft. It is like when you throw a stone into the water, the water opens.'

"Someone asked him, 'O Prophet of God, if a man is not given the joy of being able to see his heart open, and if his vision is veiled and covered with dust from his lower self and his passions, by what sign will he recognize that his heart has opened and that an expansion has taken place within him?'

"He answered, 'By this sign—that his heart will cool towards all his worldly possessions, worldly people and pleasures, and they will seem insipid. He will begin to feel like a stranger toward his worldly friends for no particular reason.' "

Standing Watch at the Doorway [126]

One day, Mevlana was standing in the market-place and was reflecting aloud. Many people had gathered, but Mevlana had turned away from them and, facing a wall, was continuing to discourse about the secrets of the Way; he continued speaking until the moment of the sunset prayer.

Then when night had fallen, the dogs of the market-place formed a circle around him. He glanced at them with love and blessing and continued to speak divine insights and subtle meanings. They shook their heads and their tails and growled with delight.

He said, "I swear by *God Most High, the All Powerful, the Compelling, aside from whom there is no power or force*, that you dogs can understand my mystic insights. From now on, you shall no longer be called 'dogs,' since you are brothers of the dog spoken of in the story of the Companions of the Cave."[34] And he recited this verse:

---

34. See *Surah al-Kahf* (the Cave) 18:9-31. Mevlana and Shams frequently refer to this story and to the "brothers of purity," so we include details of that story here. The practice of the "brothers of purity" is one that continues across religious traditions (see, also, the note to section #350):

Legend has it that some young Christians of Ephesus, accompanied by their dog, withdrew into a secluded cave in order to be able to live in accordance with their faith, and remained there, miraculously asleep, for a great length of time (according to some accounts, referred to in verse 25 of this *surah*, for about three centuries). When they finally awoke—unaware of the long time during which they had lain asleep—they sent one of their company to the town to purchase some food. In the meantime the situation had changed entirely: Christianity was no longer persecuted and had even become the official religion of the Roman Empire. The ancient coin (dating from the reign of Decius) with which the young man wanted to pay for his purchases immediately aroused curiosity; people began to question the stranger, and the story of the Men of the Cave and their miraculous sleep came to light....

The majority of the classical commentators rely on this Christian legend in their endeavour to interpret the Qur'anic reference (in verses 9-26) to the Men of the Cave. It seems, however, that the Christian formulation of this theme is a later development of a much older oral tradition—a tradition which, in fact, goes back to pre-Christian, Jewish sources. This is evident from several well-authenticated *ahadith* (mentioned by all the classical commentators), according to which it was the Jewish rabbis (*ahbar*) of Medina who induced the Meccan opponents of Muhammad to "test his veracity" by asking him to explain, among other problems, the story of the Men of the Cave. Referring to these *ahadith*, Ibn Kathir remarks

The lions of the world all bowed low
when we gave a hand to the dog
of the Companions of the Cave.

This door and this wall praise God
and comprehend Divine secrets.

Where is the eye to see the souls
that come forth from this door and this wall?
The door and wall speak subtleties:
fire, water, and earth all have stories to tell."

---

in his commentary on verse 13 of this *surah*: "It has been said that they were followers of Jesus the son of Mary, but God knows it better: it is obvious that they lived much earlier than the Christian period—for, had they been Christians, why should the Jewish rabbis have been intent on preserving their story . . . ?" We may, therefore, safely assume that the legend of the Men of the Cave—stripped of its Christian garb and the superimposed Christian background—is, substantially, of Jewish origin. If we discard the later syncretic additions and reduce the story to its fundamentals—voluntary withdrawal from the world, age-long "sleep" in a secluded cave and a miraculous "awakening" after an indeterminate period of time—we have before us a striking allegory relating to a movement which played an important role in Jewish religious history during the centuries immediately preceding and following the advent of Jesus: namely, the ascetic Essene Brotherhood (see 3:52), to which Jesus himself may have belonged, and particularly that of its branches which lived in self-imposed solitude in the vicinity of the Dead Sea and has recently, after the discovery of the Dead Sea Scrolls, come to be known as the "Qumran community." The expression *ar-raqim* (scriptures) occurring in the above Qur'an-verse lends strong support to this theory . . . ." Since it is historically established that the members of the Qumran community—the strictest group among the Essenes—devoted themselves entirely to the study, the copying, and the preservation of the sacred scriptures, and since they lived in complete seclusion from the rest of the world and were highly admired for their piety and moral purity, it is more than probable that their mode of life made so strong an impression on the imagination of their more worldly co-religionists that it became gradually allegorized in the story of the Men of the Cave who "slept"—that is, were cut off from the outside world—for countless years, destined to be "awakened" after their spiritual task was done.

But whatever the source of this legend, and irrespective of whether it is of Jewish or Christian origin, the fact remains that it is used in the Qur'an in a purely parabolic sense: namely, as an illustration of God's power to bring about death (or "sleep") and resurrection (or "awakening"); and, secondly, as an allegory of the piety that induces men to abandon a wicked or frivolous world in order to keep their faith unsullied, and of God's recognition of that faith by His bestowal of a spiritual awakening which transcends time and death.

~ Muhammad Asad, notes to "*Surah al-Kahf*," *The Message of the Qur'an*, p. 381-382.

All of a sudden the Friends appeared from everywhere, and our Master said:

> "Come, come, the Beloved has arrived!
> Come, come, the Rosegarden is blooming!"

He then said, "God was distributing alms without limit—where were all our poor needy ones?"

All the Friends lowered their heads, then they all accompanied him to the medresse singing sacred songs and whirling as they went. The sema continued that entire night, until the morning, without anyone tiring.

"I swear by God," cried our Master, "The faith that the privileged among these poor creatures have in the saints and prophets doesn't amount to a thing, unless the prophets and saints incline towards them and show them mercy."

Opening the Inner Eye [127]

Sirajuddin, the knower of God, was a reciter of the *Mathnawi,* and one of the renowned friends (May God perfume his tomb). Chelebi Husamuddin had taken this illustrious Friend under his wing.[35] He told us that one day Mevlana (May God sanctify his beloved tomb) interpreted the following verse from the Qur'an in this mystical way:

"*Men look upon that Reckoning as something far away—but We see it as near* [70:6-7]. Allah (May He be Exalted) possesses a container of salve such that if He anoints the outer eye and also the inner eye of one who is faithful with it, the faithful one will then become aware of hidden things. The mystery of mysteries will be unveiled to him, and with the eye of certainty (*ayn al-yaqin*) he will see the divine secrets in the Treasure house of our Sustainer. If God does not favor him in this way, by anointing his inner eye with this balm, he will not be able to see a single secret, even if the totality is unveiled before him.

> Even if a man were an angel,
> without the grace of God or His intimates
> how can he open his eyes?
> Without God's grace, the fire of anger
> would never be extinguished."

---

35. See section #593 of this volume regarding the beginning of the conveyance of the *Mathnawi* to Husamuddin who had become Mevlana's intimate companion and *khalifa* after the passing of Shams and Salahuddin Zarkub.

Mevlana finished by saying, "Either become a light in the eyes of the shaikh, or go away.

If you want light, become light;
if you want distance, be full of yourself and turn away."

An Offering of Roses [128]

Our Master Sirajuddin, the reciter of the *Mathnawi*, recounts that one day he went to Chelebi Husamuddin's garden: "I brought a scarf filled with red roses as an offering. It happened that Mevlana was there, and I wasn't aware of it. When I entered, I saw the Friends seated all around while Mevlana walked about the courtyard. All the verses and insights he spoke—the Friends were writing them down. I was so overcome, I forgot about the roses and left them in the place where the shoes were kept.

"Mevlana glanced in my direction and said,

'Whoever comes from the garden brings flowers as an offering;
whoever comes from the confectioner's shop
brings a handful of halvah.'

"Immediately, I brought the roses and bowing, placed them at his beloved feet. The Friends cried out and spread the petals, and the sema began."

The Whole Includes All the Parts [128b]

With respect to Sirajuddin, the Master said one day, "The entire world consists of various parts of only one being, as reflected in this *hadith:*[36] 'O Lord, guide my people for they do not know.' 'My people' refers to *all* the various parts; because if the unfaithful were not also included in these 'parts,' he would not be the 'whole.'

Everyone, good and bad, is part of a dervish.
If it's not like that, he's not a dervish."

---

36. A *hadith* is a saying of the Prophet Muhammad, emerging from his own personal wisdom and experience, not a part of the Qur'an. The body of *hadith* together with the Qur'an—along with *ijma'* (consensus) and *qiyas* (analogy)—are the basis for Islamic law and custom. A *Hadith Qudsi* is a saying of God conveyed through the Prophet Muhammad, exterior to the Qur'an.

A Heavy Bucket [128c]

One day, Parvana Mo'inuddin begged Sultan Walad: "I would like Mevlana to instruct me in private; this would be a special favor for his servant."

When Sultan Walad told his father about his request, he answered, "He would not be able to bear this burden!"

Sultan Walad pleaded the Parvana's case three times.

"O Bahauddin," Mevlana said, "a bucket that needs forty men to pull it from the well cannot be drawn up by just one man."

Sultan Walad bowed and said, "If I hadn't made the request, where would I have heard such a reflection?"

Taking Words to Heart [128d]

Sultan Walad also reported that, one day, the Parvana asked his father to give him some advice. Our Beloved Master reflected for a long time and then said, "Amir Mo'inuddin, I hear that you have learned the Qur'an by heart."

"Yes," the amir answered.

"I also hear that you have studied the *hadith* in the *Jami al-usul* as a student of Shaikh Sadruddin?"

"Yes, I have."

"You have read the word of God and that of the Prophet (peace and blessings be upon him), and you have not followed the advice offered by these glorious words. How, therefore, can you expect to follow any advice that I might give you?"

The Parvana left, weeping. After that, he reformed and acted with fairness and generosity and became an exemplary leader in the world, and Mevlana began the sema.

This Felicity Belongs to Heaven [129]

The keepers of the tradition reported that certain scholars of Konya of that era went to Qadi Sirajuddin Ormawi (May God have mercy on him) and complained about the Friends' love of music and the *rebab*, and their attachment to the sema, demanding that it be banned: "You are the chief of the religious scholars. You are an expert in Canonical Law and you sit as representative of the Prophet (peace and blessings be upon him). How can you let the love of this music spread. We can only hope that this custom will soon die out and disappear."

"This man (Mevlana), of whom you complain, is supported by God," responded the Qadi. "He is without equal in exoteric knowledge. It's not a good idea to oppose him. He knows, as does his God. 'Every sheep will be hung by its foot.' Mistakes will return to the one who makes them!"

However, these same troublemakers decided to test Mevlana with several difficult legal questions on jurisprudence, concerning different schools of law, logic, arabic grammar, philosophy, commentaries on the Qur'an, and astronomy. They gave their brief to a Turkish jurist, who went hesitantly to the sultan's palace to convey it. He found Mevlana reading a book, standing by the entrance. He put the papers into Mevlana's hands and watched from a distance.

Mevlana, without reading the papers, immediately asked for a pen and ink, and wrote at the bottom the answer to each question in great detail. In the same way that a doctor makes a potion, he subtly blended, one with another, the answers to all the questions. The Turkish jurist then took the document to the court, and, after reading the explanation to all the difficult questions, everyone was overwhelmed, ashamed, and bewildered by the extraordinary proceedings.

At the bottom, Mevlana had written: "May the wise of the world reflect on the *ayat*: *All this may be enjoyed in the life of this world—but the most beauteous of all goals is with God* [3:14]. As to the differences between the schools of law, we consider those the property of worldly people; we don't have our eye on any of that—we have withdrawn from the world and what is found there. This *rebab* gives spiritual nourishment to our dear Friends, it is needed by them. Personally, we have given it up and pleased the leaders of the religion, however because of our extreme need and distraction, we play on this strange instrument, for to please a stranger is our duty as People of God."

He then began reciting the *ghazal* of the *rebab*:

"Do you know of what the *rebab* sings—
of tears, and eyes and hearts on fire with love. . . ."

All the scholars repented and, ashamed of their behavior in the qadi's presence, admitted that Mevlana was right. They professed their admiration of his great magnaminity, worthy of Abraham, and of the immensity of his soul. Then and there, five of the most intelligent scholars became his disciples.

This felicity belongs to heaven and the stars,
not this earthly world;
it's not by force, or brute strength,
that one becomes blessed with good fortune.

The Power Is in His Hand [131]

Mevlana had a disciple, one of the most influential merchants in Konya, who had left on a pilgrimage. On the night of Arafat,[37] his wife had prepared a large quantity of halvah, which she shared with the neighbours and the poor. She also sent a large platter of the delicious sweets to Mevlana and asked him to send a blessing to her husband and remember him in his prayers.

Mevlana said, "This woman is our faithful companion (*siddiqa*). Come, eat, and partake of its blessing." All the Friends ate of the halvah and enjoyed the blessings of it—yet, still, the platter remained full. Our Master then took it and went out, towards the roof terrace. Puzzled, the Friends wondered what he was doing. A moment later, he came back from the terrace empty-handed.

He said, "I sent the halvah to our dear Friend, the merchant, so that he might have a bit of it, too."

The bewilderment and awe of the gentle Friends increased a thousandfold.

When the news of the return of the pilgrims arrived, overjoyed at their safe return, everyone went to meet them. However, this merchant, whose heart had been illuminated, came, shoeless, to visit Mevlana and to thank him. Our Master greeted him in friendship and gave him permission to return home. When he returned to his family, and the merchant's servant unpacked his luggage, his wife was amazed to see her porcelain platter.

She said, "This porcelain of mine, what is it doing with you? The date and name are inscribed on it."

The merchant replied, "I don't understand either what it is doing with me, but on the mountain of Arafat, the eve of the 'Eid, we were sitting in our tent with the other pilgrims. Suddenly, I saw a hand pierce through a corner of the tent and place this platter full of halvah

37. On the 9th of *Dhul Hijja*, the month of Hajj, all the pilgrims gather for prayer at the mountain of Arafat near Mecca from midday until evening as part of the completion of the pilgrimage ritual. It is the moment of union of the soul with the Beloved, the reflection of the Resurrection before God.

in front of us. I recognized the design as ours, but couldn't figure out how it had come there. The servants ran outside but saw no one."

Right away, the merchant's wife solved the mystery of the halvah. The merchant was bewildered at the great power of this saint, and, in the morning, he and his wife went to visit him to prostrate in his presence, weeping.

He said, "All this has happened as a result of your faith and sincerity: God Most High has manifested His power through me, His servant, as an intermediary. *All Bounty is in the hands of God, and He grants it to whomever He wills* [57:29]."

Frog Friends [134]

Every year, Mevlana and his followers would go by carriage to the hot springs, where they usually remained for forty or fifty days. On one occasion, the Friends had formed a large circle around the edge of a pool. Our Master, transported to the heavenly realms, immersed in the Lights of the Face, was conveying reflections from the Unseen. All at once, the frogs of the pool began to croak and made a terrible racket.

"What's this commotion?" Mevlana cried out in a terrifying voice. "Are you speaking or are we?"

All the frogs immediately fell silent, and not a croak was heard. When Mevlana arose to depart, he approached the edge of the water and gestured as if to say, "Now you have permission to speak."

Right away, all the frogs began to sing. Everyone present was astonished at this miracle, and almost two thousand people became his disciples that day.

With All Your Heart and Soul [135]

One day, Mevlana was on his way to pay a visit to his father, Bahauddin's tomb. That same day, the butchers of Konya had bought a bull to sacrifice, but just then it broke its rope and escaped from their hands. Everyone ran after it, but no one could catch it. In its wild flight, it encountered Mevlana. Immediately, it stopped and went gently up to him, and with the language of states, asked for forgiveness. Mevlana stroked it with his blessed hand, and when the butchers caught up, they bowed before him as well.

"You shouldn't kill this animal," said Mevlana, "let it be free!"

And so the bull was let loose, and it went off towards the countryside. When the Friends arrived, he shared his inspiration, "An animal whom they were going to kill ran away and turned to us. God, may He be exalted, in His infinite compassion has delivered it from death. Even so, a person who turns to God with all his heart and soul will be delivered from the fires of Hell and attain Paradise. There is nothing astonishing about this."

They say that this bull was never seen again—it vanished without a trace into the Konya countryside.

That glory of the pious, Shaikh Sinanuddin Najjar, the Carpenter (May God grace his spirit), told us that once our Master said, "The loss of a woman or of money can kill a worldly person, but the sweetness of mystical Love kills the dervish. God has created this world from pure nothingness, and it is to this nothingness that all must return so that something new can be born."

Ask, "What Shall I Do?" [135b]

The Shaikh also told us that, one day, Qutbuddin Shirazi (May God have mercy on him) came to visit Mevlana, who was in the midst of giving a passionate discourse on his father's *Ma'arif.* Suddenly, a carriage passed in front of the medresse, and a few of the Friends went out to see what the commotion was all about.

"It's either the noise of a carriage, or Heaven speaking," said our Master.

Everyone lowered their heads.

Then Qutbuddin asked him, "What is your Path?"

"Our path is to die and to take our wealth to Heaven. Until you die, you do not arrive at your destination. The Prophet (Peace and blessings be upon him), the most noble of the world, said, 'Unless you die, you will never attain anything.'"

"Alas," replied Qutbuddin, "What shall I do?"

"Ask, 'What shall I do,'" Mevlana answered. And then in the middle of the sema, Mevlana recited the following quatrain:

I asked, "What shall I do?"
He answered, "Ask, 'What shall I do?'"
I replied, "I want to seek a better way."
He said, "O seeker, just keep seeking and asking, 'What shall I do?'"

At this, Qutbuddin immediately became his disciple.

Mother Earth's Embrace [135c]

One of the great Friends died, and Mevlana was asked whether he should be buried in a coffin or not.

"What do my Friends think?" he asked.

That knower of divine mysteries, the mine of eternal truths, Karimuddin, son of Baktimour (May God's mercy be upon him), who was one of the leaders of the gatherings and a man of subtle insight, said, "It would be better if he were buried without a coffin."

"Why?" asked the Friends.

He answered, "A mother loves her child more than a brother loves a sister. A human being's body comes from the earth and so do the planks of wood from which the coffin is made. They are brothers to one another, but the earth is their common mother—it is more appropriate to put the body into the care of its compassionate mother."

Our Master gave his approval and added, "This idea can't be found in any book."

A Servant of His Love [135d]

The king of the qadis and magistrates, Kamaluddin of Kab, one of the distinguished judges of Anatolia, recounted:

In 656 A.H. (1258 C.E.), I went to Konya to see Sultan Izzuddin Keykavus (May God illuminate his tomb) to complete business concerning the province of Danishmandids, and to return with the royal orders and commands. By God's grace, my affairs had been quickly accomplished, and I was ready to leave. Then, a group of friends that included the great and wise of the capital, such as Shamsuddin of Mardin, Afsahuddin, and Zaynuddin al-Razi, and Shamsuddin of Malatya (May God have mercy on them) encouraged me to go to visit Mevlana. I had already heard of him and his glorious teachings from the people, but my vanity and pride, desire for wealth, and denial prevented me from taking this step—I didn't dare go. Finally, Divine grace enveloped my soul, and compelled by longing and pulled by the attraction of the heart of this sovereign of humankind, I had the honor of visiting him in the company of this worthy group.

As soon as we stepped across the threshold of the medresse, with great ceremony Mevlana came to greet me. With one glance at his blessed face, my heart melted and my mind stopped. All of us bowed in greeting, and out of all of them, he took me in his arms and said, "For so long you fled from our work, how have I finally found you here, in the middle of your work?"

"Praise be to God," he continued, "Kamaluddin[38] has turned his face towards the perfection (*kamal*) of splendor; he has become one of the perfected ones of our religion."

Then he conveyed such transcendant knowledge and mysteries that I had never heard before in all my life from the mouth of any shaikh, *qutb*, or wise man, nor read in any book. With a hundred thousand sincere longings, I joined the circle of Friends. I brought my son Sadruddin and Atabak Majduddin to him as disciples, and many of the sons of other noble and important families also became his devoted disciples.

When I had returned home, the wings of my soul were beating like a bird's with excitement in the cage of my body. I consulted my Friends and said, "I want to put on a sema and show myself worthy to be a disciple."

We looked all over Konya and could find only thirty baskets of sweets of the finest quality. They had to mix in other portions of sugar, because in those days most people lived very well and enjoyed complete ease—no delicacy, gathering, concert, or joyful banquet of delights was enough to satisfy the inhabitants of Konya and its environs.

I went to Gumaj Khatun of Toqat, the wife of the Sultan, and told her about the situation. She gave me ten more baskets of fine sugar. I was considering how for such a gathering this quantity of sweet julep might suffice, that perhaps I could make some julep with honey, for this would still not be enough.

I was still immersed in this thought when, suddenly, Mevlana appeared and said, "O Kamaluddin, if you have too many guests add more water, and there will be enough." Then, just as quickly, he disappeared like lightning. We ran after him, but he had totally vanished. We prepared the julep in the sink at the Qarata'i medresse and put it in several huge containers worthy of King Chosroes, which I then entrusted to the Sultan's servant and cupbearer, so that it wouldn't lose its potency. When we tasted it, it burned the tongue and throat, and we realized that just as our Master had said, it needed more water.

After we had added several pitchers of water, I tasted it, and it

---

38. Kamaluddin means "the perfect one (*kamal*) of the religion (*al-din*)."

was even sweeter than before. We filled ten more containers of this julep which was still even sweeter. I cried out from the depths of my heart: "This incredible miracle came from the order of our Master. We must make all kinds of dishes to go with this inexhaustible julep. Tonight I will invite all the sovereigns of the earth and the pillars of the religion." So many distinguished people came that it is impossible to render an account.

From the noon prayer until midnight, our Master immersed himself in the sema—through the strength of his friendship with God and the power of his good guidance, he controlled the assembly, overwhelming everyone, so that no one was able to move. I had tied the belt of service around my soul and was distributing the julep to the thirsty semazens. Mo'inuddin, the Parvana and the sultan's representatives were, like this servant, standing afire with a hundred thousand longings—like candles of Tiraz, in a state of bewilderment. Strange thoughts and reflections passed through my heart.

Mevlana caught hold of the reciters and began this quatrain:

"He came full of love, warmly in haste—
his soul caught the fragrance of the rose-garden of Truth.
Above all other judges, he came running today—
the Qadi of Kab in search of the water of life."

Then the sema continued and increased in intensity. Mevlana beckoned me to him, embraced me, kissed me on my eyes and cheeks, and began reciting:

"If you wish to know me, ask the nights;
ask my pale cheeks and dry lips . . ."

It was a very long *ghazal*, vast. I immediately bared my head, tore my clothes, and became a disciple of his love. After that, my situation in life improved as much as it had diminished before—my children, my descendants, my means increased infinitely, and that which he granted to my heart, that which he made me taste, cannot be expressed in any words. My chest is bursting with love, and my tongue is speechless. It is as he said:

"Whoever becomes my servant will gain the kingdom of happiness.
Whoever chooses my door will be the king of this world
and the next."

Turning Towards the One [137]

The Sultan of teachers, Sharafuddin of Kayseri (May God's peace and blessings be upon him), a second Shaf'i[39] of the age, was one of the intimate and distinguished disciples. Tadjuddin Mo'tazz built a medresse in Aksaray for him. He recounted:

One day, when I was serving Mevlana, he said, "It is not permitted for a disciple to perform the ritual prayer in the presence of his shaikh, even if he is at the Kaaba. For truly, Bahauddin Walad was once sharing divine insights when the time for prayer arrived; a group of the disciples left his presence and began to make their prayers. Some of the disciples remained immersed in the Shaikh's presence, burning with his light. By that light opening within them, God revealed to them that the faces of those who went to make the prayer were turned away from the *qibla,* so that their prayer was invalid."

Sema Is a Need [137b]

Mevlana also expressed this insight: "Sema is as obligatory for the perfect shaikh as *salaah* and the fast of Ramadan. It is optional for the sincere disciples and Friends, but they are to perform it as much as they can. Sema is forbidden to ordinary people who are neither teachers nor students of the Way. . . .

"I am not this body that is seen by the glance of the mystic lovers—I am this taste (*dhawq*), this joy that arises within the heart of a disciple from hearing our words and hearing our name. O Great God! When you receive this breath, when you contemplate this taste within your soul, consider that to be your prey, and give thanks for it to God, because that is what I am.

When you experience a moment of ecstasy
because of a meeting with the Friend,
it is that moment you find your destiny.
Take care not to let this moment slip away,
because it rarely comes again."

---

39. Imam al-Shaf'i (d. 820 C.E.) was one of the foremost Islamic scholars who began a school of Islamic law (*madhhab*), which is still followed today. The four main Sunni schools of Islamic law are the Maliki, Shaf'i, Hanafi (which Mevlana followed) and Hanbali; the main Shi'a school is the Jafari *madhhab* following the example of Imam Jafar al-Sadiq.

Food that Increases Light [137c]

Our Master continued, "Do not be so concerned about a lawful mouthful or lawful gain, since this is just income for expenditure—what is important is to know where to spend it. Many a lawful income only reaps the fruit of laziness and deceit. If you consume something that increases your love and desire for the next world and directs you to the path travelled by the prophets and saints, know that that is lawful. And if it draws you away from your love for the next world, know that it is forbidden.

This is to know, not to speak about.

Food that increases light and perfection is lawful sustenance.
From the lawful morsel come knowledge and wisdom;
from that morsel come love and tenderness.
If you find the trap of envy in it,
and ignorance and carelessness open, know it's forbidden.
Sustenance is the seed of which thoughts are the fruits—
it is a sea in which the pearl of thought is found.
From lawful nourishment, a desire to serve is born in the soul
and a firm resolve to reach the other world."

He added, "While you are able, enjoy the good things of this world, but be careful not to get too caught up in these good things or to spend too much effort on them. Use your time to follow the path and in listening to the words of the saints, so that the morsel might not devour you. It is thus that the Elect of God (Peace and blessings be upon him) said with respect to 'Omar,[40] the Prince of the faithful, (May God be pleased with him) 'Eat in the way that 'Omar does, since he eats like a real man and acts like a man.' "

Then he continued, reciting:

"The moment a morsel becomes a pearl within you,
eat as much as you can.
But if pure food turns sour in your stomach,
put a lock on your throat and hide the key.
One for whom the morsel becomes a Light of Majesty—
he may eat what he wants—it is lawful for him."

---

40. 'Omar, one of the early converts, had been a strong opponent to Muhammad and his prophethood, yet, overwhelmed by the beauty and truth of the revelation of the Qur'an, he became one of the most intimate companions, and, eventually, the third Caliph (*khalifa*) after the Prophet Muhammad, guiding the Muslim community. He was known for his fierce honesty, devotion, and fastidious integrity.

Discover the Hidden Face [137d]

During the gatherings, Shamsuddin, the professor, appeared to be bewildered and overcome with emotion in the presence of our Master, while the rest of the friends joyfully took part in the sema.

"Why do you look at me with such persistence, and why don't you join the whirling?" Mevlana asked one day.

Shamsuddin bowed and answered, "What other face is there in all the world beside your blessed face that one might want to contemplate? Your servant finds no joy equal to this contemplation."

Mevlana answered, "That's fine; may it be a blessing. However, we have another, hidden face which you cannot see with your earthly eyes. Try to discover that other hidden face and to perceive it, so that when our visible face disappears, you will be able to clearly see this other hidden face. When you see it, then you will truly know me."

Make every effort to see the Light behind the veils;
then when the veils have vanished, blindness won't increase.

O God Most Great! One mustn't stare directly at the sun—
it's brilliance will blind the eye, obscure the mind,
and you won't be able to see it.

The Hidden Ones [138]

One day, Sultan Walad (May God sanctify his unique mystery) recounted:

I asked my father for an explanation of the *Hadith Qudsi*, "My saints are sheltered within my domes, and no one knows them but Me." I wondered if "dome" referred to their physical bodies or to their lower self.

Mevlana answered, "Oh Bahauddin, that is true—'dome' refers to their characters. Certain saints have a weakness for the material world, others for voyages, and others for romance; some wish to succeed in trade, in the world of profit and loss, while others immerse themselves in the sciences. Some appear to act contrary to the laws of the prophets and thus displease people; they remain hidden under these domes and escape public recognition that way and find the peace of obscurity. Ordinary people and even the adepts of this community don't know very much about them or who they are. As the

Messenger of God said, 'Truly, God Most High has hidden Friends.'

> Some of God's Friends are hidden as they journey—
> how could they be known by worldly people?
> Their greatness is invisible to others, even for a moment.
> They and their miracles dwell in God's sanctuary.
> Even the dear servants of God (*abdals*) cannot say their names.

"A servant of God whose soul has been blessed by divine Grace is able to recognize the saints inside these 'domes'; such a servant can rise above the contradictions and receive the blessing of their guidance. The copper of their existence then becomes gold, and they find the philosopher's stone."

Then he recited:

> "To recognize the saints is the philosopher's stone for you,
> but what is this stone compared to the power of their glance."

Becoming Gold [138b]

Shaikh Badruddin of Tabriz (May God have mercy on him), the architect of the blessed tomb of Mevlana, was also renowned for his knowledge of alchemy and the esoteric sciences. During the day, he was a devoted member of the dervish circle, but at night he busied himself with alchemy, and as a result of this work, was able to convey gold and silver to the Friends.

One night, Mevlana entered his private chamber and saw him absorbed in this work. Overcome with the awe he felt at the sight of our Master, he was transfixed in his place, not knowing what might happen. . . . Mevlana picked up the anvil and handed it to him. Badruddin saw that it had been changed into gold, shining with a subtle light.

Mevlana said, "If you make gold, make it in this way . . . it is a process that needs no apparatus, no tools, nor anvil. Indeed, know that if you spend the substance of your life in this work in your usual way, when the great calamity arrives you will carry away nothing but the reputation of a counterfeiter; when your gold has become copper you will be full of regret and your remorse then will be of no use. Make efforts so that the copper of your existence might become gold and that your gold might become pearls. These pearls—it is something that cannot even be conceived of by 'so and so.'"

And he said,

"Jesus transforms your copper into gold.
If it is already gold, he transforms it into pearls;
if it is already pearl, he makes it even more beautiful—
more beautiful than the moon or even Jupiter."

Immediately, Badruddin tore his clothes and renounced his art.

Signs of Affection [138c]

Mevlana said, "Our Prophet (Peace and blessings upon him) practiced acts of devotion that he was not obliged to perform, for he was free of all legal obligations. I perform my acts of devotion out of respect for the law of the Prophet and the path he followed, and also to bring the truth of this law into the manifest world.

Until his last breath, he didn't forget his devotions for a moment.

The tranquility of outward form
    sustained by such profound meaning
is only possible in a wondrous sovereign."

He added, "All that the prophets and saints practiced, as well as the body of law that they gave us, encourages us to do the same. It is our responsibility to undertake it and to follow them."

The Friends, in awe of God, and moved by this pure mystery, recounted, "When Mevlana heard the muezzin's call to prayer (*adhan*),[41] he would kneel, in a posture of total submission and say, 'May Your Name last for eternity, O You who illuminate our soul.' He would repeat this three times and then bow, stand up, and begin *salaah* saying:

'By prayer, fasting, pilgrimage, and alms
we demonstrate our faith.
To give a present or an offering is a sign of affection.
If love were only thoughts and ideas,
the forms of fasting and prayer would not exist.'"

Through Love . . . [139]

The Beloved Friends told us that, one day, Mevlana was sharing insights regarding the benefits of *salaah* and prayers of longing.

He said, "In Balkh, there was a Friend who would jump out of

41. A *muezzin* is one who loudly chants the call to prayer (*adhan*) to gather people for the ritual prayer (*salaah*), five times each day.

bed as soon as the muezzin began calling the *adhan*: 'Allahu Akbar!' He would bow down in humble prayer for the duration. When the Friend was on his deathbed and was breathing his last, all of a sudden, the muezzin began the call to prayer (*adhan*). The dying man leapt up and began his ritual prayer just as he always had. God Most High, to reward him for these offerings of devotion, eased his death pangs. When they buried him, the angels Monkar and Nakir[42] came to this man of poverty (*faqir*) and began to question him.

"At this moment, a word came from God Most High: 'Be gentle with Our dear servant and treat him with respect, because during his life he continually remembered Our great Name and praised Us in all humility.'

Whoever shows consideration will also be considered;
whoever brings sugar will be given almond cake.
When through love, you give yourself to your Lord,
your Lord in turn will give Himself to you."[43]

Because I Lost My Heart [140]

Shaikh Muhammad, the servant (May God have mercy on him), told us:

During a very severe winter when the children would feel the cold even when wrapped in their heavy coats and beside the stoves, Mevlana would go up onto the roof of the medresse to pray and be awake until morning, offering a hundred thousand prayers and lamentations. When he would come down, after having offered the dawn prayer, I would take off his boots and find blood on his feet. The Friends wept, but he said, "Don't cry, this is just how it was for the Prophet:

The Prophet's feet were swollen from standing up all night,
and the people of Quba were upset and tore their garments.
'Not so that your past and future sins might be forgiven,'
he said, 'It is the boiling of Love, neither fear nor hope.'"

Our Master continued, "Then our Prophet (Peace and blessings be upon him) would renew his ablutions and offer the dawn prayer until it was mid-morning; then he would perform the extra mid-

---

42. Munkar and Nakir are two angels who visit the newly deceased in the grave to test their faith.

43. This reflects a *Hadith Qudsi*: He that belongs to God, God shall belong to him (*man kana lillahi kana 'llahu lahu*).

morning prayer until it was nearly midday.

"He would say: 'I was sent as a teacher, and I was taken while I was still in the school of instruction. If I don't perform my prayers diligently, my unfortunate people will become negligent and careless.'"

And then Mevlana began reciting this ghazal:

> "All these efforts and seeking are not made out of fear—
> he is free; it is the right path for one who is teaching. . . ."

Mevlana was continually saying: "In the name of God, pray, so that your means will increase and your successors and your friends will flourish, and, on Resurrection Day, you will be able to help your friends with your prayers. Surely prayers are blessed, and the one who brings his need in supplication will have his need met both in this world and the next."

The Taste of Pure Milk [142]

It was said that when Mevlana saw someone doing the ritual prayer with intense devotion he would cry, "Bravo! O eager servant, humble and modest slave! Courageous is the one who serves his master with constancy and practices his devotions for as long as he has the strength. The outer form of prayer and fasting are like a compassionate mother who little by little weans her baby that she might accustom her to the delights of food and drink so that her capacity increases for this sustenance. When the sincere servant finds strength in his acts of devotion and makes progress on the spiritual path, his capacity increases until he is able to come near the Most High (May His All-Powerfulness be Known).

> Our Sustainer said in the Qur'an:
> *Prostrate yourself and draw near* [96:19];
> through the prostration of our body, we draw close with our soul.
>
> If you wish to find a way out of this ruined prison,
> don't draw back from the Friend; *prostrate and draw near.*"
>
> [*Mathnawi* I:3607]

Tears of Blessing [143]

The wife of our Master, Kira Khatun, Lady of the World and Khadija[44]

44. Khadija was the purely faithful and beloved wife of the Prophet Muhammad (May Peace and blessings be upon them both) who was the first to support the

of the time (May the blessings of God be upon her) told us:

One night our Master was offering the night prayer in the *soffa* area in the house; he recited the *Fatiha,*[45] word for word, so slowly that those present would have had time to recite ten chapters of the Qur'an. During the prayer, tears fell from his blessed eyes so profusely that we could hear them falling.

I wept, kissed his blessed feet, and cried, "O intercessor for God's servants, the hope of the unfortunate is in your blessed hands. Alas for us . . . why all these lamentations, this weeping and sighs?"

He answered, "By God! By the grandeur of His Majestic Being and His Sovereignty, these efforts are very limited and insufficient, but I ask forgiveness of our Great and Glorious Sustainer and pray: 'O Absolutely Generous One, my power is just this much, but Your power is without limit; forgive me.' When Our Prophet heard the words: *So that God may forgive you your sins, past as well as future and so bestow upon you the full measure of His blessings, and guide you on a straight way* [48:2], he responded, 'Am I not a grateful servant?' "

Though we are full of error, Your Mercy is great.
Our apology is based on hope in Your Generosity.

What Do You Love? [150]

Someone asked one of Mevlana's disciples, "What do you see in Mevlana that has inspired you to become his student?"

He answered, "What more could I want than this—that I am associated with him and that they call me by his name—'so and so-uddin Mevlevi.' What could be better than that my name is connected to his? My soul is in love with his soul, so it moves with affection near him and is one of his friends. The secret contained in the proverb, 'Someone who loves a people is one of them' has become real for me. This is a result of the favor he has bestowed on me, and from the pull of his presence. *Truly, all bounty is in God's hand alone—He grants it unto whomever He wills* [57:29].

"As it was said:

Prophet in his mission.

45. The *Fatiha* is the opening chapter of the Qur'an, similar in content and length to the Lord's prayer in the Christian faith, it is recited at the beginning of every cycle of ritual prayer in Islam and also frequently when one is beginning an endeavor or asking for blessing for someone who has passed away.

The worth and glory of a lover
is determined by the object of his love.
O bewildered lover!
See what rank you have attained."

A Pen Always Ready [151]

Mevlana often told the Friends, "No matter what state I might be in, if someone arrives with a legal question to solve or any other kind of question, never send them away. Don't hesitate to bring them to me, so that our income from the medresse might be lawful, and I don't wish the capacity for delivering *fatwa*s to be cut off from this God-conscious family."

So, even during moments of intoxication and during the semas, the noble companions always had an inkwell and a pen ready. Even without reading the question, Mevlana would understand the situation and would always render the right answer. One day, he offered a solution to a difficult question under dispute. He gave this *fatwa* into the hands of Shamsuddin of Mardin who rejected it and took it to Qadi Sirajuddin. Shamsuddin and the Qadi attempted with all sorts of foolishness to prove the lack of foundation for the ruling. Our master Imam Ikhtiyaruddin (May the Mercy of God be upon him) was present at this meeting, and, disagreeing with them, got up and left. He told Mevlana about the proceedings.

Mevlana just smiled and said, "Convey our greetings to these masters, and tell them it is not wise to speak ill of a dervish if they haven't sorted out the situation. In brief, our Mevlana Shamsuddin has a commentary on *fatwa*s in two volumes that he bought in Aleppo for forty dirhems—he hasn't looked at this book in a long time. Tell him to look in the middle, on the eighth line, and he will find the solution to the problem."

Ikhtiyaruddin left immediately and told the scholars what Mevlana had said. They rose and begged pardon.

"It's true," said Shamsuddin of Mardin. "I bought this book in Aleppo for forty dirhems and have not read it. What a miracle! We should pay attention to the rest."

The Qadi Sirajuddin asked to see the books, and Shamsuddin's son went to fetch them. Following Mevlana's instructions, they counted page by page until the solution to the problem was found just where he had indicated. Everyone was astounded at the light of his Friendship with God and his comprehension of secrets—they acknowledged his penetrating intellect, the beauty of his miracles, and his gracious temperament. Recognizing their helplessness, they asked his forgiveness.

The Child of My Spirit [152]

Shamsuddin of Mardin told us this:

One night, I saw the Prophet (Blessings and Peace be upon him) in a dream; he was seated in a room. When I approached and greeted him, he turned his blessed face away from me. I approached from another side of the room. Again he turned away. In tears, I said: "O Messenger of God, for so many years I have borne difficulties in the hope of receiving your blessings and grace. I have tried to merit from and to deepen in the traditions and in following your example; I have tried to solve difficult theological questions. Why do you turn away from this poor one? What is the reason?"

The Prophet (Peace and blessings upon him) answered: "All that it is true, however you have looked down on our brothers, and this doesn't please us. Such an action and opinion is a grave mistake, an immense error, a shameful offense.

O you who have considered the Friends of God as separate
from God,
think how much better it would be
if you thought highly of them!

"And especially of Mevlana, who is the child of my spirit."

When I awoke, I asked forgiveness and repented. While I was fortunate enough to witness his many miracles, I had not yet been accepted into our Master's good graces. In the end, I surrendered and became one of his devoted disciples.

The Shirt Off His Back [154]

Mevlana's immersion in contemplation was so deep that if suddenly his shoe got stuck in the mud, he would simply pull his foot out and walk on with bare feet. And if beggars approached him, he would give them the cloak that was covering his shoulders, the turban from his head, the shirt off his back, the shoes from his feet, and off he would go.

Knowing [159]

The gracious queen, Gumaj Khatun, the wife of Sultan Ruknuddin, was one of Mevlana's disciples. She reported the following:

One day, I was seated in our old palace with my children and the ladies of the court. Suddenly, Mevlana appeared and cried, "You must leave immediately!"

We all ran outside in our bare feet; just then, the vaulted ceiling of the salon collapsed and fell at our blessed master's feet.

To show my gratitude, I gave generous alms to the needy and sent the Friends seven hundred dirhems soltani.

A Mountain Dancing Like a Camel [167]

One day, our Master was tired of being with people and left for the bathhouse. There was a tumultuous crowd there as well, so he went into the reservoir and immersed himself in the hot water. He stayed there three days and three nights without coming out. He was plunged in Divine revelations, seeing the heavenly lights of Divine Love.

After the third day, Chelebi Husamuddin pleaded with him to come out and join the companions. He began to weep when he saw Mevlana's blessed face so pale and weak, and he cried, "Our Master's delicate constitution is suffering; he is too thin and weak! Have pity on us, your poor companions, and break your fast with a cool sherbet. If you rest for a moment, what will be the harm?"

Mevlana answered, "Mount Sinai, in spite of its immense bulk could not withstand a single ray of Divine splendor and broke into pieces.

Our mighty God broke the mountain into pieces
with His glance.
Have you ever seen a sight like this,
a mountain dancing like a camel?

This weak servant has seen, in these three days and nights, the rays of our Lord's splendor and the lights of Divine Perfection shine over him seventy times. How is he able to bear this, without turning away from this heavenly sight?

Through Divine omnipotence the bodies of human beings
have become able to support unconditioned Light.
God's power makes a glass vessel the dwelling-place
of that Light of which Sinai cannot bear even a mote.

A lamp-niche and a lamp-glass[46]
have become the dwelling-place of that Light
by which Mt. Qaf[47] and Mt. Sinai[48] are broken open.
Know that the bodies of holy ones are the lamp-niche
and their hearts the glass:
this lamp illumines the firmament.
The light of the heavens is dazzled by this Light
and vanishes like the stars in this radiance of morning."

He rose and the sema began. There were Qur'an reciters present, and the music and whirling went on without interruption for seven days and nights.

Be as You Are [168]

The great Companions told us that the Prophet Khidr (Greetings of peace be upon him) continually conversed with Mevlana. He would question Mevlana about the secrets of the treasures of Truth, of the Unseen World, and receive answers of great subtlety.

One day, Sultan Walad was winding the cloth of his turban and couldn't get the edge of the turban straight. He undid it and began to rewind it again.

Mevlana said, "O Bahauddin! Don't keep rewinding your turban. Don't be so concerned with your appearance. Once in my youth, I, too, rearranged my turban over again, and my brother Khidr (Greetings of peace be upon him) took his companionship elsewhere, so that for a while I was deprived of his conversation."

From that day on, Sultan Walad never rewound his turban. His companions would wind it for him and simply place it on his blessed head.

Visits from Khidr [169]

In his youth, Mevlana studied in Damascus at the Moqaddamiyya Medresse. Khidr was often seen, by those with insight (*basirah*), visiting Mevlana's retreat cell of the medresse. Since then, this cell has been a place of pilgrimage of free men (*ahrar*).[49] Even so, the major-

46. This passage from the *Mathnawi* VI, 3066-3069 is a commentary on the "Light verse" of *Surah an-Nur* 24:35.

47. Mt Qaf is the mythical mountain that embraces the ends of the earth.

48. Mt. Sinai is the mountain on which Moses received the revelation of the Torah.

49. *Ahrar*: "the good" said to be the second rank in the hierarchy of saints, after simple *wali*. Some say they are three hundred in number. See *Kashf-al Mahjub* (*The*

ity of the perfected ones were unmindful and relatively unaware of the secrets of Khidr, because not everyone can see or comprehend those mysterious beings whom God conceals.

Listening to the Heart [170]

It is recounted in the tradition that Shaikh Abu Bakr Kattani[50] (May the mercy of God be upon him) had the honor of visiting the holy Kaaba. While sitting under the waterspout of the roof he saw an old man enter through the Banu Sheyba Gate (*Bab as-Salaam*).[51] The man approached him with complete dignity, greeted him, and said, "Why don't you go to the Station of Abraham?[52] There is a gathering of men there who are listening to the sayings of the Prophet; you could listen, also, and profit from it."

"O Khwaja! It is true they are discussing the long chains of transmission, but everything I might hear there I can hear here from my master, without chains of transmission," said Abu Bakr.

"To whom are you listening?" asked the unknown man.

"My heart conveys to me, from my Sustainer."

"What proof do you have of it?"

"This proof—that you are Khidr."

"Glory be to God!" replied Khidr, because it was indeed he, "I thought that I knew all the Friends of God and that none were hidden from me; now I realize that some hidden servants of God are veiled from my sight—I do not know them, but they know me. It is even as He has said in His noble book: *Above everyone who is endowed with knowledge there is One who knows* [12:76]."

O courageous one! There is hand over hand,
up to God, the Goal of all goals.

Mevlana also said, "Our Mevlana Shamsuddin Tabrizi is the beloved of Khidr (Peace be upon both of them)." Above the door of

---

Unveiling of the Concealed) of Hujwiri, trans. Nicholson, p 214.)

50. Abu Bakr Muhammad Kattani was a companion of the renowned mystic, Junayd al-Baghdadi. Later he spent a long while in retreat in Mecca, where he died in 934.

51. This is the gate to the Holy Mosque around the Kaaba through which the Prophet Muhammad would always enter.

52. The "Station of Abraham" is a special place of prayer near the Kaaba. A small structure there houses Abraham's footprint from the moments of his rebuilding of the Kaaba with his son, Ishmael.

the cell of the medresse, Mevlana wrote with his own blessed hand: "This is the lodging of the beloved of Khidr (Peace be upon him)."

Gatherings from the Other World [175]

Our Master Sharifuddin of Kayseri told us the following:

When Shaikh Sadruddin came foward to say the funeral prayers for Mevlana, he suddenly gave a great sigh and was lost to himself for some moments. Then he offered the prayers with tears of blood flowing from his eyes. Some of the prominent people there asked him what had happened.

"When I came forward to offer the prayers," Shaikh Sadruddin replied, "I saw pure beings, spirits from the Heavenly World, present there, and the spirit of our Prophet (May peace and blessings be upon him) had taken on form, and they were engaged in the prayer for Mevlana. All the angels of heaven, clothed in blue, were weeping."

For forty days, the shaikh and all the other distinguished people of Konya came and went, visiting the blessed tomb with great devotion.

Our Master Sharifuddin added, "My teacher and master of *hadith*, Qadi Sirajuddin, who was standing facing Mevlana's tomb, cried out and recited these verses:

'Would that the day the thorn of death pierced your foot
this head might have been struck by death's sword,
so that now my eye might not see this world without you.
Here I remain, at your tomb, dust covering my head.' "

Intercessions [176]

That sovereign of scholars, our Master Salahuddin Malati (May the mercy of God be upon him) said, "When I became a disciple of Mevlana, I noticed that during the course of a single day, he would send ten to twelve notes to the Parvana and other important people on behalf of the poor and the needy. They never failed.

"I wondered to myself if, on Resurrection Day, this assistance would also be possible.

"Mevlana said to me, 'Yes, by God! Why would it not be so? There will be even more for the virtuous of the community—mercies, intercessions, and generosity. As it has been said:

The virtuous of my community won't need my intercessions

on that Day of Difficulty.
Instead, they will be the intercessors,
and their word will work perfectly well.

If the sword cuts while it is in its scabbard; imagine, how effective it might be when unsheathed.'

Salahuddin continued, "Very grateful, the Friends cried out with joy."

Grasp His Grandeur [177]

One day, the Friends asked Mevlana: "We have noticed that certain of the Friends of God are prideful. This pride—where does it come from?"

He answered, "With the man of God pride is in His grandeur; it is not pride in his own opinions or passions, nor a presumption of rank. Imam Jafar Sadiq[53] (May God be pleased with him), who purified his soul and who paid no attention to the opinons of caliphs and kings, was asked about pride.

"He said, 'May God protect me! I have no pride. As soon as I left behind my own existence the Grandeur of God annihilated me and took the place of my pride. This pride comes from His Grandeur; as for me, I don't exist!' "

The pride of the tongue devours your longing.
Let go of pride and grasp His Divine Grandeur.

Happy Are Those Who Are Generous with What God Has Bestowed [182]

A wise monk in the region of Constantinople had heard of the learning, humility, and tenderness of Mevlana and, overwhelmed with affection for him, went to Konya to find him. The monks of the city came out to greet him and welcomed him with honor. The sincere monk asked to be taken to visit our Master. However, by chance, he

53. Imam Jafar al-Sadiq (d. 765) was the fifth generation grandson of the Prophet Muhammad. A spiritual pole (*qutb*), he is a connecting link for many of the sufi lineages (*silsilah*) and a common inspiration for both Sunni Muslims (as through his mother's line he was descended from Abu Bakr) and for Shi'i Muslims (for whom he was the main spiritual guide and religious leader, the sixth Imam, to whom they look for their religious law—*Ja'fariyya madhab*). He was known for both his holiness and knowledge, and the great Sunni theologians, Abu Hanifa, Malik b. Anas, and Sufyan ath-Thawri, all studied with him.

met him on the road, and when he saw him he prostrated himself three times before this sovereign of the spiritual world. When he got up he saw that Mevlana, also, was prostrating before him. It is said that our Master bowed his head thirty-three times before this monk, who cried out, tore his clothes, and said, "O Sultan of Religion! How can you show such humility and abase yourself like this before me—such an unworthy and miserable one?"

Mevlana replied, "There is a *hadith* of our sultan [Muhammad]: 'Blessed is the one to whom God has given riches, beauty, honor, and power who is generous with his wealth, chaste with his beauty, humble in his honor, and just with his power.' How could I not be humble before a servant of God or not abase myself? If I didn't do this, what worth would I have, what use would I be?"

The Radiant Peacock Lady [183]

In the caravanserai of the Minister Diyauddin, there was a woman called Tawus Khatun (Peacock lady) who played the harp and sang with a very beautiful voice. She played sweetly and caressed the hearts of her listeners. Everyone had fallen in love with her graceful beauty; her skill on the harp enraptured them.

One day, Mevlana happened to enter the caravanserai and seated himself across from her door. Tawus emerged from her room and bowing before him, placed her harp upon the hem of Mevlana's robe and invited him into her room. Mevlana accepted and spent the whole day, from early morning until the evening prayer there with her, in prayer and supplication. He then cut a cubit of cloth from his turban, gave it to her, distributed dinars of red gold to her servants, and departed.

Just then, the Sultan's treasurer, Sharifuddin, happened to pass by and overcome, fell in love with her. He sent trustworthy people to escort her to the bathhouse and to convey to her fifty thousand dinars as a *kulahbend,* or bridal dowry.

He rendered her service in countless ways and the night they brought her as a bride to his home, he asked her: "You have never seemed so beautiful or full of graceful perfection! I see you now as the Rabi'a [54] or Zulaihka[55] of our time; how is that? You are not the same as you were before; where does this elegance and splendor come from?"

She told him what had happened, how Mevlana had honored her, and described the gift of cloth from his turban with which she had fashioned a headband. Sharifuddin was overjoyed, sent grateful offerings to Mevlana, and became his devoted disciple.

Eventually, the state of Tawus the harpist rose to such a degree that the beauties of Konya and the luminous beings of Paradise became her disciples. She performed clear miracles among them and could read a person's secret thoughts. She freed all her slaves and assisted them in marrying. In the end, the caravanserai where she had lived was transformed into a bathhouse now known as *Naqshlu hammam.*

Those Who Are Hidden [186]

Sultan Walad (May God help us through his eternal secret) told us the following:

One day my father was sitting in his holy medresse. I saw three young men, clothed in red, enter, greet him, and sit down in complete presence (*huzur*).

"It is all right; you may take him," said my father. The young men immediately disappeared from my sight. I asked my father about what had happened.

"These young men are of the seven;[56] one of their number died

---

54. Rabi'a al-Adawiyya (717-801 C.E.), a woman of Basra, in what is now Iraq, is recognized as one of the major saints of Islam. Orphaned at an early age, she was captured and sold into slavery. Eventually it was her utter devotion to God that gained her her freedom. While a slave, after her duties were completed she would pass the night in prayer. One night, her owner arose and discovered her immersed in and surrounded by intense Light. In the morning he granted her her freedom. She became one of the immense sources of Light for other seekers of unity with the Divine. It is she who is credited with first clearly expressing the relationship with the Divine in the language we have come to recognize as particularly Sufic, by referring to God as the Beloved.

55. Zulaikha, known for her extreme beauty, was the wife of Potiphar, the vizier of the Pharoah of Egypt. Overwhelmed by the beauty of their servant, Joseph (who would grow to become the prophet of God), she fell in love with him. Her seductive beauty was a test for Joseph who took refuge in God and matured in his prophethood. Zulaikha, also, ultimately discovered her own reliance upon the Divine Beloved.

56. There is an idea that a core group of seven (or in some versions, forty) illuminated beings hold the spiritual well-being of humanity and all of creation in

suddenly, and they asked for our water-carrier as a replacement. He has attained a state of completion and is beloved by God. I indicated they might take him and put him in the place of the deceased."

Then he cited this *hadith* of the Prophet, "Whenever one of them dies, God replaces him by another; when the command comes, he is taken."

The Friends searched for the water-carrier, but he had vanished. After Mevlana's death, the water-carrier visited Sultan Walad, revealed certain secrets pertaining to his station and rank, and then disappeared.

The Tree of Paradise [187]

The Friend of God, the angel incarnate, the illuminated heaven, Mevlana Ikhtiyaruddin the Imam (May the Mercy of God be upon him) had a dream that he related to Mevlana and asked for an interpretation of it. He said, "Last night in my dream I saw an infinite sea, and, upon the shore of the sea, a tree resembling the Tuba tree of Paradise [13:28], extremely large and tall. Upon its branches an infinite number of great birds were perched; each sang sweet melodies and proclaimed, 'How amazing is God (*Subhanallah*)!' I was overcome by this majesty."

Mevlana responded, "This infinite sea is the vastness of God Most High. The great tree is the blessed being of Muhammad Mustafa (May God's peace and blessings be upon him). The branches are the diverse stations of the prophets and saints; the great birds are their spirits. The various melodies that they are singing, these are their subtle ideas, their secrets, and the words of their languages."

The Way of Fasting [189]

One day, Mevlana said to Sultan Walad, "O Bahauddin! If anyone asks what our path is, tell them it is fasting," and he added, "but it is much more than that! It is to die."

Then he told a short story:

A dervish arrived at the door of a house one day and asked for water. A beautiful young girl came out of the house with a ewer and gave it to the dervish, who said, "I am so thirsty, I could drink a large jugful!"

The girl cried, "Shame! Shame! A person who spends the day

---

balance through their purity and concentration on the Divine.

eating and the night sleeping, what kind of dervish is this? A true dervish is one who doesn't eat even in the evening, much less during the day."

This dervish, until the day of his death, never again broke his fast during the day, and he achieved his goal.

Desire Me with All Your Heart [190]

Sultan Walad related:

My father called me to him one day, kissed me on the cheeks and the head, showed me infinite favor, and asked, "O Bahauddin, would you like me to show God to you."

"That would be an immense blessing," I answered.

He replied, "You will see Him in ten days, if you spend the twenty-four hours of the day and night in the following way: first, for twenty-two hours according to the stars, you will occupy yourself with the affairs of this world, such as sleeping, eating, and so on. The two other hours will be used in the service of God, and so on until all twenty hours are used for your devotions and only four hours for the affairs of the world and your companions. Then, you arrive at a time when every moment will be used in the service of God, and your attachments to this vanishing world will be completely severed. After that, contemplate God as long as you wish and are able, and play in that love. All that you say or that you seek of Him will easily be obtained."

Sultan Walad exclaimed, "Inspired by my father's pure soul, I followed his instructions, and I became as he had indicated by his guidance, just as God Most High said to Moses, his intimate friend, 'Be for Me as I want, so that I will be for you as you want.'

Two days ago Love said to me, ' I'm all coquetry (*naz*).
Become complete longing (*niyyaz*) when I play.
Set aside your flirtaciousness
    and desire me with all your heart—
then, for you, I will make Myself all that you desire.' "

Everything Is Singing His Praise [191]

The wise companions recounted that towards the end of his life, whenever Mevlana began a sema, Shamsuddin of Mardin would hold a drum over his head, crying, "Truth! Truth! It is singing the praises of God! Whoever says this sema is unlawful is himself unlawful."

Then Shamsuddin related this anecdote:

"One day, Imam 'Ali (May God be pleased with him) heard the sound of a bell. He asked his companions: 'Do you know what that bell is saying?'

"They answered: 'God, the Messenger of God, and his cousin know best what it is saying.'

"'Ali then said, 'My knowledge comes from the Messenger of God, whose knowledge comes from Gabriel, whose knowledge comes from God. That bell is saying "Truth (*Haqqan*)! Truth! Truth!" and "Sincerity (*Sidqan*)! Sincerity! Sincerity!"'"

Shamsuddin continued, "If the bell of Zorastrians can say such things, imagine what the drum of the lovers of the Most Holy can say! Consider the verse: *There is not a single thing that does not extol His limitless glory and praise* [17:44]. The drum sings the praises of God; like the mountains in the story of David it echoes back: *O you mountains! Sing with him the praise of God! And likewise you birds* [34:10]!"

This was transmitted to us from that Master of teachers, Zaynuddin Razi (May the Mercy of God be upon him) who had learned from him the art of sema, and who at that time was one of the great religious scholars of Asia Minor.

The Water of Spirit that Purifies [192]

Shamsuddin of Mardin told us that, one day, he needed to go to take a bath. He got up early, at dawn, and went to the bathhouse, but when he saw Mevlana there, he became embarrassed, bewildered, and wanted to hide.

"It will do you no good to run away!" exclaimed our Master. "What is the matter? What is preventing you from coming into the bath?"

"I am ashamed before my Master and felt troubled to look upon the pure face of my Lord in my present state of such impurity," answered Shamsuddin.

Mevlana replied, "From the point of view of externals, this is good and very polite behavior, but you must look at us now because the blessed glance of real men is not less than the waters of the bathhouse. For as it says: *And we send down from the skies water rich in blessings* [50:9], which means the blessed spirit of the Friends of God.

> The meaning of this water is the spirit of the Friends—
> it washes away all your impurities.

If the servants of God can wash away one's hidden impurities, shouldn't they be able to do the same for the visible ones?

> In our stream, filth becomes pure water.
> A fly in our yoghurt becomes a falcon or phoenix."

Protecting Grace [194]

That Sultan of Knowers of God, Chelebi 'Arif (May God Sanctify his Innermost Secret) told us the following:

One day, my father, Sultan Walad, said to me, "When our Shaikh and Master Shams-i Tabrizi (May God magnify his memory) became hidden from the eye of people, and his gracious physical form as well as his glorious essence disappeared, it was a terrible loss for those of us who had been of one heart with him. My father, Mevlana, in an effort to bring peace and to put out the fire of hostility that caused this painful calamity, chose some of his Friends and his descendents and left on a journey to Syria.

"As soon as we entered Syrian territory, an army of three hundred heavily armed brigands loaded with spoils appeared, headed toward our caravan. All the travelers were terrified except my father, who continued his prayers as usual. I went to him and began to beseech him.

"He said to me, 'O Bahauddin, don't be upset, because the Commander of that army is with us.'

"He then traced a circle around the caravan similar to the circle made by the Prophet Hud (Peace be with him)—that he traced to protect his people from the destructive wind of Sarsar. When the army of brigands arrived near the caravan, no matter what they did the horses would not advance, and the brigands were dumbfounded.

"One of them dismounted and shouted, 'What people are you, and where are you from? Why can't our fine Arabian horses rush forward, why can't they take a step? Why can't we draw our Egyptian scimitars from their sheaths? Are there magicians among you?'

"The travelers replied, 'God protect us from magicians being with us! But know this—the son of Bahauddin of Balkh, our Master Jalaluddin Rumi, as well as his children and family, are in this caravan; it is the awesomeness of his Friendship with God that has bound you.

It is the terror of the partridge before the falcon;
a lowly horsefly cannot presume to cause such fear.'

"At these words, the entire company fell to the ground like leaves in autumn. The brigands came crawling forward in submission, bared their heads, and expressed their goodwill in all sincerity. They repented of their sinful life and distributed rare gifts. They accompanied us, escorting us all the way to Aleppo, and then asked permission to return to their homes.

"One who has God as his Helper, Assistant, and Protector is secure from the calamities of time and misfortunes of this world. As the poet has said:

One who has God as his protector
is guarded by the birds and the fish."

Infinite Enthusiasm [195b]

Shaikh Mahmud, otherwise known as Sahib-Qiran (May God have Mercy on him), told us the following:

One extremely cold night, I was attending Mevlana while our Master was explaining some of the meanings of words of his father, Bahauddin; the companions were writing them down, and I was drying the ink over the brazier. At midnight, Mevlana stood up and left for the bathhouse. He entered the hot water pool and sat down. For three days and three nights, the Friends visited him in small groups. On the third day, he got up and ordered the Friends to sleep a little, and when they had dozed off, he rose quietly and went without making a noise into a private niche and started to pray.

I heard him repeating, "Allah! Allah!" in a loud voice, and his words echoed from the vaulted roof of the bathhouse. Until just before the dawn prayer, he continued going into each of the niches within the bathhouse and saying prayers in each one. When dawn truly broke, and the sun, like a royal rider, mounted the heavenly sphere, he summoned everyone and we went to the medresse. When we arrived, he began the sema, and it lasted seven whole days.

One Face [195c]

Chelebi Shamsuddin, the professor's son (May God have Mercy on him), told us the following story:

One day, a terrible catastrophe occurred and all the inhabitants of Konya, who were in serious trouble, went to our Master to ask him to write a letter to the Parvana Mo'inuddin and to intercede for them. They requested that Sultan Walad be the envoy. Our Master agreed and sent off a letter asking for their pardon. When the Parvana received the letter, he kissed the paper and read it and said, "There are a hundred ways of looking at this situation; let him also present his side of the argument."

In reply, Mevlana wrote: "The goal of two beings is to have one face; could there really be a hundred sides to this dispute?"

The Parvana buried his eyes in the blessed letter from our Master and immediately pardoned the inhabitants of the city. They had been willing to give ten thousand dinars as recompense in order to be free of the difficulty. And yet, by means of one letter, our Master saved all these people from misfortune.

Choose Love [195f]

Chelebi Shamsuddin also recounted:

One day, Mevlana went with all the companions towards Shaikh Sadruddin's lodge (*zawiya*). When they came near, the guardian came out and informed them that the shaikh was not there.

"Silence!" said Mevlana, "Haven't you learned from your spiritual director that one should not give an answer, unless one has been asked?"

They continued on and went into a nearby medresse, where our Master shared such a wide array of divine insights and meanings that the Friends were rendered speechless. Then he put his ear to the wall of the medresse and shook his head.

He said, "Friends, do you know how we came to be here? The whole purpose was that this place was calling out with the tongue of its state, lamenting to God: 'What pain—will I not be honored one day with the meanings of the Friend of God?' God inspired me to come here and honor this place for an hour with sweet kernels of meaning and with the blessed footsteps of the Friends."

Mevlana also said, "Imam Muhammad Ghazali (May God have Mercy on him) stirred the Sea of Knowledge in the angelic world. He was the standard-bearer, the guide of the universe and the religious scholar of humankind, but if he had only possessed an atom of love like Ahmad Ghazali,[57] it would have been worth more, and, like Ahmad, he would have penetrated the deeper secret of Muhammad's nearness. There is nothing in the universe, no master, no spiritual director, nor guide to the Divine like love.

Choose love, love, and, in turn, be chosen;
through love you will gain true discernment."

Water Birds [196]

One day, Mevlana (May God magnify his memory) went to the room of Sirajuddin Tatari, the great religious scholar of the age, and began speaking of subtle meanings:

He said, "The divine sage, Khwaja Sana'i, and Fariduddin 'Attar[58] (May God sanctify their innermost secret) were great beings on the path of religion, but a large part of their discourses had to do with separation. As for us, the words we speak are of love, of union.

"Imam Abu Hanifa, Imam Muttalabi, and the other Imams[59] (May God be pleased with them) were architects of the world of dry land. One who, in all sincerity, has adopted the path of these powerful guides and follows them is protected from the evil of the wicked and the brigands of religion and is delivered.

"However, Friends of God like Junayd, Dhul Nun, Abu Yazid,

---

57. Muhammad Ghazali (d. 1111 C.E.) and Ahmad Ghazali (d. 1123 C.E.) were brothers, from a sufi lineage. Muhammad was a great theologian and prolific author; Ahmad was intoxicated with Divine love; eventually Muhammad al-Ghazali abandoned his brilliant career to journey more deeply within sufi practice. See *Rumi's Sun*, p.240-242, for a reflection from Shams-i Tabriz regarding the story of the two brothers.

58. Hakim Sana'i (d. 1131 C.E.), the author of *The Garden of Truth* (*Hadiqat ul-Haqiqa*), and Fariduddin Attar (d. 1220 C.E.), author of *The Conference of the Birds* (*Mantiq at-tayr*) were two renowned sufis with whom Mevlana felt in resonance. It is said that when Mevlana was young and the family was journeying from Balkh, they stopped to visit Attar in Nishapur. When Attar saw them approaching, Mevlana walking behind his father, he exclaimed, "Here comes a sea followed by an ocean!" He recognized the spiritual gifts of the son as even greater than that of his father, and he gave Mevlana a copy of his *Asrarnama* (*Book of Mysteries*) which had a profound influence upon him.

59. Abu Hanifa and Imam Muttalabi (Ash-Shafi), Al-Malik, and Abu Hanbal were religious scholars who established schools of law (*madhab*) within the early Islamic community.

Shaqiq, Adham, and Mansur[60] are water birds—swimmers completely at home in the Sea of Gnosis. One who follows them is delivered from the traps of the perfidious lower self and will surely discover the priceless pearl of the boundless Sea of Omnipotence."

*****

Bahauddin Bahri, who possessed a perfect portion of the knowledge of meaning, told us that, one day, Mevlana also said, "One who occupies himself with the words of 'Attar will profit from the discourses of Sana'i and will come to understand the secrets contained in his words. And one who earnestly studies Sana'i will come to understand the secret of the radiance of our words."

Conveying Pearls [197]

One day, that Prince of Poets, Amir Bahauddin Qani'i, the Khaqani[61] of his time, arrived with an entourage to pay a visit on Mevlana (God's Blessings and greetings be upon him). After much discussion and an exchange of questions and answers, Qani'i said, "I don't like the poetry of Sana'i, because he is not a Muslim."

"What can you possibly mean, saying that he is not a Muslim?" asked Mevlana.

"He has used verses from our glorious Qur'an in his poetry and has made them into rhymes," asserted Qani'i.

Mevlana was furious and told Qani'i to say no more: "What right do you have to speak this way about someone being a Muslim? If a Muslim were to witness the full extent of Sana'i's greatness, his turban would fall off his head. Are you really a Muslim and the thousands like you? Sana'i's virtue is recognized in this world and the World Beyond, and as for his divine words, which reveal the mysteries of the Qur'an, he ornamented them in the same way as it was said, 'We have drawn from the Sea, and we have poured back into the

---

60. These are the Friends of God intoxicated with Love of God: Junayd al-Baghdadi (d. 910 C.E.), who held his intoxication within sobriety, Dhul Nun al-Misri ("the Egyptian") (d. 859 C.E.), who focused on gnosis (*marifah*), Abu Yazid Bastami (d. 874 C.E.) mentioned many times within this volume, Ibrahim Adham (d. 777 C.E.) (see note #5 and sections #215 and 341 of this volume), his student, Shaqiq al-Balkhi (d. 810 C.E.), and Mansur al-Hallaj (d. 922 C.E.) (see sections #122, 338, 456, 526VII), all prominent saints of early sufism, close friends in Rumi's mystical universe, to whom he frequently refers.

61. Khaqani (d. 1199 C.E.) was a renowned Persian poet.

Sea again.' You haven't caught his wisdom or studied his thought, because you are content to remain on the surface of things!"

And he added:

"The dear servants of God (*abdals*)[62] use special expressions
which simple words cannot approach.
To the unripe, these truths may seem vague,
because their comprehension is veiled.

Even though you are not privy to the deepest secrets of the Friends of God, you should not deny them and throw yourself into the abyss of perdition. If you trust in them with a sincere heart, you will not have to carry the weight of your sins on the Day of Reckoning; on the contrary, the saints will provide a refuge and will intercede for you with grace."

The poet then arose, lowered his head in contrition, asked forgiveness for any indiscretion he might have committed, and declared himself a sincere and devout disciple.

*****

Sirajuddin, the reciter of the *Mathnawi* and a saint in the eyes of God (May God have Mercy on him), recounted the following as he heard it from Chelebi Husamuddin (May God sanctify his innermost secret):

One day, Husamuddin was having one of his disciples take an oath never to involve himself in illicit activities. A copy of Sana'i's *Ilahi-nama* that was covered with a cloth had been placed in front of the disciple.

Mevlana, who just happened to arrive at this moment, cried, "What way is this to take an oath?"

Chelebi answered, "I wanted him to take an oath to conduct

---

62. The *Abdal* ("substitutes," or "those who get replaced") are a rank of forty saints, but sometimes considered to be a larger group of three hundred hidden saints (*ahkyar*), only known to and appointed by God, and it is through their efforts that the world continues to exist. The term *abdal* over time has come to include a greater hierarchy of saints, all of various ranks. These pure ones serve God during their lifetime, extending blessing and spiritual support throughout the world, and may be of any age. When they die they are immediately replaced by someone else selected by God. The leader of the *abdals* is often referred to as the *Qutb* (Pole, plural *aqtab*), supported by four *autad* (Pillars), and usually remains unknown in the outer world (though some may claim that distinction); all together they work for the well-being of God's creation.

himself honestly, but I was afraid to have him swear on the Qur'an, so I covered the *Ilahi-nama* of Hakim to use."

"I swear by God, this is more effective, because the outer appearance of the Qur'an is similar to curdled milk, while these reflections expressed by Sina'i are its butter and cream," concluded Mevlana.

From That World to This [198]

Shihabuddin, the reciter, and 'Othman, the singer (May God have mercy on both of them), who were both highly regarded by Mevlana, recounted the following:

One day, at the medresse, there was a huge sema and Mevlana (Salutations and health be with him) kept losing himself in an ecstatic state. He would then go to the dais, where the Friends were reciting, bow, and offer words of apology, and then enter even deeper into his ecstasy; he suddenly exclaimed, "It is for you a subtle world; this is sufficient!"

The Friends were astounded at such humility and respect and were curious to know to whom he was speaking. When the sema was over, Chelebi Husamuddin bowed and respectfully asked Mevlana to explain his mysterious behavior.

Mevlana replied, "The innermost secret of Hakim Sana'i's spiritual essence appeared to me in corporeal form, standing beside 'Othman and Shihabuddin, playing the drum and saying gracious things. I asked his forgiveness, so that he would be pleased with us. In Truth, one should know that when people of God remember someone in the world beyond, and desire to see them, immediately that person appears, just as the Holy Spirit appeared to Mary and to our Prophet (Blessings and peace be upon them) and as spiritual forms appear to the perfect Friends of God. This is what the dervishes call spiritualization (*tarwahun*), materialization of a likeness (*tamaththul*), and assuming corporeality (*tajassud*)."

Decorate Your Self with the Knowledge of God [199]

The theologian and Friend, Khwaja Nafisuddin of Siwas (May mercy be upon him) told us that, one day, our Master went to the public bathhouse—he sat cross-legged in the bathing room, sharing many high and subtle meanings, while the Friends, deeply engrossed, sat near him.

All of a sudden, he jumped up and cried, "In this gathering, who is really of Mevlana?" Three times, he questioned them, but the Friends said not a word.

Then he continued, "If a stranger came into this bathhouse and saw your clothes in the dressing room, he would know immediately that the Friends of Mevlana are here. Now, if your clothes and your turbans are sufficient to make your presence known, shouldn't your souls be as recognizable as your clothing? At the same time that a Friend's outward form can be decorated with these things, his inward self should also be decorated, with the knowledge of God and with Truth, because it was said: 'Truly, God does not concern himself with your outward forms, nor your acts, but rather with the intention of your heart.' In every way, try to be spiritual Mevlevis, and *This is sufficient*."

Serving the Beloved [200]

Khwaja Nafisuddin told us that one day there was a large sema at the medresse. Suddenly, our Master rushed towards me and seized the collar of my jacket, and I was overcome with awe. He said, "If anyone asked you why I roll up the sleeves of my robe what would you say?"

"Whatever my Lord (*Khodavandgar*) commands," I answered.

He said, "The whole of creation is like a grand and exalted *khanaqah*,[63] the true shaikh of which is God. All the prophets, saints, and exalted ones of the Muslim community are like traveling sufis. When a sufi stranger arrives in this *khanaqah*, and does not know the caretaker, he must look to see who has his sleeves rolled up, so that he might recognize who is the servitor of this *khanaqah*—it is from him that he will learn the principles and practices of the sufis. After that he may be an intimate and sincere friend of the sufis of purity and the travelers of the way of fidelity. He can remain, work hard to follow the sufi way, and hold to the straight path. Otherwise, he will quickly be thrown out of the *khanaqah*. Now, in the *khanaqah* of this world, since the moment Adam appeared, and since the first breath was breathed, it is we who are God's servant.

"'One who serves is a friend of God' is a well-known proverb, and

63. *Khanaqah* is the Persian word for a central sufi lodge where dervishes would gather, study, receive training, and serve. A smaller lodge was referred to as a *zawiya*. In Turkish, a sufi lodge is also referred to as a *tekke*. Sometimes these lodges were attached to a medresse, adjacent to a mosque, as in the case of Mevlana's abode. The smaller lodges would house a small *masjid*—a "room for prayer" (*sajda*="prostration")—within them.

a hint is sufficient for the wise. This portion of service was transmitted to us through the Prophet of God, because he, himself, said; 'The chief of a people is their servant.' How wonderful, that through service, and the great blessings attached to it, the servant becomes the best and greatest of humankind and is in return served by everyone."

Preparing the Soul to Serve [200b]

A dear Friend told us that, one day, a certain man was being talked about in Mevlana's presence: "'So and so' said that, heart and soul, he is in service."

"Silence!" replied Mevlana. "This is a falsehood that is perpetuated by people which is often repeated. Where has he found this soul and heart with which he is going to serve others?"

Then turning his blessed face towards Chelebi Husamuddin, he cried, "God is Most Great! One should sit knee to knee with the Friends of God, because that closeness has immense effects."

And then he recited these verses:

No matter what state you are in, draw closer to the Friend,
because love is born out of intimacy.
A lover draws near through the body;
soul touches soul through seeing the Beloved.
Why do you try separation?
Why would anyone want to experiment with poison?
Pure or impure, don't go away!
Come near and increase your state of purity.

Beware of Fame [201]

Mevlana turned towards the Friends and said, "Since our reputation has grown, people come to visit us in larger and larger numbers and are more and more desirous of spiritual direction, and I have no rest from this affliction. It is true what the Elect of God (Peace and blessings be upon him) said: 'Fame is an affliction,' and 'True peace of mind is to be found in anonymity.' But what can one do, if the command comes: 'Show My attributes to My creatures; whoever sees you, sees Me, and if someone is seeking to be with you, he or she is seeking Me.'"

He continually warned the Friends against fame and said:

You should plead for mercy
to be taken far from fame.

On the Path, the heavy bonds of eminence
are like iron chains.

Opening to the Majesty of God [202]

Shaikh Sinanuddin of Akshehir,[64] one of the sweet Friends and one of the travelers of the Path of Transcendence, reported that Sultan Walad (May God sanctify his dear soul) told him this story:

One year, during the month of Ramadan, my father withdrew into seclusion for ten days and did not show his face to anyone. Then, the notables of Konya, the wise, religious scholars, people of poverty (*fuqara*), and the general populace all came together to the medresse and lamented loudly: "We can't bear our Master's absence," and they wept profusely.

I got up and went to the door of my father's retreat cell to see how he was. He asked, "O Bahauddin, what is this crowd outside?"

I replied, "All the Friends and lovers are suffering greatly due to the absence of their master."

"They are right, but tell them that they must give me another three days."

I bowed and relayed the message to the Friends. They were then so overcome with joy that they burst into sema.

Three days later, in the morning, I looked into his cell through a crack in the door. I saw that it was totally filled from the floor to the ceiling with the blessed body of Mevlana. It was completely packed, and, just as you stuff a crack with cotton, even the crack in the door was filled. Overcome, I cried out and fainted. Then, two or three times, I looked again. The last time I looked, I saw that my father's gracious body had returned to its usual proportions, as slender as before.

I saw him pat his body with his blessed hand, saying, "Be content, you have done well. Bravo for the strength you have shown. Mt. Sinai could not bear it and broke into a thousand pieces, but you have undertaken it. I give thanks for such a faithful friend, as faithful as the Companion of the Cave.

Through God's perfect power, the bodies of human beings
gain the capacity to endure this incomprehensible light.
Mt. Sinai couldn't support even an atom of it,

64. Akshehir is a town within the province of Konya, at the foot of Sultan Dagh hill.

but His omnipotence fits it within a slender vessel."

I cried out and opened the door, prostrated myself, and rubbed my face on his blessed feet.

"Oh Bahauddin," he said, "this is a secret between us. There are moments when we go towards the Majesty of God, and there are others when the Divine Presence, (May He be Exalted and Sanctified) in His infinite Grace comes to us. When we go to Him, we become thin, miserable and full of longing. When the Majestic Presence honors us with a visit, we cannot be contained within this world! How could a small retreat cell contain me, when I am filled with God?"

I left to inform the Friends. An uproar broke out in Konya and the great and lowly came to visit, offer friendship, and pay their respects to Mevlana. Mevlana bestowed grace upon each one, and then he began a sema which, without a pause, lasted seven days and nights.

Three Pearls [204]

One day, Mevlana's representative, that Sultan of the Pious, Chelebi Husam al-Haqquddin (May God be pleased with him) told us the following:

Our Master said that when God (May He be Exalted and Glorified) created the pure body of Adam (May peace be upon him), by drawing him out from within the earthly sphere and breathing into him of His Holy Spirit, He then told the angel Gabriel:

"Take three pearls from the Ocean of My Omnipotence and put them in a vessel of light, and give them to Adam the Pure, so that he might choose one."

One of these pearls was Reason, the second, Faith, and the third, Modesty. When Gabriel the Faithful showed Adam the vessel, with the divine insight of *The truly faithful one sees by means of the Light of God*, Adam looked at the vessel and chose the pearl of Reason.

When Gabriel went to return the vessel with the other two pearls to the Ocean of Omnipotence, it had become too heavy to lift. The two remaining pearls of Faith and Modesty said, "We cannot be separated from our friend, Reason; without his presence we can neither rest nor exist anywhere. Since time immemorial, all three of us have been the jewels of the mine of Divine Majesty, pearls in the Sea of our Lord's Infinite Power, and inseparable from one another."

Then the command of God was heard: "O Gabriel! Leave them and return."

With these words, Reason settled itself at the top of man's head; Faith entered his pure and sensitive heart, and Modesty took up its home in his blessed face. These three pure pearls are the inheritance of Adam's heirs. Adam's descendants who are not ornamented by these pearls and illuminated by them are deprived of this Light and this meaning. "For the wise, a hint is sufficient."

Awaiting the Command [205]

Chelebi Shamsuddin, son of the professor, told us that in the service of Mevlana there was a *neyzin*[65] named Hamza. He was a great master of his art, a very fine musician, and highly regarded by Our Master. He suddenly fell ill and died. They informed Mevlana, and some of the Friends busied themselves with preparing for his burial. Meanwhile, Mevlana arose and went to his house.

When Mevlana entered, he cried out, "O dear friend, Hamza, arise!" The *neyzin* got up, obeying this command, and began to play the reed flute, and then for three days and nights they made a great sema. That same day about a hundred deniers became Muslims. Then when Mevlana stepped with his blessed foot outside the house to depart, the neyzin immediately left for the other world.[66]

The Healing Hands of Love [207]

The theologian and Friend, the Sunni ascetic, our Master Badruddin Ma'dani (May the Mercy of God be upon him), who was a great *khalifa* and one of illumined heart, told us that there was in Mevlana's company a reciter who had a very beautiful voice but who was a hunch-back. One day, during a sema, Mevlana was transported beyond himself in Love; he came near the reciter and was even more

65. A *neyzin* is one who plays the *ney*, the reed flute that is emblematic of the Mevlevi Way. The great masterwork of Mevlana, his *Mathnawi*, begins, "Listen to the reed and the tale it tells." The *ney* is a symbol for the human being—played by the breath of the Divine.

66. This story is quite similar to a recent occurrence within the tradition. One of the finest *neyzins* of this era related that there was a *semazen* (one trained to whirl in the *sema* ceremony) who was dying, and he went to visit just as the friend had passed into a coma approaching death. While sitting with him, the *neyzin* played on his *ney* one of the passages from an *ayin*—a composition for accompaniment of the whirling ceremony. Upon hearing the *ney*, immediately the *semazen* opened his eyes, arose from his bed, and began to whirl until the music stopped. Then, after bowing in greeting, he returned to his bed, closed his eyes, and left for the other world.

overcome with ecstasy.

The unfortunate reciter, bent over as he was, continued to beat his drum with even greater love and to utter mystical secrets.

When the sema was over, Mevlana said, "Why don't you stand up straight? What is the problem?"

The reciter showed him his hunchback. Mevlana rubbed it with his blessed hand, and immediately the man stood as straight as a cypress. Overcome with joy, he returned to his house, but his wife didn't recognise him and wouldn't open the door.

"You're not my husband!" she said. The Friends told her the story of the miracle that Mevlana had performed, and, then, she allowed him to come in.

For many years after that, he served Mevlana.

Opening to the Light of Dhikr [207b]

Worship without ceasing,
but if your contemplation becomes frozen,
go and practice *dhikr*.[67]
Set reflection in motion through *dhikr*—
use it like a sun
to revive your frozen heart.

Celebrating Release [208]

Someone remarked to Mevlana, "Since ancient times, funeral processions have been led by Qur'an reciters (*hafiz*)[68] and muezzins. In this time of yours, what is the meaning of the presence of these reciters of poetry when the religious scholars and jurists of the Muslim community consider the fact that you have introduced such reciters to lead the processions to be a dangerous innovation and denounce it?"

---

67. *Dhikr* (remembrance), "mentioning God," refers to the invocation of the Divine Name or of the beloved qualities of the traditional Ninety-nine Names of God, in repeated recitation, whether chanted aloud (*dhikr* of the tongue) or silently (*dhikr* of the heart, "*fikr*") or deep within, opening to the Mystery, without words (*dhikr* of the secret, "*fikr as-sirr*"). *Remember Me; I remember you* [2:152]; *Invoke the Name of your Lord and devote yourself to Him with complete devotion* [73:8]; *Remembrance of God is the greatest* (*wa la dhikr-Llahi akbar*) [29:45].

68. A *hafiz* is one who knows the Qur'an by heart and can recite it from memory. *Al-Hafiz* (The Preserver) is one of the Ninety-nine Divine Names of God in the Islamic tradition, though it is recognized that God is far beyond any description, subtle in Essence, both infinitely intimate and transcendent.

He answered, "The muezzins, the reciters of the Qur'an, the *hafiz* who walk at the head of the funeral processions bear witness that the dead person is truly a faithful one and a Muslim. However, our reciters bear witness that the deceased is a truly faithful one, a Muslim, and a lover. We celebrate the release of the human spirit from the prison of this world and its rescue from the well of human nature. The spirit, held captive in the prsison of the body, has by the Grace of God been delivered and returned to its Source. Is this not an occcasion for great rejoicing, for music and sema, and for grateful thanks—both for him, as he rejoices in his yearning for God and returns to his Glorious Sustainer, and for those he thereby inspires to live their lives with enthusiasm and passion?

"If a person is delivered from prison and covered with honors, without a doubt this would be a cause for endless rejoicing. In reality, the death of our friends is such that we say:

Because they were sovereigns of religion
when they broke their chains, it was a joy!
They have rushed toward the fountain of happiness.
They have cast off their earthly chains—
the noble spirit has escaped from prison!
Why would we tear our garments and bite our fists with grief?"

Lightening Depression [209]

Sultan Walad told us this:

One day, I felt sad and downhearted. My father came into the medresse and saw that I was sad and said, "Are you angry with someone; you seem so downcast?"

"I don't really know what the matter is," I replied.

He disappeared into the house, and, after a few minutes, returned with his face and head covered with an old wolf-skin.

"Bou! Bou!" he cried, just as if I were a child again, as if to frighten me.

I burst out laughing and laughed until I could laugh no more and then kissed my father's blessed feet.

"O Bahauddin," he said, "if someone who loves you and brings you joy suddenly appears dressed up in a wolf skin and cries 'Bou,' does that frighten you?"

"No," I said.

"That Beloved who has caused you such joy and expansion of your heart is the same one who causes you sorrow and constricts your chest. It all comes from Him.

> Even if He puts on clothes of wrathful sparks,
> I recognize Him,
> because He has come to me many times like this
> when intoxicated.
>
> So, why feel sad for no good reason;
> why let yourself be bound by negativity?
>
> You have felt constriction,
> find the way out of your despondency—
> know that all difficulties have a common root.
> Treat your joy like a delicate plant and water it;
> when it has borne fruit share it with your friends."

"As my father spoke," Sultan Walad continued, "I experienced a profound feeling of ecstasy, and my heart expanded like a flower. For the rest of my life, I never again felt sad and was far from the troubles of the world.

"Emboldened by my extreme joy, and the intimacy I felt towards my father, I remarked, 'You've told us about the stations, the ranks, and the miracles of all the prophets and saints (Peace be with them), and you've pointed out greatness in many eminent people, but you've been silent about your own attainments.'

" 'Dear Bahauddin!' said my father gently, don't you know:

> He who praises the Sun, praises himself;
> he is saying "My two eyes are clear, not cloudy." '

"It was my father who guided me from the world of contraction toward the world of expansion, and led me from multiplicity towards Oneness:

> There is only One Beauty, but surely,
> with mirrors, this One becomes many."

Palaces of Love [209b]

My father opened the way to expansion for me, and I persisted, "Do tell us something of your ecstatic states."

"O Bahauddin," he answered, "think of Konya and all its dwellings. The houses of the merchants and the distinguished are taller and grander than those of the artisans; the sumptuous palaces of the amirs are grander than the houses of the merchants; and the domes and pavilions of the sultans are one hundred times higher and more impressive than all the rest, but the grandeur and elevation of the heavens, in comparison with these palaces, is truly magnificent and beyond imagining.

"Concerning the ranks of the prophets and saints similarly, as it says in the noble Qur'an: *Some of these messengers have We endowed more highly than others* [2:253]. Elsewhere it is said: *But indeed, We did endow some of the prophets more highly than others* [17:55] and *raised some of them by degrees above others, so that they might avail themselves of one another's help* [42:31]. There are many verses in the Qur'an that express this idea. Our stations are like the heavens in comparison with the palaces: *And God grants sustenance unto whom He wills, beyond all reckoning* [3:37; 24:38]—we are the grateful inheritors of the light of Muhammad.

> We have not built ornate palaces decorated with statues,
> like the 'Ad and Thamud, on this perishing earth,
> but, like Abraham and Noah,
> we have built Pavilions of Love in eternity.

"It is a mystic's duty to follow the Prophet (Peace and blessings upon him), who said, 'I swear by God that I have not constructed the space of even one span [for myself], nor have I hoarded gold.'"

Loving the Wood [210]

Shaikh Badruddin Mevlevi, the carpenter—a saintly man, whose heart was as pure as an angel's—told us this:

When I reached the age of puberty, I began working for very skillful carpenters taking care of the Mevlevi houses. One day, we were installing the beams in the ceiling of the large meeting hall and discovered that one of the huge pieces of timber was too short by half a cubit. We looked everywhere in the city for one to replace it without success. The master and all the carpenters were wondering what to do, when Mevlana, who had just left a sema, entered the room.

He inquired, "What are the masters concerned about?"

They all bowed and told him that this one tree was too short.

"How can this magnificent tree be too short? You must have made a mistake in measuring it," he remarked.

My master got up and for a second time measured the tree in front of Mevlana. It measured the same.

Then I watched as Mevlana went to it and lovingly rubbed the beam with his blessed hand. He said, "Such a finely proportioned beam—why would it be too short? It's the mistake of our carpenters." And he added, "Now, measure it again."

When it was measured again with the same cubit-stick, it was found to be half a cubit longer than all the others. All the master carpenters and friends cried out and were overcome. Amazed, they turned to bow to Mevlana in gratitude, when they realized he had disappeared.

That same day, the meeting hall was finished. The prophets and Friends of God (Peace be with them) are able to perform infinite miracles in the material world, in relation to transformation of both animate and inanimate beings.

That one knows, who was alive one day
and took a cup from the hand of the Beloved.
Consider the miracles of Moses and Muhammad,
how the staff became a snake,[69]
and the pillar of the mosque in Medina moaned[70]

---

69. When challenged by Pharoah to a contest with his magicians, Moses threw down his staff, which, with God's assistance, became a huge snake that swallowed up all the magician's ropes, which by sleight-of- hand they had turned into snakes, so that the magicians, too, came to have faith in the God of Moses. See *Surah al-A'raf*, The Faculty of Discernment, 7:104-125.

70. The moaning pillar: When the first mosque in Medina was being built, between its two walls a niche was built where the trunk of a date palm was used as a column or support. When Muhammed gave his Friday sermons, he would lean against this pillar. But then someone provided a pulpit for him. When he no longer leaned upon the pillar, just then the wood gave out such a sound that it seemed it would nearly break into two. The Blessed Prophet went near it, and a sound like the longing cry of a newborn baby was heard. Even so, the pillar was filled with love for the prophet, and so when it spoke, one heard and recognized the longing within it. Otherwise one might not have recognized it as more than a simple trunk of a date palm. Unless the heart is open, we usually do not recognize the ways of worship of inanimate beings. See *Surah al-Isra'*, The Night Journey 17:44: *Limitless is He in His glory, and sublimely, immeasurably exalted above anything people may say. The seven heavens acclaim His limitless glory, and the earth, and all that they contain; and there is nothing that does not celebrate His immeasurable glory. . . .*

when the Prophet stopped leaning on it.
If a lover of knowledge denies such miracles,
he just doesn't know the capacity of a Friend.

Seeing Real Beneficence [211]

The Friend and theologian, Shaikh Badruddin Yawash, otherwise known as Naqqash, the painter (May the Mercy of God be upon him), told us that one day Mevlana (May God sanctify his blessed secret), said to his friends:

"By God, all the saints allowed their disciples to beg, in order to teach them restraint and to subdue the false self. They allowed them to lift up candles and carry begging bowls, and in accordance with *lend unto God a goodly loan* [72:20] they accepted gifts of charity, alms, and donations from the wealthy. But we have closed the door of begging for our friends and put into practice the way of the Prophet (Peace and blessings upon him), who said, 'As much as you are able, don't beg,' so that each by his own effort and the sweat of his brow works to gain, or trades, or is occupied with the profession of writing. Whoever among our friends does not practice this is not worth even a single small coin. On Resurrection Day, he will not see our face. And if one of them takes something from someone, I will not turn my face toward him."

Then Mevlana recited the following *hadith*:

The Prophet said, "If you desire Paradise from God,
don't wish for anything from anyone else.
If you desire nothing from anyone, I will guarantee for you
Paradise as your refuge, as well as the vision of God."

Fruitful Work [212]

This story was told by Nuruddin Tizbazari, a shining light of the dervishes (May God illuminate his heart and his grave) and one of Mevlana's closest disciples. One day, in the middle of a discourse while sharing divine insights of the mystical Path, Mevlana told this strange story:

A dervish who had devoted himself to contemplation of God remained in a forest for forty years. He was so absorbed in his ecstasy that birds built their nests on top of his head, and he didn't even notice.

Then one day, a Pole of the Time (*qutb*) happened by and gave him a sharp blow on the back of his neck, crying, "O Miserable creature, who eats unlawful food!"

The dervish, leaving the world of intoxication for the world of reason, awoke from his torpor: "For forty long years, I haven't touched the lawful food of this world. How can you accuse me of eating unlawful food, unless you have taken up highway robbery on my behalf?"

The *qutb* answered, "Don't the messengers of the cool east wind, the morning breeze, and the north wind in the spring bear delightful scents to feed your senses and soothe your throat. These delicious fragrances are celestial food that gives you strength, but to acquire this food requires no effort on your part. On the path of the adepts such effortless gain is forbidden. Haven't you heard from the Chief of the Prophets (Peace and blessings upon him), 'Eat only what you have gathered from the hard work of your own hand and the sweat of your brow.'

"Haven't you heard that the Prophet Solomon (May peace be upon him) was served many delicious meals brought to him from Paradise which he enjoyed? And then one day, Gabriel, the Faithful (Peace be upon him), was present when this food from Paradise arrived and watched while Solomon devoured it joyfully. 'Our Prophet and King eats with such relish and enthusiasm that one would almost think that he had worked in order to obtain that food! A Prophet of God should not eat a whole platter full,' Gabriel said to one of the other angels.

"Solomon asked Gabriel, 'What are the angels saying about me?'

"Gabriel said, 'Don't you hear?'

"Solomon inquired, 'That the food that comes to one as a result of the labor of one's hands and lawful gain is better and more agreeable than the heavenly food of Paradise?'

" 'Certainly,' replied the Archangel.

"Solomon immediately repented, took up the trade of basket-making and nourished himself with food bought from that work. He also began to fast following the Prophet David's example, eating only every other day.

" 'O Messenger of God,' Gabriel said, 'Know and be informed that what makes the the food of Paradise so delicious is that God Most High has created Paradise from the labor of the devotion of the devoted, from the remembrance (*dhikr*) of those who remember Him, from the gratitude of those who are grateful, and the patience of those who endure. If you have not made an effort, you will not gain the treasure.'"

> Whoever has struggled has found a treasure;
> whoever makes a serious effort surely finds felicity.

Most of the perfect prophets, the completed saints, the great spiritual leaders of the community, the religious scholars and the wise sultans of the past earned their livelihood through some kind of manual work. *God knows best* and shows us the Truth.

A Remedy for Every Disease [212b]

Mevlana continued with another anecdote:

Moses was in terrible pain, suffering from an eye infection. "No pain is as terrible as that of the eyes," as it is said. In great distress, he took the road for Mt. Sinai, and as he went along, the plants cried out to him, "O Moses! Rub us on your eyes that you might be cured." But Moses paid no attention.

When he had finished his supplications, he added, "O Lord, I am very weak from the ailment of my eyes. I ask of God a remedy and a cure, for '*When I am ill, He heals me* [26:80].' I know that you can cure all illnesses. The plants told me their healing capacities, but I didn't accept them. What is Your command?"

The voice of God was heard: "Listen to them, so that your eyes might be healed. I have given the human being a remedy for every sickness and a panacea for every ill; I have made of it a means."

> The Prophet said that the Most Glorious God
> has created a remedy for every pain.

So when Moses turned back from the mountain, he gathered some plants from the side of the road and rubbed them on his eyes, but the pain grew even worse, and he cried out to God once more.

"O Moses!" said the voice, "I didn't tell you to take the plants straight from the fields and to rub them on your eyes without taking the trouble to prepare them. Go to the doctor's office, buy an ointment there and make a collyrium with the plants that have been ground, and put that in your eye that it might be healed, so that you might be at peace. The doctor will also profit from this simple act."

Moses (Peace be upon him) did as his Lord directed and was healed.

Offering Light [212c]

One day, Mevlana was asked why the Friends and lovers took candles, lamps, and old clothing to the graves of the prophets and saints. He responded:

If one takes a lamp to a neighbor's to light from his illuminated lamp, in this way, one then brings light to one's own dwelling. If one takes candles to the tombs of the holy ones, it is the same, as if one is borrowing light for one's own dark grave—"*Wait for us! Let us have a ray of light from your light!*" [57:13] and in your hand will be a candle in the night—*Their light spreading rapidly before them and on their right* [57:12]. Tell those of little faith to: *Turn back and seek a light* [57:13].

The Messenger of God (Peace and blessings upon him), on the night of the prayers of Berat,[71] entered into the mosque and saw that it was blazing with light from all sorts of candles, torches, and lamps.

"Who is responsible for all these magnificent lights?" he asked.

"O Messenger of God, this devoted servant," said 'Omar (May God be pleased with him).

"May God illuminate your heart and your grave, O 'Omar, just as you have illuminated my mosque."

This custom of illuminating lights in the Muslim community is a remembrance that remains from the time of 'Omar and will last until the end.

They say that 'Ali, the Commander of the Faithful (May God ennoble his countenance) had three good customs upon which human happiness depends. The first was that whenever guests arrived, he would put a bowl of honey in front of each one. The second was to clothe the poor and needy, and the third was to send lamps to all the mosques. His close companions asked him about the meaning behind these three practices.

"I give my guests who are poor travelers pure honey, so that when their mouths and palates have been sweetened, they might offer a prayer for me, in the hope that the bitterness of death might become sweet to my palate. Secondly, I make shirts and pants for the

71. The holy night of Berat, the "Night of Forgiveness" is observed with a night vigil of prayer between the 14th and 15th of the Islamic month of Sha'ban.

poor so that they might pray for me, in anticipation of that moment foreseen by the Prophet (Peace and blessings upon him) when 'He will summon men without shoes and naked'—it is my duty to cover their nakedness and to clothe them, so that I might not be covered with shame on Resurrection Day. Thirdly, if I take candles and lamps into God's sanctuaries, it is in the hope that God most High will, with His immense grace, illuminate my dark grave and not leave me in that narrow and dark tomb without light."

You should know that the candles, the lamps, the offering of clothes, and other things that one takes on a pilgrimage to visit the saints, have an effect and bestow blessings. In the books of all the religions, mention is made of candles, votive offerings, lamps, and incense being brought to the convents, synagogues, and churches, and they hope for a blessing from it. The use of incense and fragrance also brings repose to human beings as well as jinn.[72]

Remembering God [213]

One day, the Pervana Mo'inuddin (May the Mercy of God be upon him) asked Mevlana:

"In the past, spritual leaders of the dervish community (May God illuminate their thoughts) recited special litanies (*wird*) like: *La ilaha il allah*! (There is no god but God). Some dervishes from Turkestan would say, '*Hu! Hu!*'[73] and others would say, '*Illa Llah*!' (but God). Certain ascetics are moved to call out: '*La hawla wa la quwwata illa bi' llahi' al 'Ali al 'Azim!*' (There is no power or strength but with God, the most High, the Most Great!) while others recite, '*Astaghfirullah al-Azim.*' (May the Most Great forgive me!) Which one is that of our Master?"

Mevlana answered, "Our *dhikr* is: *Allah! Allah! Allah!*, because we are people of God (*Allahiyyan*)! We come from God, and it is to God we shall return."

72. *Jinn* (genies), also spelled *djinn*, are spirits mentioned in the Qur'an who inhabit the Unseen realm and, though created of fire, also have free will and can choose to be of the faithful. See Surah 72, *al-Jinn*.

73. All words in Arabic have a gender grammatically assigned to them as they do in French and Spanish, etc. Although *Allah* is referred to with the third person masculine pronoun *Hu* (*Huwa*), it is universally understood that *Allah*'s Essence is beyond gender or indeed any qualification. For the translation of *Hu* in this text occasionally "He/She" or "She" will be used and sometimes simply *Hu* in an attempt to avoid the mistake of attributing human gender to That which is beyond all our attempts at definition, limitless in subtle glory.

We are born from the Divine Essence,
and we journey to this Essence.
O my friends, bless our return!

In renouncing all that is not God, we discover Him.

If we can empty ourselves of both worlds,
we become like the letter 'h' just next to the 'l'[74]
in the glorious name of Allah!

Mevlana continued, "God spoke constantly to my father, Bahauddin Walad, (May God sanctify his inner secret), and my father constantly spoke of God and mentioned His Name. The Supreme Truth has revealed Itself to the prophets and saints through various special names. In the community of Muhammad, the name is 'Allah' and this name embraces all the other ways in which this Truth is invoked."

The Name Resounding [214]

Shaikh Mahmoud 'Arabi (May the Mercy of God be upon him) described how Mevlana would sometimes chant, "*Allah! Allah! Allah!*" all night long. He would lean his blessed head against the wall of the medresse and call out over and over again, "*Allah! Allah! Allah!*" His voice would resound with such force that the space between heaven and earth would be completely filled with the Name of our Sustainer.

He is One [214b]

One day, our Master's wife, Kira Khatun (May God be pleased with her), was in the midst of mending a tear in her husband's coat while he was wearing it. Now, it is common knowledge that one should not sew upon a piece of clothing while it is on a person's body, unless that person has something in his mouth, like a seed, a wisp of straw, or a scrap of paper, or bad luck will ensue. This occurred to Kira Khatun and she wondered whether Mevlana had put something in his mouth. Right away he said, "Don't concern yourself—you may sew in safety, because the words *Say: 'He, God, is One!'* [112:1], are firmly in my mouth. I have grasped tightly to my Sustainer."

74. In Arabic script, the letter "h" in *Allah* is attached to the "l" (the middle "a" is simply a vowel marking located above, highlighting the triliteral root of *alif*, *lam* (doubled), *ha*); the "ha" is an aspirated "h." Mevlana indicates how when the ego fixated on duality melts, empty of self (*nafs*) we become more essentially the breathing of *Allah*.

Beyond Servanthood or Kingship [215]

One day, the Parvana Mo'inuddin came to visit Mevlana, but he hid himself away. All the amirs of great distinction were kept waiting such a long time that they were losing patience; the wait was exceeding all limits, and still Mevlana would not show his blessed face to them.

It occurred to the Parvana that for the honorable amirs, who were the commanding authorities, to honor and respect the great men of religion and the shaikhs of certainty is nourishment for their souls and a refuge for them, and due to the illuminating radiance of this favor, an assistance in staying on the path of rectitude. He wondered why Mevlana avoided kings and amirs, while other scholars and shaikhs craved the attention of important worldly leaders and sought after it—he flees like a bird trying to escape a trap and distances himself from us, as one destined for Paradise distances himself from Hell.

Just as he was pondering this, Mevlana suddenly appeared from the meeting hall of the medresse and approached them like a fierce lion. He proceeded to tell the following anecdote:

"In the time of Shaikh Abu'l Hasan al-Kharaqani[75] (May the Mercy of God be upon him) Sultan Mahmoud-e Saboktegin, the Felicitous and Blessed, went to pay his respects to the shaikh. The viziers and great personages of the empire ran ahead to inform the shaikh of the arrival of the Sultan of Islam. The shaikh did not say anything, even when the sultan appeared at the doorway of the garden of the *tekke*.

"Hasan-e Meymandi, his vizier, entered, bowed, and said, 'For the love of God, would the shaikh please come and welcome the sultan, on behalf of the well-being of the dervishes and out of respect for him, so that such a royal personage will not be offended by waiting.'

"But the shaikh did not budge from his place, even when the sultan arrived at the door of the house.

"Then the vizier ran up to him and said, 'O honored teacher of the religion, have you not read in the Qur'an: *Obey God, the Prophet, and those among you who are invested with authority* [4:59]? Because to honor and glorify a chief of this world is among our duties, and par-

75. Shaikh Abu'l Hasan al-Kharaqani (d. 1033), closely connected on the inner planes to Bayazid al-Bastami, was a renowned sufi Master in Iran. Written above his doorway was: "Whoever enters my abode, feed them without asking about their faith—if they were favored by God Most High who saw them as worthy of the gift of life, then they are certainly worthy of being fed at the house of Abu'l Hasan." Sultan Mahmoud-e Saboktegin, the third Ghaznavid sultan (970-1030), known as "Sultan Mahmoud of Ghazna," became devoted to him.

ticularly a saintly one such as this sultan.'

"The shaikh answered, 'I was so lost in contemplation of the first part of this commandment which says, "*Obey God*," that I was unable to concern myself with the second: "*Obey the Prophet*," and even less so with the third, "*Obey those among you who are invested with authority*!"'

"Immediately, the sultan bowed in respect at these words, declaring himself a devout disciple of the shaikh, and then withdrew in tears.

> With sema, the musician of love sings:
> 'Servanthood is a bond and lordship a headache.'
> Know that servanthood and sovereignty are both veils
> covering the splendor of Love.
> The religion of Love is like no other—
> it is beyond the seventy-two sects;
> to a lover, the throne of kings is just splints of wood.
> The sovereigns of this world, because of their ill natures,
> can't catch even a whiff of the divine wine of servanthood.
> Otherwise, bewildered and dizzy like Adham,[76]
> they would turn their kingship upside down."

When Mevlana had finished telling this tale, the Parvana Mo'inuddin and all the amirs bowed in repentence and left in tears.

The Beloved Loves Effort [216]

Shaikh Nafisuddin Siwasi (May the Mercy of God be upon him) told us that one day Mevlana was walking in the courtyard of his blessed medresse in the company of the Friends, who were enjoying the beautiful presence of their teacher.

He said, "Lock the door of the medresse!" Suddenly, Sultan 'Izzuddin and his viziers and commanders arrived to visit Mevlana. Quickly, he went to take refuge in one of the retreat cells; from there he called out, "Tell them not to trouble themselves."

When the group had left, there was a loud banging on the door of the medresse and the sound of a person hurling himself forcefully against it. A dervish wanted to open the door, but our Master would not give him permission.

He himself went and asked, "Who is knocking like this at the

---

76. A great mystic, Ibrahim Adham, an ancestor of Mevlana's, renounced his kingdom to devote himself to God, see note #6 of this volume.

door of men?"

"The servant of servants, Amir-i Alam."

Mevlana opened the door, and the amir came in and prostrated himself before him. "O Amir-i Alam, do you know the passage in the Qur'an where it is written: *Say: 'He is God, the One'* [112:1]?" our Master asked.

"Certainly, I know it," answered the amir.

"Recite it then, so that I may hear it."

When he had recited it, Mevlana said, "God (May He be exalted) says that He is without mother, father, son or any such kin or partner, and has no similar. Now is the time of effort and the era of service. So as far as you are able, obey God, and don't rely on me because men of God have divine qualities."

And then Mevlana recited this verse: *No ties of kinship will on that Day prevail among them, and neither will they ask about one another* [23:101].

Know that on this path, there is no kinship;
piety and awe of God are the most worthy *mihrab.*[77]

From then on the Chelebi Amir-i' Alam was very devout, carefully conscious of God, and generous. After he left, the Friends were troubled by Mevlana's words.

"What will become of us!" they cried.

"Don't worry," said Mevlana. "I have exaggerated a bit. The soul, which is so cunning, is susceptible to laziness, and I was warning the amir not to encourage this laziness within his soul, so that he might as much as possible continually strive and make a real spiritual effort. God does not love those who are lazy and do nothing.

The Beloved loves this trouble;
effort even if it is futile, is worth more than sleep.
I'm an unbeliever if for an instant anyone has lost

by toiling on the path of faith and obedience.
One needs awe of God, piety, and sincerity
to gain prosperity in both the worlds.

"If I revealed what I knew about the Infinite Mercy of God, if

77. A *mihrab* is the special niche in a mosque that indicates the direction of prayer, in front of which the prayer leader (*imam*) stands. I.e., piety and awe of God are the most worthy direction of prayer and devotion.

I spoke of it and revealed it to people, they would stop making an effort and wouldn't move."

Then he added:

> "You are complete Security, but those who are immature believe, in fear, and yet place their hope in You."

A Sense of Smell [218]

It is recounted that one day a wealthy man was brought to visit Mevlana. Mevlana got up and left and went into the latrine where he stayed for a long while. Khwaja Majduddin went after him to see what was happening. He saw Mevlana sitting in reflection in a corner of the latrine.

Bowing, he inquired, "O Master, what are you doing?"

Mevlana answered, "The stench of this clogged latrine is for me a hundred times more pleasant than the society of the smelly-hearted rich, because companionship with the worldly and the wealthy obscures clear hearts and leaves them troubled."

Right away, this rich man tore his clothes and became a faithful disciple and servant. He generously distributed all his wealth among his relatives and friends, put on the dervish cloak, renounced the world, and attained his goal.

Protected by the Servants of God [219]

The elder friends and compassionate brothers of the era (May God have Mercy on them) told us that when the Mongol chief Baju's army laid seige to Konya, all the inhabitants despaired for their lives, to the point of asking one another for shrouds and forgiveness. They came to find Mevlana and appealed to him for help. After that, Mevlana, leaving by the gate of *Halqa-be gouch* ("the gate of the slaves"), went up on the hill behind the public square in Konya and occupied himself with offering the prayers of dawn. Baju's encampment was just below the hill. The Mongol officers saw the figure of our Master on top of this hill, dressed in blue and wearing a turban the color of smoke, saying his prayers in perfect tranquility while the world below was plunged in chaos.

At the time, the Mongol hordes were ignorant of the light of Islam and the security of the faith. In many Muslim cities they had demolished medresses, mosques, and minarets.

The Mongols tried to send a rain of arrows in Mevlana's direction, but no matter how hard they tried, they were unable to draw their bows. They leapt onto their horses and whipped them furiously, but not one of their mounts was able to put one hoof in front of the other to climb the hill. When the inhabitants of the city, who were watching from the tops of the towers, saw this manifestation of power, they cried out, "God is Great! God is Great!" and their cries reached the heavens.

When all this was reported to Baju, he asked for a bow and arrows and sent a volley of arrows off in Mevlana's direction, but the arrows only turned back and fell into the middle of the army. Three times, he drove his mount forward as hard as he could, but soon realized that it was not going to budge. Furious, he dismounted in order to climb the hill on foot, but his feet were bound to the ground due to the effect of the Almighty Power of "*Be!"and it is* [6:73] and he was completely unable to move.

He cried, "In truth, this man must be one of the *Yaratghan*.[78] One must not make him angry. In all the cites, in all the provinces where there is such a man, the inhabitants are unconquerable."

Mevlana said many times with respect to this Mongol leader: "Baju is a Friend of God, but he doesn't know it."

When Baju came to realize the greatness of this extraordinary miracle he said, "From now on, there will be no more war, no more conflict." The Mongol army lifted the seige of the city and went to camp in the countryside of Filubad.

All the dignitaries of the city came to visit Mevlana, to apologize, and to honor him. Then they collected great sums of money, silver, goods, animals, curiosities from afar, and brought them to Baju as gifts and as a sign of their submission. Baju accepted these gifts and pardoned the city.

Then he asked the dignitaries of the city regarding Mevlana, "Who is this man and where is he from?" They told him the history of Bahauddin Walad and the story of their flight from Balkh from beginning to end.

"I swore that I would demolish the battlements of the city. For the sake of my honor, do it," Baju requested. When the city leaders began the demolishing of the battlements, there was an outcry from the people.

---

78. "*Yaratghan*" is a designation for "God, Creator"; i.e., one of the Holy ones.

Dervishes went to tell Mevlana, who said, "Let them be demolished, since Konya doesn't need towers and city walls to be protected. A stone wall that is so easily destroyed by a slight earthquake is no protection. If it had not been for the wisdom and prayers of God's special servants, the city would have been turned upside down, like 'Ad and Thamud, as it is said: *And we turned those sinful towns upside down* [11:82], and the cries of the people would have been heard rising from the ruins.

These men are lions who come to our rescue
when they hear the cries of the oppressed.
They are incorruptible compassionate defenders
in the moments when times are hard, on a dark day.
Go, and seek them; gain their protection
before misfortune arrives.
These servants of God are merciful and patient,
with God's character, they set things right."

Mevlana continued, "My father constantly said, 'From now on call Konya the City of the Friends of God because every child born here will be a Friend of God.' While the blessed body of Bahauddin and his descendents are in this city, it will be protected from the sword. His enemies will eventually be overcome, and it will be protected from harm at the end of time. Even if one part of it is ruined and it loses its worldly power, it will never be completely destroyed. Even if it were destroyed, our treasure would remain, buried there."

Then he recited:

Even though the Mongols through war
    have brought the world to ruins,
in these ruins is a hidden treasure, so why be sad?

He concluded, "The adepts of the entire spiritual world will turn their faces in this direction, and such a joy will result that even those whose hearts are deadened will rejoice, and our insights and secrets will embrace the whole world."

Secret Journeys [219b]

Kira Khatun, Mevlana's wife (May God be pleased with her) told us the following:

One night, our master left our company. I looked for him everywhere in the medresse, in the reception rooms, all over, but without success, and what's more, all the doors were locked. We were bewildered. After everyone had gone to sleep, I, too, slept, and then suddenly, I awoke and saw Mevlana standing, offering the supererogatory night prayers. I waited until he had finished, and then I approached, bowed, and gently began to rub his blessed feet. There was colored sand between his toes; his shoes, too, were full of sand. Quite alarmed, I asked him what this meant.

"I left to go to the holy Kaaba (May God magnify and enoble it), to keep company for a moment with a dervish of illuminated heart who was longing for my friendship. This is the sand of the Hijaz. Keep it, and tell no one about it," my husband said.

"What an immense journey! What a marvellous promenade," I thought, while he recited these verses:

> A human being can journey like the heart to far horizons,
> without need for saddle or mule or any caravanserais.

The Voice of Love Is Heard Everywhere [222]

The noble and generous dervishes told us that Malik Shamsuddin Hindi, the King of Shiraz, wrote a letter to that one of sweet speech and glorious words, Shaikh Saa'di,[79] asking for a *ghazal* that would be unusual, unlike any other, containing marvellous meanings and high inspirations. He added that it did not matter who the author was, as long as it would nourish his soul.

Shaikh Saa'di wrote out for him a new *ghazal* written by Mevlana which had been sent to Shiraz around that time and which had illuminated every heart with joy. It begins as follows:

> The voice of Love surrounds us.
> We are traveling to Heaven—
> who yearns to see this splendor?

At the end of the letter, he added, "In Asia Minor, a sovereign has blessed us with his presence, and these words bear the fragrance

79. Saa'di of Shiraz (1184-1291 C.E.). His *Gulistan* (Rose Garden) is mainly in prose and contains stories and personal anecdotes. The text is interspersed with a variety of short poems, containing aphorisms, advice, and humorous reflections. Saa'di demonstrates a profound awareness of the absurdity of human existence. The fate of those who depend on the changeable moods of kings is contrasted with the freedom of the dervishes.

of his innermost secret; there are no words to compare with these, nor will there ever be. I yearn to visit him and to kiss the dust upon which his blessed feet walk. May the king know this."

When Malik Shamsuddin read the *ghazal* he wept profusely and burst into praise of it. He held a large gathering at which sacred dances were performed to the rhythm of this *ghazal*. And as a token of his gratitude, he sent numerous gifts to Shaikh Saa'di.

At last, Shaikh Saa'di came to Konya, was blessed with the honor of kissing our Master's hand, and received the glance of favor from the men of heart.

Catching a Glimpse of the Secret [224]

The most excellent among the Friends related:

One day, a great jurist came to see Mevlana. In order to test him, he asked him several questions: "Can it be said that God has a soul or not? Because if one can say that He has a soul, then what is the meaning of the words: *Every soul shall taste death* [3:185]? And if it is not allowed to use the word 'soul' in speaking of that One who is without sign, why did Jesus (Upon him be Peace) say, *You know what is in my soul, but I do not know what is in Yours* [5:116]. These two ideas appear contradictory. In the same way, if it is permitted to apply 'thingness' to God, why did He Himself say, *Everything is perishing* [28:88]?"

Mevlana answered, "The significance of the words *I do not know what is in Yours* is this—'in Your knowledge and in Your Unseen world.' For the people of unveiling, it means 'in Your secret'—*You know what is in my secret, and the secret of my secret, and I do not know what is in the secret of Your Secret*. The people of heart say it means that *You know what emanates from me into the world, and I do not know the secret of that which emanates from You into the Hereafter*.

"In regard to the expression of 'thing' as applied to God, it is allowed, because He has Himself said, *Say, 'Who is the greatest in witnessing?' Say, 'God'* [6:19]. That is to say, God is greater than others in witnessing. *Say, 'God is witness between you and me'* [6:19] on the Day of Recognition. The words *Everything is perishing* mean that everything that has been created is perishing, except the Creator (May He be Exalted), that is to say, if it is not He; and the main thing is that the exception is He, but *God knows best the Truth*!"

In that very moment, this jurist became a sincere servant and disciple, seeking the Truth.

Purify My House [225]

One day, some Arabs came to visit Mevlana and all the divine insights he expressed that day he spoke in Arabic. His final words were these:

The human being is like a vessel or a bowl. It is necessary to wash the outside, but it's even more important to wash the inside. If it is obligatory to wash the outside, it is even more of a religious duty to wash the inside, because the Divine wine can only be poured into a pure vessel. That is why God has ordered us to clean this vessel of the body, because the wine is contained inside it, not on the outside.

Purify My house, is the explanation of purity—
it is a treasury of Light
even though the talisman guarding it
is made of clay.
Though the body is the house of envy,
know that God has purified it well.

He continued, "Everyone within whom the false self and *shaytan*[80] are dead, who has purified his blameworthy characteristics, reaches God. May God protect us from only reaching the path of God."

Beholding Reality [225]

One day, when serving Mevlana, someone said, "All the prophets and spiritually advanced have trembled with fear of death and its pains."

Our Master replied, "With all respect to them; may God protect us from such feelings! Do people know what death is? Death for a

---

80. *Shaytan* (the devil) is referred to within the Islamic tradition as the impulse towards pride and arrogance within the human being. The Prophet Muhammad said, "Satan circulates within the blood vessels of the children of Adam just like blood flows within their veins." The aim is to make of one's *shaytan* a *mumin* (faithful one).

When Iblis, formerly one of those closest to God's throne, refused to bow down to Adam, in disobedience to the command of God, he said to God, "*You created me of fire, and created him of clay*" [7:12]. In other words, "My essence is of fire and his is of clay. How is it right for one who is superior to bow down to an inferior?" Iblis was cursed and banished for this sin and contention with God and resolved to tempt human beings away from faithful devotion. Yet it says in the Qur'an, *Seek refuge with God from Satan, the accursed. Behold, he has no power over those who have attained to faith and in their Sustainer place their trust* [16:98-99].

true seeker is vision of the Supreme Reality; how could one flee from such seeing?"

Prayer for the New Year [226]

On the first of the month of *Muharram*, with the moment of sighting of the new crescent moon which begins the Arab year, Mevlana would offer the following prayer:

> O God, You who are Eternal, the First and the Last! This is a new year, and I ask You to protect me in it from Satan the accursed and from the commanding self (*nafs ammarah*) which encourages evil. Keep me occupied with that which draws me closer to You, and help me to avoid the things that take me away from You—O God, You who are Infinitely Compassionate, Infinitely Merciful, in the Name of Your Mercy, O Most Noble and Generous.

Healing Words [226b]

The sultan of teachers, Shaikh Shamsuddin of Mardin (May God have Mercy on him), told us that once one of the dervishes was ill with a fever, and they came to tell Mevlana.

"Write this on a piece of paper," Mevlana ordered: "O *Umm-Muldam*! Mother of the Fever! If you have faith in God, don't give us headaches, devour our flesh, or drink our blood. Be gone from me and whomever is ill! Look for someone else who is ascribing partners to God! I am saying: 'There is no god but God, and Muhammad is His servant and messenger (*La illaha il Allah, Muhammada Rasulillah*).' Immerse the paper in water. Then give the water to the invalid to drink, and he will be healed."

The sick man drank the liquid and was cured with God's help.

Mevlana would also write three words—'*Adhan* ("call to prayer"), '*idhn* ("permission") and *pesin* ("behind")—on three cloves of garlic, or if these weren't tolerable, on three almonds. Then he would give that to the sick person who would be healed in three days.

The Spirit's Longing [227]

That glory among saints and reciter of the *Mathnawi*, Sirajuddin (May the Mercy of God be upon him), our teacher,[81] told us:

81. Sirajuddin, one of the noble disciples who was well-versed in the *Mathnawi* of Mevlana's, was one of the teachers of Aflaki, the compiler of these stories who

Mevlana constantly repeated three verses which he taught to Husamuddin, and he said, "Learn them by heart, as I have, as a remembrance from my shaikh, Sayyid Borhanuddin Mohaqqiq of Tirmidh (May the Mercy of God be upon him)." The three verses were:

The spirit has its origins in the Light of God's Throne,
while the human body consists of the dust of the earth.

The Almighty has established a harmony between them,
so that they might receive His Trust
and have the strength to bear all hardships.

The spirit is in exile, while the body is in its own country;
have pity then on this spirit, that is a stranger,
filled with longing and far from home.

Mevlana wept and then said:

Say to the one who is troubled, keep searching,
but try as you might
you'll never find a beloved as sublime as This!

Becoming a Witness for the Truth [227b]

One day, Mevlana left the city by the gate near the horse-market, in the company of a few of the Friends, on his way to visit the tomb of the Sultan of the Wise, Bahauddin Walad (May God be pleased with Him). Along the way, they came upon a large crowd gathered around someone. A few of the young men ran to appeal to Mevlana, saying: "Please do something, for God's sake! He is a young Greek; they are going to execute him!"

"What has he done?" asked our Master.

"He killed someone and has been condemned."

Mevlana drew closer. The executioners and the police bowed to him and stood aside. Mevlana then put his blessed coat around the young man.

When the chief of the police recounted all this to the sultan, he said, "Mevlana is the judge. He could intervene for a whole city if he wished, everyone is so devoted to him, much less one Greek."

The dervishes took the young man to the bathhouse, and then

---

was also the dervish of Chelebi 'Arif, Mevlana's grandson.

they went to the medresse. He declared his faith and embraced Islam while holding Mevlana's hands. He was then circumcised and a large sema began.

"What is your name?"

"Thiryanos," answered the young man.

"From now on, we will call you 'Alauddin Thiryanos,"[82] said Mevlana.

In the end, through the blessing of Mevlana's enlivening glance of favor 'Alauddin rose to such an exalted rank that the great shaikhs and the finest scholars were astonished by his knowledge and his manners, his jokes and his witty remarks.

One day, our Master asked him, "What do these priests, these excellent Christians say is the reality of Jesus (May Peace be upon him)?"

"They say He is God," 'Alauddin answered.

"Well, then," said our Master, "tell them that our Muhammad is even more God! Even more God!"

*****

One day, a group of jurists slandered 'Alauddin Thiryanos to that king of qadis, Sirajuddin Ormawi (May God have Mercy on him), saying that he was insisting that 'Mevlana is God': "This is not allowable according to the shariah of the Prophet; it is even blasphemy," they said. Several officers were sent to bring him to appear in court.

"Are you the one who is said to be calling Mevlana, 'God'?" the qadi asked.

"Not at all," cried 'Alauddin, "May God protect me! I said that our Master is one who can make God manifest! Don't you see what he has made of me? I was a stubborn denier and far from the Truth; he taught me real knowledge and made of me a scholar. He gave me understanding and helped me to know God. He led me from the invoking of the name of God and mere imitation to a true knowledge of the Supreme Being, a profound deepening of the Truth.

---

82. In another passage (#335), Aflaki relates how previously this debauched one, Thiryanos, had seen someone in a dream who had given him a good beating. Then when he had awakened and was walking along to town, he had suddenly encountered Mevlana, who said to him, "So how did you like that beating?" When he looked again, Mevlana had disappeared, and he realized it was he in his dream. It was later said that under Mevlana's guidance and grace he became such a master that even Sirajuddin and the qadis and professors of Konya were silenced by his ability to speak the Truth.

"'He who knows himself, knows his Lord'—has become the currency of my existence. If a person has not opened to the divine in his heart, he cannot know God. This is a decisive proof.

> A person without reason cannot know reason with certainty;
> understand from that who it is who knows God.

A grammarian knows a grammarian, a jurist knows a jurist; the ignorant can never know the wise, any more than the blind can see the sun. A man without God cannot manifest God in the way it has been said, 'Go and manifest My attributes to My creation.'

"Mevlana, by his illuminated conversation and education of one in service to him, is able to transform an ignorant man into a wise one; he makes him a jurist, a grammarian, a philosopher. Through his radiance, the ignorant one is transformed. In the same way, our Master's presence and his blessed breath can render the ignorant soul (*nafs*) wise, a knower of God, and endowed with reason. And more than that, he makes the man of reason into a lover of God. He makes of him even something which no one is able to become.

"Don't you see how in the alchemical process, only a speck of the philosopher's stone is needed to transform oxydized copper into pure gold; it transforms its nature. So it is not astonishing or strange that a holy person, whose nature has been transformed, who has been delivered from individuality, transformed by God's Light, can transmute into gold the copper of another's existence, can illumine another and make him reach the ocean of illumination of *All things return to God* [3:109]. There is nothing astonishing or strange about this!"

All the wise men and jurists who had accused 'Alauddin were bewildered and ashamed of themselves.

'Alauddin Thiryanos told Mevlana the entire story.

He smiled and replied, "You should have said to the qadi, 'What a misfortune for you, if you don't become God!'"

And How Do You Read? [228]

Akhi Ahmad was one of the honored people of the epoch. One day he said to 'Alauddin, "I have read as many books as a donkey could carry, and yet nowhere have I seen the sema authorized, nor have I ever heard of permission for it. What proof do you offer to support this innovation?"

"My brother," answered 'Alauddin, "has also read in the manner of a donkey, and that's why he doesn't know. Thanks be to God, I have read in the manner of Jesus and so I've come to understand the secrets contained in it."

A World of Love [229]

That glory of pious men, Shaikh Mahmoud, the carpenter, (May the Mercy of God be upon him) told us that one day Mevlana turned his blessed face towards the Friends and said, "Alas! The people of Konya are tired of our ecstatic concerts and speak ill of us behind our backs. They don't understand the delights of the sema, and show no gratitude to God, like the people of Saba.[83] It comes to these ears that they cover us with blame, but the Lord of the Day of Reckoning will chastise them for their ingratitude and waywardness. . . .

"In the end, they will repent and ask forgiveness. With complete faith, they will come to praise our children and our successors, and by the grace of our Lord Most High, the city of Konya will again flourish. The people of that time will be lovers of the sema and people of spiritual taste. The World of Love will embrace the entire universe, and all people everywhere will fall in love with our words.

"The greatness of this family will increase, and the will of God will unfold. Our Friends will be the best of humankind, in words as well as in deeds. If it pleases our Lord Most High, the people graced with blessing will come to know the secret of: *They cannot comprehend any of His knowledge except that which He wills* [2:255]."

Listen in Silence [230]

One day, Mevlana went to visit the Shaikh of Shaikhs, the King of the Traditionalists, Shaikh Sadruddin [al-Qonawi] (May the Mercy of God be upon him).

Shaikh Sadruddin welcomed Mevlana with all honor possible and then knelt respectfully on his prayer rug across from Mevlana and gazed at him. The two immersed themselves in contemplation, swimming in the Ocean of Tranquility and Divine Light.

There was a dervish present, known as Haji Kashi, who had lived

83. See *Surah* 34, *Saba* (the Biblical people of Sheba). The fate of the people of Saba is indicative of the ephemeral nature of all human power and wealth. We are reminded to be grateful to God for the gifts that come to us and to keep our focus: *Say: "I counsel you one thing only: Be ever conscious of standing before God, whether you are in the company of others or alone"* [34:46].

in service near the shaikh, had visited the Kaaba several times, and had visited many shaikhs throughout the world.

He came forward and asked Mevlana the following question: "What is poverty?"

Mevlana didn't answer.

Shaikh Sadruddin was extremely perturbed. The dervish repeated the question three times. Mevlana still did not respond, and then he got up to leave. The shaikh accompanied him to the outer door.

Then, quite furious, the shaikh shouted, "Old unripe one! Unseasonable bird! Was that the time and the place to ask a question or to speak? You acted inappropriately, but he answered appropriately, even though you were unaware of it. Go, sit down and wait, because you have just received a blow from the Unseen."

Poor Haji Kashi cried, "What was the answer?"

The shaikh replied, "This: 'When the man of poverty knows God, he is speechless.' A perfect dervish is one who is completely silent in the presence of the Friends of God; he says nothing with his tongue or his heart. In other words, 'When poverty is complete, it is God.'"

It's a mistake to speak hearsay in the presence of seers—
it just reveals our unawareness, our deficiency.
It's more profitable to be silent before one who sees,
that is why we have been told: *Be silent* [46:29].

[*Mathnawi* IV: 2071-2072]

A True Knower of God [231]

A dervish asked Mevlana, "What sort of person is a true knower of God?"

He answered, "One whose pure temperament is untroubled by adversity. 'He who knows the Truth remains constant,' and is able to transform all murkiness into pure water."

And then Mevlana said,

"O my soul! Could a wisp of straw ever remain still in
running water?
How could loathing ever take up residence
within the spirit and soul?"

The One Who Keeps You in Love [232]

One of the dear dervishes told us that, one day, Mevlana asked for an inkwell and a reed pen and wrote in huge script on the wall of the medresse, "To abstain from spiritual food is forbidden, but God best knows the Truth!"

He also asked one of the dervishes to record on the page of a book: "The proof of the beloved's exquisiteness is the tears of the lover, and that is the miracle of the prophets (Peace be with them all)."

Stay in love with the One who keeps you in love
and seek for the One who keeps you seeking.

Under His Eye [233]

One day, Mevlana was commenting on the verse: *The One who created me and is the One who guides me* [26:78]. He said, "He created me, to serve Him, and He guides me in the ways of serving Him. *And [He] sees your comings and goings among those who prostrate themselves before Him* [26:219]—in the loins of the fathers, and the wombs of the mothers."

*****

Fakhruddin Adib, one of the finest of the Friends, told us that one day, our Master, in the middle of a large assembly, commented on this *hadith* of the Prophet (Peace and blessings upon him): "I have only seen God in a red garment." Everyone was speechless and overwhelmed by the explanation.

According to another version, it was this *hadith* upon which he commented: "My Lord appears to me only in a red robe." Overcome with meaning, he recited this *ghazal*:

There is a light within these red hairs
beyond sight, higher than the spirit—
if you wish to connect yourself to it,
arise and tear away the veil of passion.
This subtle spirit has taken on a face,
with its eyebrows, eyes, and dark complexion—
Our Lord Beyond Description
appeared in the form of Mustafa, His prophet.
This form is the annihilation of form;
his narcissus eye was like the Resurrection.
Wherever his glance fell upon creation,
a hundred doors flew open with God.
When the bodily form of Mustafa disppeared,
all of creation began to cry, "God is Great!"

"If one dreams of wearing red or of seeing red," Mevlana observed, "it means pleasure and joy; green denotes asceticism; white, awe of God; and blue and black are the colors of mourning and sorrow. But *God knows best!*"

When You See Him, Don't Look Anywhere Else [233b]

One day, Mevlana was present at a meeting held by the Parvana, in the company of various religious leaders and distinguished people of the community.

"God exists for those who contemplate His works, but is absent for one who seeks to grasp His Essence," he declared. "If one strives desperately to find Him, one can only arrive at something other than He, but if one is patient, one reaches Him. God is more obvious than the sun. One who, after having seen Him, still looks for a logical explanation is lost.

One who looks for proof of God's existence,
is himself faulty, blind, and disgraced.

To be without a goal is to have no existence, or if one has, it is only for the sake of abasement. The ascetic loves service and worship; the knower of God loves the One whom he serves. The ascetic is like one who is ill, while the knower of God is like a physician."

Prepare Yourself for the Light [233c]

Once, the practice of sema was being discussed in the presence of Mevlana (May God sanctify his innermost secret).

Mevlana said, "First acquire a capacity for sema, then devote yourself to it. Yesterday, I put sugar to my nose, but it could not catch the fragrance, because it had not yet gained the capacity."

Gain a capacity for paradise, and be reborn with new life.
If you go unprepared into a mine,
you won't bring back a single bit of gold.

If you don't wish to get lost underground,
take refuge in the light—
it remains above the earth.

If you yearn for the light, prepare yourself;
if you desire *houris*, be purer than a *houri*.

If you don't gain a pure heart like Gabriel,
how will you find the road to real men?

To be dead and seen by God is better
than being alive and deprived of His Glance.

Seek Like-minded Friends [234]

Mevlana would constantly pray for the Friends, "May God protect you against obvious fate."

The dervishes asked what he meant, and he answered, "Obvious fate is associating with strangers and those not on the path. By God! The company you keep is a powerful thing! The Prophet (Peace and blessings upon him) said, 'Avoid the company of those not of your kind.'"

And as the poet has said:

Flee the friend who is not of your kind!
O great ones, find a good companion!
Seek out the company of like-minded people,
or you'll find yourself, like the bear, in the mouth of a dragon.[84]

Mevlana continued, "On this subject, my master, the Sultan of the poor ones, Shamsuddin Tabrizi (May God increase the mention of his name) said, 'The sign of a disciple who has gained acceptance is that he absolutely does not speak with strangers, and if by chance a conversation were to begin, he just sits there, like a hypocrite at the mosque, a child in school, or one who is restrained in prison.'"

Poverty Is My Livelihood [235]

One day, Mevlana was expressing divine insights in the medresse, and many of the prominent people of the city were there.

He said, "I have never been delighted in a harmful desire, nor made presumptuous by any compensation.

Though poverty boxes my ears until I'm close to death,
I would never sell liberty for slavery.

I renounced the taste of greed. For forty years now, contentment with little has been my nourishment, and poverty has been my livelihood.

---

84. This is an allusion to the story of "The fool who trusted the bear," on "putting trust in the fawningness and good faith of the bear," *Mathnawi*, Book II:1932-1992.

May God protect me! In my heart no greed exists.
Through contentment, it holds a whole world.
If he gives me sour milk, I don't desire honey,
because every benefit has a care that accompanies it."

After that he added, "All perfection, all beauty claimed by someone, whether in act or in word, in which that person takes pride—according to the situation, he may say, 'I am the Truth (*ana'l Haqq*)!'—those who are liars join Pharaoh and his kind, but not the sincere, the venerated, who one day raise their head, having reached this perfection, so that the truth of their rightful character is verified by humankind."

One "I" is cursed; the other blessed.
God's Mercy keeps faith with the true,
while the other is struck down.

In the Name of God! [237]

One day, as he was walking in the courtyard of the medresse, Mevlana said: "In the Name of God—one who holds tight to Him cannot be conquered; one who trusts in Him cannot be in loss! May my repentence be in the Name of God. May the joy in my heart be in the Name of God, and my intoxication and my gratitude."

Morning Prayers [238]

That king of representatives and God's holy saint, Shaikh Mevlana al-Kabi (May the Mercy of God be upon him), one of the great and noble companions from the kingdom of the Daneshmandids, told us the following:

One day we were at our Master's medresse in the company of Shamsuddin of Mardin (May god have Mercy on him) at the time of the dawn prayer. The dervishes wanted Mevlana to lead the morning prayers, because when someone prays behind a God-conscious prayer-leader, it is as if he were praying behind a Prophet. Mevlana accepted. Then he recited many unusual and marvellous prayers and *wird* which no other shaikh had ever formulated.

Among the prayers he recited that day, I kept these as a remembrance:

With God's help, I am prepared for any fear with "There is no god but God" (*La illaha il Allah*); for any sorrow or sadness with "May it be as God wills" (*Mashallah*); for any benfits with "Praise be to God" (*Alhamdulillah*); for any ease and abundance with "Thanks be to God" (*Shukrulillah*); for all astonishment with "God is Subtle beyond all knowing (*Subhanallah*); for any sin or errors with "May God forgive me" (*Astaughfirullah*); for all scarcities with "God is enough for me" (*Hasbiyallah*); for any event of destiny with "I trust in God" (*Tawakkaltu 'alallah*), for any calamity with "We belong to God and to Him we shall return" (*Inna lillahi wa inna ilayhi raji'un*); for any obedience or disobedience with "All power and strength is with God, the Most High, the Most Great" (*La hawla wa la quwwata illa billahil 'ali il 'azim*).[85]

Light Upon Light [239]

Shaikh Mevlana al-Kabi continued to relate that when Mevlana had completed the morning prayers, he would continue with great feeling:

> O Beloved God! Grant me light in my heart, light in my tomb, light in my hearing, light in my sight, light in my hair, light on my skin, light in my flesh, light in my blood, light in my bones. Place light in front of me, light behind me, light below me, light above me, light to my right and light to my left! O great God, increase my light, give me light, make me light, O Light upon Light (*nur ala nur*), through Your Mercy, O Most Merciful of the Merciful.[86]

Fakhrunnisa, the Glory of Women [240]

Our Friends of subtle glance, the exemplary brothers, told us that in the time of Mevlana there was in the city of Konya a woman, a Friend of God and perfect being, who was known as Fakhrunnisa, the "Glory of Women," (May God be pleased with her). A pious and sincere woman, she was known as the Rabi'a of her day. The great of the world and the knowers of God who lived by the heart, all loved and revered her. She was perfect and endowed with manifest miracles beyond measure. Fakhrunnisa loved to be in the presence of

---

85. This recitation of prayers has continued as part of the daily *wird* recited by Mevlevi dervishes. See *The Mevlevi Wird*, translated by Camille Helminski with assistance from Cuneyt Erolu, Mahmoud Mostafa, and Amer Latif, The Threshold Society, 2000.

86. It is said that a version of this Prayer of Light (*Du'a an-Nur*), a prayer offered at dawn by the Prophet Muhammad (See Hadith collections: al-Bukhari #8.328 and Muslim #380), was recited by Mevlana every morning; it continues to be recited by Mevlevi dervishes.

Mevlana, and he, as well, would sometimes come to visit her.[87]

There was a time when her disciples were encouraging her to go to Mecca on pilgrimage, and she herself received inner guidance to do so.

"Let me consult Mevlana first, because I can't possibly go without his permission and his direction. I'll do whatever he orders."

She went to visit Mevlana. Before she began to speak, he immediately said, "It's a very good idea and a blessed journey. Let us hope that we will be there together."

Fakhrunnisa bowed her head and didn't say a word. Her friends and followers, puzzled by her response, wondered what had taken place during the meeting. That night, Fakhrunnisa stayed at Mevlana's house and they continued speaking together. After midnight, Mevlana went up on the terraced roof of the medresse and continued his night prayers. After he had finished his prayers, he became very excited, and through the roof opening, called Fakhr-unnisa to join him up on the roof.

When she came up, he said, "Look!" pointing at the sky. "Your destination is here." Fakhrunnisa saw the Kaaba circumambulating Mevlana's head, circling around him like a dervish in his sacred dance. It was clearly visible, without any doubt or supposition. Fakhrunnisa, that poor one (*faqira*), let out a cry and was plunged deep into ecstatic bewilderment.

After a while, she came to herself, bowed her head, and renounced her intention. Mevlana's reply was this beautiful *ghazal*:

> The Kaaba circumambulates around the abode of one idol.
> O Lord, who could this be, so distraught and full of longing?
> Compared to her, the full moon is a broken plate
> and her sweetness puts sugar to shame.
>
> All the Masters of the Way, all the faithful angels, bow to her,
> crying, "O adored one, for the love of God, have mercy on us."
> The creatures of a thousand foam-covered seas are the shell
> that contains this pearl of Love.

87. One may still visit Fakhrunnisa where she rests in the garden beside the mosque on Tea Garden street in Konya. In recent years, for various reasons of renovation and road rerouting, it was decided to reconstruct her tomb. As Shaikh Suleyman Hayati Dede was then the acting spiritual head of the Mevlevi order in Konya, he was asked to be present when she was exhumed. He told us of how, when her body was uncovered, it was totally intact and the fragrance of roses filled the air.

From the direction of Honor and Glory, such a high reflection!
She is the Kaaba's paradise, its *houris*, its joy,
its pleasure and celebration.
In her overflowing light, one sigh of worship
is a whole Divine verse.

Listen to this tale and be aware
that one of the sun's atoms has befriended an idol.
O you who are the Shams of Tabriz of Mercy and Compassion,
a sun bestowing a thousand blessings,
your words have become like a jug full of wine—
let's drink of it forever.

O Soul of My Soul, Speak! [241b]

Sultan Walad told us:

One of the dervishes complained to my father that some scholars had asked him why they called the *Mathnawi* a Qur'an, and that he had told them that it was a commentary on the Qur'an.

My father was silent for a moment and then exclaimed, "Why would it not be? Miserable ones! There is no question that the lights of the Divine secrets are contained in the words of the prophets and the Friends of Gods. The Word of God pours forth from their pure hearts like a stream from their tongues.

Certainly, the word is to be found in the heart;
the tongue is just a guide for speech.

Sometimes it's expressed in Syriac,
sometimes in the seven oft-repeated verses of the *Fatiha*,
sometimes in Hebrew, sometimes in Arabic.

Whether like this or like that, O Soul of my soul,
O Khusraw, with lips of Shirin,[88] speak to me
in whatever language You choose."

When this explanation, from the mouth of this man of vision, arrived at the ears of the scholars, they realized their error, asked forgiveness, and joined the Brotherhood.

---

88. Khusraw (Sassanian King Khusraw II) and Shirin (the Armenian princess) were two lovers whose story was recounted in the *Shahnamah* and later romanticized in Nizami's (d. 1209 C.E,) *Khusraw and Shirin*.

A Key to Paradise [243]

One day, Mevlana Shamsuddin Tabrizi (May God magnify his memory) was in the blessed mosque and said:

"If you wish to see the prophets, look at Mevlana! He possesses the manners of the prophets, those who received true revelations, not just dreams or inspirations. The nature of the prophets is purity of heart and being bound to the satisfaction (*rida*) of the men of God.

"Now, Paradise is when Mevlana is satisfied, but Hell is when he is angry. He is the key to Paradise. Go and look at him, if you wish to know the meaning of the saying: 'The scholars are the heirs of the prophets.' And other things upon which I won't comment . . . If I had remained without a shaikh, I would never have remained. A thousand mercies upon your spirit. May God Most High grant Mevlana a long life! O Lord, bestow him upon us and us upon him! Amen!"

Gracious Wisdom [244]

One day, Shamsuddin Tabrizi said, "At this moment, there is no one in all the inhabited world like Mevlana. He can speak with the specialists about jurisprudence, grammar, or logic, and he speaks more powerfully than they do, and with a more subtle taste. Even if I toiled for a hundred years in these fields, I could never acquire a tenth of his knowledge nor of his merit. In my presence, he pretends not to know this, because of the perfection of his graciousness."

The One I Know [244b]

Sultan Walad recounted that his father, Mevlana, was speaking in the medresse about knowing God and said, "The true disciple considers his spiritual director to be beyond anyone. One day, someone asked a student of Abu Yazid (Bastami) who was greater, his shaikh or Abu Hanifa.

"He replied, 'My shaikh.'

"He then asked, 'What about Abu Bakr?'

"The student replied, 'My shaikh is greater.'

"He then listed all the companions of the Prophet (peace and blessings upon him), and finally asked, 'Who is greater, Muhammad or your shaikh?'

" 'My Shaikh,' he replied.

"At last, he cried out, 'Who is greater, God or your spiritual director?'

"To which the Friend replied, 'I have seen God in my shaikh; I know nothing beyond this: my shaikh is all!'

"Someone else was asked, 'Is God greater or is your shaikh?' And he answered, 'There is no difference between these two great beings.'

Since God is not directly seen,
these prophets are representatives of Truth.
No! What am I saying!
To think they are two is ugly, unseemly."

Exaltation and Humility [245]

According to Sultan Walad (May God sanctify his unique mystery), one day, Mevlana was present for the mourning ceremony after the death of Shoja's child. All the qadis, shaikhs, amirs and *akhis* had gathered and were occupied in a discussion about the various degrees of elevation and superiority.

Mevlana said, "True elevation is towards the future life, towards God, and not in relation to the world and its creatures. In this world, there is a risk to loftiness, because the higher an object rises, the further it will fall, and the more it will then break into small pieces." And he recited:

The human being mounts the ladder of "we" and "I,"
but a fall is bound to occur.
One who rises high above others is a fool—
his bones will only break more easily
when he falls from his exalted place.

Bravo for one whose passions have been subdued,
whose character is good, and whose morals are beautiful.

Sultan Walad commented, "The manifestation of our Great Master, my grandfather, was through grandeur and exaltedness, with my father it is humility and great gentleness. In a Friend of God, grandeur and gentleness are equally divine."

He Is With Those Who Love Him [246]

Sultan Walad continued:

One day, my father said, "When a Friend of God leaves this world, his journey is one hundred thousand times greater than during his life, because his journey is within God, who is Infinite. And until the Day of Reckoning His hold will remain over His disciples and those who love Him.

"As it has been said,

God is the Creator—what have his servants created?
God endures, even when the servant departs.

"'God will be with his servant until Eternity.' And that is sufficient."

Patiently Draw Near [248]

Sultan Walad also recounted:

One day, Mo'inuddin, the Parvana, came to pay a visit on Mevlana. I told my father and sat down, waiting with the Parvana. He waited and I apologized for the delay, and repeated to him what Mevlana had said many times: "I, too, have affairs to take care of, ecstacies, and immersions in the Absolute. The amirs and the friends cannot always see me. Let them be occupied with their own business and the affairs of the people. We will go to visit them."

The Parvana continued to maintain a humble attitude. Suddenly, Mevlana emerged. The Parvana bowed and said, "Bahauddin offered many apologies and was very gracious, but I imagined that your lateness was a teaching for me: 'Parvana, for people in need, waiting is bitter and painful.' By your lateness, I have gained the advantage of learning this."

"Excellent thought," said Mevlana, "but the principle is that when a petitioner arrives at someone's door, and he has a disagreeable voice and appearance, he is sent away quickly, so they don't have to keep listening to him or see his face. If the one who arrives is beautiful and has a pleasant voice, even though he is a beggar full of supplications and entreaties, one doesn't grant his request for a crust of bread right away, but rather says, 'Have patience while the loaf is baked,' so that they might keep listening to his voice. Just now, we were late because your entreaties and your love, your supplications were pleasing to the men of God, and we wanted you to draw even closer to God and be more accepted by Him."

As Mevlana spoke, the Parvana prostrated himself, full of amazement and said, "The goal of your servant in coming to see *Khodavandgar* was to let people know that I, also, am a servant of Mevlana and one of those attached to this threshold."

When he returned home, he sent the dervishes six thousand soltani as a token of his gratitude for the mercy that had been bestowed upon him. The narrator added that this sum was taken to Chelebi Husamuddin's house so that he could divide it among the companions.

Enduring Faith [249]

Sultan Walad continued:

One day, my father was describing the infinite joys to be discovered through sincerity and pure faith:

"All the learning that one might possibly acquire in this world is useful only up to the moment one is put into one's grave and no further; it is not transportable to the World Beyond.

> Know that this learning you've acquired will be left behind—
> you will not remain, nor will the knowledge you choose.

But faith is a gift from the Beyond and will accompany one on one's return voyage."

And on this subject, he told us the following story:

When I was young, I had a friend in Damascus. We studied the *Hidaya*[89] together, and later he was appointed to be the qadi in Malatya. When the Mongol commander, Bahadur laid seige to Malatya and pillaged the town, he seized the qadi's fortune. Finally, Bahadur gave the order that my friend be castrated, that his testicles be removed.

"O great commander!" he cried, "May God support you with His Spirit. Everything has been taken away from me, except these testicles which I brought with me from my own country—why would you take them away?"

This pleased the commander; he restored the qadi to good favor, granted him many benefits, and reinstated him as a qadi.

I am telling you this story in order for you to know that the qualities of real bravery and generosity are the true faith that the human being brings with him from the country of the World Beyond of *Am I not your Lord* [7:172], and that he will take with him when he returns to that Eternal world. One must protect these qualities and not dis-

---

89. The *Hidaya* referred to here is probably the *Hidaya* on *fiqh* (principles of Islamic law) of al-Marghinani d. 1196), a Hanafi scholar.

sipate them in the company of the weak, so that one doesn't become impotent and deprived of the joy of the pure ones of Paradise.

A real man isn't known by beard or penis—
or the king of men would be he who has a member
as big as an ass's.
Anyone who acts shamefully towards a friend—
and blocks the way for men—
it is he who is the unmanly man.

Planting Seeds of Generosity [249b]

"One day," said Sultan Walad, "two jurists came to visit my father and brought a small quantity of lentils, but were ashamed that their present had so little monetary value." He recounted that Mevlana then told them the following anecdote:

God Most High conveyed the inspiration to his Elect, peace and blessings upon him, that the faithful were to give money and goods, each according to his means. At this command, some brought half their fortune, and others brought a third. Abu Bakr gave all that he owned, which amounted to an enormous sum; others gave camels, gold, and weapons. Among the Companions was an old and poor man, the sole provider for his children, who only had three dates and some barley bread. He gave his humble offering to the Prophet and then sat down in a state of bewilderment. The Companions began to laugh secretly, but the Elect of God (Peace and blessings upon him) who realized they were making fun of the man, stopped them: "Shall I reveal to you a secret from the Unseen?" he asked.

"O yes, Messenger of God!" the Companions cried.

"God Most High has lifted the veils to show me that all the money you gave was on one side of the scale, and the three dates and barley bread of this poor man was on the other, and this small amount weighed more than all the rest."

Everyone bowed and applauded Muhammad's vision of this secret but asked for an explanation.

"This poor man gave up his only possessions, while you still kept some of yours. A little can be a lot in the eyes of the Supreme Being. Think of the tiny seed that is put into the earth. With the grace of God, it is transformed into a tall tree that bears much fruit, because it has been entrusted to God. Therefore one must give the obligatory alms to the poor and to the servants of God, and in doing so, one entrusts it to God. Because as it has been said: *Alms arrive in the hand of the Merciful before they fall into the hands of the poor; alms are only for the poor and the needy* [9:60]."

The poor among the emigrants (*mohajarun*) and the helpers (*ansar*) were filled with faith and happiness.

Sultan Walad continued, "Overjoyed, the two jurists then declared themselves disciples and servants of Mevlana."

The Seeds That Keep Blooming [251]

Sultan Bahauddin Walad told us one day:

My father said, "O Bahauddin, look carefully at me! When the seed of my teaching has taken root in your heart, you will understand—reflect deeply on my teaching and really try to absorb it and if you do, felicity will be yours. Know that the body of the prophets, the saints, and their friends will never perish. A seed thrown into the earth may appear to die and disappear, however, at the end of a few days, it comes to life and grows into a tree. In a similar way the body of the prophets and the Friends of God will also come to life again."

Keep Serving [251b]

Sultan Walad recounted:

One of the employees of the government came to my father to repent for his actions, and to speak about finding a different occupation. My father told him this story:

In the days of the Caliph Harun ar-Rashid there was a prefect of police who was visited every day by Khidr (Peace be upon him). He repented of his past misdeeds and retired from his work, whereupon Khidr stopped visiting him and completely disappeared.

The poor prefect was very upset. That night, he heard a voice in a dream: "Your spiritual station was based on your work." The next morning, the prefect immediately went to the Caliph and asked for his job back.

"What does this mean?" asked the Caliph. The prefect told him about the dream and Harun ar-Rashid agreed to reinstate him.

Khidr again began to visit the prefect, and the prefect asked Khidr to explain the mystery. He said, "Your elevated spiritual rank comes from your work in the administration, where you show respect for the poor and the weak and where you deliver the oppressed from the grip of tryants—know that this is worth more than thousands of mystical retreats. You must not give up this important and dangerous job, because as it has been said: 'One who is blessed in some work—let him continue to do it.'"

Upon hearing this story, the government employee accepted anew his occupation, resumed his work, and received Mevlana's favor.

Blessed Are the Strangers [252]

Sultan Walad continued:

One day, our Master Shamsuddin Tabrizi was talking about Mevlana and said, "The secret of Mevlana is like the secret of Islam—hidden and strange. See how his secret is like: 'Islam began as something strange, and will return to being a stranger; blessed are the strangers.'"[90]

Seeing the Friend [253]

One day, Shamsuddin Tabrizi said to Mevlana: "I followed a shaikh called Abu Bakr, in the city of Tabriz. He was a basket-maker, and what experiences of God I received through him! But there was something in me which he did not see and that no one saw. But our Great Master, Mevlana, saw it."

Sultan Walad later commented, "The Sayyid (Burhanuddin) loved Sana'i like Mevlana loved Shamsuddin of Tabriz."

Sincere Beneficence [253b]

Sultan Walad continued:

It was my father's custom, before he had taken up the way of poverty, to give lessons at the medresse, and in each cell there were two or three students. Each time he left the medresse, he would slip into the cells and place twenty or thirty dirhems, or sometimes ten, appropriate to the needs of each one, under the rug of each student. When they would lift their rugs to shake off the dust, the students would find the money; astonished, they would bow before his generosity and kindness.

---

90. This is a *hadith* of the Prophet Muhammad.

From the beginning of my father's spiritual journey until the very end of his life, like the Caliph 'Omar, all that he did, he did out of a sincere love for God and never just for people or out of hypocrisy.

The Depths of Dhikr [255]

Sultan Walad recounted:

One night, my father was saying his prayers and I was seated beside him. He stood up and was saying, "Allah! Allah! Allah!" over and over. After a while, I saw that his blessed mouth was open, but his lips were no longer moving. The words, "Allah! Allah!" now were coming from a place deep within his chest.

Inhabitants of the World of Bliss [256]

Sultan Walad also recounted:

One day I told my father, "The Friends say that when they don't see our Master, it causes them pain, and their happiness vanishes."

He answered, "Whoever is unhappy without me has not known me; only he has truly known me who is also happy without me—when he has understood me, that is, my inner meaning." And he added, "O Bahauddin, whenever you are in a state of bliss, know that this state is my presence within you." Then he recited:

If you look for us, look for us in happiness,
for we are the joyful inhabitants of the world of bliss.

Learning to Fly [258]

According to Shaikh 'Izzuddin Kusa, one of the attained ones, Mevlana said: "A bird that flies away from this earth might not reach heaven, but still it will distance itself far enough from the traps of this world to escape them. If someone has become a dervish, even if he does not reach perfection, he will at least be free of the worldly traps, unlike the crowd in the marketplace. His burden will become lighter, and it will be as it has been said: 'The lightly burdened will be saved, and the heavy will be lost.'"

Someone asked our Master, "What about 'so and so', who sometimes acts shamefully, what will his fate be?"

"Don't be concerned," Mevlana said, "because he is like a bird whose feathers are fully grown; he can fly wherever he wants. However, one does need to be concerned about a bird whose feathers have not yet grown, for if it leaves the nest, it will be devoured by the cat."

Love Overlooks Faults [259]

According to Sultan Walad, our Master Shamsuddin Tabrizi (May God sanctify his powerful secret!) expressed the following at a meeting:

"Perhaps you have not found a faithful friend, but I have, and it is Mevlana (May God extend his shade)!"

Turning his blessed face towards Mevlana, he added, "You have come, unique in all the world, and have carried the ball from the field. You have intoxicated everyone with your love!"

In the middle of a gathering, one of the highly regarded Friends was praising Mevlana, "How great is Mevlana's glory and how intense his light! He inspires such awe!" However, at the same time, he was denying such qualities in Shamsuddin Tabrizi.

Mevlana Shamsuddin responded, "That which Mevlana believes, the way that he follows—if these were empty, vain things, how could he possess such glory and light? On the contrary, Mevlana is guided by Truth, not by falsehood. You say again that Mevlana deserves to be attended by fifty devoted Friends of God—how could these saints let themselves be guided by a blind person? Then, you say that the Friends of God reveal themselves by certain signs—who are you to know such signs? When a human being finds himself to be helpless, that helplessness can bring clarity or darkness. Iblis' helplessness deepened him in darkness, while powerlessness made the angels bright.[91] Miracles are like this—such are the signs of God. When one feels helpless, one should prostrate."

A few of the dervishes remarked in Mevlana's presence, "Our Master is detached from the world, while Shamsuddin is not."

"This observation comes from your dislike of Shamsuddin," replied Mevlana. "If you liked him, you would not see greed or any unpleasant behavior.

A contented eye overlooks faults
that an irritated eye is inclined to see.

"'Love renders you blind and deaf'—to your beloved's faults. When you begin to perceive faults, it is because love is fading. Don't

91. See *Surah* 15:26-49 and 17:61-65: *And behold! We said unto the angels, "Prostrate yourselves before Adam"—whereupon they all prostrated themselves, save Iblīs. . . .*

you see how a compassionate mother never complains about her child's excrement, but loves him with all her heart and soul. She never turns away from him, and, even more, she isn't ashamed of his lame donkey, even if it kicks and is ill-behaved."

Pearls from the Ocean [259b]

"Mevlana is like a diver who throws himself into the deep sea of meaning, and I am the merchant who buys his pearls," said Shamsuddin Tabrizi. "The pearl is with us; I am speaking about it, but you keep thinking about money. God's way is like this—the way passes through Aksaray, and one must cross over the bridge indicated: *And they have striven hard in God's cause with their possessions and their lives* [9:88].

"First of all, one must distribute one's wealth, and after that there are many things to be done. 'But first one must pass by Aksaray' means that one must first find a man of God to follow,[92] and then one must seek union with God."

And Who Is a Saint? [259c]

The illustrious disciples reported that when Shamsuddin Tabrizi came to Konya a great uproar broke out among the eminent people of the city, who questioned whether or not he was a saint. Everyone had their opinion and sought him out in order to try to understand, but he avoided the great mosque, the gatherings, and crowds.

When Shamsuddin Tabrizi did find himself in a meeting, he was often interrupted when speaking. One day, he said, "Someone who interrupts me is like Sharif Lahawari who sank in dark waters. He saw in a dream that he was sinking in dark waters and that he waved two fingers and cried, 'O Shamsuddin, take my hand! Please take my hand!', but it did not do him any good—he didn't pay attention.

"After that, in my presence, he again attempted to explain the difference between the miracles of the prophets and those of the saints: 'The prophets can perform miracles whenever they wish.'

"I said to him, 'What a distance between you and the saints!'

"He continued, 'For some, grace is ever-present, for others it is

92. A city not far from Konya along the silk road trade route, "Aksaray," means "white palace." "Ak" has the meaning of "white," "light," "bright"; a "saray" is a palace or large house. "Aksaray" also has the meaning of the "full moon"—i.e., the man of God is a palace of light. Like the Prophet Muhammad, often referred to as the "full moon," the human being of God radiates light, enabling one to find one's way.

not; some can choose to enter a state of grace, while for others, it is involuntary.'

"I replied, 'Your idea of a Friend of God and his state is just a creation of your own fantasy.'

"When I rejected his ideas, he thought it was from envy and hate," continued Shamsuddin Tabrizi. "On the contrary, my character is such that I say prayers for the Jews. When someone curses me, I say, 'May God guide him!' I offer a prayer: 'O God, send this person something better to do, more pleasant, than to insult me—let him rather praise God and occupy himself with God's world.'

"Why are these people chasing me around, demanding to know whether I am a Friend of God or not? What good could it do you?

"It's like when they told Juha: 'Look, people are bringing trays of food!'

"'What is it to me?' he asked.

"'They are taking them to your house.'

"'So then what business is it of yours?'

"This is a good example of the reason why I avoid the company of people; so that such people through imitation might not fall into trouble."

Mevlana and Shams [259d]

Someone said to Mevlana, in Shamsuddin Tabrizi's presence, "I love you, and for your sake, I love others," and recited this verse of Majnun:[93]

> Out of love for her I love those who are black;
> for love of her, I even love black dogs.

"If by 'others' you are referring to Shamsuddin Tabrizi, if you had said that you love me for his sake, I would have been happier and more pleased than with what you said," commented Mevlana. "What you are saying is that through loving one person one is then able to love another. This can only come about if the person loved consents to have the other dependent upon him."

The person who had recited Majnun's verse did not answer but simply lowered his head and got up and left.

93. Majnun was a poet who fell madly in love with Layla. Due to the extremity of his love he was given the name "Majnun" which means "the mad one."

*****

Mevlana was disclosing certain divine insights at a gathering: "Our prophet (May the blessings of God be upon him) left us this tradition, 'Conceal the time of your departure, your gold, and your route,' as well as 'One who hides his secret is the master of his affairs.' And that is good advice and very appropriate. But why would I want to hide anything from Shamsuddin? One would also be a muslim if one were to apply the opposite meaning of this proverb: 'He who reveals his secret is the master of his affairs,' but where is such a man?"

*****

One day, our Master Shams of Tabriz was with some of the close companions and said, "Last night I had a dream in which I was speaking with Mevlana, and I recited *Everything is perishing except His Face* [28:88], and I added, '*except* the face of the friends and that friend is you!'

Whether one sees the friend or his apparition (*khayal*),
everything but that is imagination.

"There are people who belong to this world, and people of the hereafter, and those who belong to God. Shibli is of the second, and Mevlana is of the people of God. What has come to me from Mevlana belongs only to me and three other people." His intimate friends asked him who the three other people were.

He answered, "Shaikh Salahuddin, Shaikh Husamuddin and our Master Bahauddin (Sultan Walad). May God be pleased with all of them and with their followers, until the Day of Reckoning! Amen. For the sake of our trustworthy Prophet."

Silent Ecstacies [260]

Shaikh Nuruddin, Kamal Khorsaf's father (May the Mercy of God be upon him), one of the eminent ones, told us the following:

In the beginning, I was a disciple of Shaikh Sadruddin. I attended his *dhikrs* and went about in his service. It was his custom, every Friday after the prayer, to hold a gathering in his *zawiya*—all the wise scholars, dervishes, and commanders would gather in accordance with: *And when the prayer is ended, disperse freely on earth, and seek to obtain something of God's bounty* [62:10]. The shaikh would pose a question, or express a subtle idea, which everyone would then discuss. There would be quite a tumult, and the shaikh would not say anything until, with comments at the very end, he would close the conversation.

One day, many prominent people were present when, suddenly, Mevlana appeared. Shaikh Sadruddin got up immediately and went to greet him, along with all the distinguished men. However, our Master sat down at the edge of the sofa. The shaikh extended a warm invitation for him to sit at the head of the prayer rug.

"It is not appropriate," said Mevlana. "How could I face my Lord?"

The shaikh then suggested that they each sit on half the prayer rug.

"I cannot answer to God concerning the appropriateness of that either," said Mevlana.

"A prayer rug that is not of use to Mevlana is not appropriate for us either," said the shaikh, and he rolled it up and put it aside.

Then Mevlana fell deep into a meditative silence and sat without moving for so long that all present were plunged into ecstasy. Meanwhile, Shaikh Sadruddin had bowed his head and rubbed his forehead upon the floor; I saw that he was drenched with sweat. Suddenly, Mevlana cried out, "Allah!" Then he rose and left, saying, "May God grant you success!"

The shaikh, as a result of the intoxication into which he had been plunged, fell silent and was lost to the world for three days and three nights. All the great ones present were amazed by Mevlana's awesome power and demonstrated their devotion. As for me, I immediately declared myself a disciple and entered his service. Thanks be to God for the blessings He bestows upon us!

The Adventures of the Nafs [261b]

One day, the Atabak Majduddin, the Parvana Mo'inuddin's son-in-law, asked Mevlana for permission to take a retreat in his medresse. He consented and the Atabak went into retreat in one of the cells. However, after a few days, he was overcome by hunger, and could no longer bear it, because he was accustomed to the pleasures and luxuries of this life. He had a friend who was his confidant in his struggle—he told him of the state of despair to which hunger had reduced him. They made a plan, and one night, they left the cell and went to his friend's house. He prepared a duck cooked in butter with peppered rice for them. After the meal, they returned to the cell and went to sleep. In the morning, Mevlana, as was his custom, came to the door of the cell.

He put his finger on the door and inhaled: "That's strange," he said, "The smell of duck and rice is coming from this cell, not austerities. One must entrust oneself to a shaikh of pure soul, so that he might always accompany one through one's difficulty and lead one to the goal."

The two friends emerged from the cell and fell at Mevlana's feet, asking forgiveness, "Given the existence of such a powerful presence, such an ocean of mercy, to continue to mortify our flesh in a solitary retreat seems an unfortunate effort."

Sharing the Water of Life [261f]

One day, our Master went to the bathhouse, and the dervishes went on ahead to wash the room and perfume it in order to prepare it for him. They turned away the people who were there, and returned to meet Mevlana. By the time they all arrived, the lepers and the other sick and afflicted people had returned in full force. The disciples gave them a hard time and tried to force them away from the water. Mevlana shouted at his companions to leave the invalids in peace. Then he took his clothes off and entered the water; he came up close to them and poured the same water over himself. Everyone there was amazed by his magnaminity and intense generosity. That king among scholars, Amir Badruddin Yahya, who happened to be present, was so overwhelmed with joy that he sang out:

> "You came from God, a mercy for the people.
> What beauty is not within you!"

And God Grants Sustenance to Whom He Wills [261g]

"When I was an amir," said Bahauddin Bahri, "I often used to visit Chelebi Husamuddin to converse with him, and he too, would sometimes come to our house, but I had never had the chance to meet Mevlana. One day, when the Chelebi paid me the honor of a visit, I was delighted to see Mevlana climbing up the stairs behind him. He said, 'O Amir Bahauddin, so you wish to grab Chelebi Husamuddin from us?'

"'We are both among those devoted ones who are overcome by our Master,' I said, bowing. Meanwhile, he came and sat down in a leisurely way. I thought about preparing something to eat.

"'Just some small thing,' he said.

"I got up to go, but he said, 'Call the servant, so that he might bring it.'

"I spoke to the servant in Greek, 'What is there that is ready?'

"'Since we just ate,' he replied, 'I've put hot water into the pot to wash the bowls.'

"Mevlana said, 'Bring the pot!' And he asked for a plate and a bowl and with his own hand put something from the pot on it. I saw that it was beautiful fried meat and rice cakes, so delicious and incomparably tasty. We were amazed and asked how such a meal could appear from an empty pot.

"'It is from God,' he said, 'Please eat.' While Chelebi and I were eating our share, he left the table and went to pray. And it was as a result of this that I left behind fortune, family, and lands, and was accepted into the Brotherhood to become our Master's servant and disciple."

Keeping the Heart Clear [261j]

A group of merchants, old friends of Jalaluddin Faridun, often came to visit him and showed him great loyalty. One day, they asked if he would introduce them to Mevlana.

They added up their fortunes and told Jalaluddin that they would like to give it to the dervishes. They also declared that they would like to renounce the world totally and become dervishes themselves.

"Give this to Mevlana as a sign of our good will, to see what he will say and in what way he will use it," they insisted.

When Chelebi Jalaluddin told Mevlana about the merchants, he was not pleased, and taking a jug of water went into the bathroom toilet area where he stayed a long time.

To the merchants waiting outside, he seemed to have been gone forever, and they complained to Sirajuddin Tatari, asking what the reason was for the delay.

When Sirajuddin Tatari went into that constricted spot, he saw Mevlana standing in a corner.

"O Sirajuddin, what a distance there is between us and the world!" our Master reflected. "What importance could the world possibly have for me, and what did it mean to the Prophet (Peace and blessings be upon him)? How did his companions feel about the world? In truth, the smell of this dirty room pleases me more than all the money in the world and all its inhabitants.

"Please convey my apologies to these people; let them organize the distribution of their wealth with their own hands among the people of the heart and those who are entitled to it. If they are sincere followers of the path, they will do so without trickery or hypocrisy, and the reward will be greater, easing the burdens of my dervishes."

He refused to take even a penny from this fortune. The merchants distributed all their fortune to the dervishes, put on semas, and becoming disciples, joined the Brotherhood.

Medicine from the Unseen [261k]

The Friends told us that Sultan Ruknuddin in Erzinjan asked the doctor, 'Alauddin Erzinjani, to prepare various remedies for him, which the doctor did, spending about three thousand dinars soltani and carefully mixing the ingredients into a sweet paste for him. His son said to him, "You are a generous man. Friends visit you constantly and ask for your remedies, and responding to their need, you will continually give them to them. You are losing a lot. The way to solve this is to put you in a secluded room (*khalvet*) and put a lock on the outside of the door, so that no one will know you are there."

That same day, after having locked the door, the doctor busied himself making remedies with the help of his wife. Suddenly, they saw the curtain part and Mevlana appeared from behind the stove and stepped into the room. The doctor and his wife, overcome with awe, were glued to the spot, totally overwhelmed. After a moment, the doctor regained his senses and put all of the remedies into a golden bowl which he offered to Mevlana.

Mevlana put his finger over the bowl and said, "There is in our heart a terrible longing, a suffering that all the medicine in the world could not heal, nor provide one rest from it."

Both the doctor and his wife began to weep. Mevlana pointed to the locked door; the lock opened, and he left.

They ran after him, but he had vanished without a trace. In that moment, both the doctor and his wife, in complete sincerity, became lovers and disciples. Before this, 'Alauddin did not believe in saints and spoke ill of them. Overcome by this love, 'Alauddin took his wife to Konya where they became devoted disciples. All this had taken place in Erzinjan.

Fish in the Ocean [261n]

The great free ones (*ahrar*) told us that the dear dervish, Amir Gurji, one of the sincere disciples, decided to go to Damascus on business. He went to see Mevlana, and asked for his blessing, and then left. When he arrived in Damascus, he saw Mevlana standing in a shop, beckoning to him. He cried out and fainted.

When he came to, there was no one in sight. He finished his business, and when he got back to Konya, he immediately went to tell Mevlana what he had seen.

"Men of God are like fish in the ocean—they put their heads out of the water wherever they wish," Mevlana replied.

Amir Gurji bowed and told the other dervishes about the appearance of Mevlana in Damascus.

What Are You Drinking? [261o]

The perfection of Mevlana's generosity and mercy and his good manners were developed to a very high degree. One evening at a sema, he was deep in ecstasy and lost in the contemplation of the face of the Beloved when, suddenly, a drunk pushed his way into the sema and like a crazy person threw himself against Mevlana.

The esteemed Friends hit him.

Mevlana said, "He is the one who has drunk wine, but it is you who are acting like nasty drunkards."

"But he's a Christian!" they replied.

"Yes, he is a Christian (*tarsa*), but why aren't you afraid (*tarsa nistid*)?"

The dervishes bowed their heads and asked for forgiveness.

Bad Character, Heavy Load [261s]

Shaikh Mahmoud, otherwise known as Sahib-Qiran, told us the following anecdote:

One day a dear Friend, Companion of the Cave,[94] Jalaluddin the

94. A "Companion of the Cave," an intimate of the heart, refers to Abu Bakr the close companion of the Prophet Muhammad who accompanied him on his journey from Mecca to Medina. Enroute, while pursued by the Meccans, they hid in

butcher, told us that someone said in the presence of Mevlana: "'So and so' has such a bad character and such a heavy load; just like that famous proverb: 'Bad character, heavy load.'"

Mevlana responded, "The origin of this proverb is this: long ago there was a very just sovereign of noble character. When he would walk about, near the gate of the city, he would pass the shop of a potter who was quite elderly. Whenever the sultan would come through the gateway, the potter would praise him profusely and shower him with good wishes.

"The sultan happened to pass by again on the day of Nowruz.[95] 'Old man, ask of me today whatever you desire, whatever you wish,' he said to the potter.

"'Long live the sovereign of the world,' said the potter. 'Command each of your courtiers and every soldier in your army to buy a jug or bowl from me at the price I want and then to carry it to the sultan's arena.'

"The sultan gave this order: 'Whoever loves me, buy a jug from this old man.'

"All the soldiers, amirs, and prominent people of the city bought a jug for one gold dinar and brought it. However, among the sultan's entourage was a minister of heavy spirit, dishonorable, and of bad character. He heard the order after everyone else and came in person to buy a jug. The old man, who was quite intelligent, showed him a bowl upon which he fixed the price of one hundred dinars.

"The minister argued and disputed the price; finally, out of necessity, he bought the bowl for a thousand dirhems.

"However, the old potter insisted, 'I will let you have it at this price only on the condition that you carry me on your back to the sultan.'

"Grudgingly, in spite of himself, unable to do otherwise, the minister paid the thousand dirhems and then lifted the old man onto his back and went to take the bowl to the sultan.

"As soon as they arrived, the sultan cried, 'Old man, what is this? What is the reason for this shameful treatment?'

---

a cave. Doves nested in the rocks and a spider wove a web across the entrance, so that the Meccans thought no one was there, and the two companions were able to reach freedom. During this time in the cave it is said that the Prophet Muhammad conveyed many secrets to Abu Bakr and the lineage of the Naqshbandi Sufis and their silent dhikr originates with these moments.

95. This is the Persian New Year, which is celebrated with the spring equinox.

"'Bad character, heavy load!' replied the potter. 'If he weren't always so stingy, he might have only paid one dinar and taken the bowl and not exposed himself to this humiliation and irritation. He has destroyed his precious honor due to the vices of his lower self; he has brought this degradation upon himself.'"

Listening for Need [261v]

Shaikh Nafisuddin of Siwas (May God have mercy on him) said:

Mevlana ordered me to go and buy some good *khotab* for two dirhems. In those days, it was possible to buy a plate of *khotab* for one dirhem. Immediately I went to get it. He took it from me and rolled it up in a napkin and went off.

I walked quietly behind him until he reached some ruins where I saw a bitch lying with a litter of puppies. Mevlana gave her all of the food. I was deeply moved by his compassion and mercy.

He told me, "For seven days and nights, this poor creature hasn't eaten anything, and she cannot leave because of her little ones. God conveyed her entreaties to my ears and ordered me to console her."

*****

The same narrator told of a large sema at the Parvana's house. Mevlana, at a certain moment, went into a secluded room and began to offer *salaah*. Meanwhile, Gurji Khatun sent a large platter of *khotab* for the dervishes to eat. Suddenly, a stray dog ran in and ate most of the *khotab* and defiled the rest. The dervishes were furious and wanted to beat it.

"Leave it alone," said Mevlana. "That dog needs that food more than you do, and its appetite is more honest than yours."

Everyone bowed in agreement.

Tasting the Light [264]

The unique Amir Tadjuddin Mu'tazz al-Khorasani (May God have mercy on him), accepted by the Friends of God and one of the close disciples of Mevlana, was an influential commander and a benefactor who built schools, *khanaqahs*, hospitals, and caravanserais in Asia Minor. Of all the sultan's officials, he was the one Mevlana loved the most and whom he called his compatriot. Whenever the amir would visit Mevlana and the dervishes, they were overjoyed—since Mevlana considered him to be one of his special disciples and a sincere student, with a deep thirst for knowledge, he would become more heated in his response, offer deeper commentaries of Truth and share more secrets of the path.

One day, when the amir was visiting as was his custom, Mevlana told him, "Those who have not been able to detach from their own personal identity, nor set aside their egoism, and yet talk about the World of Non-existence are like a man who cries out from the depths of a well, 'I am the greatest,' and can only speak about how important he is.

"But those who have been delivered from self-importance and their self-existence, cry from the rooftops, 'I am the lowest!' with a cry of true humility—we consider the spiritual stations of these people to be very high; everyone knows they are speaking from a lofty place. It is like someone who has put garlic in his mouth but pretends to smell of musk, while another perfumes himself with musk and claims to smell of garlic. But the soul of the mystic whose sense of smell has been sweetened by this *hadith*: 'I smell the fragrance of mercy coming from Yemen,'[96] has a good sense of smell and can recognize the difference between musk and manure instantly, as well as the cry of the falcon from that of the sparrow. Like the great discerner, 'Omar, the real knower can tell the true from the false, and the high from the low, as has been said, 'The truly faithful one is intelligent, wise, and can discern, because he sees with the light of God.'

He who sees with the light of God
can discern the beginning and the end.
God has indicated, '*Their marks are on their faces*,'
so the eye of the mystic is intent on the face.

"In effect, as God has said, *Their marks are on their faces, traced by prostration* [48:29]. Now, Amir Tadjuddin!" Mevlana concluded, "Sharpen your sense of smell, and if you catch no whiff of the divine coming from a person, quickly turn away from them.

Try to detect the scent of God on a dervish's lips;
if your search is a serious one, you will become his intimate friend.

"Animals in the fields take on the color of the plants and the for-

---

96. This *hadith* refers to the sweet fragrance of faith that Muhammad was perceiving coming from the saint in Yemen, Uways al-Qarani, whom he knew through the Unseen but had never met.

age they eat," continued our Master. "Some become green, and others, blue, black, or yellow. God's servants graze in the plain described by these words: *And remember, spacious is God's earth* [39:10]. They drink from those springs which give eyes to the heart, and they are so replenished with light that they actually become the light of God."

And he recited:

He who eats straw and barley will be sacrificed,
but he who is nourished by the light of God
will himself become the Qur'an.
If ever you taste this edible light,
you will throw away both bread and oven.

Then Mevlana said, "And our Prophet (Peace and blessings upon him) was like this, bathed in this celestial light."

And at these words, the Amir Tadjuddin, bowed his head upon our blessed Master's feet and felt his faith grow a thousand-fold. He immediately asked to build a dergah for the dervish friends.

Mevlana replied:

We will not build ornate palaces decorated with statues,
like the 'Ad and Thamud, on this perishing earth,
but, like Noah and Abraham,
we build Pavilions of Love in eternal felicity.

"The people of meaning must follow the Messenger of God (Peace and blessings upon him), who said, 'By God, I have never built even a span nor hoarded gold.'"

The amir returned to his palace and sent three thousand dinars of poll tax money by his representatives to Mevlana, who promptly refused it. Greatly disturbed, Mevlana observed, "What a distance there is between us and the preoccupations of the world!

I yearn for a like-minded soul,
whose beauty is like silver, not ugly coins."

Finally, Sultan Walad intervened and pleaded with Mevlana to accept the money and to allow the construction of some small unpretentious houses beside the medresse for the use of those serving there. Under Sultan Walad's direction, these were built.

The Glance of Love [265]

Some of the intimate Friends who had attained a special station and were illuminated by the lights of sincerity told us the following:

One day, when Mevlana was in his medresse he said, "Shamsuddin Mardini is a Friend of God, but he, himself, does not know it; let us help him come to know himself. There are Friends of God who do not realize their saintliness. Others are conscious of their own Friendship with God, but are not able to recognize the saintliness of others. There are also perfect and noble Friends of God who with the eye of certainty (*'ayn al-yaqin*) and the truth of certainty (*haqq al-yaqin*) know their own Friendship with God as well as that of others. These are the perfect cupbearers who have drunk from the spring of *Kawthar* of Muhammad.[97] One day, Shamsuddin received a glance of favor from one of the men of God and through this blessed glance (*nazar*), he became an incomparable knower and Friend of God."

The Friends conveyed to Shamsuddin the good words that Mevlana had said about him: "Today, at the medresse, in front of so many great mystics, Mevlana said such-and-such, speaking so highly of your favor!"

Right away, Shamsuddin bowed his head and, full of joy, cried, "It is as the sultan, Mevlana, has said," and he recounted the story.

"One day, when I was a young man and was studying at the medresse in Aleppo, suddenly a dervish entered and asked me for water. Without hesitation or excuses, I got up and gave him water and placed before this poor one of wounded heart the little bit of food that I had. I saw that as a result of my thoughtful gesture, this dervish became happy, and he looked at me in an extraordinary way. This sweet look filled me with an exquisite joy. When I came to my senses, the dervish had disappeared, but the ecstasy I experienced from his look never left the palace of my soul.

"However, when I arrived near Mevlana, and witnessed his magnificence, and was the object of his blessed glances, it seemed to me that the sweetness of the first glance, in comparison with the second, was less than a drop of water compared to the ocean or an atom of dust in the presence of the great luminosity of the sun. Thanks be to God—it is through his blessing and guidance that I have become a great knower of the Friends of God."

---

97. *Kawthar* is one of the springs of Paradise whose water is an unending source of abundance. See *Surah al-Kawthar, surah* 108.

Initiation [268]

A poor one saw Mevlana in a dream. He dreamed that he accepted him as a disciple and cut his hair.[98] In the morning, he told his dream to the noble Friends who immediately wanted to take him to see Mevlana, so that he could become an initiate. They referred to the Holy Qur'an: *This is the real meaning of the dream I had; my Sustainer has made it a reality* [12:100].

As soon as Mevlana saw the poor man, he cried, "At last! This is the one whose hair I cut last night and whom I have already accepted. That is sufficient."

May I Not Take Another's Place [270]

One day, Mevlana went into the bathhouse, but then immediately left and put his clothes on again.

"Why did our Master leave so quickly?" the Friends inquired.

"The attendent turned someone away from the bath to make room for me," Mevlana replied. "I felt such shame that I began to sweat and had to leave."

Calling to God [270d]

One afternoon they were playing the *rebab* and Mevlana was delighting in ecstasy. One of the Friends entered and cried, "They are calling the afternoon prayer!"

Mevlana was silent a moment. Then he said, "No, this is also an afternoon prayer. Both are calling to God—one is an external form of worship and service, and the other is an internal way by which one comes to love and knowledge of God."

Men and Women are Welcome [270e]

One of the dervishes was getting married:

"If God pleases," said our Master, "Let us hope that she will become a spiritual friend."

98. As part of the initiation ceremony, a shaikh cuts some of the hair of the new dervish as a token of the cutting away of the binding of worldly attachments in recognition of his deepening focus on the Divine and his servantood.

Even Though You Conquer the World . . . [270f]

A dervish was complaining to Mevlana about the mean things that someone else was saying and was very critical of his behavior.

"One may conquer the world," said Mevlana, "and yet you can't conquer the tongue."

The Fools of Paradise [272]

One day, Kira Khatun (May God be pleased with her) asked what might be the secret within the *hadith*, "Most of the people of Paradise are fools": "What does this mean?"

Mevlana answered, "If they were not fools, how could they be content with Paradise and its streams? The place where one can gaze upon the Beloved—that is Paradise and its streams. The Prophet (Peace and blessings upon him) said, 'Most of the people in Paradise are fools; the Highest Heaven is reserved for the Masters of the Heart.'"

Mevlana then recited these verses:

If in Hell I were to grasp a lock of Your hair,
I would be ashamed of being of the elect in Paradise.
For if I were called to Paradise without You,
those vast fields would be a tight prison to my heart.

He said, "The people of low aspiration who limit themselves to contemplation of the Garden remained deprived of the sight of the Gardener," and then he recited:

Paradise without seeing Her is both Hell and the enemy.
This splendor has burned me—so what of the glory
    of lights of eternity?

He continued, "One day, companions with enlightened hearts saw Rabi'a al-'Adawiyya running with a torch in one hand and a jug of water in the other. They called to her, 'O Sovereign Lady of the World Beyond, where are you going, what are you doing?'

"'I am going to set fire to Paradise and to extinguish the flames of Hell and so remove the two veils that obstruct our way, so that our spiritual goal will be made clear and the servants of God might serve Him free from the motives of hope and fear. If there were no hope for Paradise or fear of Hell, no one would worship God or obey his laws.'"

Then Mevlana recited these verses:

Why would this hypocritical body ever bow in prayer
without the hope of roast meat and the halvah of Paradise?

And he said, "But the goal of sincere lovers is union with the Beloved, and the two worlds depend upon this union.

Even if one is a lover of sugar, one destroys the soul
by loving other than God the Most Beautiful.
To ask of God other than God
is illusion and ultimate loss.

Someone said to Shaikh Matoridi,[99] 'Ask for whatever you wish.' He answered, 'I wish not to wish!'"

Becoming a Ruby [272b]

One day, Mevlana was passionately sharing divine insights at a gathering where all kinds of people were present. He told the following story:

"A Turk who had just arrived in the city happened to come to the door of a medresse. He saw that the courtyard had been swept and freshened with water; some jurists were sitting there with their tall turbans and elegant clothing. Just then, he saw the doorkeeper of the medresse approach and serve each one a portion of bread, meat, and other food, which was their allotment from the religious foundation, giving each his share. All this impressed the Turk so much that the very next day he left his family and his village, dressed himself in a turban and robe, went directly to the medresse, and, after greeting the teacher, sat down next to him. This teacher happened to be a *faqir*, and could perceive that the Turk was not a scholar but had come with some other intention.

"He said to him, 'My dear friend, it is not by putting on a robe or a turban, by external appearance, that one becomes a scholar or jurist. One must exhaust oneself and struggle for many years, constantly repeating the same things over and over again, becoming smoky from the lamp, in order that a beggar might become someone by the grace of God and His Favor, and so that through his existence,

99. Shaikh Abu Mansur Muhammad al-Matoridi (d. 944) lived in Samarkand and, following in the footsteps of Abu Hanifa, one of the main founders of the schools of Islamic law, developed his own branch of Islamic theology. He was the author of *Kitab al-Tawhid* (*Book of Oneness*).

the initiated and the raw might learn to be a true human being.'

"Now, those who worship only the externals, who are attracted by appearances, and content with externals, who take on the dervish cloak simply for the sake of appearances and do not know, do not see, and do not grasp the essential meaning within are like that Turk. Years of suffering are needed before a man can become a real human being of 'the moment (*dem*).'"

And he recited:

It takes many years by the grace of the sun
for a ruby to gain its brilliant color and glow.
For a sack of skin to become musk, O my student,
it must graze many years in the meadow.
My heart and soul have grown thin as a thread,
so that the end of this thread became apparent to me.
Through asceticism, the body pales
in order to chase phantoms from the heart.

Can You See Him? [272c]

Shaikh Mahmoud the Carpenter, the intimate of the free and perfect ones, told us of an immense sema that took place in the blessed medresse. Shaikh Fakhruddin Iraqi, one of the knowers of God of the era, was transported into a state of ecstasy. He was crying out and had thrown off his robe and turban. In another corner, Mevlana was whirling, while the Doctor Akmaluddin and the religious scholars and amirs watched attentively.

When the sema ended, Akmaluddin said, "O true master, Shaikh Fakhruddin Iraqi will soon have lovely dreams."

"If he turns his head in this direction while he sleeps," replied Mevlana.

Then Mevlana looked upon him with a glance of favor and the Parvana Mo'inuddin, with Mevlana's permission, invited Fakhruddin to go to Toqat, where he built a large tekke and installed him as the shaikh. Shaikh Fakhruddin was always present at the sema gatherings at the medresse and continually spoke of Mevlana's greatness.

"No one has ever really understood our Master. He came as a stranger into this world, and he left as a stranger," said Fakhruddin.

"He came into this world
and appeared to us for just a few days,

but he left so quickly
I don't know who he really was."

Fish Leaping from the Stream [272d]

One day, in the midst of sharing divine insights, Mevlana said, "Regarding the water of this stream, where fish abide—they don't raise their heads out of the water unless you cast some bits of bread upon it, only then will they turn around those bits of bread. Likewise with the stream of wisdom that flows through the channel of our spirit—unless you cast upon it the purity of your search, true faith, and sincere devotion without hypocrisy, the fish of our meanings won't raise their heads out of the stream, in response to the need of the listeners and seekers; they won't be caught on the hook of any fisherman. It takes humility and the practice of poverty—for it is bewilderment and deep need that produce benefit: *Who is it that responds to the distressed when he calls out to Him* [27:62]?[100]

If God Most High has created the heavens,
He has created them for the purpose of satisfying needs.
Whatever grew has grown for the sake of those in need,
so that a seeker might find the thing he sought.
Until the tender-throated infant cries,
how should the milk for it
flow from the mother's breast?"[101]

---

100. *Who is it that responds to the distressed when he calls out to Him, and who removes the ill [that caused the distress], and has made you inherit the earth? Could there be any divine power besides God? How seldom do you keep this in mind!*

101. See *Mathnawi* III, 3204; 3208-3213, *Jewels of Remembrance*, p. 31.
It was Mary's painful need that made the infant Jesus
begin to speak from the cradle.
Whatever grew has grown for the sake of those in need,
so that a seeker might find the thing he sought.
If God most High has created the heavens,
He has created them for the purpose of satisfying needs.
Wherever a pain is, that's where the cure goes;
wherever poverty is, that's where provision goes.
Wherever a difficult question is,
that's where the answer goes;
wherever a ship is, water goes to it.
Don't seek the water; increase your thirst,
so water may gush forth from above and below.
Until the tender-throated babe is born,

One Who Is Free [272e]

One of the dervishes was sad. Mevlana said, "Sadness arises from attachments to things of this world. Each moment that you are free of the world, when you see yourself as a stranger, when in the midst of all the colors that you experience and all the tastes you appreciate you realize that you will not remain in this world but are leaving for another, then you will not be sad. 'Blessed is the one who keeps company with the people of jurisprudence and the wise, who spends time with the poor and humble.' "

He added, "A man is free if he does not get upset at the wrongs done to him; the generous man is one who does not punish those who deserve to be punished."

As he said:

"As long as we wear this dervish robe,
let us never be angry or cause each other harm."

Witnessing the Microcosm [274]

One day, one of the dervishes encountered Mevlana, and bowing he said, "How disgusted and tired I am of this miserable world! I wish that God would allow me to go to the other world. At least I would find peace there, because God Most High is there."

"How do you know He isn't here?" Mevlana said and added:

"The world, and everything in it, is not outside yourself;
search within your own being for all that you desire.
The whole universe is within you."

I am with You [274b]

One of the dervishes went to a large gathering one day where everyone was reciting *surahs* on different subjects and commenting, each trying to outdo the other. The dervish kept silent.

Mevlana questioned him, "My friend, why are you not also taking a turn?"

"There are a lot of important people here, and I doubt myself," said the dervish.

"You must open your mouth, since I myself would speak," said Mevlana.

---

how should the milk for it flow from the mother's breast?

It Is Your Heart He Sees [275]

The Plato of the era, Khwaja Akmaluddin (May God reward him) went to pay a visit on Mevlana who happened to be at Chelebi Husamuddin's house that day. Akmaluddin arrived wearing elegant clothes of scarlet cloth and flung over his shoulders was a sable cloak. Right away, Mevlana whispered something in his ear, and immediately Akmaluddin bowed and gave his clothes to the singers and left.

Chelebi Husamuddin asked him, "What did Mevlana say to you, why did you bow; what happened?"

"I suddenly saw myself, and how ridiculous I must appear to a man of God, in these rich clothes worthy of a society lady," answered Khwaja Akmaluddin. "I realized it was not appropriate attire and I felt ashamed. Just then Mevlana whispered in my ear, 'Be at peace; don't worry or feel ashamed, because the clothing of our soul, which is the body, has no value for us. So what value could a cloak against the rain, which is an external thing, have? Remember the *hadith*, "Truly, God does not pay attention to your faces and your actions. He only pays attention to your heart and your intentions." Make an effort so that it is you who gives value to your garment, and not the garment that gives you value.'

"This favor he bestowed on me brought me such pleasure that I gave my clothes to the singers as an offering of gratitude." And for the rest of his life, Akmaluddin never again wore fancy clothes.

The Blessings of Garlic [276]

Those who were devoted to him and in his service told us that Mevlana loved garlic, just as Haydar, the Lion of God, 'Ali did.

Often he would break a fast of ten or fifteen days, or even twenty or thirty days, with cloves of raw garlic, saying, "Mostafa (May peace and blessings be upon him), often told the Commander of the Faithful, 'Ali (May God be pleased with him), 'O 'Ali, eat raw garlic!', for a mysterious reason which he alone understood."

Sustaining Love [277]

Kiraga,[102] the mother of Chelebi 'Arif (May God bless their innermost secret) told us:

---

102. "Kiraga" is another name for Fatima, the wife of Sultan Walad and daughter of Salahuddin Zarkubi, Mevlana's close student and dear friend who had traveled with him from Balkh.

For almost a month, I didn't see Mevlana eat anything. I was just newly married then, and Mevlana was my teacher.

One day, he said, "O Fatima Khatun, do we have any yoghurt in our house?"

"Yes," I replied, "but it is very sour."

He asked me to put it in a large bowl and give it to him. He said, "Crush twenty cloves of garlic and put it in the yoghurt to give it the taste of garlic."

At midnight, I saw him come back, and he asked for it. He dipped some pieces of stale, mouldy bread in the yoghurt and ate all the bowl contained. I tried to taste just a little of this yoghurt, and my tongue immediately blistered, it was so acid. Even so, Mevlana licked the bowl, gave it to me, and began the extra night prayers, continuing until dawn.

When the dervishes regathered, he immersed himself in the sema and did not rest for seven days and nights. On the eighth day, he went to the bathhouse and stayed there for the following week. Everyone was amazed at his strength and power.

The Throne Verse [281]

An important person asked Mevlana: "Why is one meant to recite the Throne Verse after each of the prescribed prayers?"

He answered, "The Prophet (May God's peace and blessing be upon him) said, 'Whoever recites the Throne Verse after every prescribed prayer, God Most High will lift up his spirit to Himself.' What could be better and more wonderful than for God Himself to take your soul with His own hands and to pour upon you the grace of His mercy? Certainly, Mustafa recited the Throne Verse constantly and encouraged his followers to do so as well. The merits of the verse of the Throne are greater than God's Throne itself."

Wings of Prayer [281b]

One day, Mevlana said, "Whoever sees my tomb and has faith and trusts in my Friendship with God, God will gather him among the forgiven. Especially if that person comes in perfect love, in sincerity without hypocrisy, in truth without similitude, in certainty without doubt, and visits the tomb and performs prayers there. . . .

> From praying so much, my existence
> has become a prayer;

whoever sees my face, a prayer flies to him.

Prayer is like an arrow, and the 'amens' of the companions are the feathers of that arrow."

Ask, O my heart, whatever you wish!
the gift is in cash, and the King is here.
The beautiful moon-faced one won't say,
"Go away until next year."

Uncovering the Kernel of Truth [281c]

One day, the dervishes were discussing the seven different ways in which the Qur'an was recited by Sa'inuddin, the Qur'an reciter, who was considered to be the Abu Hafs and the Qalun of his time. Every night, Sa'inuddin had to read the entire Qur'an, before he could go to sleep.

Mevlana said, "Sa'inuddin can count the walnut shells well, but he has no part of the wonderful kernels within." Then he added, "'The Book of God is based on four things: expression, allusion, subtleties, and truth. Expression is for the people, allusion is for the adepts, subtleties are for the saints, and truth for the prophets.'[103] This dear friend is continually occupied with the expression, so the secrets have remained veiled to him."

Immersing in the Qur'an, Dying in Love [282]

One day, Sa'inuddin declared emphatically, "Last night, out of love for Mevlana, I recited the entire Qur'an."

"How is it that you did not die?" he asked.

Our reader bowed his head and began to weep.

Then Mevlana recited:

If the Beloved shines in your heart,
atom by atom, you will take on His form.

If We had revealed a book to the mountain,
it would have split apart, crumbled, and disappeared.

You would indeed see it humbling itself, breaking asunder out of awe of God [59:21].

---

103. This is a saying attributed to Jafar as-Sadiq (see note to section #177); see *Spiritual Gems, the Mystical Qur'an Commentary Ascribed to Jafar al-Sadiq*, translated by Farhana Mayer, Fons Vitae, p.1.

And what meaningful insights he continued to express about this!

"One night, when Imam Abu Hanifa began his evening prayer," Mevlana told us, "he recited the chapter in the Qur'an which begins: *When the earth quakes with her mighty quaking, and yields up her burdens* [99:1]. When he arrived at the verse which says: *He who has done an atom's weight of good shall behold it* [99:7], he gave a great sigh and lost consciousness. They say that he remained unconscious seven days and nights on his prayer carpet due to the awe he experienced from the secrets within these Qur'anic passages. When you recite the Qur'an, recite a small amount carefully, so that it draws you in, not so much that you are driven away due to your carelessness. This is the secret contained in these words: 'How many a reciter of the Qur'an has been cursed by the Qur'an!'

The Qur'an is a shy bride who only lifts her veil
when she sees faith's palace empty of turmoil."

The Ecstasy of Sema [284b]

It is said that when Mevlana became intoxicated during a sema he would grasp the singers by the arm, and, continuing to whirl, he would tap his foot and then pronounce blessings: "O God, bless Muhammad and bless the family of Muhammad!" and then would begin again.

Don't Waste Your Time [285]

One day, the barber was trimming Mevlana's beard and mustache and asked him how he would like this done.

"Just enough to show the difference between a man and a woman," he replied.

The next day he said, "I am jealous of the qalandars who have no beards." Then he quoted this *hadith*: "It is good fortune for a man to have a thin beard, because a beard is a man's ornament—when it is thick, it creates pride in him—that is a danger."

He added, "A thick beard is pleasing to the sufis, but in the time it takes to comb and groom it, a true mystic (*'arif*) has already reached God."

And He Is With You [286]

Our Master stood at the door of the medresse; the dervishes were all gathered.

He turned his face towards them and said, "By God! There is only one person in the world, and that person is always with you, is there for you, makes an effort for you, and wants you."

"And so it is said:

I remain here in the prison of this world as a benefit!
What do I have to do with prison? From whom did I steal?"

The dervishes expressed their gratitude, bowed, and rejoiced.

The School of Mystical Love [286b]

The son of Modarres related that Mevlana said:

"Khwaja Faqih Ahmad (May God have mercy on him) would continually say, 'Day and night for forty years, I have practiced asceticism, mortifying myself so that the illness of scholarship might leave me, so that I might remove this veil, but traces of it are still left. The clearer the tablet of the heart, the nearer one is to God—the Preserved Tablet (*lawh-i mahfuz*)[104] is certainly more exalted than the tablet of one who has memorized the Qur'an (*lawh-i hafiz*).'

"My father, the Sultan of the Wise, Bahauddin Walad (May God be pleased with him), often told me: 'Even if I didn't possess the knowledge that my religious studies would indicate, no matter—the world of meanings is mightier than mere learning.' And he would recite:

I have purified my heart of learning and found a Friend;
I have left the shadows of existence and discovered clarity.

"Now, a rare person is needed, one who upon leaving the school of jurisprudence enters the school of poverty and finds God.

Just as the school of jurisprudence
has requirements for completion
know that the school of divine love also has its rules."

Beyond Words [287]

One day Mevlana said to that connaisseur of the knowledge of God and the Eternal, 'Alauddin Theriyanos (May the mercy of God be

104. The Preserved Tablet (*lawh mahfuz*) is the Book of God upon which the destiny of beings and the sacred books are written. See *Surah al-Buruj*, The Great Constellations 85:22. Rather than listening to interpretations about the Qur'an from others, one must look to the Book of God, the completed human being, for real knowing, and find the meaning within oneself.

upon him): "If anyone asks, 'Who is Mevlana?' tell them, 'Someone you do not see; someone you do not hear.' That is to say, 'You cannot see his grandeur nor comprehend his secrets.'"

Then he added, "To greedily chew ten maunds[105] of bread and let the pieces fall into the folds of your robe is easy enough, but it is extremely difficult to actually eat a single maund of bread. The external scholars of this world grind up knowledge and scatter the bits about. If they had even once actually eaten knowledge as they should have, which is to say without reading, they would have been delivered from the effort of chewing and would have adopted silence as a profession.

Flee from words—avoid the trap—
so you don't get hooked.

"At the end of his life, Khwaja Hakim Sana'i (May God have mercy on him) was whispering something—his companions leaned an ear closer to his mouth. He murmured:

'I repent of everything I ever said, because words
make no sense,
and meanings cannot be expressed in words.'"

Music Prevails [287b]

The Parvana Mo'inuddin wanted to appoint the son of Vizier Tadjuddin to the position of Qadi of Konya; he was a well-educated and worthy man, but rude and conceited and far from the world of the Friends of God.

"I will accept the position with these three conditions," he said, "The first is that you ban the *rebab*. The second is that you throw out all the old bailiffs, the executioners of the court. And the third is that you give the new judges a stipend, so that they are not tempted to take money from the people."

The Parvana replied, "I will accept the last two conditions and put them into practice, but I cannot possibly ban the *rebab*, because it was encouraged by a great sovereign."

Because of this, the son of the vizier refused the position.

When Mevlana heard this, he cried, "Bravo! O blessed *rebab*! Praise be to God, because the *rebab* has taken the hand of this person and de-

105. The "maund" weight varied from region to region . . . from about 24 pounds to 80 or even 160 pounds.

livered him from the clutches of the judgment of being a judge." Eventually, all of his children became disciples of Mevlana's family.

Becoming the Mirror of God [290c]

Mevlana was speaking of divine meanings with a man of high station:

"You have reached the degree of gold," he said, "but you must become even more than gold. You must arrive at the moment when you enter the furnace and begin to melt, and submit to the blows of the smith on the anvil of mortification, so that you might become a ring worthy of Solomon or an earring worthy of adorning the cheek of a sovereign. Now, all these human beings are mortals and pretend to be Muslims through imitation. They will become true seekers and reach their goal when they enter the furnace of Divine Love and bear the blows of misfortune on the anvil of patience. If they can withstand impossible situations, in which they are the victims of rough injustice, and reach purity of heart, they will become the mirror of God. This is sufficient!"

The Ocean of Bewilderment [294]

The renowned Friends told us that one day, in a gathering of people of merit in Tabriz, the King of Teachers, the Sultan of Judges, Mevlana Qutbuddin of Shiraz (May the Mercy of God be upon him) recounted the following:

When during my youth I arrived in Konya, I became a close companion of the distinguished men of the region. We were a group of twelve friends who were all extremely well-learned, each one well-versed in the different branches of knowledge. We delved into many marvellous books, and I was particularly gifted at finding obscure and astonishing points such that no one could counter in response.

However, the moment I saw the blessed face of Mevlana, none of them remained in my mind. I realized that everything had been erased from the tablet of my soul and that I could no longer remember anything.

The secrets contained in *God effaces or confirms whatever He wills—for with Him is the source of all revelation* [13:39] were revealed to me, and I realized that Mevlana had captured me by the perfection of his power and, having cleared from my heart the totality of the sciences, had left it empty.

As it was said:

When, out of forgetfulness he has closed the door of reflection,
no matter how much skill one may have, nothing can be done.
Since they can make you forget or remember,
know they have power over all people's hearts.
Recite: *It made you forget all remembrance of Me* [23:110].[106]
Surely, they have the power to cause one to forget.

"I was lost in the sea of bewilderment," Qutbuddin of Shiraz continued. "All of a sudden, Mevlana began to share divine insights. Among his reflections he instructed us in all the questions and subtle points we had prepared, citing them one by one; he shared subtle references and he took them to such a point that the minds of the wise of the world were stupefied and in awe.

"When he had finished, I stepped forward with my friends to declare myself a devoted disciple and servant. In truth, from that day on, I realized that there was no limit to the sea of mystical knowledge and that I was a part of that sea."

A Sea Without Limits [296]

The honorable Friends, intimates of the joyful holy precinct (of Mecca), (May God magnify their memory) told us this story concerning Gurji Khatun, the Queen of the Era, the Lady of the World, the wife of the Sultan (May God have mercy on her). She was one of the sincere Friends and a close disciple of Mevlana's family, and she burned with a constant desire to see Mevlana.

One day, due to various circumstances, she wanted to go on a trip to Kayseri. The Sultan could refuse her nothing because she was a noble person and strong minded. So when she was beside herself, not knowing how she was going to stand the burning caused by separation from Mevlana, the Sultan summoned a painter who was

106. See *Surah al-Mu'minun* (The Faithful) 23:109-111: "*Behold, there were among My servants such as would pray, 'O our Sustainer! We have come to believe [in You]; forgive, then, our sins and bestow Your mercy on us: for You are the truest bestower of mercy!'—but you made them a target of your derision to the point where it made you forget all remembrance of Me; and you went on and on laughing at them. [But,] behold, today I have rewarded them for their patience in adversity: truly, it is they, they who have achieved a triumph!*"

considered to be another Manes[107] in painting and drawing, who was so skilled that he could have said to Manes himself, "My skill renders you powerless." He was called 'Ayn al-daula-i Rumi. Gurji Khatun gave him robes of honor, and then ordered him to paint a portrait of Mevlana and that he must paint it with extreme beauty that it might be the companion of her soul on her journey.

'Ayn al-daula went to visit Mevlana, along with several trusted officials, to tell him about this. He bowed and stood at a distance, but before 'Ayn al-daula could say a word, Mevlana said, "It's a good idea, if you can do it—go ahead."

'Ayn al-daula picked up his pens and approached. Mevlana was standing. The painter glanced at him and began to draw. On a piece of paper he drew a very delicate likeness, but then he realized that it was not even close to what he had seen. He drew another drawing on another piece of paper, and this time a completely different figure emerged. He drew another, and another, until there were twenty different drawings. Each time he drew, and looked again, he saw Mevlana in a completely different way.

Totally bewildered, 'Ayn al-daula cried out and fainted. Then he broke his pens in two, and recognizing his powerlessness, prostrated.

Just then, Mevlana began to recite this *ghazal*:

Who is this being without color or sign that I am?
How can I see myself as I am?
You said, "Bring the secrets amidst us."
Where is the middle in this center that I am?
How can a soul in movement and at peace
  like mine still itself?
The sea that I am has drowned within itself;
what an astonishing sea without limits I am!

Still weeping, 'Ayn al-daula took the drawings to Gurji Khatun. She put them in a chest and kept them with her, whether she was at home or on a journey. Whenever she was carried away by the longing to see Mevlana, the moment she would see his likeness, she would find peace.

---

107. Manes was the founder of Manichaeism and reputed to be a very fine painter.

One Step Ahead [297]

Shaykh Kamaluddin-i Tabrizi al-Khadem (the Servitor) (May the Mercy of God be upon him), who was the chief servitor of the sacred tomb recounted that among the miracles of Mevlana's that he witnessed on the route from Aleppo to Damascus when he witnessed Mevlana's hidden bravery was the following:

The camel-driver who was leading our caravan was insisting that we camp at a certain place. Mevlana would not consent. The camel-driver, looking for a quarrel, advanced towards him and said, "I will not go further."

Mevlana quickly struck him just above the ear and the man immediately fell down. Mevlana tied his hands securely and putting him over his shoulder continued onward for several miles. At last, he halted in a fertile spot full of good vegetation and said to the camel-driver, "O drunkard! Maybe you have no pity or compassion for us, but aren't you concerned for your camels? The other spot was a dry place where the Mongol army will camp tonight, and they will destroy everything in that area."

It happened that the Mongol army did arrive in their footsteps, place after place, and devastated the province of Aleppo.

Transformation [299]

According to the great free ones (*ahrar*) (May God be pleased with them) Mevlana was walking in the market one day, when he happened to pass the shop belonging to Shaikh Salahuddin Zarkub, the goldsmith (May God sanctify his innermost secret).

When the staccato sound of the hammering made by the goldsmiths reached Mevlana's blessed ears, he began to whirl. A considerable crowd gathered, and then Shaikh Salahuddin was informed that Mevlana had begun whirling outside his shop. The shaikh told his apprentices to keep hammering on the sheets of gold: "It doesn't matter if some are ruined."

Mevlana continued whirling from the middle of the morning until the afternoon prayer. Then he ordered them to stop—it was then that the reciters arrived. The sema began again in earnest, and Mevlana recited the *ghazal* that begins:

> A treasure has revealed itself in the goldsmith's shop.
> O form! O spirit! O character! O beauty! . . .

When the shaikh went back into his shop, he saw that it was completely full of gold-leaf, and that all of his gold-beating instruments had been transformed into gold. He cried out and threw himself at Mevlana's feet. Then he gave orders for everything in his shop to be given away. He abandoned his goldsmithery and became instead a gem in the golden ring of the circle of dervishes. It was because of this favor from Mevlana that he gained his renown. They say that the shaikh's apprentices hid the golden anvil. They sold it and used the money to pay for many semas and made a gift of the remainder to the Friends.

Halvah of the Heart [301]

One day, Mevlana was in the garden of the *Khalifa* of God among His creatures, Chelebi Husamuddin (May God bless his secret), attending a large sema that lasted from dawn until the afternoon prayer. Just then, having stopped the music, Mevlana lifted his blessed arms and said:

"Come everyone—loosen your sashes. Travelers have arrived from far away and are asking for warm halvah. They have been drawn here by visions of fresh halvah."

All of a sudden, a group of worthy men arrived in Konya from Turkestan and Bukhara. They had been told that Mevlana could be found that day in Husamuddin's garden. Even though they were covered with dust from the trip, they had come directly, just as they were, to meet this sultan.

Just when they had been graciously accepted into his presence and had the joy of gazing upon him, at that moment, the Queen of Women, Fakhrunnisa, the Glory of women in the universe (May God be pleased with her), placed a platter of fresh homemade halvah in front of them.

Mevlana beckoned to them to eat, saying, "*Partake of all the lawful, good things which God has provided for your sustenance* [16:114]. For if you had asked for the feast of Jesus [5:114], it would have appeared here in this lodge. Of what importance is halvah? O God! don't ask for sweets from men of God, but rather pray that your difficulties might be solved and that the power of the soul might become your nourishment."

Draw Near Through Adab [304]

One day Mevlana entered the dervish cell of Chelebi Badruddin, the professor's son, and saw him sleeping with the *Illahi-nama* of Hakim Sana'i behind his back.

He said, "Our Master Sana'i is present, while you are lost in sleep! *Adab*[108] is preferable to all the acts of devotion, so learn to be polite, so that you might not become the cause of anger or the target of wrath."

And he added:

"We seek from God the blessing of *adab*—
for a rude man is deprived of God's grace.
The impolite not only harm themselves—
they set the far horizons aflame.

O happy is the soul of one intelligent enough to have perfected his external and internal *adab*. In whatever house you hear the word of God, God Most High will be there; wherever the *hadith* are remembered, the Messenger of God will be present. Wherever the words of the Friends of God are recited, their spirits will be present. And that is sufficient."

Unfolding Meanings [305]

One day, Shamsuddin, the professor's son, was sleeping in his dervish cell and, out of forgetfulness or negligence, had placed the *Mathnawi* behind his back.

Suddenly, Mevlana entered and saw the book like that: "Our words—have they come only to end up behind your back? By God, by God, from the place where the sun rises to where it sets this meaning will take hold and will become known in all regions. There will be no gathering where it will not be recited, even in the churches and temples; all the nations of the world will don the garments of

108. *Adab* is one of the primary principles of Sufism. One seeks to observe courteous and truly loving, appropriate behavior in every instance, both with one's fellow human beings and internally, within oneself, and with God, as one moves into nearness with the Divine, until, as it is said, "When, through his, or her, voluntary devotions, my faithful servant draws near to Me, then I love him, or her, [with an even greater Love] and I become the ear with which he hears, the eye with which he sees, the tongue with which he speaks, the hand with which he grasps, the foot with which he walks." (*Hadith Qudsi*, a saying of God conveyed through the Prophet Muhammad outside the Qur'an). Also "*I become his/her ear and eye.... He/she sees with the divine light of God.... His heart didn't contradict what he saw.*" [53:11-12].

these words and will delight in them."

And Be Steadfast [307]

Sultan Walad asked, "Why do some people sometimes have faith in the Friends and then become cool and hesitant?"

Mevlana responded, "These people are like the mad who sometimes say reasonable things even though for the most part they are absorbed in illusion and foolishness. However, true good fortune belongs to the one who never steps foot outside of faith and sincerity and who walks straightforward on his way: *Those who say, 'Our Sustainer is God,' and then steadfastly pursue the right way* [41:30[109]; 46:13], because steadfastness is the station of the sincere and true (*siddiq*)."

Come to Know Me [308]

A dervish told Mevlana, "So and so is such a wine-drinker, but he never gets drunk."

Mevlana responded, "Maybe he pours it down the collar of his robe, because the characteristic of wine is that it intoxicates—when it no longer has that effect, it is vinegar. It's like this for those who are imitators of the sacred law and the mystic path—they read the Word of God and repeat the words of the Friends of God, but they find no pleasure in it, nor does it increase their longing, nor are they brought to joy. They obtain no benefit from what they read; they chew but do not eat. Truly, knowing God is better than calling upon God, and the aim of '*That they might serve Me* [51:56]' is '*That they might know Me.*' That is what is sought."

Be Patient in Adversity [311]

Ikhtiyaruddin, one of the great companions, told us that one day he

---

109. See *Surah al-Fussilat* (Clearly Spelled-out) 41:30-33: *[But,] behold, as for those who say, "Our Sustainer is God," and then steadfastly pursue the right way—upon them do angels often descend, [saying:] "Fear not and grieve not, but receive the glad tiding of that paradise which has been promised to you! We are close unto you in the life of this world and in the life to come; and in that life you shall have all that your souls may desire, and in it you shall have all that you ever prayed for, as a ready welcome from Him who is much-forgiving, a bestower of grace!"*

And who could be better of speech than he who calls [his fellow human beings] unto God, and does what is just and right, and says, "Truly, I am of those who have surrendered themselves to God"?

was sitting with Mevlana, who suddenly got up and said, "Peace be upon you!" and then sat down.

We saw no one and were astonished when he continued, "Come closer—*do as you have been ordered; you will find me, if God wills, among those who are patient in adversity* [37:102]."

Then Chelebi Husamuddin, who was also present that day, bowed and asked what was going on.

"I saw a very angry-looking, blue-eyed person with yellowed skin who approached me and greeted me with 'Salaam,' and said, 'I am fever; I am called, "*homma.*"' I gave him permission to stay with me as a guest for three days."

Mevlana immediately began to tremble. At the end of the three days, the fever ceased, and he no longer had to endure it. Accompanying Mevlana, all the companions had also become ill with him, and now, they, too, were all restored to health.

Only Give What You Really Value [315]

The close companions, the well-educated brothers (May God hold them in His mercy) told us that sometimes Friends and faithful ones would bring gold and silver coins and secretly place them under the felt carpet where Mevlana would sit. Our Master accepted it out of regard for the Friends and would say nothing.

However towards midnight, when he got up for prayer, he would take all the coins and throw them into wells. The refined companions, because of their need, asked him why he did not distribute the money among the Friends, why he had thrown it into the wells.

He answered, "The sign of love and perfect friendship is to give to one's friends the things one loves the most and not what one loves the least or is poisonous. Since all the goods and means of this world are a mortal poison, mediocre, and without benefit, I would regret giving my Friends something that would cause me harm or pain. For this reason, it is better that I don't give it to you, that I withhold it from you."

And he reminded us of the *hadith*: "Put your hand on your heart, and that which you would like for yourself, do the same for your brother."

If something does not pass your approval,
then do not pass it on to someone else.

Keeping You from the World [316]

One day, our Master's wife spoke to him of the difficulties of poverty she was experiencing.

Mevlana answered, "Don't think that I am withholding the goods of this world from you; on the contrary, I am withholding you from the world."

No Strings Attached [319b+320]

In Mevlana's presence they were speaking of how Atabak Arslan-Toghmush had built a large medresse and afterwards had written into the charter of endowment the conditions that the professor of this medresse would have to belong to the Hanifi sect, be a sufi, and give lessons in jurisprudence. Also, those of the Shafi sect were not to be allowed to enter.

"According to Ibn Mas'ud's[110] conveyence, a gift or good deed that has conditions attached to it is not pleasing to God," Mevlana commented. "What one does, one must do out of love of God and to please Him, without conditions, purely for God's sake. For this the reward is multiplied. The Atabak's donation is like this:

"An Indian dervish found himself in the company of a rich merchant of Nishapur. Before meeting this merchant, the dervish had walked everywhere barefoot in complete tranquility of spirit and never noticed the rough thorns or stones.

"The merchant felt sorry for him, though, and gave him his own shoes. The dervish offered up prayers of thanks for the merchant and set off, walking briskly. Then the merchant from Nishapur kept giving him orders: 'Go that way! Walk this way! Step carefully on that rock! Be careful—don't get scratched by those thorns!'

"The Indian was very quickly fed up, took off the shoes, and gave them back to the merchant, saying, 'Here, take them back—it does me no good to be constrained in this way. For thirty years, I have walked barefoot without any restriction, and I cannot now be a prisoner of gratitude because of a pair of shoes.'

"If you wish to be delivered of all bindings, learn to give without strings attached: *And do not through giving, seek yourself to gain, but patiently turn to your Sustainer* [74:6-7].

110. Ibn Mas'ud was a companion of the Prophet and one who related many of his teachings.

As long as I have my cup of sour milk in front of me,
I'll pay no attention to the cup of others, or to their wealth.
Misfortune can torment me and threaten me with death,
still I will never exchange freedom for slavery."

Watch What You Serve to Whom [321]

Mevlana was sharing insights into the meaning of this verse:

Don't tell the Sultan's secret to anyone,
and don't spread sugar out for flies.

He told us this:

A person had left for a certain city with the intention of robbery and fraud. Suddenly, when he arrived in one of the districts of the city, he saw a young boy holding a roll in his hand and eating it. He asked for a piece, but the boy refused. The man insisted.

"Moo like a cow, and I will give it to you," said the boy.

The swindler looked around in all directions; he didn't see anyone. Driven by intense hunger, he let out a "Moo" just like a cow, then he said to the boy, "Now, give it to me."

The boy replied, "No, I will not give it to you; my mother and father told me, 'Don't give it to a cow, because hay is better for cows.'"

If sugar could excite a donkey,
then he'd have given him a hundred-weight pile.

Likewise, it is not helpful to tell words of wisdom and the secrets of the free men to just anyone; instead, consider it your duty to veil them. As it has been said, "Don't give wisdom to those who are not worthy of it, because you will be unjust to wisdom." If someone is not appropriate for these secrets and incapable of beholding them, it will be of no benefit to show them to him and will make the uninitiated arrogant.

Distillers of Secrets [324]

The noble dervishes told us that one day Mevlana was reading the words of Fariduddin 'Attar (May the mercy of God be upon him).

A fool said, "These are just the words of an attar-maker."

"Imbecile! Then who am I?" shouted our Master.

Real Generosity [325]

A Friend asked Mevlana, "What is this place '*la-mekan*'[111] that you speak of?"

"Placelessness (*la-mekan)* is the soul and the heart of the human being," he explained.

A Sufi asked, "What is grace?"

He answered, "It is generosity which arises from the soul and heart as we journey towards God."

Heart and soul are the generosity of a dervish.
It's from these that all generosity flows.

The Support of the Teacher [326]

Those who carefully study the traditions told us that once there was an enormous gathering, to which all the great ones had been invited. The son of one of the nobility, a gentle soul, overcome with sincere devotion, became a disciple.

An envious person said, "Has this man reached God; has God forgiven him?"

Mevlana replied, "First He forgave him, and then He revealed Himself to him, and then He made him seek us and sent him to us. Because the Divine custom is that first God accepts His servant and then shows him the road to His other servants, so that through the blessing of their company and training he learns appropriately. He then is supported and enabled to draw near to the Lord of Glory.

"As the Prophet said, 'If there were no teacher, I would not have known my Lord. The shaikh is to his people like the prophet is for his community.' If I had not had a teacher, I would have failed: 'Whoever has no shaikh, has no religion.'"

Being Grateful for the Gifts [327]

A serving girl in the harem was complaining to Mevlana about what little resources she had.

"If they gave you a thousand dinars and then cut off your ears,

---

111. "*La-mekan*" means "no-place": the metaphysical concept of the detachment from place.

"My place is the Placeless; my trace is the traceless . . ." See Mevlana's *ghazal*, "I Am Not," *Love Is a Stranger*, Rumi, translated by Kabir Helminski, Threshold Books, 1993, p.56.

your nose, and your other limbs, would you consent to that?" he asked.

"No!" replied the serving girl.

"Then, why do you claim to be so impoverished? Why not appreciate the true value of the gifts that you have and give thanks for those? Make the patience of the poor your capital. *Give thanks to God for his blessings, if it is truly Him that you serve* [16:115]."

Increase is promised to one who is grateful,
as nearness to God is recompense for prostration.

Are You Worthy of Being His Prisoner? [328]

One day, two distinguished people were arguing, hurling foolish insults at each other.

One said, "May God take you, for being a liar." And the other said, "No, on the contrary, may God take you, because you are the liar."

Mevlana suddenly arrived at their room and said, "No! God will not take either one of you. May He take me, because we might be worthy to be taken, worthy of being captured by Him."

The two men bowed their heads, made peace with each other, and became devoted students.

May God Increase Our Knowing [330c]

One day, Mevlana was speaking and became quite passionate as he shared divine insights:

"Woe to the one who has known us and woe to the one who has not known us, the one who has not perceived that the goal of creation is to know our Creator: *Except that they know Me* [51:56] . . . . That is to say, unfortunate is one who has not known God and has missed the opportunity, and unfortunate is one who has known God but hasn't recognized His Majesty and been grateful.

Many a beloved remains unknown
by those unfortunate ones ignorant of Love.

Truly, the most cruel separation is one that comes after one has seen one's Beloved and found union. We seek refuge with God—may He protect us from that!"

The Lamps of Heaven [330d]

That Scribe of Books of Secrets, Bahauddin Bahri (May God have mercy on him), swimmer in the seas of mystical meanings, recounted this:

We had all gathered with all the companions around Mevlana, in the house of his son-in-law, Khwaja Shihabuddin. The friends were immersed in the light of Mevlana's presence.

Suddenly, Mevlana arose and cried out, "Welcome, O Lamp of God!" and sat down again. We saw no one; Chelebi Husamuddin and Sultan Walad questioned him.

He replied, "The spirits of spirit-beings and of the generous men continually visit the men of God; one of them is the Lamp of God (*Misbah Allah*) from whom all the other lamps of Heaven draw their light."

The Realms of the Mathnawi [330e]

Those noble guardians and recorders of Mevlana's words asked Mevlana one day, "Is one or another of the volumes of the *Mathnawi* superior to another?"

He answered, "The merit of the second book and its relationship to the first is like the relationship of the second heaven with the first; and the third with the second and so on with the sixth in relation to the fifth. Similarly, the *'alam-i malakut* (Angelic Realm) is superior to the *'alam-i mulk* (Realm of Sovereignty—the visible world), the *jabbarut* (Realm of Power) to the *malakut*, and so on until infinity.

"Likewise, according to the verse, *We did endow some of the prophets more highly than others* [17:55]—'We have preferred some people, some things, and some secrets over others': this hierarchy of merit and superiority is found in every created thing and being.

"The words of a human being are his or her scent; through the scent of his breath (*nafas*), one can know his soul (*nafs*), unless one's sense of smell has been spoiled by illness," Mevlana observed.

> "Just as musk and garlic linger on the breath,
> so do sincerity and falsehood.
> If you are unable to distinguish between a friend
> and someone who has ten hearts,
> complain about your own bad sense of smell.

From the Qur'an comes the divine scent of God; from the *hadith*, the scent of the Prophet, and from the *Mathnawi*, our scent.

"If one sincerely studies the words of Fariduddin 'Attar, one will grasp the secrets of Sana'i. And if one reads the words of Sana'i with sincere faith, one will grasp our words and find joy in them."

Accepting Invitations [334]

That Friend of God on earth, Fatima Khatun, the daughter of Shaikh Salahuddin (May God be pleased with her) told us the following:

In the time of my father, one night, the sincere Friends invited Mevlana to a sema in forty different places.

"We'll come!" he said, accepting every invitation.

He then arose and went into seclusion with my father where they prayed and engaged in worship until dawn.

In the morning, each of the Friends returned from the forty semas with one of Mevlana's shoes, which he had left behind at the sema at each of their houses, one shoe of the right foot and one of the left. Each told the story of that night and the amazing things that had taken place, saying, "Last night Mevlana did such and such in our home." They then spoke with each other and their amazement caused an uproar in Konya.

Mevlana and my father, Shaikh Salahuddin, had not moved from their place, but Mevlana in his perfect generosity had appeared to each one of the Friends and had fulfilled their wishes. All the doubting shaikhs and distinguished people of Konya, astonished by the news, gave up their testing and acknowledged Mevlana.

Finally, all the shoes were given away to the great ones of the era and to the people of faith. One of the shoes came to my father, Shaikh Salahuddin. It was this shoe that Chelebi 'Arif (May God sanctify his innermost secret) took as a present to Suleyman-Pasha of Kastamonu and which served him infinitely.

Water, in which one of these shoes had been soaked, when given to the ill would cure them, with God's permission. Pregnant women gave birth more easily with the help and blessing of Mevlana's relics (May God bless his innermost secret).

Bringing Flowers into Bloom [337]

Two friends were quarreling and refused to make peace.

One day, in the midst of uttering divine insights, Mevlana said, "God Most High has made two kinds of people—one is like the earth, solid and unmoving, because of his density and heaviness; and the other is like water, always flowing. Now when water flows onto the earth, a hundred thousand rose-gardens bloom, because of the blessing of their coming together—trees, flowers, and fruits come into being to nourish body and spirit. Now these two friends who are arguing with each other and have broken apart, one must take on the quality of earth and the other that of water and through extreme humility be like it. If they mix with each other and practice harmony, then God, through the blessing of that union and tranquility, will bring forth a thousand delightfully fragrant herbs of peace and joy, and rosebushes of fidelity and purity, and various plants of tranquility and happiness will grow."

Then he added, "Now, Nuruddin, your brother has taken on the quality of earth, he won't budge and will not hasten to make peace with you, so you, who are like water must exert yourself, and difficult as it might be, go to him, so that the spirits of the friends might be at peace and they might thank us and praise God. *Whoever pardons his foe and makes peace, his reward rests with God* [42:40]."

And then he recited this verse:

Since God has said, "*Peace is best* [4:128],"
set aside the quarrel, O unique one!

The two friends immediately bowed and were truly reconciled.

Under the Command of Love [338]

Sultan Walad (May God sanctify his secret) praised the era in which he lived. "This epoch is truly a good time to live in which all men are believers and full of sincerity," he observed. "Although there are some deniers, they have no power."

"O Bahauddin, how can you say that?" asked Mevlana.

Sultan Walad responded, "Because in the past, Mansur al-Hallaj was taken to the gallows for saying, 'I am the Truth (*Ana'l-haqq)*,' and the life of Abu Yazid al-Bastami was continually threatened. They put to death many of the noble shaikhs of past eras. As it was said, "*They put to death the Prophets against all right* [2:61]. All this happened in past eras, but praise be to God, in this era in each verse composed by our Master there are thousands of expressions like 'I am the Truth!' and 'May I be exalted!' And no one has the audacity to utter a word of objection."

"The others were at the station of being a lover, and lovers endure difficulty," said Mevlana, smiling.

"It is good for the friend to suffer pain;
it is good for aloeswood to be in the fire.

We now abide in the station of being a beloved; the beloved issues orders and is obeyed—he is a sultan of the spirits, the prince of souls, and the governor of intellects.

Shams of Tabriz walks above the heads of the spirits—
lay your head, not your foot, on the place where his foot steps."

And on another occasion, he said,

"Love is mad, and we are the mad of the mad.

The *nafs* (ego) tries to command, but we command the command."

What Remains? [338c]

Mevlana sent a group of Friends on a mission to Kayseri. They returned with tales of the Parvana's hospitality and of the extraordinary deliciousness and variety of the food he had offered them.

Mevlana became angry with them and said, "Shame on you for such exaggeration. You're puffing up with pride, saying, 'We've eaten this and that and carried this and that away.'

O you who've seen such fine fatty food, arise;
see what's left when you go to the latrine."

They immediately asked forgiveness and repented.

Call Out in Need [341]

A disciple asked Shaikh Ibrahim Adham (May the Mercy of God be upon him) to teach him the greatest name of God. The Shaikh ordered him to be thrown into the Tigris. Fighting for his life, he cried out. They kept submerging him until he was in danger of drowning.

Then in extreme need at last he called, "Allah! Alllah!" At that very moment a wave cast him up onto the shore, and he was saved.

The Shaikh said, "The greatest ineffable name of God is the one that comes as assistance for His servant when in his powerlessness he calls out in utmost necessity. *Who is it that responds to the distressed when he calls out to Him* [27:63]? It is our intense need that merits His response."

As the poet said:

It was Mary's pain and supplication
that caused the infant Jesus to speak.[112]

The Blessing of the Face of the Friend [342]

Sultan Walad (May God sanctify his unique secret) told us:

I was at the medresse, deep in spiritual conversation with Akmaluddin the Physician when my father suddenly came in the door. He laid his blessed head on my knees and said, "O Bahauddin, look upon us a long while!"

"Will I see your blessed face on Resurrection Day like this?" I asked.

"By God," Akmaluddin cried out joyfully. "I believe that anyone who has seen our Master's blessed face, even once in this world, on Resurrection Day he will intercede graciously for all his loved ones and his whole tribe."

"Tomorrow, God will forgive all the doctors of the world, because of you," said my father. "Whoever has seen us will not face Hell. The day will come when this medresse will be completely destroyed, in the unfolding of time, but those travelers who pass by here will never go to Hell."

As he said:

You are so beautiful! May the evil eye stay far from you!
Happy the eye that has seen you!
What a rare gift to look upon your face!
Happy the ear that has heard your name!

Likewise Sultan Walad (May God sanctify his secret) said this about his father:

The flames of hell won't burn anyone who even for a day
has glanced upon him or heard him utter explanations.

Nothing in This World Exists Without a Purpose [346]

One day, some religious students from Jand and Khojand arrived and asked our Master the following question, "In this world of form, what is the point of a mouse?"

112. See *Surah Maryam* 19:16-33.

Mevlana responded, "Nothing in this world of form exists without a profound purpose. If there were no mice, snakes would destroy the world and human beings. The mouse eats the eggs of the snakes and destroys them, otherwise the world would be overrun by them. The explanation of the particular qualities within every atom of the universe and within the human being is infinite."

They all bowed and became his disciples. He then told the following story:

The Elect of God (Peace and blessings upon him) was seated one day within the *mihrab* of the mosque of Quba[113], surrounded by his noble companions. Suddenly, a snake slithered through the open door and hid under our Prophet's robe.

The snake pleaded, "O Messenger of God, I am fleeing an enemy. Since you are the refuge of both worlds, protect me!"

After him, a hedgehog appeared and also called out, "O Messenger of God, deliver my prey up to me, since my children are waiting."

The Prophet, peace and blessings upon him, ordered that the hedgehog be given some entrails, and the animal, well-satisfied, left.

"O serpent," said Muhammad, to the snake who was still under his robe, "Your enemy has left. You can come out now and be on your way."

The snake answered, "Before I go, let me show you what my talent is." Whereupon he wound himself around Muhammad's waist, like a belt, and was about to bite him mercilessly.

The Prophet offered the snake his little finger, so that he would bite a joint and not reach his flesh. When the snake lifted his head to bite, Abu Hurayra (May God be pleased with him) who carried in his chest: 'The cloak of every community is a sage and the sage of my community is Abu Hurayra,'[114] and who had upon his head the crown of kindness, opened his bag, out of which jumped a black cat who tore the snake to pieces with its claws and then quietly went over to the Prophet.

At that moment, the Prophet said, "Love of the cat is part of the faith; love, even if it is a cat," and gently stroked it's back.[115] The

113. The mosque of Quba, located near Medina, was the first mosque constructed after the emigration of Muhammad and his community from Mecca to Medina.

114. This is a *hadith* of the Prophet Muhammad.

115. This anecdote reminds one of the love and special care that the Prophet Muhammad continued to have for cats. As did Mevlana, the Prophet honored all of nature, encouraged by the words of the Qur'an. Even a cat's comfort was more

power of the blessing attached to this caress was such that no matter how many times a cat is thrown from a roof it will always land on its feet and its back will not touch the ground. That day, the Prophet offered many prayers of blessing for Abu Hurayra. They say that Abu Hurayra had twenty or thirty cats in his house that he cared for. To anyone who wanted one, he would give one as a gift and then reserve for himself one of its offspring.

*****

It is said that when Muhammad held out his little finger to be bitten by the snake, it cried out, "O God, Ahmad[116] has considered poor me to be the most feeble of his members and has abandoned me. O You who are the Protector of the weak, come to my assistance."

Immediately, Gabriel, the faithful Archangel, appeared with a gift for the Prophet—a ring with its gem—and reinforcing the little finger, appointed it the possessor of the signet ring and the companion of the Seal of the Prophets. From this comes the custom which will last from now until the Day of Reckoning of wearing the signet ring on the little finger and on no other. This is so that we might remember the power that the prayers and supplications of the weak and miserable have in the eye of God.

Softening Hearts [348]

One day, Mevlana was sitting with the Friends beside a stream. Directly in front of them was a large rock.

"How will that large rock become earth?" Mevlana asked.

"Perhaps through a series of cycles and changes in form," someone answered.

Mevlana said, "Yes, it eventually becomes earth, but it takes many years. Like this rock, our hearts are of earth. They may exist in a hard and constricted state embedded in shame, until they also dissolve.

> The words, the teachings of the Prophets are beyond compare,
> but has the stone felt their breath?
>
> Hearts like these that claim 'mine,' not recognizing 'ours,'

important to him than his own. It is recorded that once when he was sitting, a cat fell asleep near him upon the edge of his cloak. When he needed to rise, rather than disturb the cat, he cut the fabric off around the cat, leaving her resting peacefully.

116. "Ahmad" ("the most praiseworthy") is another name for Muhammad.

are like the hearts mentioned in this verse:
your hearts hardened and became like rocks, or even harder [2:69].

A heart like this needs to be transformed, to receive God's beneficence, it's not enough to just have the capacity for transformation.

It's my desire to transform a heart like this
and make it drunk with Love.

You have in your possession a philosopher's stone
that can complete this transformation.
You can change a river of blood into the flowing Nile.

God is Merciful and loves to forgive
and will transform bad deeds into good."

And We Have Honored the Children of Adam . . .[117] *[349]*

An example of Mevlana's praiseworthy qualities and his kindness is the following:

One day he went to the hot springs with a group of honored Friends. Chelebi Amir 'Alim went on ahead to tell all the bathers to leave, so that Mevlana could enjoy the waters alone in the company of his Friends, and he ordered enough red and white apples to be brought to fill the pool.

When Mevlana arrived, he saw men hurriedly getting dressed in the vestibule in a state of embarrassment. And he also saw that the surface of the pool was covered with apples.

Mevlana said, "O Amir 'Alim, are apples more important than the feelings of these men? You put them outside, and you put apples in their places! Each one of them is worth thirty apples, so what place is this for apples?[118] The whole of the world and everything in it—isn't it for the sake of the human being (*adami*); and isn't the human being for the sake of that moment (*an-dami*)?

---

117. See [17:70-72]: *Now, indeed, We have honored the children of Adam, and borne them over land and sea, and provided for them sustenance out of the good things of life, and favoured them far above most of Our creation: [but] one Day We shall summon all human beings [and judge them] according to the conscious disposition which governed their deeds [in life]: whereupon they whose record shall be placed in their right hand—it is they who will read their record [with happiness]. Yet none shall be wronged by as much as a hair's breadth.*

118. As he often does, Mevlana is making a play of words in explaining his meaning, here between *si baha* (thirty) and *sib-ha* (apples).

The goal of the universe is the human being;
and the goal of the human being is the moment.

If you love me, tell everyone to return to the warm water and let no one, good or evil, healthy or sick, be left outside. Then I, too, can enter as if their parasite and rest a moment."

Overwhelmed, Chelebi 'Alim bowed, and beckoned everyone to return to the pool. Only then did our Master put his blessed foot into the water.

The Song of the Reed [350]

The distinguished religious scholars among the Friends (May God magnify their remembrance) told us that one day Mevlana was commenting on the secrets contained in the *hadith*: "The first thing created by God was the reed pen," alluding to that passage from the Qur'an: *Nun. Consider the pen, and all that they write therewith* [68:1]. He recounted:

"One day, the Elect of God (May God's blessing and peace be upon him) explained the secrets of the brothers of purity[119] to 'Ali (May God ennoble his face) and said, 'Never reveal these secrets to

119. At the time of the Prophet Muhammad, there was no formal "sufism (*tassawuf*)." It was, as is sometimes said, a "reality without a name," an inner dimension of the *Islam* (self-surrender) conveyed by the Prophet—he and his close companions immersed in the Presence of the Divine through prayer and remembrance of God (*dhikrullah*) within their daily lives. At that time there was a group of poor ones, "brothers of purity (*safa*)," many from foreign regions and countries, who in their devotion to the Way opened by Muhammad spent their time near the Kaaba in prayer and *dhikrullah*. Because they sat on a verandah or large bench (*suffa*) they were referred to as the "people of the bench (*ahl-i suffa*)." Some say the word "sufi" originated in reference to them, either from "*suffa*" or in regard to their purity (*safa*). It is noted that verse 28 of *Surah al-Kahf* alludes to them: *And contain thyself in patience by the side of all who at morn and at evening invoke their Sustainer, seeking His countenance . . .* [18:28].

Later, also, as an outgrowth of this companionship, the "Brotherhood of Purity (*Ikhwan as-Safa*)" was begun as a society of spiritual friends around 951 C.E. in Basra. They compiled one of the first encyclopedias, the *Rasa'il ikhwan as-safa* which included philosophical, metaphysical, and scientific knowledge, and sought to maintain an ethic of self-sacrifice and inner purification. Numerous "sufi" orders (*tariqah*) began to form in the 12th and 13th and following centuries, usually around a major sufi mystic whose example of being and devotion was particulary inspiring and illuminative.

See, also, the note to section #126 of this volume regarding the Essene tradition and the Companions of the Cave of *Surah al-Kahf.*

the irreverent; do not divulge them, and remain steadfast.'

"For forty days, 'Ali bore the burden of this secret, but finally, like a pregnant woman, he could contain himself no longer; he could no longer breathe. He went out to the countryside and found a deep well; he put his head into the darkness and began to speak the secrets, one by one. His mystical rapture was so intense that he began foaming at the mouth. The foam, mixed with his saliva, spilled into the well. When his energy was completely spent, this sovereign of the secret, 'Ask me!' found tranquility.

"A few days later, a reed began to grow from this well—it grew until it reached a great height. A shepherd of enlightened heart came by and saw the reed growing out of the well. He cut off a piece, made a few holes, and on this flute he began to play, day and night. The shepherd's music was that of a lover, and he played without stopping while his sheep grazed. News of his exquisite flute playing spread throughout Arabia, and bedouins, from the east and west, came and wept with joy at the beautiful sound. Even the camels made a circle around him and stopped grazing to listen. From mouth to mouth, word of this music was carried until it came to our Prophet (Peace and blessings upon him), who asked for the shepherd to come to him.

"When he began to play, all the Companions who were with the Prophet that day were plunged into such ecstasy that they lost consciousness. The Messenger said, 'These melodies are a commentary on the secrets I communicated to 'Ali in seclusion.'

"However, unless a person has some purity from the people of purity (*Ahl-i safa*), he won't hear and or be able to enjoy the secrets of the brothers of purity in the melodies of the flute, because as the Prophet said, 'Faith consists completely of ecstatic tasting (*dhawq*) and passion (*showq*).'"

As Mevlana has said:

Since I have no confidant to entrust with my longing for You
like 'Ali I sigh into the depths of the well.
It foams and a reed grows upon its edge—
the reed laments; my secret is revealed.
Be silent, O reed, because we aren't intimates—
because of this secret, forgive—us and the reed.

One of the primary principles guiding their practice is the Prophet's counsel on *Ihsan* (the Beautiful): "Worship God as though you saw Him, and if you do not, know that He sees you."

The Opening of a Door [351]

Sultan Walad told us that, one day, someone asked Mevlana if he didn't think the voice of the *rebab* was quite strange.

"It is the sound of the door of Paradise creaking that we hear," said Mevlana.

Then Sayyid Sharifuddin joined in: "We hear the same sound, but why is it that we don't become as enraptured as our Master?"

"It's not at all the same," Mevlana replied. "What we hear is the sound of the opening of the door, and what you hear is the sound of it closing."

And as he said:

When wisdom's harp begins to sing
they say a door opens to the Gardens of Paradise.
Listen carefully for the sound of this door,
you who are far away.
Happy is the one fortunate enough to hear it.

Figs of Blessing [353]

One day, one of the Friends brought some figs from the orchard of the brethren to our Master. Mevlana took one and said, "What a fine fig, but it has a pit in it," and he put it back in the basket.

Quite taken aback, the dervish thought, "How can a fig have a pit?" Then, he got up quietly and, taking the figs, left. After a while, he returned with another basket of the figs and put them down in front of Mevlana.

This time, Mevlana took one and broke his fast with it, saying, "This fig does not have a pit." Then he made a sign to Shaikh Mahmoud, the server, to pass them around to the Friends. The disciples were all perplexed.

When the dervish left, the Friends followed him, since they were mystified and wanted to ask him about the way in which he had obtained the figs.

He told them, "I have a Friend who is a gardener. I picked the figs from his garden without his permission, since he was not at home, telling myself that I would pay him later, and I brought them to our Master. But Mevlana, through the light of his Friendship with God, knew that I had not paid for them and refused to eat them. That is what the pit in the fig was. So, I went back to the garden of this same friend, and found he was at home. I purchased some fine figs and asked him for a receipt. Then Mevlana accepted them, ate these figs, and bestowed favor upon me."

Burning with the Fire of Love [356]

The following anecdote was told by Bahauddin Bahri:

At the end of autumn, and the beginning of winter, Mevlana came to visit my water wheel. At this time of year, the water had begun to freeze, but he took off his clothes and entered the pool and stayed there for a long time. Anxiously, I followed him and saw that he was sitting under the spout with the water flowing over his blessed head; where he sat, the cold water came up to his throat. He remained in this position for three days and three nights and no one could say anything.

In desperation, I cried out and tore my clothes. I called out to warn him, "In this season, cold water is harmful, and your body is extemely thin and delicate. I'm afraid that you'll catch cold."

"People who are cold might, not real men," he answered.

Just then, Mevlana left the pool and began the sema. He continued the sema for nine days and nine nights, without stopping or sleeping for a single moment. All the while he continually shared secrets of the path and recited *ghazals*.

Hunger! [357]

On another occasion, our Master performed the sema for seven days and nights without eating anything. His intimate Friends prepared a delicate meal, easy to digest, hoping that he might eat something.

Mevlana said, "O greedy self! Be patient and hear my words. Do not eat this food. If you eat it, it will eat you!" He would not eat anything, and then he began reciting:

> "Once you've tasted this food of light,
> you'll throw earth on bread from the oven.
>
> Hunger! Hunger! Hunger! And then the return!"

And he continued to whirl.

Demonstrate Your Love [360]

Our Master Salahuddin told us the following:

One night, I was in my cell reading the *Mathnawi* when Mevlana suddenly appeared. He took off his blessed shirt and gave it to me with gracious generosity.

"It is a duty to demonstrate our love (*muhabbat*) through our acts," he said. "Alamuddin Qaysar gave me a gift of two thousand soltani as an offering of gratitude."

Salahuddin accepted the shirt and brought it as a gift to Gurji Khatun. She then gifted him with two thousand dinars.

A Sema for the Noble Women of Konya [361]

The following was related according to the perfect Companions:

Every Thursday evening, all the noble ladies (*khatun*) of Konya would go to the house of Aminuddin Mika'il, who was one of the Sultan's special representatives, for a gathering led by his wife. They begged her to invite Mevlana, because they knew that he held her in special regard and conferred upon her limitless favors; he referred to her as *Shaikh-i khawatin*, "Spiritual Director of Ladies." When this gathering had begun and everyone was concentrated in tranquil presence (*huzur*), Mevlana, himself, without anyone informing him, arrived just after the night prayer, all alone, without any following.

He would sit down in the middle of the ladies who made a circle around this *qutb*. In the middle of the rose petals that they threw upon him for keepsakes of blessing and the rose water they scattered, until the middle of the night, perspiring profusely, he would be occupied with sharing divine insights, secrets, and moral council.

Finally, serving girls who recited Qur'an, accomplished tambourine players, and female flutists would begin to play, and Mevlana would begin to whirl. The women would be plunged into such ecstasy that they no longer could distinguish their heads from their feet, nor their heads from their hats. They would pour all their jewels and gold ornaments into the shoes of this Sultan of Unveiling (*kashf*), in the hope that he would accept something and thus bestow favor upon them, but he wouldn't even glance at any of it. After performing the dawn prayer with them, he would leave.

No other Friend of God or prophet had such a custom, except the Chief of Messengers, Muhammad (May God's blessings and peace be upon him). Arab ladies (*khatun*) would come to learn from him and question him about the secrets and subtleties of religious law. This was a lawful special piety particular to his exalted character.

The husbands of these women of Konya would gather outside the palace with Amaluddin and have their own spiritual conversation (*sohbet*) and keep guard so that other rough people would not become aware of these secrets.

Awakened Dreams [364]

One day, while sharing divine insights, Mevlana said:

A dervish of enlightened heart went to see an amir, who was one of his companions. He said to him, "Last night, in a dream I saw such and such."

The amir was irritated and thought, "Do dervishes sleep?"

The shaikh understood his thoughts and cried, "May God keep us from it. A dervish dreams while awake."

And as the poet said:

The Prophet said, "My eyes sleep,
but my heart never sleeps in regard to humankind."
The knower of God sees delightful dreams while awake.
Sprinkle some of his dust upon your eye.

Immediately, the amir bowed and asked forgiveness.

Greeting the Sun and the Moon [365]

According to the great *ahrar* (May God be pleased with all of them), Mevlana, at the rising of the sun and the first appearance of the moon, would stand and face these heavenly bodies, and say, "*The sun and the moon and the stars are subservient to His command. Do not the creation and the command belong to Him? Blessed is God, the Sustainer of all the worlds* [7:52]."

And then, in respect, he would go on his way.

When Even Poison Is Honey [366]

One day, someone asked Mevlana, "Is it possible for a dervish to commit a sin?"

Mevlana answered, "If he eats when he has no appetite. It is a great sin for a dervish to eat if he isn't hungry. Because if a man is extremely hungry, he can even swallow poison without coming to any harm, but when one is full, even sugar becomes poison. When someone of enlightened heart is really hungry, everything is permitted." And so he said:

You're the victim of your lower self, O careless one—
drink blood in the dust.
For one of enlightened heart, even poison is a honeyed antidote.

From His Mouth [367]

Mevlana told the following anecdote about the way the Prophet (Peace and blessings upon him) taught and his good manners:

"'Ubay ibn Ka'b (May God be pleased with him) was one of the foremost among the Companions, one of the oldest and wisest, but he was not very eloquent. The Prophet, with extreme humility and his Muhammadan kindness, recited for him the entire Qur'an with the correct pronunciation and melodious voice. So that, 'He heard the whole Qur'an from the mouth of the Messenger.' And in this way 'Ubayy finally learned the Qur'an and the correct way to recite it.[120]

"It is also conveyed that the Elect of God (Peace and blessings upon him) recited the whole of the glorious Qur'an to Gabriel the Trustworthy, seven times, and that first Gabriel recited it to him seven times while the Messenger listened. During the Night of the Ascension, he recited it seventy times in the presence of the Most Exalted Creator."

It is also transmitted that Chelebi Husamuddin, that Sultan of Khalifas, (May God sanctify his holy innermost secret) read aloud the entire *Mathnawi* seven times in the presence of Mevlana. It was a sema of the spirit. The divine treasures and esoteric secrets concealed within the *Mathnawi* were revealed to him. Letter by letter, 'alif' by 'alif', he resolved all the difficult parts, and then he transcribed it in liquid gold adding the indications for the vowels. All the great *khalifas* who heard it from Husamuddin's high authority and made a copy—these are unsurpassed authentic copies worthy of trust.

Make Me a Gift of My Faults [369]

One day in the blessed medresse, Mevlana was sharing divine insights. He said:

120. 'Ubay ibn Ka'b became recognized as the greatest reciter of the Qur'an (after the Prophet Muhammad, Peace and blessings be upon him). He memorized and collected the entire Qur'an during the lifetime of the Prophet Muhammad and became one of the foremost teachers of Quranic recitation.

One day, a shaikh saw that one of his students was holding a stick in his hand and asked him about it.

"It is to hit you with if you disobey the rules of the Way," answered the student.

"You are a true disciple and a Friend on the path," his shaikh responded.

Caliph 'Ali said, "May God hold in His Mercy a man who makes me a gift of my faults."

He also said, "Through good character, I get along well with people."

"How do you do this?" someone asked.

He answered, "As much as possible I try to help them advance, and if they don't accept my help, I leave them be. I must speak, but they don't have to listen."

I have shown you the straight path;
if you turn away, it is your choice.

Immersing in Prayer [371]

The noble companions (May God hold them in His Mercy) told us that one Friday Mevlana said, "We must go to the Mosque of the Citadel."

All the companions prepared themselves, and they went to the mosque. Mevlana went into a corner and pronouncing the "Allahu akbar!" of the ritual prayer remained in the standing position. The imam finished his recitation of the Qur'an and completed his sermon. The congregation completed their prayer, and the sultan, the military commanders, the scholars, and the people of poverty left; Mevlana remained in the standing position. In perfect politeness, the companions also left, because his presence (*huzur*) filled them with awe and no one felt able to accompany him.

On the next Friday he was still in the mosque. When the sultan, the nobility, the scholars, and the shaikhs of the community assembled again for prayer, they saw that Mevlana, in complete reverence and humility was now bent in the second position of bowing (*ruku*). The great Shaikh Sadruddin embraced Qadi Sirajuddin and they wept so intensely while deeply contemplating this that it cannot be described.

"If worship and faith and prayers are what this man is engaged in, then we are making fools of ourselves and have no idea what we are doing," Qadi Sirajuddin exclaimed, and, in tears, they departed.

On Monday, Mevlana returned to himself from this spiritual immersion and went to the bathhouse. From there he returned to the blessed medresse, where he immersed in sema for three days and three nights.

Honor Even the Walls [373]

One day a Friend was hammering a nail into the wall of one of the cells of the medresse.

"Our medresse is the abode of the Friends of God, and this cell belongs to our Master Shamsuddin; aren't you afraid to hammer a nail into it? You must not do this—it is as though you were hammering a nail into my heart," said our Master sternly.

Such was the respect he had for the blessed medresse.

A Turban Joining Head and Heart [375]

Various Friends (May God be satisfied with them) told us that a distinguished young man, from the Sayyids[121] of the City (Medina) of the Prophet, came to visit Sultan Walad one day. He was accompanied by other Sayyids from Konya who introduced him as the son of the custodian of the Prophet's tomb.

He was wearing an extraordinary turban that he had wound around his head with one of the ends falling to his heart, while the other end was rolled in the way that the Mevlevis call *shakar-aviz.* Sultan Walad showed him great respect and spoke with him about various meanings and secrets of the Path, *in the clear Arabic tongue* [26:195]. The young man demonstrated great devotion and good will and asked in all sincerity to become a disciple. He asked for a written permission (*ijazat*) and they gave this to him in Arabic.

After that, Sultan Walad asked him, "This mode of *shakar-aviz* is a special custom of Mevlana's and is particular to the Mevlevis; other shaikhs have not adopted it. Where does it originate?"

"In great antiquity," replied the young Sayyid. "We are descended from Abraham, the Friend of God, and the Quraysh tribe—since the time of Abraham, the Friend of the Compassionate, we have kept the keys of the holy Kaaba, and those of the Prophet's tomb are, also, under our care. Whenever the keys or the Messenger's two blessed

121. "Sayyids" are descendents of the Prophet Muhammad.

sandals or other of his relics are needed, the custodians of the tomb—our fathers and our ancestors—have given them to the Sayyids. With our permission they convey them throughout the Islamic community. They gain benefit from this, and so, year after year, members of this community have brought their revenue to us as a recompense, to be granted to the inhabitants of the city (Medina) and to those who live close to this great spiritual power, according to their rank and their virtue.

"Also, a tradition that comes from our ancestors and that is recorded in the *Book of Secrets of the Ascension (Kitab-i Asrar-i Mi'raj)* affirms that when the Prophet (May Peace and blessings be upon him) rose on the Night of the Ascension as *Limitless in His glory is He who transported His servant by night from the Inviolable House of Worship at Mecca* [17:1] and was honored with: *He drew near, and came close* [53:8], he was honored with seeing the Face of the All-Powerful and was looked upon with a favorable eye, and, becoming fortunate, was shown that which he needed to see. He heard the secrets of the revelation directly without intermediary."

Something happened between the lover and his beloved!
O you who are neither one nor the other,
what has happened to you?

"When in blessing he returned for the sake of his mission to his people, he saw a figure above the Heavenly Throne of amazing beauty, such that he had never seen before, in the highest rank of the angels or among any of the other inhabitants of Heaven."

With my eye I see a moon beyond sight;
no eye has ever seen such as he, nor ear heard of his like.

"The Prophet was overcome with love and intoxicated with the grace and beauty of this figure and felt a great attachment to him. He saw that he wore upon his head a turban wrapped in the *shakar-aviz* style and that he was wearing clothes of striped cloth from Yemen. Extremely bewildered and agitated, the Prophet asked the Great Confident of Divine Secrets (*Namus-i Akbar*), that peacock of the heavens (Gabriel), about this figure: 'I saw many marvelous and unusual forms in each celestial sphere when I journeyed to Heaven, as it was said, "No created thing exists without there being a likeness of it under the Throne." However, none of them enraptured me or attracted me as much as this figure does. Who is he and what is the nature of his secret? Is he an angel close to God, or a Messenger, or a perfect saint?'

"Gabriel answered, 'This beautiful figure is a person descended from Abu-Bakr, the Truthful, who will appear among your community at the end of time, and will fill the world with the lights of your secrets and truths, bestowing beauty. And God Most High will give him a foot, a pen, and a breath such that all the people and the rulers will become his friends and devoted followers; he will be the secret of the light of the manifest world bringing purity to your religion.'

"As the poet has said:

Reveal to us the treasure hidden in:
Truly, We have opened before you a manifest victory [47:1];
tell us, again, of the spiritual secret of Mustafa.

"Gabriel continued, 'And in every way, in conduct and appearance, he will be like you!'

"As the Messenger (Peace and blessings upon him) said, 'There is no prophet who did not have his like among his community.'

"Gabriel concluded, 'And his name is Muhammad and his other name, Jalaluddin. His discourses will explain the secrets of your traditions and will illuminate the profound meanings of the glorious Qur'an.'

"At this, the Prophet smiled with intense joy. When he returned in blessing to his glorious home, he began wearing his turban in the same way that he had seen. He told the Companions, 'Let one end of your turbans hang down, because Satan doesn't do so, and turbans are the crowns of the Arabs.'

"He let one end of his turban hang down to his heart and tied the other end at the nape of his neck in the *shakar-aviz* style. From that time until now, we of the Quraysh tribe have followed this custom of the Prophet. And it is said that the wise shaikhs and adepts of Khorasan do the same.

"That day when the Prophet spoke of it, from immense happiness, Abu-Bakr, the Truthful, gave everything he owned to the Prophet and the Companions as a token of his gratefulness.

"It is reported that when the Prophet (Peace and blessings upon him) was about to die, Abu Bakr was weeping in deep distress. The Prophet asked, 'O Truthful one, dear friend, why are you crying? What is the reason for these endless tears?'

"He replied, 'Adam the pure, Noah the Confidant, and all the other noble prophets had long lives and for many years taught among their people; you who are the sovereign of them all, who said, "Adam and those who come after him are under my banner"—you are making the last voyage at the age of sixty-two years; for this reason my heart is filled with sadness. I am overcome that a sultan such as yourself must go so quickly. I wish that you could have stayed a thousand years here on earth like Adam, so that mortal men could have been blessed with your presence for a longer time.'

"'Don't be sad,' said the Messenger. 'One single day full of mercy of my mission is equivalent to a thousand years of time of the other prophets. That which has manifested for my community and that which will manifest, that which has occurred for the wise of my community and that which will occur did not occur even after many years for the people of other eras. Did you not know that I have said, "The wise of my community are like the prophets of Israel?" O Truthful One, may your perfumed heart be at peace. Today all openings are closed except the opening of Abu Bakr. All windows have been closed except those of Abu Bakr and of those who are like him. Know that one day my secret will emerge from one of the sons of Abu Bakr and will once again light up the world, so that your goal will be completely fulfilled.'

"Abu Bakr bowed and became full of joy. The Prophet, that very moment, departed. Throughout the centuries, we Sayyids have hoped that one day we would see the figure that the Prophet beheld and of whose appearance he spoke, and thus have the honor of being connected with that luminous unfolding. Praise be to God! We have attained that happiness; this felicity has been granted to us, and our goal has been realized!"

This is what that the pilgrims from Mecca reported to us and we heard it repeated in all its detail by the worthy Sayyids of Medina.

They cannot describe his perfect nature!
The reality is two hundred times greater.

The Freedom of Fasting [377]

Some religious scholars were discussing how to subdue the lower self (*nafs*). Mevlana said:

There was a dervish who performed acts of devotion and mortifications for many years. One day, he addressed his *nafs*: "Who are you and who am I?"

His *nafs* responded: "You are you, and I am I."

Then he set off on foot to perform the Hajj, circumambulating the Kaaba numerous times, and experienced all sorts of trials.

Again he asked: "Who am I and who are you?"

Again, his *nafs* responded, "I am I, and you are you."

He tried all sorts of religious devotions, but he was unable to subdue his ego self. Then, he began to fast and practiced the mortification of hunger.

Finally, he asked, "Now, how is it?"

This time, his *nafs* answered, "I am annihilated, and you are you. *God knows best the Truth.*"

This indicates that no religious practice can conquer the lower self and cause it to be truly surrendered (*muslim*) like hunger.

O you who are a prisoner of your craving for food,
if you can wean yourself, you will be saved.

Don't Hestitate! Give Something to the Poor Ones. [379]

Shaikh Mahmoud, otherwise known as Sahib-Qiran, told us that after the death of Sahib Fakhruddin one of the great Friends saw him in a dream and Sahib Fakhruddin was very happy and content.

The Friend asked him, "You were called Abu'l-Khayrat (Father of Beneficent Deeds). How did our Lord Most High receive you in the other world?"

"Among all the acts of beneficence that I performed, none helped me find favor in God's eyes as much as this—I had a tree brought from my country for the construction of Mevlana's tomb. That is why God Most High received me with such grace and mercy."

After the death of Mevlana, Sahib Fakhruddin had shown great respect to the Friends and served Sultan Walad in many ways. He also enveloped Chelebi Husamuddin with kindness and so was rewarded for all his good deeds.

As the poet has said:

You will rest in the shade of any kindness that you do!
Don't hestitate! Give something to the poor ones.
If you sow a single kernel, you'll reap a hundred ears of corn.
Why are you looking puzzled?
Don't hesitate! Give something to the poor ones.

All Souls Shall Taste of Death but Not All Hearts [380]

It was reported by Fakhruddin Divdest that, one day, Mevlana was sharing divine insights at a large gathering at the Pervana's house:

Mevlana spoke, "The faithful do not die; they are transported from one abode to another."

Shaikh Tadjuddin-i Ardebil, who was the shaikh of the Parvana's *khanaqah*, and a virtuous and articulate man asked, "If that is the case, why did God say: *Every soul will taste death* [3:185; 21:36; 29:57]?"

Mevlana replied, "In actuality God said, 'all souls (*nafs*)' and not 'all hearts (*qalb*)'. Either become all heart or find a place within the heart of a truly faithful one in such a way that, like that truly faithful one, you will not die. If you make of yourself a heart, you will never become counterfeit coin. If however, you abandon yourself to the passions of the self, then the Prophet's saying: 'All *nafs* must taste death' will apply to you."

Everything Is Perishing Except His Face [381]

One day, Mevlana was commenting on the Qur'an and shared an unusual meaning of the verse: *Everything is perishing, except His Face* [28:88]. He said, "God Most High did not wish to praise Himself or to boast about His superiority to His servants in relation to the eternal pre-existence and the future, so as to say, 'I am eternal, while you are perishing.' On the contrary, He invites us to Mercy by saying, 'Disappear in Me, like a drop of water in the immensity of the sea, so that within Our noble Face you will become eternal.' "

As Mevlana said:

All is perishing except His Face;
If you don't have that Face, don't try to exist.
One who is annihilated within Our Face,
the saying "All is perishing" will not apply to her.
Whoever is included in that "except"
escapes negation and does not die.

[*Mathnawi* I: 3052-3056]

Wherever You Turn[122] [382]

One day, Mevlana was again sharing divine insights at the Parvana's house and explaining at length regarding the heavens, the earth, the stars, and the creation of the world: "The appearance of this world is a revelation for the people of God who know the true meaning of reality."

"Then why did the Elect of God say, 'The world is a decaying carcass'—how can that be?" asked Tadjuddin-i Ardebil.

Mevlana answered, "Don't deliberately seek the world, that it might not be like a carcass and that you might not be like the dogs who look for such things to devour. Anything you might occupy yourself with apart from God is a carcass or worse than a decaying carcass. Rather always seek for God and in this way become worthy of contemplating Him, so that you might see Him in all things. Then the words, 'Whatever I saw, I saw God in it,' might become the ruler of your eye."

In the Kitchen of Love [383]

It is conveyed that, one day, some of the Friends who were artisans complained about the injustice of miserable tyrants.

Mevlana responded, "In the bazaar of the butchers, they don't kill dogs, even though they may deserve to be killed; they always slaughter sheep—they bear this burden. God shows greater mercy to the faithful, and so necessarily their burden is also great, but the mercy reserved for them is infinite."

Then he added:

In the kitchen of Love, only the good are killed.
They don't slaughter the infirm or those of ill character.
If you're a sincere Lover, don't flee the slaughter;
the only one that can't be killed is already a carcass.

These words consoled the Friends; they thanked him and accepted bearing the turbulent injustices of the time.

Be Watchful in Humility, in The Manner of The Prophet [384]

The wise friends told us that, one day, Mevlana related:

---

122. This selection is also a reflection of the verse that traditionally completes the Mevlevi sema (whirling ceremony): *And God's is the east and the west: and wherever you turn, there is the Face of God. Behold, God is infinite, All-knowing* [2:115].

"Satan, he who is pelted with stones, was standing outside the Quba mosque, waiting to enter and visit the Prophet, but Mustafa (Peace and blessings upon him) would not give him permission and kept him from entering.

"Then Gabriel, the trustworthy transmitter came from the Glorious Presence and said: 'Give our Satan permission to visit.'

"When Satan entered, he humbly sat down in a lowly place and said, 'O Messenger of God, do you know who I was and what my rank and work used to be?'

"'Tell me,' said the Messenger.

"'For thousands of years, I was master of the empires of the celestial spheres and taught humility, servanthood, and endurance of hardship.

"'As you saw on the night of the Ascension, my pulpit was at the foot of the Glorious Throne. A thousand angels were present at my assemblies, and not for a thousand years would they attend such a meeting.

"'But for a small mistake, I became an eternal outcast, and the collar of damnation was hung around my neck: *Go forth, then, from this angelic state—for behold, you are henceforth accursed, and My rejection shall be your due until the Day of Reckoning* [38:77]. Because of that, I became despised by human beings and deprived of the company of the angels. God appointed Adam, abandoned on earth, to mastery and chose him to be His vicegerent, while I was cursed.

"'Now, O Muhammad, see and be afraid—do not become presumptuous because of being the Praised one (*Muhammad*), nor overly joyous in being the beloved (*habib*) of the All-Powerful, because there is no end to His ruses and His traps. Be on guard, always, so that your deepest self will always be in awe of Him.' And he wept piteously.

"This is why the Prophet (Peace and blessings upon him) was busy until his last breath in combating his lower self (*nafs*), showing great courage in the lesser *jihad* and the greater.[123] He did not rest for the blink of an eye, nor did he sleep for a moment. His heart was always on fire, and his eyes bathed in tears. As a result of the fear of his lower self *(nafs)* within, he would let out a whistling sound like that of a boiling kettle. He said, 'I am the one among you who knows God the best and is most in awe of Him.'

123. The word *jihad* means "struggle." The Prophet taught that the lesser *jihad* was the struggle for outward justice and practice of faith; the greater *jihad* is the struggle with the inner self and the continual polishing of the heart.

"He never ate barley bread to satiety, nor did he sleep fully, out of concern for the well-being of others. True following is to act, and to become, like him."

And then Mevlana cried out and began the sema. He wept infinite tears and was so overcome that he remained standing for seven days and nights.

Eat Less, Speak Less, Sleep Less [385]

The glory of the companions, Chelebi Shamsuddin, the son of the professor, may God have mercy on him, told us that, one day, Mevlana was sharing divine insights from his retreat cell with the close Friends.

He said, "In a human being's body, there are three thousand snakes. One single mouthful of food enlivens a thousand snakes. If you eliminate one mouthful out of three, a thousand snakes within your soul (*nafs*) will die, and if you eat two mouthfuls less, two thousand snakes will die. If you eat one additional mouthful, a thousand snakes of your egoistic desires are enlivened, but if you give up one mouthful, a thousand die. If it pleases God, may God Most High grant us and all the Friends the capacity to eat less, speak less, and sleep less. So be it, *O Lord of all the worlds*!"

This is what Mevlana said, but *God best knows the Truth*!

Follow the Example of the Lovers [388]

Some of the exalted Friends related that certain foolish jurists had strongly reproached the companions saying that it is not permitted to prostrate before a created being.

"Miserable creatures!" said Mevlana, "If someone had saved me from Satan and that executioner, the commanding self (*nafs al-ammarah*), had set me free, and given me new life, why would I not bow before him or even give my life for him?

"For instance, the sovereign of the era became angry with someone and hands him over to the harsh executioner, who ties his hands and neck and takes him to the place of execution and is about to cut off his head. But just in time, one of the prince's courtiers brings a royal ring of safety (*anngoshtari-ye aman*) so that the condemned man is, instead, set free and dressed in a robe of honor.

"The unfortunate man, thus delivered, asks, 'This generosity, this good deed, this life that has been restored to me, to whom do I owe it?'

"He tries to find him, and they tell him, 'It was "so and so" who demonstrated this generosity.'

"With great happiness, in all sincerity and humility, he falls at the feet of his benefactor, and prostrating in front of him, praises him, saying, 'O you who have given me life, you are the Khidr of the day. You have granted me life again, and always, until my dying moments, I will consider it my duty to thank my benefactor and to pray for him.'

"It is the same for the Friends of God and God's creatures. They show compassion by delivering them from this place of chastisement that is the world, from the hand of accursed Satan, and from the power of the rebellious commanding self. They deliver them from the abyss of perdition and the dangerous roads, and bestow upon them sincerity (*ihklas*) and guide them on the straight path towards proximity to God the Most Generous.

"Why would people not prostrate in gratitude and all sincerity, and why would they not consider this an obligation? In the way of mysticism and truth, gratitude towards the Friends of God, bowing down before them and honoring them, is gratitude to God. To prostrate oneself in this way is really reverence for God—it is a duty for a person who has received the generosity of such a Friend and who has been brought from an inferior station to a better one.

"On the other hand, it is not permitted for him to bow down before those who have not shown this generosity—that would be infidelity: *Those are the ones who denied the truth and the profligates* [80:42]. These dear Friends close to God are not concerned with such people, because if suddenly, out of imitation, he were to prostrate, he would become a denier. While on the other hand, the one who knows God, if he does not bow before one loved by God, he would be unfaithful. It is a personal obligation for human beings to honor the followers of the Messenger, who are loved by God and accepted by His Messenger, because it was said: "*Say, 'If you love God, follow me, and God will love you* [3:31],' so that in this way they may share in that state of being loved. *And Peace be with those who follow the guidance* [20:47]."

Witnessing the Unity [389]

One day, Mevlana was speaking about the meaning of union among the Friends of God and the prophets (Peace be upon them all):

"Two individuals were engaged in an argument and appeared

before the judge (*qadi*), who asked one of them to provide witnesses. He left and brought back two sufi dervishes as witnesses. The judge asked for another. The man brought another two dervishes, but the judge wanted still more.

"'Instead of two witnesses,' said the man who had come before him, 'I have brought four people. Why do you want still more witnesses?'

"The *qadi* answered, 'Because even if you were to bring forty thousand of those who really are as one, it wouldn't matter—in reality by their union, the Friends are but a single soul, because, "The truly faithful are in reality a single soul."'"

And Mevlana has said:

The souls of wolves and dogs are separate from one another;
the souls of the lions of God are in unity.
When you see among them two friends united,
they are at the same time one and yet six hundred thousand.

The Faithful One Is a Mirror [390]

One day, Mevlana was sharing subtleties of the *hadith*: "The faithful one is a mirror for the faithful." He said, "*Mu'min* (the Faithful) is one of the names of God and also applies to his servants; when we say, 'The faithful one is a mirror for the faithful,' it means that God reveals Himself in this mirror.

The Creator of souls made a mirror of water and clay
and has held it up before Him.
When the sun shines into a mirror,
what can it say but, 'I am the sun?'

That means that God, the *Mu'min*, manifests Himself in the mirror of His faithful servant; if you wish to see God, look into this mirror.

When the iron of my existence was polished by His love,
it became a mirror that reflected the universe
and was no longer metal."

He Is With You [391]

One day a group of religious scholars asked Mevlana the following question: "How can you explain: *And He is with you wherever you may be* [57:4]?"

His answer was this parable:

"It is like the presence of spring that enters every particle in the universe and through which everything comes to life and begins to smile—every flower, every small bit of earth, every stone, every color is illuminated and adorned by spring. Still spring does not come in the same way to the thorn bush and the stone as to the rose and sparkling ruby. And likewise, the intimacy of God's presence with the soul of the prophets and saints is not the same for the ordinary person; the relationship of a sovereign with his intimate courtiers is not the same as with his grooms and donkey-drivers and attendants.

Since God is together with everyone,
seek the togetherness He keeps with the aware.

"The togetherness of a professor with a new student at the beginning of his studies is not the same as with a student of theology who can offer proofs. *And this is sufficient.*"

All the religious scholars bowed their heads and declared themselves disciples.

All In Good Measure [393]

A Friend was complaining to Mevlana about his lack of resources and constrained circumstances.

Mevlana responded, "If God Most High gave you your portion for fifty years in one large amount, what would you do, and where would you put it to save it?

"God is Generous and Wise. From his storehouses in the Unseen beyond direction, the All-Powerful conveys to you your daily portion, so that you will not become rebellious and disobedient. *If God were to bestow in this world abundant sustenance to His servants, they would behave on earth with wanton insolence* [42:27].

"And those who came before, because of their wealth, became transgressors, and were pretentious enough to rudely ask, '*To whom belongs the kingdom?*', and to say: '*I am your Lord All-Highest*' [79:24] until, having lost the dominion (*mulk*), they brought disaster upon themselves. Take care! Don't say that He doesn't bestow upon you. Remember what God has already given you, what you have received in the past. Don't forget to thank Him for His Grace and abundant generosity.

Don't be concerned about the future; stop worrying—
remember all the food you've already been given to eat."

Bending the Bow in Submission [394]

The Friends endowed with divine knowledge, the knowers of God (*'arifin*), told us that one day an important person came to visit Mevlana and asked him what one must do to avoid suffering at the moment of one's death.

Mevlana responded, "Death is like the Khwarazm Shah's[124] bow, very tight and tough—even an adept archer or bowman cannot draw it. Unless one has had lessons from a master, one cannot draw the bowstring (*zeh-i*) to one's ear, and if one is not strong enough to do that, one will hear no accolades of 'Bravo (*zehi*)!' Therefore one must practice for many years, and first become able to bend a light bow, in order to acquire the strength to bend the bow of the Khwarazm. Now, this lightweight bow, that prepares us for death, is the servant's perseverance in acts of devotion and charity—generosity with his goods and with his body. When the patient servant has learned to be generous and thus progressed on his spiritual journey, when the angels responsible for taking your soul come to find you and reclaim your soul, you can readily give it up to them, without any pain or sorrow. You will not refuse to return the loan that God has entrusted to you, for it has been said: *Truly, God bids you to deliver all that you have been entrusted with unto those who are entitled to it* [4:58], and also, as in this passage which describes the way the angels gently gather up the souls: *By those who gently release souls* [79:2], your limbs won't hurt you any more, and there will be no more pain or suffering.

"But those people who have not practiced generosity nor learned how to give will not yield up their souls with joy and goodwill but will continue to be stingy even at that moment. For this reason, they will be taken by force, as it is said: *By those who pluck out the soul violently* [79:1], and that will be painful and will seem like suffering; they will not want to leave this world.

> If you are faithful and gentle, your death will be of the faithful;
> if you are unfaithful and bitter, your death will be that way."

---

124. Khwarazm, one of the oldest centers of civilization in Central Asia was located around the basin of the lower Amu Darya River (now NW Uzbekistan). In the early 1200's it stretched from the Caspian Sea to Samarkand. Though in 1221 it was conquered by Jenghiz Khan and became a part of Mongol territory, the Khwarazm Shah (King of Khwarazm) and his horse-archers were renowned for their outstanding strength and skill.

Making Devotion Fruitful [395]

One day at a gathering, a prominent person asked, "Can one make progress on the spiritual journey without a shaikh?"

Mevlana answered with this anecdote:

There was a dervish who was continually repeating a *dhikr*, of his own, without having been taught by any guide, and was putting immense effort into it. One night, he saw a light come out of his mouth and fall to the ground. Troubled by this, he went to find a shaikh and told him his dream.

The shaikh told him, "Such is the *dhikr* that one practices without the instruction of a shaikh of true certainty." He then learned a *dhikr* from this shaikh. That same night, he saw the light came out of his mouth, but this time it shone up to the Throne of God, as it says in the Qur'an: *To Him good words rise and good deeds—He upflifts them* [35:10].

You must know that without the instruction of a shaikh there is no way to find the right path. Without a spiritual director, all acts of devotion remain fruitless and without light: "One who has no shaikh has no religion."

Entrust your hand only to your shaikh's hand;
God guides him and holds him by the hand.

As Slippery as Mercury [396]

A dervish, who was tormented by his passions, saw his *pir* one night in a dream—he placed a bowl full of mercury in front of him and put a diamond-like sword in his hand. Every time he tried to cut the mercury in two with the sword, it kept rejoining again. Exhausted, he woke up and saw his spiritual director standing beside his bed.

"Until the moment of death," his *pir* said, "one must not give up the struggle with the bodily desires; as much as is possible do not slacken in the effort to subdue the passions, because until the ego soul dies, you will not be free of its tricks.

Kill it in combat, struggling courageously;
God will reward you with union with Him.
Until you die, your struggle will not be uprooted.
Without the completion of the stairway,
    you will not reach the roof."

Of Shaikhs and True Friends [397 & 398]

One day, Mevlana told us the following:

"Someone asked a shaikh, '"So and so . . . uddin" is the disciple of which shaikh?'

"The shakih answered, 'What are you talking about? He is dying to be a shaikh himself!' " and Mevlana recited this verse:

For anyone who has found life in love
not to be a servant would be unbelief.

And he added, "One who has found the sweetness of being a servant and a disciple doesn't wish to be a shaikh at all during his life.'

"Similarly, a distinguished person sent a message to a shaikh saying, 'Send me a friend to keep me company, someone with whom I can have a conversation.'

"The shaikh replied, 'A friend is rare and often not possible to find. However, I can send him as many shaikhs as he likes.' "

Loved by All [399]

One day, Gurji Khatun light-heartedly asked 'Alamuddin Qaikar, "What miracle did you witness Mevlana performing to be so delighted with him, to become his disciple, and to love him so completely as you do?"

"May the Lady of the World live a long life! The least of Mevlana's miracles is this: a prophet is loved by his people, and a group imitates its shaikh, but with one accord, all the people and their sovereigns love Mevlana, delight in his presence, and consider themselves honored to receive his teachings. What miracle could be greater than this?"

Gurji Khatun placed robes of honor over his shoulders and showered favors upon the companions.

The Boat Is Waiting [400]

One day, in Mevlana's presence, a few Friends were speaking about the way some hypocrites were denigrating and mocking the Friends. Mevlana said:

When, at God's command, Noah (May God's peace and blessing be with him) had completed building the ark, unfortunate Canaan, due to obstinacy and pride, in company with the deniers mocked him, saying, "Of what use is a boat in a dry desert?"

After the construction had been finished, time passed, and the Qur'an commentators say that for two entire years people defecated in the boat—the ark became filled with filth, and there was nothing Noah could do to prevent it. He lamented to God Most High.

In the end, God sent a deadly sickness that could only be cured by human feces. The doctors of these people agreed that that they would have to eat human excrement as a remedy. In their shame, the people each secretly went to the ark to eat the feces until none remained.

Then God the Sublime and Exalted sent rain falling for forty consecutive days: *the waters gushed forth in torrents over the face of the earth* [11:40; 23:27], *And it moved on with them into waves that were like mountains* [11:42], the water rose from below and *they were overwhelmed by the very thing which they were wont to deride* [40:78]—the flood drowned them all. If one rejects pious people and mocks these mysteries, there will be no blessings but rather great loss. Those who navigate the flood of affliction watch in ambush—the bow of power is within their strong grasp. May the Friends endure; in time we will see the results.

And so we said:

> If the gardens of the impious seem green for a day or two,
> never mind—by a secret way, I can touch their roots.

Sultan Walad referred to this invisible flood when he said:

> O you who deny our way, O enemies of our King,
> the time is near when our flood will overwhelm all of you.

Everyone was drowned in the flood of misery, and most of those who died, died without faith and disappeared. As a result of God's stringency, they perished so that not even a trace of them remained in the world. *And say: "The truth has now come to light, and falsehood has withered away; for, behold, all falsehood is bound to wither away* [17:81]."

> If Noah hadn't had God's help, why would he have overturned
> the world?
> He was like a hundred thousand lions in one body.
> He was like fire and the world, the threshing floor
> of the gathered harvest.
> Since they didn't respect the tithe to be paid,
> the harvest was set ablaze.

Meeting Is a Mercy [401]

That Master of Sultans, Fakhruddin Divdest, the learned, told us that once our Master entered the gathering hall of his medresse and saw the Friends assembled there.

"By God!" he said, "Gather together and be always at peace, for as it is said, 'Meeting is a mercy and separation a punishment.' If one leaves a sheep all alone in a field, it laments and doesn't gain weight—it dies or the wolf tears it to pieces; it should stay amid the flock. In the same way, a tree planted all by itself will only grow well in rare cases. Thus meetings and union where there is no hypocrisy have a great influence.

> It's customary to take a companion on a journey;
> you'll encounter difficulties
> if you travel alone far from the known road.
> Gather yourself, for gathering is a mercy,
> and so I might tell you that which is."

Choose Harmony [402]

Similarly, Mevlana said:

Nushirvan the Just, King of Persia,[125] was asked, "Which is best—intellect, wealth, or power?"

"The unity of human beings and the meeting of friends," he answered. "In other words, wherever there is harmony and cooperation, the three qualities you mentioned will also be found. Harshness and rudeness are of no use."

Mevlana added:

> If you are rough and rude, your commands will be ignored.
> Treat others gently, so they don't act prickly like hedgehogs.

Pray for Friendship [403]

One day, Mevlana gave the Friends the following advice:

As much as you can try to be in the company of a shaikh, and benefit from all he can teach you, for the rest is worthless. If this is not possible, spend time with the Friends, and if this is not possible,

125. Nushirvan the Just, also known as Chosroes (Khusraw), was the King of Persia in the 6th century.

contemplate their words. And if this is not possible, spend your time in worship of God, praying in all humility that you might be granted the privilege of finding such a fellowship, and asking for the protection of a spiritual friend, as Moses did.

The protection of a Friend is better than reciting the Name of God.
This is what our Muhammad has said.

Forgiveness [404]

That King of Scholars, Fakhruddin the Professor, May God have mercy on him, told us the following:

One day, I went with Mevlana to visit the tomb of his father, Bahauddin Walad. After having performed the ritual prayers and reciting litanies, he meditated for some time. He then asked me to fetch an inkwell and reed pen. When I had brought them, he stood up and went to the tomb of his son, Chelebi 'Alauddin. On the side of the tomb which was whitewashed in plaster he wrote in Arabic:

If just the virtuous could place their hope in You,
to whom could the sinner turn for refuge?

To whom might the vile man direct his entreaties,
if, O Generous One, You only accepted the good?

Mevlana said, "I saw that in the world of the Unseen my Master Shamsuddin Tabrizi had made peace with and forgiven he whom I have just mentioned. He pardoned him and interceded for him, so that he has become forgiven by God.

Merchandise no one gave a glance at He has purchased,
thanks to the intervention of this generous one.

Just think what he might do for those accepted by God
who already have received His mercy!"

The Qur'an Bears Witness [405]

One day, the reciters of the Qur'an of the city of Konya asked Mevlana to comment on the meaning of the *hadith*, "How many a reciter of the Qur'an has been cursed by the Qur'an!" He responded:

Most of the Qur'an consists of commands and prohibitions and encouragement of good *adab* inwardly and outwardly. Some recite the words, *Be constant in prayer, and render the purifying dues* [4:77], but then they do neither. Others recite the words, *God enjoins justice, and the doing of good* [16:90], and then they behave in an unjust and oppressive way, betraying the trust put in them and engaging in what is wicked and shameful. Through the tongue of its state (*zaban-i hal*), inevitably the Qur'an damns them and on the Day of Resurrection will testify against their souls.

One day, this word will bear witness against those who heard it.
I called you my "water of life," and still you played deaf.

On the contrary, those who follow the way of the Qur'an, obeying the counsel of the wise and not wandering from the straight path, are referred to in this way: "The Qur'an shows him mercy."

Ask the meaning of the Qur'an from the Qur'an itself,
or from one who has burned away his desires.

An Ongoing Conversation [408]

One of the great Friends told us the following:

One day, Mevlana asked for an inkwell and a reed pen and, himself, wrote these verses on the door of the medresse garden:

Know the word of God and that of His servant:
the human being says, "Hu" and God says, "O man!"
How beautiful—the "Ha" of God and the "Hu" of His servants![126]
A tumult, a lively conversation, arising between God
and those here.
A presumptuous man cannot see his sovereign;
God requires the lamentations of those who have sinned.
There is no place for self-conceit on this path—
what is required is a lean body and a broken heart.

126. Mevlana refers here to the way in which God calls to the human being and the human being to God, as in verse 1-3 of *Surah 20, Ta Ha: O Man! (Ta Ha!) We did not bestow the Qur'an on you from on high to make you unhappy, but only as an exhortation to all who stand in awe* [20:1-3], and such passages as *Ihklas* 112:1, *Qul: Hu wallahu Ahad (Say, "He, God, is One")*, in which the human being is counseled to call upon God, "Hu," remembering the Encompassing Presence of the Divine, and as in *Surah An-Nas* [114], seeking refuge in Him.

Sweet Silence [409]

Chelebi Badruddin, the professor's son, told us this:

One day, Mevlana wrote something on a piece of paper and gave it to me:

For the dervish, repose, pleasure, and contentment are greater in a state of silence. But for you, in silence boredom increases and anguish takes hold of you—how can this be? Can it be good? When God shows Himself and throws aside the veils, is there any place for speech?

I am not all tongues, like a comb,
but rather all eyes, like a mirror.
So that my traces might not be revealed,
I cry out secretly.

In Him, we die to ourselves;
through Him we remain—in Him;
the Truth itself speaks for us.

This person is like a silkworm spinning a cocoon around itself—he imagines that he is doing some good work, but he is wrapping himself in his own prison and turning this world of light into a dark and obscure place.

"O Lord, increase my bewilderment!" said Abu Bakr. In his whole life, Abu Bakr, the Truthful, conveyed no more than seven sayings (*hadith*) of the Prophet Muhammad.[127]

And He Is Always Ready to Respond [411]

One day, the scholars of the epoch asked Mevlana about the mystery contained in this *hadith*: "Actions are judged by their outcomes." To explain the circumstance when this *hadith* was spoken, Mevlana told them the following:

In the time of the Messenger (Peace and blessings upon him), a young man who was famous for his debauchery suddenly died. His parents, saddened and embarrassed by the situation, buried him

127. Abu Bakr, one of the two closest companions of the Prophet Muhammad, kept silence about what the Prophet shared with him, except for seven *hadith*. Others who were near the Prophet readily shared many of his utterances, whereas Abu Bakr immersed in the meaning.

quietly in the middle of the night. In the morning, the faithful archangel Gabriel came to the Messenger with the following message: "Go and pray at his tomb." The Elect of God asked why he had been given this order.

Gabriel returned to the Presence of Almighty God and came back, saying, "God has said: 'This young reprobate, in his last moments, said, "I bear witness that there is no God but God and that Muhammad is His servant and His Messenger," and he asked for My forgiveness. In that very moment I received him into My Mercy and I pardoned him his sins.'"

The Prophet was very joyful and said, "Actions will only be judged by their outcomes."

Never look upon a denier with disdain,
there is always hope that he might die
as one who is surrendered (*muslim*).
God has said, "Even if you are debauched
and a worshipper of idols,
whenever you call Me, I will respond."

Mevlana added, "There is no benefactor or generous being as ready to pardon as God is with regard to His servants who are sinners and criminals." Then he told the following little story:

Asma'i, one day, on the pilgrimage road, struck a bedouin Arab a few times with his fist in a dispute over water. He immediately repented and went searching for the bedouin for a long time, so that he could ask his forgiveness, but he could not find him. When he climbed the Mountain of Arafat,[128] he found the Arab praying for him: "O Lord, don't make Asma'i suffer because of me, because he did not know what he was doing."

Asma'i fell at his feet and cried, "It is I who must pray for you!"

"Quite the opposite," said the bedouin. "My name is '*Mohsin* (benefactor),' and I must act in accordance with my name and ask for forgiveness for you."

Now, imagine what God, our Absolute Benefactor will do for us on the Day of Reckoning.

---

128. The gathering on the Mountain and plain of Arafat is the culmination ritual of the Hajj, the pilgrimage to Mecca. It is as though all of humanity is standing before God on the Day of Resurrection.

A Lover Cannot Sleep! [412]

One day, nobles of the city came to visit Mevlana, and he shared insights about the verse: *One whose bosom God has opened wide with willingness towards self-surrender unto Him* [39:22]. He said:

When this verse was revealed, they asked the Messenger, "Is there a sign to indicate this expansion of the chest and opening of the heart?"

He answered, "Yes, when the Light of God enters the heart, it opens and expands, and the sign of this is that this heart withdraws from the world and inclines toward the life of the Beyond. Before death overtakes him, he prepares his provisions for the journey; he divorces himself from the world before the world divorces him."

The day when the Messenger (Peace and blessings upon him) died, the vastly truthful 'Aisha[129] (May God be pleased with her) cried and lamented. But she did not lament in the way that you might, saying, "Alas, horses, goods, wealth, power, family!" Rather, she cried, "O you who do not sleep on a bed! O you who do not wear silk! O you who do not eat your fill of barley bread! O you who sleep only on a mat!"

On the day that our Prophet died, he was lying on a mattress stuffed with palm bark so thin that the marks of the palm fibers were imprinted on his sweet and blessed thighs. From a wooden bowl beside his mat, he took water to spread on his forehead and chest saying, "O Great God! Help me against the pangs and anguish of death."

Another sign of the expansion of one's heart and chest is that one turns one's face towards the life of the Beyond and one seeks Paradise, but there is much suffering to bear along the way; it is not an easy journey—one does not obtain a treasure without suffering, nor fortune without misfortune . . . *as a reward for all that they did* [32:17; 46:14].[130]

Anyone who is seeking the perishing world must chase the sleep from their eyes, take the long road and endure fatigue, otherwise they will not succeed in gaining the world. Even so, someone who is

---

129. 'Aisha was the wife of the Prophet Muhammad, the daughter of his beloved companion, Abu Bakr as-Siddiq. See also note #145 of this volume.

130. *No human being can imagine what blissful delights, as yet hidden, await them in the life to come as a reward for all that they did* [32:17].

For, behold, all who say, "Our Sustainer is God," and thereafter stand firm [in their faith]--no fear need they have, and neither shall they grieve: it is they who are destined for paradise, therein to abide as a reward for all that they have done [46:13-14].

in search of Paradise, fleeing Hell, and pleading with God, how could he expect to arrive at his goal while sleeping, eating, and resting. One who looks for God does not slumber; one who is fleeing from Hell must not sleep.

> O amazing! How can a lover sleep?
> Sleep is forbidden to one in love!
> O David! He lies who lays claim to My love
>   and yet sleeps when night appears, forgetting Me.
> When night descends, the lover becomes frenzied.
>   Come lovers, leap up and bestir yourselves!
> The sound of the water is here—
> if you are thirsty, how can you sleep?

Purifying Water [413]

That dear Friend, Husamuddin, the currier, told us that Mevlana once was standing in the doorway of the stable and was looking at a stream that flowed nearby, passing through the city. He saw that the water was very dirty, and after having looked at it a long time, he cried, "O poor water! Go, and be grateful that you don't enter inside their bodies, or you would see what you would become. God willing, the Holy Sovereign will purify you and render you sacred by His Holy Purity."

And this is what he said commenting on the Name of the Most Holy and Pure:

> When the water has become useless and impure,
> and the senses turn away from it,
> God carries it to be cleansed
> by the generosity of the sea of Truth.
> The following year, she returns, her robe trailing with her.
> "Where were you?" "In the Sea of Beauties."
> She replied, "I arrived dirty, but became purified;
> I received a robe of honor and am now returning to earth.
> Come! O polluted ones, come to me,
> since my character has taken on the quality of God.
> I will accept all your ugliness;
> I can even gift a devil with an angel's purity.
> When I become dirty, I will return above,
> I will go to the Source of the source of all purity.

There, I will take off my soiled dress,
and God will once again give me a pure robe.
Such is His work and mine is like this;
the Lord of the worlds is the beautifier of the world."

[*Mathnawi* V: 200-208]

In Heaven Is Your Provision [414]

One day, Mevlana was reflecting on this passage: *And in Heaven is the source of your earthly sustenance and of all that you are promised for your life after death* [51:22]. He told how a Friend was searching for heavenly nourishment, and along the way he found a jug of wine, but he did not take it, saying, "I am hoping for a heavenly revelation." He returned to his house that night and found that the children were crying from hunger, and the family was angry with him.

"God sent me daily bread, but in my stubbornness I did not take it," said the Friend.

A robber who was listening through the window heard the story and, figuring out where the jug was, ran like Hamza[131] to find it. He found the jug but was disgusted to find that a black snake was sleeping inside it.

"Perhaps this dervish told this story especially to defend himself and his children," he considered. He very carefully plugged up the mouth of the jug and threw it through the Friend's window.

The Friend was astonished to discover the jug, now full of gold; he prostrated and gave thanks to his Creator. "I swear that the meaning of the Qur'an is true. God protect us from thinking that it might ever lie," he cried.

O You who have shown us that Your place
is where there is no attachment to place,
You have made these words apparent:
In Heaven is your provision.

A Lighter Soul [414b]

Mevlana wrote in his own books:

There are many advantages to eating little: if a person does so, he will have better physical health, a better memory, brighter com-

131. Hamza, known for his valor, was the much beloved uncle of Prophet Muhammad.

prehension, a clearer heart, a lighter soul, and will sleep less, have a more penetrating glance, a healthier nature, be content with fewer provisions, offer more abundant assistance and have a more generous character.

Muhammad bin al-Yamani[132] said, "I adopted perpetual fasting because I questioned six kinds of people about six different things, and they all gave me the same answer. I asked doctors what remedy healed the best. They answered: 'Hunger and eat little.' I asked sages what helped the most in the pursuit of wisdom and they answered, 'Hunger and eat little.' I asked the devout what was the most useful for worshipping the Most Compassionate, and they answered, 'Hunger and eat little.' I asked kings, what is the best spice and nourishment, and they answered, 'Hunger and eat little.' I asked lovers how best to obtain the favors of the beloved, and they answered, 'Hunger and eat little.' "

Abu Talib al-Makki[133] said, "The truly faithful one is like the flute; his voice is only beautiful when his stomach is empty."

> Keep an empty stomach and like the flute cry out with longing;
> keep your stomach empty, and speak mysteries like the pen.

Fasting—Physician of the Body, Guardian of Souls [414c]

There is a saying in Arabic: "The best of acts is to starve the satiated stomach and to fill the starved stomach," or in other words, "Starve your overfull stomach, and fill the stomach that is aching with emptiness." Some have said: "the stomach of the friend"; and others have said: "the stomach of the soul"—and then wait, for that which is able to nourish the spirit!

Fasting is the physician of the body and the guardian of souls. Through their acts of devotion, it cleans the bodies of the sick and the lazy, and it delivers the soul from loneliness and isolation. Each time your existence is annihilated, this state of annihilation flowers into a real existence.

Al-Hakim was asked, "What is the mystery of purification?"

He answered, "Real purification is that of mystery."

"We have learned what the exterior form of this purification is,

---

132. Muhammad bin al-Yamani (d. 881) was a well-known philosopher and theologian who was born in Samarqand.

133. Abu Talib al-Makki (d. in the 990's), a well-known hadith scholar and sufi ascetic was the author of *Qut al-qolub (The Nourishment of Hearts).*

but what is the soul of it?" they continued to ask.

Al-Hakim replied, "The soul of purification is the purification of the soul which expels harmful qualities. Purification is intended to remove the obstacles that prevent one from approaching God, to generate one's own secret, and to purify the character that remains distant from God."

The Mystery of Gratitude [414d]

There are three types of gratitude. The first is the gratitude of the common people for food, drink, and clothing, which are perishable things. The second kind of thankfulness which is of the elite is for the remembrance and grace of the Benefactor which has descended into their hearts, for the pleasure and sweetness which do not belong to this world below but which are rather the sign of acceptance by God. The third, which is the gratitude of the elite of the elite, is for the vision of the beauty of the Infinite Bestower of Bounty, such that the importance of all the joy of this world and of the future life, and of everything other than God, becomes loathsome in one's heart.

Someone said to Sana'i, "Only one out of a thousand people understands what you are talking about."

He answered, "It is for that person that I speak."

Three Kinds of Hearts [414e]

Mevlana said:

It is said that there are three kinds of hearts: the abandoned (*matruh*), the wounded (*majruh*), and the expanded (*mashruh*).[134] The abandoned heart belongs to one who has heard the Truth but does not act accordingly; the wounded heart belongs to the faithful, and

---

134. See *Surah al-Inshirah* [94]: *Have We not expanded your chest* . . . And so allowed space for the opening of the heart. It is reported that the angel Gabriel appeared to the Prophet Muhammad, opened his chest, and removed the impurities remaining in his heart:

Have We not expanded your chest and removed from you the burden which weighed down your back,

and increased your remembrance? So, truly, with every difficulty comes ease; truly, with every difficulty comes ease.

So when you are free from your task continue to strive, and to your Sustainer turn with loving attention.

[94:1-8 complete]

the expanded heart belongs to the knowers of God.

When God wished to manifest His creative power and His attributes, He created the world; when He wanted to reveal His own Self, He created Adam.

Someone asked Sufyan ath-Thawri,[135] "What is the sign of God?"

"It is God," he answered.

"What use is the intellect?" the man asked.

"Intellect is powerless, and that powerlessness serves to reveal the existence of the All-powerful," said Sufyan.

Three Kinds of Speech [414f]

Speech is of three kinds: the first comes from the passion of the self (*nafs*), the second from intellect, and the third from love. Speech which arises from the self is troubling and insipid, giving neither pleasure to those who speak, nor profit to those who listen. That which arises from intellect is accepted by the wise and gives pleasure to the listener and the speaker, and speech that arises from love renders enraptured those who listen and those who speak.

Strength from Heaven [414g]

'Ali (May God ennoble his countenance) said, "I did not tear down the door of Khaybar by bodily force nor by strength resulting from food, but rather through strength that came to me from the Celestial Realm (*malakut*). My relation to Ahmad (Muhammad) is like that of light to the sun."

Someone who sees himself as of little value and little worth is gracious, a lover, and delightful. However, a person who holds his own existence in high regard and who watches the roads carefully in order to protect himself is a person whose spirit is heavy and who is frozen and dead.

But *God knows best*!

Hold to the Most Beautiful Thoughts [415]

Someone entering the cell of a dervish who was on a retreat said to

---

135. Sufyan ath-Thawri (d. 778) was a famous traditionalist and ascetic who wrote one of the earliest commentaries on the Qur'an and founded a school of Islamic jurisprudence. He said, "Beware of filling your stomachs, for doing so hardens the heart."

him, "Why do you stay alone like this?"

"The moment when you entered, only then I found myself alone—you separated me from God," said the dervish.

Uways al-Qarani said, "If a person comes near me without greeting me, I am very grateful to him, because he would have occupied my attention at that moment, which would cause pain and suffering."

"Blessed is one who is with people in body, but whose heart is with God Most High (*hadith*)." For God, there is no greater act than subtle thought: "Among you, the one who is the closest to Me is the one with the most beautiful thoughts."[136]

Guarding the Gates [415b]

Try to write beautifully, because this is one of the keys to daily sustenance. Fast, because fasting is one of the keys to the secrets of hearts. Serve pious men and visit them, because that is the greatest of occupations. Hunger is a cloud out of which emerges wisdom and the light of the eye; it is the door of devotion, the key to the door to the Unseen, and the way to sincerity and certainty.

Surely, God is with those who are conscious of Him and who do the good [16:128]. This means that God grants tranquility in this world to one who avoids doing wrong to another, and if someone does wrong to to him unjustly, then he forgives the wrong that has been done to him and erases it from his heart.

> Guard your tongue, if you wish to be secure.
>
> O tongue, you are the cause of my suffering;
> I will cut off your head, so that you don't cut off mine.[137]

Be Wakeful with Solomon [416]

One night, a large sema was held at the Parvana's house and scholars, shaikhs, as well as amirs of the sultan were there. Until midnight, Mevlana was occupied with the sema, immersed in ecstasy.

The Parvana Mo'inuddin whispered in the ear of Sharafuddin,

---

136. This is similar to another *Hadith Qudsi*: "I am within My servant's conception of Me." See section #534 of this volume.

137. These passages are reminiscent of a saying of Hazrati 'Ali: "O tongue, you are an endless treasure! O tongue, you are also an endless disease!" He cautioned people about letting words fly unconsciously: "Words are like arrows. Once loosed from the bow, they cannot be taken back."

Khatir's son, "Watch over our Master for a few moments, so that I might sleep a little and regain my strength in order to serve these distinguished people."

Just then, in the middle of his whirling, which amazed the vaults of heaven, Mevlana began to recite this *ghazal*:

> If you don't sleep for a night, what will it matter?
> If you don't knock at the door of separation,
> what will it matter?
> If you sleep just a little at night until dawn
> for the heart of the Friends—what will it matter?
> If Solomon goes seeking the ants,[138]
> so that the ants become Solomon, what will it matter?
> If by your presence my two eyes are illumined,
> what does it matter if Satan is blind?

The Parvana tore his clothes and fell to the ground and asked for forgiveness, because his name was "Solomon." The unfortunate minister, overwhelmed by Mevlana, this sultan of the spiritual world, served him loyally and humbly like an ant until dawn truly appeared.

Under the Cloak of Blessing [417]

The masters of certainty related the following from Muhammad Sayyid-abadi, that King of chivalry (*futuwwah*) and Purifier of the region of Rum, whom Mevlana called "my *akhi*":

It was harvest time, and I had gathered an enormous pile of grain and a huge pile of winnowed wheat, when suddenly the Mongol army appeared on the plains of Konya, destroying the harvested crops and pillaging.

Mevlana had given me a coat, and I told my servant, "Throw this coat over the pile of wheat, so that by his blessing our harvest will be safe." God knows, and *He suffices as witness*, that the Mongols pillaged near and far, but not one bale of hay or grain of our wheat was touched. I took these provisions to the city and set up tables for

---

138. See the story of Solomon and his army approaching the ants: *Surah an-Naml* 27:15-19.

So he smiled, amused at her [the ant's] *speech, and he said:*

"O my Sustainer! so direct me that I may be grateful for Your blessings which You have bestowed on me and on my parents and that I may do the good work that will please You; and admit me by Your Grace among the ranks of Your righteous servants." [27:19]

the travelers. As I entered Konya, I encountered Mevlana, who approached me, smiling: "*Akhi*, if you had ordered it, everything would have been delivered."

My Saints Are Under My Domes [418]

According to Shaikh Sinanuddin of Akshehir a dervish once asked what was meant by these words: "My saints are under My domes."

After expressing various insights, Mevlana said, "When you spend time with Friends of God or dervishes drunk with mystical love accept with full sincerity that which in their characters is acceptable to your nature and that you comprehend. Leave alone what seems disagreeable in their actions and morals, and don't repeat it to others, so that they don't jump to the wrong conclusions and cause harm. If it were not for these domes of bad morals, they would not remain in this world but would quickly die and join the *abdals* and the beings of the Unseen world. To help humankind and to uphold the universe, God hides his saints in these 'domes' of faults so that lovers with discernment might be distinguished from those who are deniers and who have no discernment. *So that God might distinguish the corrupt from the good* [8:37].

"The sober work constantly to better human beings and to establish external integrity, while those who are intoxicated recklessly occupy themselves with destroying external appearances. Those who are sober are the intelligent, and those who are drunk are the lovers. The perfect ones (*insan al kamil*) are at the same time sober while intoxicated; their domain is to rectify the external and the internal. The lovers rest in the embrace of God while the scholars and intelligent work hard to improve this lowly world."

Patience and Perseverance [419]

One day, the Friends were complaining about the envy and malicious gossip of those who opposed them.

Mevlana responded, "Five terrifying and powerful people were the enemies of Moses (Greetings of peace be upon him); he put up with their hostility and was patient. Finally, God Most High uprooted all five from the world and submitted them to the power of Moses; He made the Prophet Moses victorious over all of them. One of them was Qarun, who believed he had the right to be arrogant because of his immense wealth; he perished—swallowed up by the earth: *And thereupon We caused the earth to swallow him and his dwelling* [28:81].[139] The second was Samiri, who argued with knowledge and was overthrown by his casting of gold: *But then, so they told Moses, the Samaritan had produced for them out of the molten gold, the effigy of a calf* [20:88]. The third was Balaam who boasted about his ascetism and became subject to metamorphosis: *His parable is that of an excited dog* [7:176]; he became the dog at his threshold. The fourth was Uj ibn 'Anak (Og the son of Anak), who quarreled, relying on his own strength and giant stature, but at the hand of Moses he perished. The fifth was Pharoah the damned, who was the proud ruler of Egypt and its waterways and led such large armies, yet he was drowned in that same water, and perished at the head of his army.

"The enemies of the prophets and the saints will act similarly until the Day of Resurrection, and they are not few in number. There is test after test, O my son! *And all this is ordained by the will of the Almighty, the All-Knowing* [6:97; 36:38; 41:12].[140]

It is test after test, O my son!
For whoever knocks at the door, there is a witness.
Truly in each era, a Friend of God stands;
the testing continues until the day of Resurrection.

---

139. See Surah 28:76-78:

When [they perceived his arrogance,] his people said unto him: "Exult not [in thy wealth], for, verily, God does not love those who exult [in things vain]! Seek instead, by means of what God has granted thee, [the good of] the life to come, without forgetting, withal, thine own [rightful] share in this world; and do good [unto others] as God has done good unto thee; and seek not to spread corruption on earth: for, verily, God does not love the spreaders of corruption!"

Answered he: "This [wealth] has been given to me only by virtue of the knowledge that is in me!"

Did he not know that God had destroyed [the arrogant of] many a generation that preceded him—people who were greater than he in power, and richer in what they had amassed?

140. See also the reflections of Shams of Tabriz in *Rumi's Sun*: "The Sanctuary of the Heart," p.251:

It was said, "*The one who enters into it finds peace* [3:97]." There is no doubt that "it" is the heart. *Are they, then, not aware that We have set up a secure sanctuary* [within the heart], *while all around them people are being carried away* [29:67]? *Outside of the sanctuary of the heart, the devil lurks—he whispers in the breasts of men* [114:5]. A hundred thousand times he carries them away with fears and doubts and despair. But the Truth nurtured the Prophet Abraham in the midst of the fire, the Truth completed him. The Prophet Moses was brought up and nurtured at the hand of the enemy through God's grace.

Yes, the Prophet knew this about the favor and guidance of God, so he said, "First the Friend and then the Path."

Remember these words:
There is no community where there has not been one who warns [35:24]."

Forty Mornings *[420]*

Chelebi Jalaluddin told us that, one day, a dervish asked Mevlana about the secret contained in: "For forty mornings, He kneaded the clay of Adam with His hand."

"Why did He not do this during the night or during the day?" asked the Friend.

Mevlana answered, "If God had kneaded it during the night, all of His creatures would have been dark and heavy, and if he had created during the day, all would have been light and luminous. He created during the morning so that half of all people would be dark, unfaithful, rebellious, and outcast, and the other half would be luminous, faithful, happy, and surrendered: *Among you are such as deny this truth, and among you are such as have faith in it* [64:2]."

And so he said:

"Our spirit is like the day and our body is like the night;
in the middle of the night and the day, we are like the dawn."

Increasing Knowledge *[421]*

Sultan Walad told us this:

After I finished my studies in Damascus and had distinguished myself in various areas of knowledge, I arrived in Aleppo. There, I handled all the questions that the scholars put to me, vanquishing their debate, and no one could add to it.

When I returned to Konya, all the worthy people of the city gathered at my father's medresse. He asked me to comment on several subtle questions as a gift for him from the journey. I unfolded certain subtle thoughts so thoroughly, since I was without equal in this area of knowledge, that I imagined he would be very pleased and would have nothing further to add.

Quickly, my father reviewed all the subtleties which I had conveyed and then explained even further in such a manner that everyone was astounded; reciting by heart, he added many additional proofs and, amid exoteric explanations, wove in esoteric explanations, crying out with joy. I tore my clothes and fell prostrate at his feet. All the scholars present were bewildered by his intelligence and discernment and, amazed, enthusiastically applauded.

Who Is Listening? [425]

One day, the Minister Fakhruddin kept insisting to Sultan Walad that Mevlana give him some advice and some teaching. He waited from dawn until the middle of the morning, but Mevlana remained in contemplation and only cried out from time to time, "God is Great (*Allahu Akbar*)!"

When the minister finally left, Sultan Walad greeted his father and asked what the meaning of this was.

Mevlana responded, "Fakhruddin is an insensitive man whose soul has not been awakened. He ignores the world of meaning and has no delight in comprehension. With whom would I speak and what would I say?

> With whom would I speak, since his soul has no ears?
> The ecstasy of an explanation is for someone who can hear.

"His inner thoughts keep stinging me, and the beautiful brides of the World of Truth flee into the interior of the harem, since he is not of those who are intimate.

Mevlana continued, "One day, a poet was deep in the composition of his verses when someone threw a stone against his door. He ran to open it but saw no one there; this happened three times. Then he said, 'Since there is no one there to talk to, to whom should I speak? Yet my work is interrupted.'

"However, Fakhruddin's end will be praiseworthy."

God Is Sufficient [426]

The dear Friends told us that Mevlana expressed these insights regarding the cultivation of modesty and contentment with little:

We turn away from those of our Friends who hold out their hands to ask for the riches of this world, because we have closed the door of begging for our Friends. We have been taught to give, not to take.

> The Prophet said, "If you desire Paradise from God,
> desire nothing from anyone else.
> When you desire nothing from anyone,
> I am your guarantee for *the Garden* and the vision of God."
> [*Mathnawi* VI: 333-334]

May We Be Brought Near [427]

It was reported that Khwaja Majduddin of Maragha had a young slave girl of Greek origin whom Mevlana called 'Siddiqa' (the truthful one).

She often reported seeing miracles, saying, "I saw a green light. I saw a red light, and a black light. I saw an angel. The spirit of such a saint, or the soul of such a prophet appeared to me."

Majduddin was discouraged, and feeling jealous, said, "How is it that the slaves of my house can see mysterious entities, while I am deprived?"

He recounted all of this to Mevlana, who answered, "Yes, the light is in the pupil of the eyes—to some people this light manifests as beautiful beings, to others as self-restraint to lead them to the one who is the beloved in the harem. If one is distracted along the way by external beauties, drawn this way and that, then the internal, pure wife will remain veiled from the khwaja. Whoever beholds a door to the World Beyond open and to whom God Most High reveals Himself is rendered helpless, as some have said, 'How great is My glory.'[141]

"Others can strive and struggle and cry, but God will not show them anything until they are favored by His special sight and are among those who are brought close to Him."

At these words, Majduddin bowed, overcome. He organized a sema for the dervishes, and distributed gifts to the Friends to express his gratitude.

May the Fire Not Burn You [428]

At the monastery of Plato on the outskirts of Konya there was a very wise elderly monk. Whenever the Friends went to the monastery, this monk would serve them in every way and demonstrate his faithfulness. He particularly loved Chelebi 'Arif.

One day, the Friends asked him to share with them the reason for this faithfulness, what he thought of Mevlana, and how he had met him. The monk responded:

> What do you all know of him? As for me, I saw him perform innumerable miracles and astonishing things, and I became his sin-

---

141. Bayazid al-Bastami, overcome by God's Presence, uttered: "How great is my glory!" See the story of the meeting of Shams and Mevlana, section #93 of this volume.

cere and faithful servant. I had read about the past prophets in the Gospel, and I saw the same qualities in his blessed person, and I had faith in his truth.

Once, Mevlana came to this monastery and made a retreat of about forty days here. When he emerged, I grasped his blessed robe and asked, "God on High has said in the glorious Qur'an with respect to the Fire: *And every one of you will enter into it: this is, with your Sustainer, a decree that must be fulfilled* [19:72]. Since we will all enter the fires of Hell, in what way will your religion be favored over my religion?"

Mevlana said nothing. After a few moments, he made a sign to me and headed back towards the city—I quietly followed in his footsteps. Suddenly, at the edge of the city, he went into a bakery where an oven was aflame. He took my cloak of fine black silk and wrapped it with his cloak, threw it into the oven, and then sat in a corner in contemplation for some time. Dense smoke came out, and no one could speak.

After a while, Mevlana said, "Look!" I saw the baker remove our Master's blessed cloak from the oven and put it around him. It was completely clean and unharmed, while my silk robe inside it had been completely burned and reduced to nothingness.

"This is how I will enter the Fire, and this is the way that you will enter it," he said.

I immediately bowed and became his disciple.

Aim for a Love That Is Real [429]

Kaluyan-i Naqqash and 'Ayn al-Doula, two Greek painters who excelled at their art in the representation of figures, had become disciples of Mevlana.

One day, Kaluyan mentioned, "In Constantinople, there is a painting in which the figures of Mary and Jesus have been depicted—it is without equal as are they. Painters from all over the world have come, but have not been able to reproduce such figures."

'Ayn al-Doula, moved by an intense desire to see this icon, soon set out and stayed for a year in the large monastery in Constantinople where it was; he served the monks who lived there. One night, when the opportunity opened, he put the painting under his arm and left. When he arrived in Konya, he went to visit our Master.

"Where were you?" he asked.

He related the story of the painting.

"Let's see this charming painting—it must be beautiful!" said Mevlana.

After having looked at it a long time, he said, "These two beautiful figures are complaining bitterly about you. They say, 'His love for us is not real; he is a false lover.'

"How is that?" asked 'Ayn al-Doula.

"They say, 'We don't sleep, and we never eat—we stay up all night and fast all day, while 'Ayn al-Doula has abandoned us—he sleeps at night and eats during the day; he doesn't accompany us.' "

"It is absolutely impossible for them to sleep and eat; they cannot speak. They are figures without a soul," said the painter.

Mevlana said, "You who are a figure with a soul, who possess so many skills, who were created by an Artist who created the entire universe, Adam and *all that is in the heavens and on earth,* how can it be that you have abandoned Him and have fallen in love with a painting without a soul or any insight? What benefit can come from these figures that are not conscious? What profit can you hope to get from them?"

Immediately 'Ayn al-Doula had a turning of heart, bowed, and embraced Islam.

Being Brought to God [430]

Shaikh Mahmud Sahib-Qiran told us the following:

There was a distinguished merchant whose son, a devoted lover of mysticism, asked for permission to become our Master's disciple. His father wouldn't allow it. At last, he held a large gathering and Mevlana cut the young man's hair.[142]

The merchant, who was a companion of Shaikh Awhad-i Khu'i, whispered in his ear, "Will my son reach God through his own efforts, or is it Mevlana who will convey him there?"

Awhaduddin, who was one of the devoted lovers of Mevlana, told the merchant not to ask such a question.

Mevlana overheard and said, "Let him speak; there is nothing wrong in it. I swear by God, this boy reached God first, and then he became my disciple. If the attraction of Divine favor had not pulled him, he would not have come running to our side."

Shaikh Awhaduddin let out a cry and tore his clothes, and then a magnificent sema began.

142. The cutting of the hair is a symbolic gesture indicative of an initiation. See also section #268 of this volume.

Coming into Unity [431]

Shaikh Mahmoud also told us the following:

In Sahib Isfahani's caravanserai, there was a very beautiful prostitute who had many female slaves working for her. Mevlana passed by there one day, and she ran towards him, bowed, and fell at his feet in sincere humility.

"O Rabi'a! Rabi'a!" Mevlana cried. The slave girls heard him, and they all ran out and fell at his feet.

"Bravo, O heroines," Mevlana cried, "Your great patience bearing this burden and efforts in subduing lustful desires has allowed the chastity of pure women to manifest itself."

One of the distinguished men of the era criticized him, saying, "It's not appropriate for a great man like him to occupy himself with prostitutes of the tavern and to flatter them this way."

Mevlana replied, "This woman walks about with one color, she shows herself as she really is, without hypocrisy. If you are a man, do the same and renounce duplicity, so that your exterior is the same color as your interior, because if it is not, it isn't worth anything."

In the end, this beautiful woman repented, as Rabi'a had, freed all her slaves, gave away her dwelling, and became one of the blessed of Paradise. Demonstrating her devotion, she rendered many services to the Friends.

Unbinding [432]

It is related that at the Aksaray gate there was a blind man of clear heart. One day, he was begging for bread, for the love of Mevlana. Akhi Qaysar's son, Akhi Chuban, was nearby. Just then, Mevlana passed by and threw his waistband to the blind man and then continued on his way.

"Take a hundred dirhems, and wrap that waistband around my waist," Akhi Chuban said to the blind man.

The blind man refused, "Even if you offered a thousand dinars, I would not give it up; I will bind it to my neck and take it to my grave."

He spent that night lamenting, crying out, "O Lord! For the sake of the waist around which this waistband was bound, deliver me from the ties of this place and receive my soul, so that I might quickly be freed from the bindings of this world."

At that moment, a voice was heard, "This blind man has been delivered from the bindings of this life and has become immersed in eternal life."

Akhi Chuban wrapped the belt of longing around him and arranged this poor man's funeral with great honors, doing all that was necessary to take care of his affairs and the performance of the mourning rites.

A Religion of Love [435]

The King of Teachers, the Heart of Men of the recent era, the Sea of Knowledge and Tradition, who could unite both fundamental and jurisprudential knowledge, Mevlana Zaynuddin 'Abd al-Mu'min of Toqat (May the Mercy of God be upon him), was a teacher of great scholars and unique among the men of Anatolia. He was called a second No'man, a Sea of 'Oman[143] of insight. Due to his awe and piety and his knowledge of legal decisions (*fatwa*) he was a second Abu Yusuf[144]. This humble servant (Aflaki) is one of his poor students. He told us the following story at an assembly of scholars in Toqat, in the medresse founded by the Parvana Mo'inuddin (May God bestow His forgiveness upon him):

In the time of our Master, I was in Konya as a Qur'an tutor under Mevlana Shamsuddin Mardini, at the medresse of Jalaluddin Qarata'i (May the Mercy of God be upon him). One day, a group of distinguished men were speaking in the presence of Shamsuddin Mardini about Mevlana and his illustrious heritage, remarkable personal qualities, his Muhammadan character, and marvellous miracles. The shaikh, in perfect sincerity, enthusiastically approved all that was said, and tears came to his eyes; everyone present also wept.

In the deepest recesses of my heart, I felt some reservation, asking myself why such a wise and great sovereign, who was such a scholar could involve himself in dances and the sema, and if he might not be authorizing acts contrary to religious law. Surely this behavior is not permitted under religious law. However, I kept my thoughts to myself.

The next morning, I happened by chance to meet Mevlana.

143. The Sea of 'Oman is another name for the vast Indian ocean.

144. Abu Yusuf, Yaqub bin Ibrahim, was the student and successor of Abu Hanifa (No'man bin Thabit), the great traditionalist and initiator of one of the primary schools of Islamic law. Abu Yusuf authored *Khitab al-Kharaj*.

Shamsuddin of Mardin arrived at the same time and bowed and kissed Mevlana's hand, and I followed my teacher's example.

Mevlana then turned to me and said, "O Master Zaynuddin, there is a question of law that I know you have studied: in the case of necessity and hunger which could lead to death, is it not permissible for a man to eat dead and unlawful things? Is this not permissible, so that human life might continue and not disappear and for the good of religion? This is the view which is established among the scholars. Now, for men of God there are circumstances and necessities which are similar to hunger and thirst and which can only be cured by semas, dances, melodic songs, and mutual ecstasy. Otherwise, the terror caused by Divine manifestations and the lights of God's Splendor would dissolve the blessed bodies of the saints and they would be reduced to nothing, like ice in the July sun.

To maintain this spiritual body,
the sun withdraws a moment from this snow.

"It is to this situation that the Prophet referred by saying, 'Speak to me, O dear red-complexioned one!'[145]

"Excuse us, because this desperate hunger and this pitiless thirst have become our kingdom. This abhorrent state is better than a lawful state, a bitterness perferable to sweetness, incredulity better than faith. Of this we have made the religion for lovers.

I am in the state in which you see me;
you know of what I lament.
There is a strong pull within my soul,
and I know who is attracting me;
I would like to rest, even for a moment, but I can't.

The ruin of lovers can't be restored,
nor can it be expressed in words.

Knowledge acquired at the medresse is one thing,
and love is something else."

Zaynuddin said, "The awe that Mevlana inspired in me caused me to fall into such an ecstasy that I lost consciousness for a long

---

145. "Humayra ('red-haired one' or 'red-complexioned one')" was Muhammad's name of endearment for 'Aisha, his beloved wife. When almost overwhelmed by love of the Divine, he would call out to her to speak to him. See also section #550 of this volume.

while. When I came to my senses, I bowed my head upon his blessed feet and asked forgiveness. In all sincerity, I became a disciple, as well as a lover of the sema to such an extent that it became my soul's complete nourishment."

All the scholars present agreed with him and their faith deepened through his sharing of the story.

Be a Story That Is Pleasing to Remember [437]

Sultan Walad told the following to Salahuddin Malati who told us:

At the end of his life, my grandfather (Bahauddin Walad), the Great Master (May God preserve his innermost secret), gave my father the following advice: "O Jalaluddin Muhammad, I am returning to God! I will be brought near the Lights of His Essence.

We are born of His Essence and to Essence we return.
O my friends! Pray for our journey.

"Those who return to the World Beyond, those who are directed to the Great Assembly, convey news to their predecessors about the morals and behavior of their successors and what has happened to them. O Great God (*Allahu Akbar*)! Make a great effort, so that I can be happy and glorious in His presence and that I might not be embarrassed and bow my head with shame. Put this advice in your ear like a golden earring:

Men are just stories,
so be a tale that is pleasing to remember."

My father did as he was told, even one hundred thousand times better; he eventually reached such a perfection that he said:

O my heart! Due to your dissolution and intoxication,
you don't speak the words of a father,
nor do you have the desires of a son.

You Are Health [438]

It was reported that Bahauddin Bahri had fallen seriously ill while visiting the hot springs, and no one thought he would live. Mevlana ordered that, wrapped in his night clothes, he be taken to the great pool in the center. There he immersed him in the water so many times it was impossible to keep count.

All the Friends had given up hope and remarked, "No doctor has ever prescribed such strange treatment for a patient! No one has ever seen anything like this!" But no one dared say anything; only the patient's son, Salahuddin, let out a cry.

Then our Master, himself, pulled Bahauddin from the water and told him to rest for a while. When Bahauddin got up, he asked for something to eat. He was completely cured and left, saying:

You are the remedy—when you arrive and reveal your face,
the army of troubles turns its back and disappears.

Stay Clear of Fools [439]

One day, our Master was sharing insights about those who are deniers and ill natured. He said:

A scorpion was walking on the edge of a stream. A turtle encountered him and asked him what he was doing.

"I am looking for a way to get to the other side, because all my family and my children are on the other side."

The turtle, full of compassion for this stranger, took him on his back, as if he were one of her own family, and began to swim along the surface of the water to the other side. When they got to the middle of the stream, the scorpion felt the desire to sting with his tail and began to strike on the shell of the turtle.

"What are you doing?" the turtle asked.

"I am showing my cleverness," replied the scorpion. "You demonstrated your generosity by easing my suffering, so I stung you—to show my kindness."

Immediately, the turtle dove under the water, and the worthless scorpion joined the snakes in Hell.[146]

Mevlana then recited this verse in Arabic:

Come on, kill this evil within you—hurry!
Don't leave it alive. For, surely, it's a scorpion.

And he also recited:

Even if a fool agrees with you,
through his stupidity he'll cause you trouble in the end.
The love of a fool is like that of a bear,
for whom hate is love and love, hate.

---

146. This ancient fable is related in *Kalilah wa Dimnah* by Ibn al-Muqaffa'.

Coming to Clarity [444]

The great companions related the following:

Khwaja Shamsuddin-i Attar (the druggist) (May God have mercy on him), was one of the disciples who had reached nearness with God and was one of the masters of the domes of the Infinitely Beneficent One. Sometimes he would drink wine, and when he was drunk he would speak of secrets and say miraculous things.

One day, completely drunk, he went to find Mevlana and asked him for a candle, a beautiful companion, and delicious food to eat. Mevlana ordered that he be taken to a cell and that a candle be placed in front of him. He brought his wife for him as the beautiful companion and prepared all sorts of sweetmeats. When Shamsuddin sobered up and he came back to his senses, he saw that he was in a cell of the medresse with a woman sitting beside him. Like one who is mad, he cried out, "What is happening?!"

His wife told him what had happened. He cried out and tore his clothes, cast earth over his head, and wept tears of blood. Mevlana took him in his arms, spoke kindly to him, and forgave him. Immediately, he prostrated in front of Mevlana and gave up all thought of drinking wine and living a wayward life and repented sincerely. For the rest of his life, he never again even ate during the day.

The One without Need Loves Our Need [445]

One day, while sharing divine insights, Mevlana said:

God Most High tells us, "I love the longing (*niyaz*) of My servants so much that if they did not reveal their suffering and abject state and supplicate Me, I would lift from them their wish to entreat Me. I would show them My need—My Majesty without need (*niyaz*) loves those who are in need."

A Bird of God [448]

Mevlana Ikhtiyaruddin, the imam (May God be satisfied with him), told us that one day, he quietly followed Mevlana as he went to Chelebi Husamuddin's garden. Ikhtiyaruddin swore under oath, in the name of God, the Most Glorious and Generous, that with his own eyes he saw Mevlana walk between heaven and earth, about one cubit above the ground:

"I fainted, and when I got up, Mevlana had gone on about his affairs. One day, in secret, he whispered to me, 'One must not be less than a bird, if one is a bird of God's Throne.

I am a bird in the Garden of Heaven;
I don't belong to this earth.
For these two or three days,
they've made a cage of this body for me.' "

No Fear for Provision [449]

Certain of the Friends who were poor were complaining about their lack of money and how tired they were. Mevlana told them this story:

In the time of Mustafa (Peace and blessings upon him) there was a terrible shortage of food. One of the Companions had a sack of barley flour. He complained to Muhammad, saying, "What is it possible to do now when life is so dear?"

"Sell your barley flour and trust in God," said the Prophet.

Following the direction of Muhammad, this Companion hoisted his flour onto his shoulder and began to auction off the flour among the Companions saying, "Who will buy a sack of barley flour?"

However, no buyer stepped forward.

One person said, "I have provisions for a month; that is enough for me."

"I have enough food for ten days," said another.

"I have enough for two days," replied a third. "When nothing more is left, there is always the Great Provider."

Then a poor man said in his turn, "I have only a mouthful, but tonight I will break my fast to eat. I do not need any provisions."

The Elect of God (May God's peace and blessing be upon him) had distributed alms—he had given to each one the strength to trust in God and not to be concerned about food, and enabled each of them to hold high their banners in the way of the kings of Truth.

The first companion was ashamed. The Prophet said to him, "You have enough provisions for two months, and still you are complaining! That's not acceptable—God won't give you gifts from His Abundance."

Immediately, the Companion gave the flour away as alms, repented, trusted in God, and was strengthened by spiritual nourishment.

Come on! Trust in God;
don't let your foot or your hand tremble.
Your daily bread is more in love with you
than you are with it.
If you don't rush, it will come to your door.
If you make haste, you'll get a headache.
You are not like those delicate beauties,
that they should keep you without nuts or raisins.

The Friends asked forgiveness, gave thanks, and found tranquility.

Turning Earth to Gold [450]

One day, Mevlana said, "Intelligent men have with great suffering and difficulty extracted gold and silver from the earth and from stone, and brought them to the surface, so that other people might enjoy them; while others make an opposite effort to hide gold and silver in the earth, so that no one might profit from it. In the end, they will leave this world naked and without provisions, and this fortune will be left as an inheritance for others.

At the end of your life, you will leave incomplete,
with your affairs in disorder and your bread unbaked.
You might, through enforced taxes, collect gold like sand,
but one day you will die. It will be left for someone else.

"One who transforms earth into gold is a true man, but he is also a man who transforms gold into earth," observed Mevlana. "Praise be to God! In both, we are champions:

We have learned from God the art of being human;
we are a hero of mystical love, a friend of Ahmad."[147]

Light Keeps Shining [451]

One day, Mevlana excused himself to the Parvana, saying:

The being of a dervish is like a ship on the sea of God's Power; he does not have control; at times, the winds toss the ship about where it may not wish to go. *For God always prevails in whatever His purpose may be* [12:21].

147. Ahmad, "The Highly-Praised One," is another name for the Prophet Muhammad ("The Praised One"), the "true human being" who is continually praising and giving thanks to God, sharing the radiance of Spirit.

Whoever contemplates the light contained in: *For, truly, God does what He wills* [22:18], will have no conflict in his heart and will have compassion for all creatures. A kind act done out of love for God, for His pleasure, is better than the light of the sun and the clarity of the moon. A benefactor's bones may go into the earth, but their light does not stay in the tomb. Try this—if you take the light of the sun and put it into a tomb, it will emerge; it will not stay there. This discourse has no end. Even so, the goodness of the valiant is like this. When a good man goes into the tomb, the light of his good acts and the brilliance of his good name still shine forth forever.

Goodness is like the sun,
it can't be hidden.

The Parvana bowed, and served the Friends in innumerable ways from that time on.

Customs of the Noble [452]

It is recounted that after our Master's death, a group of fanatical jurists and well-known ascetics of external devotion went beyond all bounds, and in the presence of the Parvana complained, "The sema is absolutely forbidden. We accepted Mevlana practicing it when he was alive, that was allowed for him, but now it seems that his followers have adopted this innovation in all seriousness and practice it openly. It is your duty to forbid such things; you must strongly oppose it."

The Parvana arose and went to see Shaikh Sadruddin and told him what had happened. That day, all the distinguished people of Konya were present at the meeting.

The Shaikh said, "If you accept my view, if you trust in the words of the dervishes, and if your faith in the great being of Mevlana is firm, I beg you, in the name of God, not to say anything, not to interfere. Ignore these ill-intentioned people, and do not oppose it, because to pay attention to them would be to turn away from the saints, and that would be unfortunate.

"Truly, the innovations of the perfect saints of God are like the customs (*sunnah*) of the noble prophets (Greetings of peace be upon them all). The saints know the wisdom that is behind such things; everything that flows from them is not without the command of the Almighty. And so it has been said, 'The good innovations that open from the Friends of God are like the illuminated customs established by the prophets (Greetings of peace be upon them).'"

The result of this conversation was that the Parvana rejected this disagreeable idea and asked forgiveness. The group of argumentative people dispersed, and they were never again able to gather themselves.[148]

Returning Home [453]

The Generous ones told us that one day our Master's wife (May God sanctify her innermost secret) said:

"Our Master should live three hundred years, no four hundred years, in order to fill the world with truths and insights!"

"Why? Why?" asked Mevlana. "We are not Pharoah or Nimrod. What do we have to do with this dusty place? How can we find a place of tranquility here? In order to deliver a few prisoners, we have been locked up here for a few days, in the prison of this world; one can only hope that we will soon return to the Beloved Friend.

What a difference between this earthly world
 and the Essence of Purity.
From where have we come? Pack your bags!
 What sort of place is this?!

"If it weren't a help for the situation of these unfortunate creatures, I would not have remained even a moment in this earthly world." Then he recited this noble verse:

I have stayed in the prison of this world only to be of benefit.

---

148. See the reflections of Shams of Tabriz regarding "Rats and Cats," *Rumi's Sun*, p. 250:

Many shaikhs are the waylayers of the religion of Muhammad. Like rats, they work to turn the house of this religion upside down. But there are also cats among the dear servants of God who work to clear away these rats. Even if hundreds of thousands of rats were to come together, they could not muster enough courage to even look at a single cat, because the majesty of the cat prevents them from being able to gather together. And cats are a community among themselves. If rats had the courage to gather, if they could join together and if a few self-sacrificing rats were among them, then the cat could catch one of them, and while he was occupied with it, the others could scratch the cat's eyes out, jump onto his head, and certainly could kill him. Or at least, they could escape. But the fear within them prevents them from gathering together. A rat is the symbol of dispersion, and a cat is the symbol of gathering.

Otherwise, for what reason would I be here?
Whose money did I steal?

During the days when he was preparing to leave this world, for three days and nights, he did not speak to anyone, and no one was able to speak to him.

Mevlana's wife came to him, bent down, and asked why he was so withdrawn, what was troubling him.

"I am considering death and what it will be like," he answered.

"See the souls of these lions in the forest, fearing their end;
at the sight of the Lion of Death, even lions piss blood."

She cried out and lost consciousness for some time.

During these days, he would walk about in contemplation in his blessed medresse, and would cry out and heave profound sighs. His cat was there then, and she would come towards him, mewing and crying.

Mevlana, smiling, said, "Do you know what this poor cat is saying? She is saying, 'You are about to depart for the sublime Kingdom, you are returning to your original homeland. I, poor one that I am, what will I do?' "

All the Friends cried out and fainted. After Mevlana's death, this cat would not eat or drink for seven days and nights, and then it died. Meleke Khatun, Mevlana's daughter, wrapped the cat in a shroud and buried it near Mevlana's blessed tomb; after that halvah was shared among the Friends.

No Shirt Left [455]

According to Chelebi Husamuddin, one day, Shaikh Sadruddin, accompanied by the distinguished dervishes, came to visit Mevlana during his illness.

Everyone displayed their affection for him, and the shaikh, painfully moved by the situation, said, "May God cure you right away, and may this be a blessed elevation. We can only hope that you make a full recovery. Our Mevlana is the soul of human beings, and his good health is a gift to us all."

Mevlana answered, "May your wishes for good health be for your own sake. Between lover and Beloved, there remains only a thin silk shirt—don't you want it to be removed and the light to be joined with the light?"

He said:

"Even if one's robe is of silk or Shoshtar cloth,
to embrace without a veil is more pleasing.
I have cast off my body; She has cast off imagination—
I am delighting in the completion of union."

The shaikh and his companions began weeping and departed. Mevlana recited this *ghazal* while all the dervishes cried out and rent their clothes:

What do you know of the Sovereign who keeps me company
in the world of secrets?
Don't look at my face of gold, for I have a foot of iron.
I turn my face completely towards this Sovereign
who brought me into this world,
and applaud a thousand times the One who created me.

Show Them the Moon [456]

One day, Mevlana gathered his most intimate Friends together and said:

"Don't be afraid of my departure, and don't be sad, because the light of Mansur al-Hallaj (May God be pleased with him) after one hundred and fifty years manifested itself to Fariduddin 'Attar (May the Mercy of God be upon him) and became his spiritual director.

"In whatever circumstances you might find yourself, remember me, so that I might show myself to you. Whatever clothes I might be wearing, I will always be with you, and I will pour into your hearts the currency of inspiration. Like our Sultan Muhammad, the Messenger of God (May the most perfect salutations be upon him), I say, 'My life is a blessing for you, and my death is also a blessing for you. My life is to bestow guidance, and my death is for Divine grace.'"

Then he said:

"In this world here below, I say, 'Show them the way.'
In the World Beyond, I say, 'Show them the moon.'"

The Friends cried out, bowed their heads, and wept profusely.

One Single Soul, One Attachment Remaining [457]

At the moment of Mevlana's death, Kira Khatun cried out and tore her clothes saying, "O light of the world! O soul of humanity! O mystery of this breath, this moment (*an dam*)! In whose hands do you place us, and where are you going?"

"Where am I going? In truth, I will not be outside your circle," he answered.

"Will there be another like our Master?" Kira Khatun asked.

"If there is," he answered, "He will also be myself."

And he added:

"There is only one single soul in the world;
it is ashamed of outer appearances.
This soul takes on a human form, but it is myself."

And he continued, "I have two attachments in this world, one for you and the other for my body. When through our Sovereign's grace, this body is stripped away and I become single, and the world of Unity reveals itself, this attachment for you will remain."

Parting Counsel [458]

It is said, also, that during the time Mevlana was confined to his bed, there was a terrible earthquake that lasted seven days and nights; the tremblings went beyond all bounds. Many houses and garden walls were demolished, and the world was turned upside down. At the seventh shaking, the Friends cried out and asked for help from God Most High.

"Yes, the poor earth wants a tasty morsel to eat, and we must give it to her," said our Master and then gave the following advice to the Friends:

"I recommend that you remain conscious of God (*taqwa*) in secret and in public, eat little, sleep little, speak little, and avoid comitting sins and errors. Fast assiduously, keep yourself upright, and renounce all lusts. Endure people's unjust behavior, but break off association with fools and rough people. Keep company with honest and generous people, because the best of human beings are those who are the most useful, and the best speech is that which is brief and gives guidance."

And he added:

"To turn away from earthly passions is the way of princes;
to abandon them completely is the power of prophets.

Praise be to God alone, and peace be upon him who witnesses His Oneness!"

O Refuge of My Soul [459]

Sirajuddin Tatari (May the Mercy of God be upon him), that theologian and dear Friend, told us that Mevlana, when he was departing from this world, called him near him and taught him the following prayer. He told him to say it continually, at times of ease as well as when times were difficult:

O Lord God! Through You I breathe; You are the refuge of my soul! O Lord God! I want Mevlana to be my intermediary who will bring me close to You; I ask that well-being might bring me near You, so that I might praise You continuously and mention Your Name always. O Lord God! Do not give me an illness that might make me forget You, or disturb my longing for You, or which might interrupt my delight in glorifying You, and neither give me good health that would make me rebellious and increase my pride and carelessness. By Your Mercy, O You Most Merciful of the merciful!

A Real Treasure [460]

At a sema, a dervish of enlightened heart was hoping to ask Mevlana, "What is poverty?"

Just then, in the midst of the sema, Mevlana recited the following quatrain:

Poverty is the substance and anything else the accident.
Poverty is health—anything else is disease.
The entire world is trickery and pride;
poverty, rather than this world, is the treasure, the aim.

The dervish wept and fell to the ground at Mevlana's feet, declaring himself a sincere disciple.

A House in Ruins Lets in the Light [463]

The theologian and man of poverty, Ikhtiyaruddin the Imam (May the Mercy of God be upon him), the glory of God's servants, reported that Chelebi Husamuddin said:

The last day of Mevlana's life, I was seated at his blessed bedside;

our Master, my spiritual director, was leaning against me.

Suddenly, a very beautiful man appeared, and his spiritual nature was apparent. His gracious beauty was so marvellous that I lost consciousness. Mevlana got up and received him with honor, and asked for the bedding to be put away. This young man stayed there for a while, so I went to him and asked him who he was, and what he wanted.

"I am Azrael, the Angel of Resolution and Decision. I have come on the orders of the Most High to ask what Mevlana will command. Happy are the clear eyes able to see such a form! Such was the pure sight that could behold the Supreme Being."

While overcome by this awesome sight, I heard Mevlana say:

"Come closer, O my soul!
O Messenger from my Sovereign's court!

Do as you are ordered;
you will find me, if God so wills, among those who are patient
in adversity [37:102]."

He asked for a bowl of water into which he submerged his blessed feet. From time to time he would put some of the water on his chest and wipe his blessed forehead, saying:

"When the Beloved brought us a cup full of poison,
we drank it joyfully,
since it was from His hand.
Our body might be under the earth,
but our heart is above the sky.
Although we might seem dead, in reality, we have come to life.
The soul is like a pure mirror, and the body is like dust upon it;
when we're covered with dust, our beauty isn't so apparent.
Surely, both these abodes are His dominion.
Serve Him and be happy, as we have also served."

Once again he rubbed water on his forehead and chest, saying:

"If you are a true and sweet believer, death will be truly sweet,
if you are bitter and in denial, death will also be like that."

This is how we were when the reciters arrived, and began reciting the following quatrain:

Far from you, the heart becomes resentful,
due to its own weakness, when far from you.

Bitterness is in the mouth of every bilious heart;
far from you, even sugar burns with envy towards you.

The Friends cried out, wept, and moaned.

"Yes, the Friends are upset, but what good is it, since the house is already in ruins?" our Master asked.

"See my ruined heart, and look kindly on me;
the sun shines kindly on such ruins.

Our Friends call to me from this side, and our Master Shamsuddin calls me from the other side. *Respond to God's Messenger's call, and have faith in Him* [46:30]. It is time to go.

All of this existence emerged from nothingness;
once again it is captured in nothingness.

The Divine Order is this way eternally;
Judgment belongs to God, the Most High, the Magnificent [40:12]."

They say that Sultan Walad, as a result of his service and concern for Mevlana, had become very thin and weak from lack of sleep. He cried out, wept, tore his clothes, and refused to sleep.

That night, Mevlana said, "O Bahauddin, I am fine. Go and rest for a while."

After Sultan Walad bowed and left, Mevlana recited the following *ghazal* which Chelebi Husamuddin wrote down:

Go, rest your head and leave me alone;
I am ruined, let me wander tonight in my pain.
All night we are alone with this troubling passion,
all night until dawn.
If you wish, come and be merciful, or go and torment me.
The King of all Beauties is not compelled to be faithful.
O pale-faced lover, be patient and faithful!
Overwhelming, His heart is unbreakable like stone—
He kills, and no one tells Him, "Pay the blood price."
Death is the only remedy for such longing;
so how can I tell Him, "Cure this pain"?
Last night, in a dream, I saw an old man in the street of Love;
he beckoned to me, saying, "Come to us!" . . . .

This was the last *ghazal* he composed.

Everyone Loves the Sun [464]

The Sultan of the Knowers of God, Chelebi 'Arif (May God sanctify his innermost secret) told us the following:

When Mevlana's sacred spirit returned to the Presence of Divine Majesty beyond compare, Mevlana Ikhtiyaruddin, the Mevlevi Imam, who was an angel incarnate, was present.

"I placed the silken body of our Master on the bier and began to wash him with complete respect, great reverence and awe," said Ikhtiyaruddin. "The intimate Friends poured the water over him, and before it would fall to the ground, they would drink every drop, just as did the companions of the Prophet (Peace and blessings upon him). When I put my hand on his blessed chest, Mevlana suddenly moved. I cried out and my face fell to his chest and I wept. Just then, he grasped my ear with his right hand so tightly that I fainted. It was as if to say, 'Don't breathe and don't be so bold.' Overwhelmed, I remained bewildered.

"I heard a mysterious voice which said, '*The Saints of God have no fear or sorrow* [10:63]. The truly faithful don't die but are transported from one dwelling to another.'

Azrael has no power over, nor access to, the lovers;
it is love and passion that pulls lovers.

"When they carried his body outside on the bier, all the distinguished and everyone present uncovered their heads; men, women, and children lamented so loudly that it seemed as though it were Resurrection Day. Everyone followed the bier, crying loudly, tearing at their clothes until they were half-naked. Members of all the different religious communities and nations were there: Christians, Jews, Greeks, Arabs, Turks and others, each carrying aloft their sacred books. From each tradition, they read verses, from the Psalms, the Pentateuch, and the Gospels, and mourned aloud. The Muslims were not able to contain the crowd with their staffs and swords; the gathering could not be dispersed.

"News of the great uproar was brought to the Sultan and the Parvana, his minister. The chief monks and priests were summoned and asked what this had to do with them, since this sovereign of religion was an imam and guide for those of Islam. 'Knowing him, we understood the truth of Jesus and that of Moses and all the prophets. We witnessed in him the behavior of that of the perfect prophets, as described in our books. If you Muslims can say that he was the Muhammad of your time, we recognize him as the Moses and Jesus of our time. Just as you are his sincere companions, we are a thousand times more his servants and disciples. He said the following:

> Seventy-two sects hear from us their secrets;
> we are like a flute, with one note, in harmony
> with two hundred religions.

"'Mevlana was the sun of Truth which shone on human beings and granted them its grace; all the world loves the sun, which illuminates everyone's house.'

"Another Greek priest said, 'Mevlana is like bread, which is needed by everyone; have you ever seen a starving person run away from bread? And you, what do you really know of him?'

"All the distinguished fell quiet and did not say a word. Then, from another direction, numerous *hafiz* began to softly recite marvellous verses of the Qur'an; a sorrowful murmur of mourning arose, and sweet-voiced muezzins called the faithful to prayer as though it were the Resurrection. Twenty groups of excellent singers sang the funeral songs that Mevlana had himself composed. The sound of drums, flutes, and trumpets raised a great noise, as though announcing the good news of: *When the trumpet-call of Resurrection is sounded* [74:8].

"Early in the day, we took the coffin from the blessed medresse and began to walk. It fell into pieces six times during the procession, and each time a new one was constructed. When we finally arrived at the illuminated tomb, night had fallen."

Leaving the World of Separation [465 and 466]

Chelebi Husamuddin had asked our Master, "Who will say the funeral prayer for you?"

"Shaikh Sadruddin would be best," was the answer.

All the great scholars and qadis wanted to say the prayer, but this favor was reserved for that unique person, Sadruddin (Konevi).

Chelebi Husamuddin also told us the following:

The Qadi Sirajuddin came to visit our Master, who was ill. I was holding the cup containing a potion, and offered it to him so that he might moisten his lips, but he paid no attention to it. I gave the cup to the qadi in the hopes that he would accept it from him, but he didn't.

The qadi left, and I saw Shaikh Sadruddin enter. He took the cup from me and offered it to our Master, who then drank a little and gave it back to him.

"Alas, what will become of us without our Master's blessed existence?" asked Sadruddin.

"After us, you, too, will leave the world of separation and be brought to the world of union, and reach your true goal," Mevlana answered.

May God Sanctify His Mystery [467]

Mevlana (May God sanctify his precious mystery) was transported from the world of dominion (*mulk*) to the world of the Heavenly Realms (*malakut*) on Sunday at sunset, on the 5th of Jumada'l Akhar of the year 672 A.H. (December 17, 1273 C.E.).

> This king of pure thought has gone to that country of Light,
> dancing as he goes.

Greetings from a Friend [472]

Bahauddin Bahri (May the Mercy of God be upon him) told us that, one day, Chelebi Husamuddin (May God sanctify his pure mystery) said:

Seven years had passed since the death of my shaikh, and I hadn't seen him in a dream. I looked for him in that other world, realm by realm, but had not been able to find him, and no one could give me a sign of him, for he had no signs.

> Who would look for a sign of you, since you have no sign?
> Who will find your place, since you have no place?

Not knowing what to do, my strength was waning. Suddenly, one day when I was walking in the garden, I saw that the door of the ninth heaven opened:

"O Chelebi Husamuddin, how are you?" I heard our Master say.

I saw nothing more. However because of the grace in this blessing of this majesty without qualities asking, "How are you?", I have for years been plunged in contemplation of that Being beyond compare.

And Chelebi added:

> "There are thousands of assemblies beyond,
> but this assembly is even more beyond,

because it is even more without a sign
within this world that has no sign."

Sharing Secrets [473]

The dear Friends told us that, one day, a distinguished person asked Mevlana (May God sanctify his precious mystery), "During the night of Muhammad's ascension,[149] what secrets did God share with Muhammad and what secrets did Muhammad share with Him? What happened between them?"

"The Creator (May his Power be exalted and His word be magnified) conveyed seventy thousand secrets full of light to Muhammad, peace and blessings upon him," Mevlana answered. "Then He said, 'According to your choice, you may reveal thirty-five thousand of these mysteries to whomever you wish among your intimate friends; hide the other thirty-five thousand, and don't tell them to any of the good and pious.'"

"The Prophet told his noble Companions some of the secrets. He conveyed ten thousand to the ear of the Caliph 'Ali (May God ennoble his countenance); and the rest he hid in the deepest part of his secret inwardness.

"But, one day, he heard the brothers of purity (*safa*) and the loyal (*vafa*) Companions speaking of the secrets that he had kept hidden from humankind: 'Who told you these secrets; where does this knowledge come from?' he asked.

"'The same one who ordered you not to speak of them and to keep them hidden—He told us without an archangel or a prophet as an intermediary.'"

And so Mevlana said:

"Unknown to Gabriel, the trustworthy,
I have another Gabriel who is trustworthy.

The Prophet's amazement grew a thousand times greater when he realized their proximity to God and His acceptance of them, and his

149. *Al-Mi'raj* is the ascension of the Prophet Muhammad through the heavens into the Presence of God. It is recounted that during a very difficult time in the life of the Prophet, he was resting in prayer one night near the Kaaba in Mecca when he was transported to Jerusalem and from the Dome of the Rock, mounted upon the angelic steed, Buraq, and accompanied by Gabriel, lifted into close proximity with God. He then journeyed on beyond the lote tree, two bow lengths or nearer, into the very Presence of God. (See surah 17 and surah 53.)

affection for them increased.

"Thanks be to God, the Supreme Truth has allowed us to know secrets which the brothers of purity would long to know and by which they would be overwhelmed."

As Mevlana said,

Be quiet, so that if I am permitted, at my last breath,
I will tell you a secret that even the brothers of purity
were never told.

Mevlana continued, "When the Caliph 'Ali was overcome by these secrets and the lights that appeared from them, crying out and overwhelmed, he went out into the desert. He put his head into a well and cried out into it, sighing deeply. He spoke his innermost insights; deep in ecstasy, he cried out, 'Even if the veil were lifted, my certainty could not be greater.' "[150]

Devotion Is Recognized [475]

It is also recounted that Mevlana had a student, a Friend of God, named Nizham Khatun, who was an intimate friend of Fakhrunnisa. She wanted to put on a sema for Mevlana and to serve the Friends. She possessed nothing other than a veil from Bura in Egypt that she was keeping to use as a shroud for her funeral. She told her servants to sell it in order to host the sema.

The next morning, Mevlana came to Nizham Khatun's house and called out to her: "O Nizham Khatun, though you may be poor, don't sell your veil, because you need it. See! We have come for your sema."

The sema began in her home and lasted three days and nights.

There Is No Longer Anyone in This House [478]

One day, in his blessed medresse, Mevlana, transported by the sema, gave away all his clothes to those present and danced unclothed except for his long shirt. Then his shirt became untied, and Chelebi Husamuddin quickly jumped up and put his own cloak around him, and the sema continued. Mevlana was in a state of ecstasy for three

---

150. The secrets shared by Muhammad which Ali spoke into the well grew into a reed nearby which was then fashioned into a reed flute (*ney*) through which these secrets were expressed. It is in remembrance of this that Mevlana begins his *Mathnawi*, "Listen to the reed!" [*Mathnawi* I:1] For more details, see section #350 and #593 of this volume.

days and nights due to this divine intoxication and composed this *ghazal*:

As a result of my drunkenness and dissolution,
I can no longer distinguish water from earth.
I can no longer find anyone in this house.
If you are sober, perhaps you can find someone here.
I know this, the gathering is held on your behalf,
but I don't know if wine or meat is served.
On the inside, you are the soul of my soul of my soul,
and on the outside, you are the sun of the sun! . . .

To Be in the Company of the Saints [481]

There was in Konya, an eminent person known as Tadjuddin Motasadder (he who sits in the honored place), and he was indeed used to sitting in the place of honor and was in the habit of dominating gatherings. He absolutely denied the existence of saints and refused to recognize Mevlana, or to accept the company of the Friends united through the Heart.

One night, Tadjuddin had a terrifying dream in which he saw himself at the door of Hell, and in this dream, he saw what it is like. He saw a damned person being taken in irons and shackles from one place in Hell to another. There, four people said, "Miserable good-for-nothing, recite what the saints have said, if you wish to be delivered from this heavy and painful burden."

The condemned man pleaded with them to be taught some of the saints' words. They taught him some of Mevlana's verses, and when he had recited these verses, his chains and shackles fell off, and he went on his way to Paradise with the breezes of felicity.

Tadjuddin woke up and ran to Mevlana's medresse.

Mevlana came towards him saying, "O Master Tadjuddin, this unhappy person has been delivered from the flames of Hell and has reached the Kingdom of eternal delights as a result of our blessing. The words of the Friends of God can bestow great blessing on those who call to them for help, but to be in their pure company is even greater; imagine where one might arrive through the blessings of their love."

Tadjuddin bowed and, along with his wife and children, declared himself a disciple and faithful servant.

Under His Protection [485]

The King of the chivalrous (*fityan*), Akhi Ahmad Shah (May God have mercy on him), the chief of the Akhis of Konya was an exceptional man. He was wealthy and lived a comfortable life. He commanded thousands of debauched soldiers. He told us the following and it has become part of the oral tradition:

After Mevlana's death, the Mongol sovereign, Keyghatu Khan, entered Konya at the head of a large and well-equipped army. Nearly fifty thousand men camped on the plain that surrounded the city and were about to destroy and pillage this capital of the Seljuks and massacre the inhabitants.

One night, in a dream, Keykhatu Khan dreamed that Mevlana grasped him tightly by the throat and, almost strangling him, cried, "Konya belongs to us. What business do you have with our people?"

Keykhatu Khan woke up in a very agitated state and sought forgiveness. He wondered what this dream meant and sent an ambassador to ask to be permitted to enter the city, to bathe, and to tell the dream to the eminent men of the city.

Accompanied by Akhi Ahmad Shah, they brought him to Sultan Walad and told him what had happened. Sultan Walad gave Keykhatu Khan permission to visit the city with two or three thousand Mongols soldiers, but not to take possesion of it.

When Keykhatu Khan arrived at the royal palace, all the notables of the city came and brought him unusual gifts. Then Akhi Ahmad Shah arose, and along with several young men, presented Keykhatu Khan with a very ornate belt studded with precious stones, some fine horses, and numerous other rare gifts. Akhi Ahmad Shah then had an audience alone with him and after kissing his hand, sat facing him.

"Father Akhi, who is the person sitting beside you?" Keykhatu Khan asked, quite agitated.

"Actually, I am alone; I see no one else," replied Akhi Ahmad Shah.

"What?! What are you saying? I see a man of medium height, with grey hair and a pale face, and a brown turban on his head, with Indian cloth over his shoulder. And he is looking at me in a very penetrating way," replied the emperor.

Then Akhi, with his great insight, understood that this was the figure of Mevlana and answered, "O sovereign of the world, your Majesty is looking at a great Sultan, the son of Bahauddin Walad of

Balkh, our Master Jalaluddin, whose body rests in this land."

"Yesterday, I had a dream that he grabbed me by the throat and told me that this city belonged to him. Now, O Akhi, I declare that you are like my father. I renounce the terrible plans I had and repent. I will not harm the people of Konya. Does this sovereign of the World of Knowers have any successors, any family?" asked Keykhatu Khan.

"Yes, his son, Bahauddin Walad, is the shaikh of our city; there is no man of God in the world equal to him, and he is the sovereign of the adepts of mysticism and gnosis," Akhi answered.

"Then, it is our duty to visit him," said the Emperor.

Keykhatu Khan then went with his courtiers and Akhi Ahmad Shah to visit Sultan Walad. He was so impressed with the profundity and elegance of Sultan's Walad's teaching that in goodwill and all sincerity of soul he declared himself a disciple.

Sultan Walad put the Mevlevi *sikke* on his head[151] and took a special interest in him. He told him about the difficulties his grandfather, Bahauddin Walad, had had in Balkh, the Kharazm-Shah's ingratitude, and the events which followed. Everyone then went to visit the sacred tomb, and Sultan Walad began a sema which continued until the time of the noon prayer. He kept reciting the following quatrain:

> Leave the world be—it doesn't belong to you;
> when you enter it, it's not by your command.
> If you happen to gain wealth, don't take pride in it;
> and your life—remember, it doesn't belong to you.

The Emperor Keykhatu Khan's eyes were wet with tears of joy; he kissed Sultan Walad's hand and returned home content. The people of Konya renewed their sincere devotion and their service.

151. It is part of the initiation ceremony for a Mevlevi dervish to have the shaikh place the *sikke* on his head. The tall felt hat (*sikke*) that is characteristic of Mevlevi dervishes is representative of the tombstone of the ego.

Chapter IV
Shams of Tabriz

The deeds of the Sultan of the Poor, God's Secret among humankind, perfect in state (*hal*) and in word (*qal*), Mevlana Shams al-Haqq w'al Din Muhammad bin 'Ali bin Malakdad at-Tabrizi (May God sanctify his innermost secret).

The Strength of the Sun [486]

It is reported that one day Mevlana Shamsuddin Tabrizi said:

"When I was in school, and not yet an adult, sometimes I would go thirty or forty days without eating, because the way of Muhammad inspired such love in me. If they even mentioned food, I would hide my hands and my face.

"Yet, if the inhabitants of the habitable quarter of the world are on one side and I am on the other, I would respond to them; I would not give up speaking; I do not jump from branch to branch. The habitable quarter is the space where men live; the other three-quarters is uninhabitable because of the consuming strength of the sun.

"When one speaks of a difficulty, I give answer upon answer, response after response. My words hold ten answers or proofs for each one."

May Your Name Be a Remedy [487]

One day, Mevlana said, "The wise of the exoteric world know our Prophet's traditions, but Mevlana Shamsuddin (May God magnify his mention) knows our Prophet's mysteries (Peace and blessings upon him), and in me his lights are manifest (Peace be upon him).

O Shams-i Tabrizi!
You comprehend the Prophet's mysteries;
may your sweet name be a remedy
for those who have fallen in love!"

No One Can Describe You [488]

Those spiritual directors (*pirs*) of the past, told us the following:

The adepts of the mystical path and true knowers of God of Tabriz called Shamsuddin "the Perfect Man (*kamal*) of Tabriz'. Certain mystic travelers called him "Shamsuddin the Flyer (*perande*)," because of the miraculous ability he had to rise above the earth, to fly from place to place.[152] At the beginning of his training, he was a disciple of Shaikh Abu Bakr of Tabriz, otherwise known as Sellabaf, the basket-maker (May God have mercy on him).

Later, when his mystical training and the perfection of his ecstatic states went beyond the limits of human perception, he set out on his travels in search of the most perfect man of God and the most excellent of teachers. He traveled to all regions of the earth in search of the men of God, *traveling through the land seeking of God's bounty* [73:19].

He contemplated them all in obedience to: "The earth has been gathered for me, and I have been shown its places of rising and setting. The kingdom of my community extends to the east and the west, on land and sea, near and far."

Shamsuddin of Tabrizi visited many *abdals*, *autads*, and *qutbs*, those veiled ones on the path of blame, adepts of meaning and of form, and other learned individuals, but he found no one who could meet his vastness. The spiritual directors whom he met became his servants and disciples.

He continued to travel and search for the Beloved. Then, he concealed the blessed mirror of his existence in felt clothing and disappeared from view, into the world of mystery and the veiled domes of divine ardor.

Mevlana spoke of him like this:

Our Master's cheeks amaze the beauty of a Joseph,
even though he was the most beautiful of all mankind.
The day birds cannot bear his rays,
how could the night birds wish to see him?

O you, whom Adam and his descendants
have not seen, even in a dream,
whom should I ask to describe your beauty?

---

152. *Tayyi zamin* is the capacity he had to rise in the air and to be transported long distances from place to place, a recognized gift granted to certain advanced saints.

I have asked everyone, and no one can describe you.

Keeping Company with the Sun [488b]

Shamsuddin wore clothing of black felt, and everywhere he went he would stay at a caravanserai. After this Friend, soul of the world, had journeyed from place to place around the world, from station to station, he arrived in Baghdad, that abode of peace.

There he happened to meet Shaikh Awhaduddin Kirmani (May the Mercy of God be upon him).

"What are you doing?" Shamsuddin asked the shaikh.

"I am looking at the moon, in this dish of water."

"If you don't have a boil on your neck, why don't you look at it in the sky? Find a doctor to cure you, so that you'll be able to see the real object of sight in everything you gaze upon."

"From now on, let me be in your service," replied the shaikh with longing.

"You wouldn't have the strength to bear my company," answered Shamsuddin.

The shaikh persisted, "Oh please, accept me."

"On one condition—that in full public view, in the middle of the Baghdad bazaar, you drink wine with me."

"I cannot," was the answer.

"Then bring me some wine."

"I cannot," he responded.

"Then at least keep me company while I drink," said Shamsuddin.

"I cannot."

"Then be gone from real men! As it says in the Qur'an: *Did I not tell you that you will never be able to have patience with me* [18:74]?[153] You are too weak and powerless to be an intimate friend of God or to keep me company. So it is not your work to keep me company; you are not a man of my companionship. You must sell for a cup of wine all the disciples and the honor of this world—this is the work of the men of the arena, that of those who know. I don't take disciples. I will take a shaikh, but not just any shaikh, only the one who is perfect and has attained the Truth."

In spite of Awhaduddin's pleas, Shamsuddin refused to accept

153. This is the response of the Prophet Khidr to Moses when he failed the test that Khidr had set him, continuing to question Khidr's actions. See *Surah al-Kahf*, 18:60-82.

him. "You cannot be my spiritual companion, only the son of Bahauddin Walad of Balkh (May God sanctify his power and mystery)," he said.

Much later, Shamsuddin of Tabrizi met Mevlana in the public square in Damascus. At that time, Mevlana was involved in his religious studies.

The Meeting of Two Seas[154] *[489]*

It is conveyed by the old Friends skilled in sailing the Ocean of attainment of Reality:

On the 26th of Jumada al-Akhar 642 A.H. (November 29, 1244 C.E.), Mevlana Shamsuddin arrived in Konya, the capital of the Seljuks, and went to stay at the caravanseriai of the sugar-sellers. Mevlana was, at that time, a professor of religious studies in four important medresses. The great scholars would accompany him on foot, walking beside his stirrups.

They likewise recount that, one day, Mevlana left the medresse of the cotton merchants riding on a mule, accompanied by various worthy scholars walking beside him. As they passed in front of the sugar merchants caravanserai, Shamsuddin appeared out of a doorway and seized our Master's bridle.

"O Imam of Muslims, who was greater Abu Yazid Bastami or Muhammad?" he asked.

Mevlana later told us: "Due to the awesomeness of his question, it seemed as though the seven heavens had split apart, one from the other, and had fallen to the earth. I felt an immense fire rise in my body to the top of my head and saw smoke rise from this spot to the foot of the heavenly Throne."

Mevlana replied, "Muhammad, the Messenger of God is the greatest of mortals; what is Abu Yazid in comparison?"

"Then why, in spite of his greatness, would the Prophet say, 'We have not known You as we should have,' while Abu Yazid said, 'How exalted I am! How great is My dignity! I am the Sultan of Sultans!' "

---

154. See another version of their meeting in sections #83-94 of this volume. The place of their meeting in Konya, situated on a corner of the current *Mevlana caddesi* (Mevlana street) not far from the mosque of Shams of Tabriz, is referred to as the place of "the meeting of two seas," in reference to the meeting of Khidr and Moses (*Surah al-Kahf* 18:60-65), and acknowledgment of the vast Sea of Meaning flowing through each of them.

Mevlana answered, "Abu Yazid's thirst was satisfied with one sip, and the jug of his understanding was full; the light he received was proportionate to the opening of his heart. However, when the Elect of God was seeking water, his was thirst upon thirst. His blessed chest had become that *vast plain of God* [4:97] through: *Have we not opened up your heart* [94:1]? He continued to thirst, and every day his yearning for proximity with God increased. Of the two claims, our Prophet's is the greater. When Abu Yazid found God, he was satisfied and did not look beyond, while the Elect of God (May Peace be upon him) advanced further every day. He saw, day by day, hour by hour, the Divine lights and the magnificence and power of Divine Wisdom increase. For this reason, he said, 'We have not known You as You deserve to be known.'" . . .

Immediately, Mevlana Shamsuddin cried out and fell to the ground. Mevlana got down off his mule and told the imams to depart. Mevlana held Shamsuddin's head on his knee until he came to himself and then, taking his hand, they left for our Master's medresse. They spent a long time together there as companions, sharing spiritual conversation.

Mysteries in Seclusion [490]

Mevlana and Shamsuddin did not leave the retreat cell for three entire months, day and night, observing continual fasting. No one had the audacity to interrupt them. Mevlana stopped his professorial duties, teaching, and sermons, and spent his time in contemplation of this greatest saint.

All the important people of Konya were in an uproar, demanding to know what was happening, who this person was and where he came from. They wanted to know why Mevlana had renounced his old friends, his devoted family and honored position, and was occupied with him. Such a great person, who was himself the son of a great saint, how could he be taken away by one person?

Burning in bewilderment, various people said all sorts of stupid and ridiculous things but remained powerless before this Truth. Even the disciples who were close to Mevlana didn't know what sort of person Shamsuddin was.

It was during this revelatory time in seclusion that Mevlana Shamsuddin offered a hundred thousand marvelous questions and answers, precisely to the point. Such a spiritual immersion and conversation had never been seen or heard from any shaikh or *qutb*.

Offer Everything [491]

That Sultan of Mystics, Chelebi 'Arif (May God sanctify his innermost secret) told us this anecdote which Sultan Walad (May God magnify his memory) had told him:

As a test and a trial, Mevlana Shamsuddin Tabrizi asked my father for a servant. My father took by the hand his wife, Kira Khatun, who was, in her perfection, the most beautiful and gracious woman of the epoch—she was a second Sarah and the Mary of her time because of her chastity and virtue—and he brought her to him. However, Shamsuddin said, "She is my soul sister. It wouldn't be appropriate. A gentle young man would be better."

Immediately, Mevlana brought his own son, Sultan Walad, who was as beautiful as Joseph. "We can only hope that he is worthy to bring you your shoes."

"He is my dear son," said Shamsuddin. "Now, if there is a way of procuring some wine, I will drink it instead of water, since I can't do without it."

Immediately, my father left. I saw him go, himself, to the Jewish quarter, fill a jug, carry it back, and place it before the eyes of Shamsuddin. Shamsuddin cried out, tore his clothes and bowed his head upon my father's feet. Overwhelmed by Mevlana's strength of soul and obedience, he said, "I swear by God, the First who has no beginning and the Last who has no end, that from the beginning of the world until its end, there has never been, nor will there ever be, a heart-ravishing Sultan with a character like Muhammad's such as you!"

Then he bowed and became his disciple, saying, "I wanted to reveal the extent of Mevlana's forbearance; his vast inwardness goes beyond the limits of speech."

O my son, there are a hundred thousand tests
for one who claims to be a leader.

Speech falls silent, for how could it describe him?
How can that which perishes ever encompass
    that which has no end?

Even if every hair on my body became a tongue,
I couldn't describe a single one of your thousand graces.

Diving into Spirit [492-493]

The old companions and noble Friends (May God be pleased with them all) told us that Mevlana said:

As soon as our Master Shamsuddin reached me and engaged in spiritual conversation with me, immediately the fire of love burst into flame in my heart. In complete command, he told me, "Don't read your father's words any more!" Following his orders, I stopped for some time. Then he told me, "Do not speak to anyone!" And for some time I kept silence. However, my words had been a source of spiritual nourishment for the Friends and mystical lovers and wine for their pure spirits. Without them, the Friends became intensely thirsty. Through the energy of their aspirations and complaints the evil eye fell upon Mevlana Shamsuddin."

The Friends of Certainty and True Lovers told us that at the beginning of our Master's spiritual journey he studied Bahauddin Walad's words in depth. Shamsuddin came in the door, and three times told Mevlana, "Don't read them! Don't read them!" The source of transcendent wisdom opened, bubbling up in his blessed heart, and he no longer concerned himself with his father's words.

Setting Books Aside [494]

It is reported that when Mevlana first met Mevlana Shamsuddin, he used to read the *divan* of Motanabbi[155] at night.

"You are wasting your time," Shamsuddin told him. "Don't read it anymore."

Even though he said this once or twice, Mevlana continued reading it, and was very absorbed in it. One night, while he was carefully reading it, he fell asleep and dreamed that he was having an intense discussion with the scholars and jurists, and that he won the argument. Then, in the same dream, he regretted what he had done, asking himself, "Why did I do that? Was it necessary?" He went to leave the medresse.

At that moment, he awoke and saw Mevlana Shamsuddin enter. Mevlana Shamsuddin said to him, "Did you see what you have done to these poor jurists? All this difficulty comes from your reading Motanabbi's *divan*."

155. Ahmad ibn al-Husayn Abu al-Tayyib al Jufi al Kindi al-Motanabbi (d. 965 C.E.), born in Kufu, was one of the most renowned classical Arab poets.

It is recounted that another night, Mevlana had another dream in which he saw Mevlana Shamsuddin holding Motanabbi by the beard. He led him to Mevlana and said, "Do you actually read this man's writing?"

A thin and feeble-looking man, Motanabbi pleaded, "Deliver me from Shamsuddin and don't disturb my *divan* again."

Eventually, Mevlana renounced religious studies and teaching, put a red turban on his head, his cloak from India over his shoulders, and began to practice austerities and the sema. As he said,

In all the land, I was the foremost ascetic and preacher.
My heart's destiny made me a lover celebrating you.

Be Watchful of Your Tongue [495]

Mevlana Shamsuddin traveled one day from Kayseri to Aksaray and arrived at a mosque there.

After the night prayer, the muezzin said sternly, "Leave the mosque and find somewhere else to stay."

"Forgive me, I am just a stranger and want nothing. Please let me rest," said Shamsuddin.

The foolish muezzin, out of ignorance, treated him badly.

"May your tongue swell," said Shamsuddin as he left the mosque and departed for Konya.

The imam of the mosque arrived to find the muezzin in his death agony with a swollen tongue and asked him what had happened. The muezzin managed to ask him to go and look for the traveling dervish who had left him in this terrible state.

The imam followed in Shamsuddin's footsteps and caught up with him at the river of Qalqal. The imam bowed and begged him, "He is a miserable one who did not recognize your greatness," making sincere apologies.

"*It has been determined*; the judgment has been brought down. However, I will pray that he dies as one who is faithful and is not chastised in the next world," said Shamsuddin.

The imam was a man of enlightened heart whose faith was sincere, and he became a disciple. When he returned to the mosque, the muezzin was dead.

Roses from the Unseen [496]

The knower of God gifted with the light of dawn, Sirajuddin Tatari

(May God have mercy upon him) recounted that Mevlana told him the following:

In the midst of a terrible winter, Shamsuddin was having a conversation with the intimate Friends; they were seated in a secluded corner. One of the dear ones expressed the longing for a bouquet of roses. Shamsuddin got up and went outside, and then returned carrying a beautiful bouquet of roses which he placed before him. Everyone bowed.

"This isn't a miracle," he said. "This comes in response to the request of the Friends. In response to your sincere devotion, God has sent this gift from the invisible world."

Sometimes, Mevlana said, "Our Shamsuddin was as powerful as the Messiah in the way that he could draw souls to follow his blessed soul. His breath was a life-giving breath (*nafas*). His knowledge of alchemy was without equal as was his knowledge of astrology, mathematics, theology, philosophy, astronomy, logic and dialectics. There was no one like him throughout the world. However, when he talked with men of God, he set all this aside and chose instead the world of surrender, seclusion, and oneness (*tawhid*)." He said,

"When I found a single page in the book of your love,
I left forgotten three hundred pages of learning."

Give to God a Goodly Loan [498]

Chelebi Husamuddin (May God bless his innermost secret), in his youth, served Shamsuddin in all humility. When the Friends saw the respect and reverence he showed him, they, too, served him in all sincerity.

One day, Shamsuddin said, "O Shaikh Husamuddin, this is not the right way to proceed. Religion requires money—give something and serve so that you may draw closer to us."

Husamuddin immediately got up, went to his house, took everything he had in the way of furniture, goods, money, even household utensils and the jewelry of the women in his household, and placed them before the eyes of Shamsuddin. He also had a vegetable garden that was like a paradise in the village of Filiras. He sold it and poured the money into the blessed shoes of Shamsuddin. He prostrated, weeping, and gave thanks that a sovereign such as Shamsuddin would make a request of him.

Shamsuddin replied, "Yes, I hope through God's grace and the spiritual beneficence of true men, that after today, you will advance to such a station that you will be the envy of perfect Friends of God and the brotherhood of purity, and loved by them. Even though people of God don't need anything and are detached from the two worlds, the first test to which the lover must submit is the abandonment of the world; the second is the renunciation of everything other than God. A disciple cannot enter the Path through his own desire, unless he serves and gives his wealth. Isn't the verse, *As for one who gives and is conscious of God and has faith in the good of the ultimate end* [92:5-6],[156] inscribed on the banner of the *siddiq* (the truly faithful one, Abu Bakr)? True friends are in need of a true friend.

Take the purse full of gold,
and Lend unto God a goodly loan [73:20].
If you lend even a bit of gold,
you will receive a hundred thousand mines.

"Any disciple or lover who is able to give his spiritual director money is also able to sacrifice himself. A sincere lover is attached neither to religion nor to the world."

Shamsuddin would only accept a single dirhem of all that was offered to him. He returned all Husamuddin's wealth to him, and bestowed infinite favors upon him beyond description.

Eventually, Husamuddin attained such a rank that the Friends of expanded heart (*sadr*) would rest their heads upon his heart, and Mevlana gave him the title of the "Guardian of the Treasures of God's Throne." The six volumes of the *Mathnawi*, consisting of twenty-six thousand six hundred and sixty couplets, were a commentary on his innermost secret and were revealed as a description of him.

The Secret of the Lamp [499]

It is recounted that, one day, our Master Shamsuddin said, "Bastami was veiled. For sixty years he never ate watermelon. They asked him,

156. See *Surah Layl*, 1-7:
Consider the night as it veils [the earth] in darkness, and the day as it rises bright!
Consider the creation of the male and the female!
Verily, [O men,] you aim at most divergent ends!
Thus, as for him who gives [to others] and is conscious of God,
and has faith in the truth of the ultimate good,
for him shall We make easy the path towards [ultimate] ease.

'Why don't you eat it?' He answered, 'I don't know how the Messenger of God cut it.' How could such a person who doesn't know how the Messenger cut watermelon inform us about his knowledge that is even more hidden and difficult?"

Shamsuddin said, "If I yell at a hundred year old unbeliever, he becomes a believer. If I yell at a believer, he becomes a saint and enters Paradise."

"Someone asked me, 'Who is Satan (Iblis)?' and I answered, 'you, because at this moment, we are immersed in Idris;[157] if you were not Iblis, you, too, would be immersed in Idris. If you had the slightest trace of Idris in your being, what concern would you have for Iblis? If you had asked me, 'Who is Gabriel?', I would have answered, 'You are!' "

Chelebi Jalaluddin, who was a king among the Friends, told us that when Shamsuddin first arrived in Konya he found three dirhems *soltani* on the road to the *Halqa be-gush* gate. "This is for my expenses," he said to himself.

In those days, a dirhem was worth one hundred and twenty *pul*, and a thin, white, round flatbread cost one *pul*. Every night, he ate half of a flatbread and gave the other half to a poor person. When the provisions were gone, he put on his shoes and left for Syria.

In his early youth, he broke his fast only once every twenty or fifteen days. In the course of a week, it was rare that he would eat anything.

When he decided to make the journey to Syria, he disappeared. Mevlana recorded the date of his departure, saying to Chelebi Husamuddin, "Our dear Master, who calls to the Good, the quintessence of spirit, the secret of the lamp-niche, the lamp-glass and the lamp,[158] the Sun of Justice and Religion (Shams al-Haqq wa'l Din), he

---

157. See *Surah* 21:85-86: *And [remember] Ishmael and Idris,*
and every one who [like them] has pledged himself [unto God]:
they all were among those who are patient in adversity,
and so We admitted them unto Our grace: behold, they were among the righteous!

158. See *Surah an-Nur*, 24:35:
God is the Light (Nur) of the heavens and the earth.
The parable of His light is,
as it were, that of a niche containing a lamp;
the lamp is enclosed in glass, the glass like a radiant star;
lit from a blessed tree—an olive-tree
that is neither of the east nor of the west—
the oil of which would almost give light

who is the hidden light of God among the ancient ones and the contemporary (May God prolong his life and allow us to meet in Goodness) left on Thursday 21st of Shawwal 643 (March 11, 1246).

It was said that Shamsuddin spent only one dinar a year, and that once a week, he would break half of a flatbread into a bowl of sheep's-head broth and eat that. One day, the cook saw his state and added a bit of butter to his broth. From that moment on, he no longer went to the shop of a sheep's-head merchant. He was always on his feet and continually journeying.

Mevlana became extremely agitated when Shamsuddin left and did not rest or sleep, day or night. He became intoxicated and spoke mysterious things.

Look Inside [500]

One day, on his travels, Shamsuddin met a debauched shaikh who played with beauty—he loved to contemplate beautiful faces.

"Hey! What are you doing?" Shamsuddin asked.

"A beautiful face is like a mirror. I am contemplating God in this mirror," replied the shaikh.

"As it was said:

Our glance is pure, for in reality,
we don't gaze upon you with the eye of passion and desire.
Your beauty is the mirror of God's grace;
this is the grace that I contemplate within you."

"Fool!" cried Shamsuddin. "Perhaps you see God in the mirror of matter, why don't you look for Him in the mirror of your soul and heart—why don't you seek inside yourself?"

Immediately, the dervish bowed and asked forgiveness.

A single favorable glance from Shamsuddin guided him; he attained perfection, saw the reality of his own being, and understood the reality of our Master Shamsuddin.

Recognizing Gold [503]

It is recounted that Bahauddin Walad (May God bless his innermost

---

even though fire had not touched it: light upon light!
God guides to His light the one who wills to be guided;
and God offers parables to human beings,
since God has full knowledge of all things.

secret) had a disciple called Qutbuddin Ibrahim. He was a man of subtlety, with an enlightened heart. One day, Shamsuddin became upset with him.

Qutbuddin's ears closed, and he could hear nothing. After some time, our Master Shamsuddin inclined towards him again, and his deafness disappeared. However, some constriction remained in Qutbuddin's heart.

Shamsuddin said, "My friend, I forgave you some time ago, and I am glad that I did so. Why are you sad? Be happy!"

However, Qutbuddin's condition did not change. Then, one day, he met Shamsuddin in the bazaar and in all sincerity, bowed, and proclaimed his faith, saying: "There is no god but God, and Shamsuddin is the Messenger of God."

The crowd was incensed and cried, "Beat him!"

A man came forward to attack Qutbuddin, but Shamsuddin let out such a cry that the man died on the spot. The people in the bazaar, completely overwhelmed and bewildered, bowed and became devoted servants.

Then Shamsuddin took Qutbuddin by the hand and led him out of the bazaar.

"I am named Muhammad[159]—you should have said, 'Muhammad is the Messenger of God,' because people do not recognize gold if hasn't been minted as familiar currency."

Relevant Revelation [504]

One day, there was a discussion about the prohibition of hashish.

Mevlana Shamsuddin said, "Our friends are excited by hashish, but it gives rise to illusions of the devil. Even angelic illusions are worth nothing, so how could the illusions of the devil be worth anything? I wouldn't even be satisfied with a real angel. So what of a devil? Instead of hashish, which renders them stupid and senseless, our friends should taste the pleasures of the Infinite World of Purity."

Someone objected, "There is a prohibition against wine in the Qur'an, but not hashish."

"Each verse had its own reason for being revealed," Shamsuddin answered. "Hashish was not used in the time of the Prophet (Peace be upon him); if it had been, he would have ordered them to be killed.

159. The full name of Shamsuddin was "Mevlana Shams al-Haqq w'al Din Muhammad bin 'Ali bin Malakdad at-Tabrizi."

Each verse was revealed according to need, according to a particular situation. When the Companions recited the Qur'an at the top of their voices, in the presence of our Prophet, it troubled his blessed spirit. Then, this verse was revealed: *O you who have attained to faith! Do not raise your voices above the voice of the Prophet* [49:2]."

Love of the Homeland Is Part of the Faith [505]

It is recounted that during a gathering of shaikhs in Mevlana's time (May God be pleased with him), a sufi cried out, "Alas! What a shame that Bahauddin Walad of Balkh's gracious son is following a boy from Tabriz and submits the land of Khorasan to that of Tabriz."

Shamsuddin responded, "This sufi's claim is ridiculous! He doesn't have the sense to know that no importance belongs to the land; if a man of grace had arrived from Istanbul, it would be the duty of a Meccan to follow him. The Prophet said, 'Love of the homeland is part of the faith.' How could the Prophet have meant Mecca, which is of this world? Faith is not of the earthly world, so everything concerning it is of the Other World. 'Islam began as a stranger,' from the World Beyond. Since it is a stranger and comes from the World Beyond, how could he long for Mecca?

"Peace."

A True Friend [507]

It is recounted that some of the great scholars whose hearts had been enlightened called Shamsuddin, "God's sword of justice" because he either killed a person who angered him or wounded his heart. One hundred thousand jurists were but a drop in the ocean of Shamsuddin.

Even so, our Master Shamsuddin always said, "A true friend is one who is, like God, able to have disagreements with his intimate friend and tolerate his difficult and ugly behavior without becoming angry. He overlooks his mistakes and failings and does not permit negativity and opposition to enter his heart. The All-Merciful is like this—not disturbed by the sins, vices, and contradictions of His servants. He bestows their daily portion on them in perfect kindness and royal compassion. Such is perfect love and friendship!"

As Mevlana said:

"You are Divine Grace and Mercy.

Whoever takes refuge in you
is accepted despite his mistakes."

A Bright Light [508]

One day, a group of women passed by at a distance from where Kamal (the perfect one) of Tabriz was standing. He said, "A bright light burns in the midst of these women. Such clarity must come from Mevlana's mine of lights."

They looked to see who this could be and discovered that it was Meleke Khatun, Mevlana's daughter (May God be pleased with her). Kamal of Tabriz invited her to his house, where he showed her great respect and hospitality.

Mirrors of Light [509]

Sultan Walad told us the following:

One day, my father was praising Mevlana Shamsuddin in the highest terms possible, describing extensively, beyond all limits, his spiritual attainments, miracles, and power. Compelled by the faith and joy in my heart, I went to Shamsuddin's cell, bowed, and stood outside his cell.

"O Bahauddin, is this a joke?" he asked.

"Today, my father spoke at length of your grandeur and your glorious qualities."

"By God, I am not even a drop in your father's ocean of grandeur, but I am a thousand times more than he has said," Shamsuddin replied.

I went to see my father and, bowing, told him what Shamsuddin had said.

"He acknowledged his light, and showed his grandeur, but he is one hundred times more than he has said," was his answer.

True Friendship [510]

It is also transmitted that, one day, Mevlana Shamsuddin said:

I will tell you in secret, so that Mevlana does not hear. We have abandoned the ancient ones, because there are more men of merit among the current ones. After Muhammad, the Messenger of God (Peace and blessings upon him), there is no one who has spoken like Mevlana has spoken.

A single small coin (*pul*) from Mevlana is worth one hundred thousand dinars to me, as it is for his devotees. Whoever finds access to me submits himself to him; a door was closed, and he opened it. I only know Mevlana in an imperfect way—every day I can see states of soul and actions that were not there the day before. Try to increase your understanding of Mevlana, so that later you will not be in loss. *When He shall gather you all together unto the Day of the Last Gathering—that Day of Loss and Gain* [64:9]. He has a beautiful face, and he speaks beautiful words, but don't be satisfied with that; be aware that behind these words is something else. Seek that!

When it comes to words, some words are false, some true. That which is hypocritical is to say that the soul of all the saints and their spirits long to have found Mevlana and to sit with him. That which is true is to say that the soul of the prophets does have this longing: "Would to God that we had lived during his time and heard his words!"

Don't lose this opportunity. The one who is the most sincerely devoted will be the first to enter the Kingdom of God. I am a friend of Mevlana, and I am certain that he is a Friend of God. A friend of a Friend of God is also a Friend of God. That is certain.

The sun is always shining upon him, since his face is always turned towards the sun. The back of this sun is for others. No book is more of benefit than the forehead of the Friend, but not everyone is a perfect Friend. Some are a tenth, others a twentieth. If they had the capacity, they would draw close to him into seclusion. But most friends are a thirtieth. The one who unites together (*al-Jami'*) these thirty parts is God.

In All the Forms I Love [511]

Sultan Walad recounted that, one day, Mevlana related the following:

Our Master Shamsuddin had a wife named Kimya. One day, she became angry with him and went to the gardens of Meram outside Konya. Mevlana said to the women of the medresse, "Go and bring Kimya Khatun back, because the heart of our Master Shamsuddin is greatly attached to her." A group of the women set off to find her.

Meanwhile, Mevlana went to see Shamsuddin, and found him sitting in his room speaking with Kimya and caressing her. Kimya was sitting there in the same clothes in which he had seen her earlier. Mevlana was astonished, because the women who were going to look for her had not yet left. Mevlana left and took a walk around the medresse to allow them their delight in privacy.

A bit later, Shamsuddin called out, "Come inside."

When Mevlana entered, he saw no one there with him. He asked about the mystery: "Where did Kimya go?"

Shamsuddin responded, "The Most High loves me so much that He appears to me in all the forms I love; just now He came to me as Kimya, and showed Himself to me in her form."

An Immense Sea [513]

According to the perfect companions, one day certain envious jurists, negative and opiniated, asked Mevlana, "Is wine lawful or forbidden?" Their intention was to discredit Shamsuddin's honor.

He responded in figurative terms: "It depends on who is drinking it. If you poured a goatskin of wine into a large lake, the lake would not be changed. It would still be permissable to use this water for ablutions and for drinking. But a drop of wine will render the water in a little bowl impure. Similarly, a person who falls into the salty sea, takes on the characteristics of salt.

"This means that Mevlana Shamsuddin can drink wine because he is as immense as the ocean. However, if he had a nature like yours, even barley bread would be prohibited to him," he answered.

"This is not so, but if it were, O earthly bird,
know that the Red Sea doesn't notice a carcass that falls into it.
He is not less than two pitchers and a bowl full[160]
that he could be sullied by a drop.
Fire does not harm Abraham but terrifies a Nimrod.[161]
For a Friend of God, poison is a delicious remedy,
but if a student drinks it, his consciousness darkens."

Ah, the Melon! [517]

Sultan Walad told us that Shamsuddin sometimes asked his disciples and friends for watermelon. Succulent melons would be brought. After he had eaten, he would throw the rind at them,

160. It is traditionally accepted that if a drop of impurity falls into a container of water this is the minimum amount of water sufficient to maintain the ritual purity of the water for ablutions.

161. Though the ruler Nimrod attempted to destroy Abraham by throwing him into the fire, for him with God's Grace the fire became cool, like roses.

crying, "Miserable Creatures! What have you brought?"

This would open for those disciples and friends the world of revelation and visions from the Unseen and veils would be lifted.

A Devoted Servant [518]

Sultan Walad told us the following:

One day, my Father gave a passionate speech, praising our Master Shamsuddin's dignity and greatness. He spoke of his advanced station, the miracles he could perform, his ability to penetrate the secrets of hearts, and other capacities beyond expression in words. Such praise left the Friends totally bewildered.

He also recited this verse:

Shams of Tabriz walks above the head of spirits.
Put your head, not your foot, where he puts his.

I was overjoyed to hear my spiritual director openly praised like this in the presence of the generous companions. I went running to our Master Shamsuddin's cell, bowed, kissed his hands, and rubbed my eyes with them to express my deepest friendship.

Shamsuddin was astonished by my behavior: "O Bahauddin, you show me such honor and affection, such that you have never shown to people of the Way!"

I replied, "My father described your greatness so magnificently that we have all gone crazy. If I were to live a thousand years and were in your service one hundred times over, my father's words would remain forever etched in the soul of your sincere servant," and I added:

A conqueror of the world is your hungry slave,
a beggar with a basket, knocking at your door.
If heaven served your dust a hundred years,
still it would not have fulfilled one day's duty."

"O Bahauddin! What Mevlana has said about us is true. I cannot say it is not. However, I swear by God that one hundred thousand such as Shamsuddin of Tabriz are not even a single atom of the sun of Mevlana's glory.

In the rays of your sun which enlighten the world,
this mote that we are is as nothing.

"After so many revelations, proximity of lights, and witnessing the World of Mystery which is my absolute domain, still I have not been able to reach even the foot of Mevlana, much less his true reality."

The Unity of God [519]

The Friends (May God be satisfied with them all) recounted that Mevlana told them the following:

Shamsuddin was asked, "What is the Oneness of God (*tawhid*)?"

He answered, "The Oneness of God is such that to question a spiritual director about it is a reprehensible innovation. All things belong to God, come from God, are created by Him, and return to Him. As for that which belongs to God, *To God belong the heavens and the earth and all that they contain* [5:120], and as for that which comes from God, *Whatever good thing comes to you, comes from God* [16:53]. *Say: All is from God* [4:78; 2:5]. As for that which has existence through God, *The heavens and the earth stand firm through His command* [30:25]. And as for that which returns to God: *Unto God all things will have been brought back* [2:210; 3:109; 8:44; 22:76; 35:4; 57:5], *All that exists returns to Him* [11:123], and *With Him is all journeys' end* [42:15; 5:18; 64:3].

"Whoever knows that his body is a recent creation, knows that God is Eternal; whoever knows that his body is unjust, knows his God is Faithful; whoever knows that his body is faulty, knows God to be Truly Beneficent."

I Would Have Given My Life [521]

Our Master's friendship and spiritual love for Shamsuddin was so profound that after his departure if someone claimed to have seen him, Mevlana would be beside himself with joy. Immediately, he would untie his turban and take off his cloak and give it to the person who pretended to bring this good news and would shower him with gifts and give thanks to God.

One day, someone reported to him, "I saw Mevlana Shamsuddin in Damascus." Mevlana was so delighted that he gave him everything he was wearing—turban, cloak, shoes and stockings.

Then one of the dear Friends said, "It's a lie! He never saw Shamsuddin."

Mevlana responded, "It was for his false news that I gave him my cloak and my coat. If his news had been true, instead of clothes,

I would have given him my life and sacrificed myself for him."

By Heart [522]

The old companions, the chief among the Friends, *May blessedness be with them and a beautiful return*! [13:29], recounted that one day there was a grand ceremony in the *khanaqah* of Nasirrudin the Vizier (May God have mercy upon him)—they were installing a great man as shaikh for the *khanaqah*. All the religious scholars, shaikhs, and knowers of God, the sages, amirs, and distinguished people were in attendance. Each one spoke regarding various areas of knowledge and religion, discussing them in depth. During all this talking, Mevlana Shamsuddin was sitting in a corner like a hidden treasure.

All of a sudden, he jumped up and angrily shouted: "How long will you go on preening, talking about 'so and so' said 'such and such', and prancing about in the arena mounted on a saddle without a horse? Isn't there anyone among you who can say, 'My heart informed me about my Lord'? How long will you keep walking around with someone else's walking stick?

> The foot of those who offer learned proofs is wooden,
> and a wooden foot is wobbly.

These words that you talk about from the *hadith*, the commentaries on the Qur'an, the wisdom of the wise, and so on, are words of people from some other time during which each of them sat upon the throne of humankind; they conveyed to us their insights from the states that they each experienced. Since you are the real men of your time, where are your secrets and your words?"

They all remained silent and bowed their heads in remorse.

He continued, "Since the time of Adam, every child that comes from the world of Nothingness and places his foot into existence, be he prophet or saint, has his own rank and work to accomplish. There have been some who receive divine revelations (*wahy*) and others who have recorded them. Now, try to be both, the place of the revelation of God and the recorder of divine revelation, so that you might hand on that which has been given to you.

"Say: 'I am but a mortal man like all of you, but I have received revelation' [18:110; 41:6]. Mevlana knows the purpose of the revelation of this verse. 'Ali, the Commander of the Faithful (May God be pleased with him) was with the Elect of God (Peace and bless-

ings upon him) during the ten days before Ashura.[162] During these nights, the Prophet ate nothing. He looked at 'Ali, and saw traces of weakness in him; he said, 'I am not like any of you.' It was then the revelation arrived: *Say: 'I am but a mortal man like all of you, but I have received revelation that God is One. . . .'* The difference is: '*I have received revelation.*'

In body, you're an animal, but your soul is angelic,
so you can journey on earth as well in the heavens.
He is outwardly a man *like you*,
but through his seeing heart he *receives revelations.*

Revelations came to the Prophet through Gabriel, and also through the heart, just as he received this: 'I have such a moment with God in which no prophet sent with a mission nor archangel close to God can enter.' And 'God speaks through the mouth of 'Omar.' This hasn't happened for you. When it does occur for someone, people look towards him."

Then he recited this quatrain:

O You for whom those sated with the world are hungry
    for union,
the courageous fear to lose You.
What chance have gazelles before Your eye,
when Your glance has captured this world's lions?

Then Mevlana arose and threw himself into the pool of the *khanaqah*, and that day, there was a wondrous sema. So many scholars and distinguished people became disciples and devoted servants that it was impossible to count them.

A Tranquil Earth [523]

One day, Shamsuddin was revealing certain divine insights at a gathering of religious scholars:

---

162. These are the first ten days of the Islamic month of Muharram which is the beginning of the Islamic lunar calendar, the "New Year." Ashura, "the tenth" of the month, was the commemoration day of the arrival on land by the Prophet Noah after his journey in the ark, as well as the moment Moses was saved from the Egyptians. Later, it also came to be the day of remembrance of the beloved grandson of the Prophet Muhammad, Husayn, who was martyred that day at Karbala, but for the Prophet Muhammad it was a special time of fasting in remembrance of God with gratitude.

"The purpose of all this reading, and study, and struggle is to render the soul obedient, to humble the rebellious soul, as did Aaron, brother of Moses. It is like the yoke around the neck of an ox, which tames him and helps him work the earth in complete tranquility. Then the receptive earth can receive the seed, and instead of thorns and dry brush, all sorts of nourishing grains and aromatic plants can grow, and from this mud (*gel-ha*), roses (*gul-ha*) blossom. Unless it is knowledge through which one can surrender, it is nothing but suffering and affliction, not a blessing.

> Knowledge through which you haven't surrendered—
> pure ignorance is a hundred times better."

A Glance of Love [524]

Sultan Walad (May God sanctify his innermost secret) recounted the following anecdote:

One day, while my father was in retreat, he went deep into the ecstasy of nothingness and remained immersed for several hours. When he returned from this World of Mystery and bewilderment of the spirit, I begged him to tell me about it.

"O Bahauddin, I saw a person in Baghdad who had been practicing mortifications and living an ascetic life for many years. He was weeping. His body was emaciated and thin, and his face was pale. He had undergone great hardships, and his attainment was such that he would lay out his prayer mat on the surface of the Tigris River and perform *salaah* there. Yet, in spite of all his power and proximity to God, this was his prayer: 'O God! O Sovereign! Bestow upon me greater ecstasy, a better bewilderment than this, because I receive no benefit from these things.'

"At that moment, I whispered in his ear, 'Mevlana Shamsuddin is in Damascus, appearing at gatherings and glancing at people there. Go there, so that this sovereign of Love might see you in this state and might smile upon your suffering, so that you might be granted what you are seeking and that from within your heart that which you are looking for might manifest.'

"This dervish of wounded heart took my advice and right away went to find our master, Shamsuddin, in Damascus. The appearance of this suffering person was pleasing to the eye of Shamsuddin, and he smiled when he saw him. Immediately, a light and an ecstasy coming from the World of Mystery appeared in the seeker's heart, and he began to whirl up to the stations of the highest Heaven. He achieved that perfection which is the goal of the perfect knowers of God. *And God grants sustenance unto whom He wills, beyond all reckoning* [3:37; 24:38].

O my son, a *faqir* might bestow upon you only a glance,
but this glance can take you to the Highest Heaven."

Revealing Dreams [525]

The great *khalifas* (May God increase their dignity) told us that, one day, Mevlana told the Friends the following:

At the beginning of my spiritual journey, when I began to experience moments of illumination, I continually read the words of our Great Master [Bahauddin Walad] (May God be pleased with him) and had to have them always in the pocket of my sleeve. When Mevlana Shamsuddin forbid me to read them, I stopped, out of the respect I had for his blessed insight.

One night, I had a dream that I was seated among some Friends at the Qarata'i medresse, and I was reading our Great Master's book. As I awakened, Mevlana Shamsuddin entered the door and said, "Why have you begun to read this book again?"

"May God protect me! I have not read this book for a long time," I answered.

"How is it then that you were reading it last night at the Qarata'i medresse? Most dreams are made of thoughts and memories. If it had not been in your thoughts, it would not have appeared in your dream."

From that moment on, for as long as Shamsuddin lived, I was no longer occupied with it.

Reaching Perfection [526]

The dear Friends told us that, one day, Shamsuddin was sitting with Mevlana and many important people of Konya were present:

He said, "I want a disciple such that all the perfect shaikhs and knowers of God who have attained the goal are powerless to perfect him, one who has no capacity for perfection, whom no one has been able to help. I will take on the responsibility of guiding him to perfection and show him God without doubt or hesitation. It is as it was said: *I shall heal the blind and the leper, and bring the dead back to life by God's permission* [2:49]. In the presence of the All-powerful, *'Be!' and it is* [6:73; 36:83], no one refers to capacity.

> If capacity were required to receive God's action,
> no non-existent being would have come into existence."

All the Friends bowed and blessed that immense power.

> The lordship of Shams of Tabriz is above the seven azure spheres.
> Beneath his knee, predestination's steed is tame
> even though rebellious and ill-tempered.
> All the difficulties that the adepts cannot solve
> are, for him, just pleasantries and play.

May the Mercy of God be upon him and may his memory be magnified until the end of time.

*****

Some of the teachings of Mevlana Shamsuddin follow
(May God magnify his dignity):

Surrender, Satisfaction, and Remembrance *[526, I]*

One day, Shamsuddin was discussing mysticism at Mevlana's medresse. He said, "God (May He be exalted) asks three things from all of His creatures; first, submission; second, fulfillment of proper behavior; third, remembrance. Submission is worship; proper behavior is being God's servant, and remembrance is knowledge of God (*ma'rifat*). Remove your burden from someone else and carry his; give up desiring something from others and give them what they desire. They are looking for riches, you must seek poverty; they desire honor and glory, and you desire humility.

Someone asked, "What is knowledge of God?"

Shams responded, "The life of the heart through God (May He be exalted). That which is living annihilate, and I refer to your body; and that which is dead enliven, and this means your heart. That which is present allow to be absent—and that means this world. That which is absent cause to be present, and that is the world of the Hereafter. That which exists make non-esistent, and that means the passions; and that which does not exist bring into being, and that is intention.

"True knowledge of God is within the heart, while the profession of faith is on the tongue, and service is by the body. If you wish to escape from Hell, serve; if you want to reach Paradise, obey God; if you desire intercession, make the prayer of an intention; if you desire the Master, turn your face towards Him, so that you find Him immediately. Whoever knew me has tried to reach me; whoever desires me looks for me. Whoever seeks me will find me, and will chose nothing other than me."

Someone asked, "What must I do to reach you?"

"Leave behind your body and come! The veil beween the human being and God is the body, which consists of four things: the private parts, the gullet, wealth, and fame. This veil is a special one and it prevents us from seeing true obedience, recompense, and miracles. But *God knows best the Truth*!"

Never Tiring of the Friend [526, II]

A special sign of the knower of God is that he never tires of remembering his Friend and can never have enough of that friendship. There is no food more delightful than the food of remembrance eaten in certainty at the table of contentment.

The distinguishing signs of a knower of God are three: a heart occupied by the thought of God, a body that serves God, and an eye intent on closeness with God. Another sign of a knower of God is that he is not interested in this world or in the next, and that his Master is foremost in his heart and cannot be replaced by anyone. Knowledge consists of three things; a tongue which mentions God, a heart which remembers Him with gratitude, and a body capable of patience. A body in which there is no knowledge is like a village without a well. A body that does not abstain is like a tree which doesn't bear fruit, and a body without shame is like a stew without salt. A body incapable of making an effort is like a slave not needed by his master.

Four things are precious: a rich person who patiently bears difficulty, a poor person content with his portion, a fearful sinner, and an abstinent scholar. From knowledge, one must derive benefit; from work, well-being, and from discourse, good advice. He who pursues the goods of this world cannot ignore profit and loss; he who looks to the Hereafter cannot set aside obedience and service; he who looks for the Master cannot avoid tests and suffering; he who looks for knowledge is destined for rejection and exile. One who expects to find the comforts of life in mystical knowledge will continue to suffer, and one who endures suffering patiently will attain ease.

Whoever pursues glory, will soon be rejected; one who looks for wealth will remain in poverty, and one who is patient in poverty will attain wealth. A wise man must possess three qualities: compassion, absence of greed, and abstinence. The two best qualities are knowledge and forbearing compassion.

Real Wisdom [526, III]

Someone asked him about wisdom (*hikmat*).

He answered, "Wisdom is of three sorts: word, action, and sight. Wisdom of word belongs to the religious scholars, wisdom of action to the devoted worshippers, and wisdom of sight to the mystics. One who is wise does not become angry with someone who opposes him, nor does he hate someone who mistreats him.

"They said to Abu Yazid [Bastami], 'You walk on water and in the air!' He replied, 'A piece of dry wood can also walk on water, and birds also fly in the air; magicians can go in one night from Mt Qaf to Mt Qaf.[163] The work of real men is to not attach their heart to anything except God Most High.' "

Contentment [526, IIIb]

If a mystic gives his heart, he will receive love like those described in the Qur'an: *People whom He loves and who love Him* [5:54].

I have seen nothing more beautiful than humility. Be satisfied with what you have in your hands and have no expectation of what is in the hands of others. The glory of prophets is their prophethood; that of the wise, their humility; that of saints, their compassion; that of the poor, their contentment with little; that of the rich, their generosity; that of the worshippers of God, their solitude (*khalvat*). Keep

---

163. It was a common belief that "Mt Qaf" was a mythic mountain range (the Caucasus (*kaf-kaz* = "unknown mountain"), which encompassed the world, so "to go from Mt. Qaf to Mt. Qaf" was "to go from one end of the earth to the other." It is said in the Qur'an: *In time they will come to understand . . . Have We not made the earth a resting-place [for you], and the mountains [its] pegs? And We have created you in pairs; and We have made your sleep [a symbol of] death and made the night [its] cloak and made the day [a symbol of] life* [78:5-11] *. . . whoever wills, then, let him take the path that leads towards his Sustainer!* [78:39].

your religion through generosity and good character. You cannot escape death nor can your portion flee from you.

As it was said, "Your daily portion is fixed in advance as well as the length of your life; a greedy man will remain deprived, a miser will be accused, the envious will grieve, but a mystic will be the object of God's mercy." To try to change your predestinated fate is useless; you cannot live beyond your appointed time—you will not reach your desired goal. However, you will not be deprived of your daily portion, nor will you be given that of another. So why are you killing yourself?

O child of Adam, wealth is in contentment with little. There is security in solitude, freedom in the absence of desire, friendship in lack of envy, joy in patience. There is no glory for the greedy person, nor is there humiliation for the person who is content. The free man becomes a slave because of his immoderate desires, and the slave is freed through contentment.

The Net of Love [526, IV]

Prayer takes away shame, but pride takes away religion. A greedy man is like the devil—where there is greed, there is aquisition; where there is acquisition, obstacles present themselves; where there are obstacles, there is discord, and where one finds discord, infidelity appears, and where infidelity appears, there, also, is fire.

In the same way, if you put aside the body and reach the soul, you reach that which is contingent; God is eternal. As the Qur'an says: *Limitless in His Glory is God* [21:22; 36:83]. How can that which is contingent reach the eternal? What relationship is there between earth and the Lord of Lords? For you, that by which you are freed is your soul. If you put your soul in your hand and bring it to Him, what will you have done?

> For a lover to bring the gift of his life
> is to bring cumin to Kirman.

What profit could there possibly be in taking cumin seeds to Kirman? Or what honor, since Kirman is the source? It is a royal court. God has no need. Bring God your need, since He has none and loves those who do. Your supplication can intercede, and you can leap out of these contingent affairs. Something will reach you from the Eternal, and that something is Love. The ambush of love will overtake you, for *He loves them and they love Him* [5:54]. Through the Eternal, you will see the Eternal: *No human vision can encompass Him, but He encompasses all human vision* [6:103].

These words have no end, nor will they end, and we will not see their completion until the Day of Resurrection.

The Sustenance of Sema [526, IVb]

One day, they asked Mevlana Shamsuddin about the secret of the sema, and he replied:

For men of God, Divine manifestation and sight of God takes place more frequently during a sema. Those who take part leave this world and their individual existence behind and are taken to other worlds, where they meet God.

There are semas which are not lawful—if a dancer raises his hands and feet without ecstasy, he will be chastised in hell—those who have said that this kind of sema is forbidden and an act of infidelity have performed a great service.

A dancer who raises his hands in ecstasy will assuredly reach Paradise. There is a sema that is lawful. For those who practice mortification and asceticism performing the sema brings tears and tenderness.

There is also a sema which is an obligation. For these ecstatics, sema is a personal obligation and a duty, like the five daily prayers and fasting during Ramadan. Just as eating bread and drinking water in case of need, this is a religious duty for ecstatics, because it sustains their life. If one of the people of sema starts turning in the East, another begins to turn in the West—they are aware of each other's states.

Beauty and Stringency [526, V]

Someone said, "Mevlana is all kindness (*lutf*), but Mevlana Shamsuddin has both kindness and wrath (*qahr*)."

Someone else said, "Everyone is like that." He then said to Shamsuddin, "My intention was to refute them, not to blame you."

Shams responded, "Fool! How dare you interpret my words and then make excuses for yourself. He attributed to me the qualities of God, of both wrath and beneficence. These words weren't from the Qur'an, nor the traditions of the prophet, they were my words he spoke.

"How can you say that everyone possesses the wrath and beneficence that are attributed to me? How could they belong to everyone? If they had such intelligence and *adab*, they would reach the same attainment as Bayazid, Junayd, and Shibli[164] in two days and drink from the same cup. If they speak of the work of these shaikhs in front of him, just hearing about it does him no good. Even with all that, they remain veiled from God."

He added, "Mevlana possesses a perfect beauty (*jamal*), while I have both beauty and ugliness. Mevlana has seen my beauty, but he has not seen my ugliness. From now on, I will set aside hypocrisy, so that he will see me in my totality, my beauty and my ugliness.[165]

---

164. Bayazid is another name for Abu Yazid Bastami, Junayd is Junayd al-Baghdadi who was a source of inspiration for many of the sufi lineages and included in their *silsilah* (See note for section #196); Shibli is Abu Bakr Shibli (d. 946 C.E.), who under the intense guidance of Junayd attained Friendship with God.

165. See further words of Shams regarding this in *Rumi's Sun*: "*Balancing Gentleness and Stringency*," p.429:

There are certain things which I cannot say—I have said a third of it. They declare that, "Such and such a person is all gentleness, nothing but pure gentleness." They think that perfection is to be in a state of continual gentleness. However, it's not like that. One who is all gentleness is incomplete. It would never be appropriate to say about God "He is all gentleness," because then you will have abolished the attribute of stringency in Him. Both gentleness and stringency are needed, but these attributes must be in their appropriate places. The ignorant have both stringency and gentleness but manifested in an inappropriate or improper way.

Someone said, "Everybody has stringency towards enemies and gentleness for friends." But not everyone recognizes who is a friend and who is an enemy. . . .

Just as with the words of the Commander of the Faithful, Ali, "Love your friend but not excessively. Bear in mind that one day you may bear a grudge against him! Don't behave with hatred towards your enemy either, because perhaps one day you may become friends!" And *It may be that Allah will ordain love between you and those of them with whom you are at enmity* [60:7].

To distinguish between an enemy and a friend
you will need to live your life again.
There is many an enemy who looks like a friend.
What you need is that friend who is true.

To "live life again" is for the person who has not been able to be liberated from his/her first self and hasn't been able to find a new self. But the one who has found a second life has the promise—*truly we shall quicken with good life*" [16:97]—he/she sees with the light of God. He recognizes his friend and knows his enemy. His/her stringency goes where it should, and his/her gentleness also goes where it should. In reality, though, both return to one thing.

"The sign of a person who has found his way into my company is that the company of others becomes cold and bitter. It is not that he becomes cold and continues conversation anyway, but rather that he has no wish to speak with them at all."

As the poet said:

Because of other travelers, you're traveling;
stop spending time with others.
Otherwise you'll keep being tested
and tied to that travail.

A Familiar Friend [526, Vb]

The Prophets (Peace be upon them) have each informed us about the others.

Jesus said, "O Jew, you have not known Moses well; come be with me in order to know Moses better."

Muhammad said, "O Jews and Christians, you have not known Moses or Jesus well; come be with me, in order to know them better."

The prophets all inform us about each other. Their words explain and illuminate each other's words.

The Companions asked the Prophet, peace and blessings upon him, "O Messenger of God, each prophet told us about those who had come before. Since you are the Seal of the Prophets, who will make you known?"

He answered, "He who knows himself (*nafs*) knows his Lord: he who knows my self knows my Lord."

In other words, Muslims are those who make known Muhammad's state and his words. However, he who is most learned is furthest from the goal. The more abstruse his thought, the further away he is.

Prostrate yourself in the dust at his door;
this is an affair of the heart, not the forehead.

May God be exalted! Everything sacrifices itself for man and man sacrifices himself for his Self: *We have honored the children of Adam* [17:72]. God did not say, "We have honored the heavens and the Throne." Even if you rise to God's Throne, it's worth nothing. Your heart must open.

The suffering of all the prophets, saints, and the pure was for this. It was this they were seeking. Everything is within a person;

when a person knows himself (or herself), he knows all. Passionate need and the quality of stringency are both within you. *Lead my people for they do not know* [3:163-164] which is to say, "Guide all my parts." These are the parts in denial, but they are within.

> Good and bad are both within the dervish;
> if it were not so, he would not be a dervish.

If they were not parts [of a whole], then there could have been something separate. How could a whole have known only the universals and not the particulars? What part could remain outside the whole? But *God knows best the truth.*

May God Save Us from Hypocrisy [526, VI]

"Benefit from the big city." In other words, through serving a shaikh who is a perfect knower of God. "And be careful of the villages"—in other words, associating with those who are imperfect.

> O friend, if you must be covered with dust,
> then take it from the highest hill.

"One who eats with someone whose sin has been forgiven will also be forgiven." However, the food referred to is not bread, but spiritual nourishment which God has set aside for the martyrs. *They will be nourished in joy* [3:169-170]. When the lustful soul has been subdued, the human being becomes a martyr, a witness (*shahid*) to the faith of surrender (*islam*), and fights in the struggle (*jihad*)[166] of life. One who eats of such nourishment with one who has been forgiven, he also will be forgiven his errors; if not, thousands of hypocrites and Jews ate food with Mustafa.

---

166. The greater *jihad* ("struggle"), referred to is the struggle with the egoic self. For instance, see *Surah al-Muzzammil,* O Thou Enwrapped One 73:20:

Behold, [O Prophet,] your Sustainer knows that you keep awake [in prayer] nearly two-thirds of the night, or one-half of it, or a third of it, together with some of those who follow you. And God, who determines the measure of night and day, is aware that you would never grudge it: and therefore He turns towards you in His grace.

Recite, then, as much of the Qur'an as you may do with ease. He knows that in time there will be among you sick people, and others who will go about the land in search of God's bounty, and others who will struggle in God's cause: recite, then, as much of it as you may do with ease, and be constant in prayer, and spend in charity, and lend unto God a goodly loan: for whatever good deed you may offer up in your own behalf, you shall truly find it with God—yea, better, and richer in reward.

Someone said, "But according to their belief, he was not someone whose sin had been forgiven."

I said, "By partaking of nourishment from a single bowl, belief that his sins have been forgiven becomes true—this is the reward of faith; the sign of soundness of faith. Being a muslim is to work against lustful passions; infidelity is to conform to them."

For one who has attained to faith, this means: "I am engaged in the struggle against the passions." Someone else says, "This is not my work; I cannot do it. I will pay the tax and live my life as best I can."

The Prophet accepted that declaration and gave a certificate which said, "If someone harms a *dhimmi*,[167] it is as if he has harmed me as well as the person who is bound in pledge."

Another person says, "I have attained to faith, and am disgusted with my passions." He says, "I am white," but he isn't; he is black. He says he is a falcon, but he is a crow.

It is the duty of one who is faithful to give thanks that he is not unfaithful, and the duty of the one who is unfaithful to thank God that he is not a hypocrite. In truth, a hypocrite is worse than a denier. *Truly, the hypocrites shall be in the lowest depth of the fire* [4:145].

Among the traditions that are not widely known is this one: "When Hell is emptied of its inhabitants, a group of people will come to inspect those lowest regions. The doors will blow open and closed, like the doors of a ruined and empty house. Yet, the groans of the hypocrites will be heard, and the people will ask: 'Who are you? The house is empty, but you are still here!' They will respond, 'We are the hypocrites, who have despaired of of salvation.'"

It was the Qadi of Damascus, Shamsuddin Joveyni, who taught this *hadith*, but it has not become well-known, except by those who can penetrate its higher meaning. Now, what is hypocrisy? May it stay far from us and our friends, be it hidden or open hypocrisy! As for secret hypocrisy, a great effort must be made to rid the human heart of it, with the help of God Most High!

---

167. "*Dhimmi*" was the term used for a person of another faith (especially people of the Book, i.e., Christians and Jews) under Islamic rule. A *dhimmi* had protected status and was allowed to maintain his or her original faith. They paid a tax rather than engaging in military service.

Following Muhammad [526, vii]

At a gathering, people were discussing whether the world had existed eternally. Shamsuddin said:

Of what importance is the eternity of the world to you? Find out whether you are eternal or newly created! Use your time in this life to discover your own situation, not to research the eternity of the world!

The purpose of the world is for good works, because a good action brings tranquility to the soul. Tranquility of the soul opens one's need for God, and it causes faith in the life hereafter. A person might have a hundred thousands skills and artful knowledge, but if there are no good works, there is no need for God or belief in the Hereafter; one has nothing. If there is no knowledge, no Arabic or Turkish, but there are good works, it is the honor and the glory of this world and the world to come. Everyone is pursuing knowledge and profit; pursue good works, which is the kernel, the rest is just the outer shell.

The Infinitely Compassionate is seated on the Throne [20:5]. In the exoteric teaching, "to be seated" means "to take possesion of," as in this verse:

Bishr took possession of Iraq
without a sword or spilling blood.

Besides their saying, "*He sat*," and without asking how or why, "we believe this without looking further," what can one understand from this?

What has been said about the word, "*Ta-ha*," besides the exoteric commentary that *Ta-ha* is the name of the Prophet Muhammad (Peace and blessings upon him)? Another interpretation is that it means, "O man!" and another, "Press your foot on the earth (*Tah al-arda*)," because the Prophet was standing up all night on one foot. He had begun doing this after the night prayers since the order came to offer superogatory prayers, *Stay awake* [17:79]. He would stand for so long on one foot that it would begin to swell.

The Prophet's foot became swollen from standing all night;
out of love for him, the people of Quba tore their tunics (*qaba*).

Then he heard the command, "*Tah*" ("Press!"), and took this to mean, "Put your other foot on the ground, and don't stand on one foot, because We did not send the order for you to keep vigil at night in order to cause you pain."

I am not asking you about these external commentaries that have been given. Don't tell me what has already been said. Now it is known that one must read the interpretation of these words from the Preserved Tablet (*lawhim mahfuz*); the extent of this Tablet is beyond imagining.

Our Sovereign said, "Don't perform service for Me, because I feel shame before you." Our Prophet, peace and blessings upon him, replied, "O don't say that to me, because this prohibition could cause love for You to chill in my heart, You might become cold in my heart."

The Sovereign responded, "Then I will not prohibit it." Another moment, He said, "I swear, by your soul and your head, that I have no need of this service. Do not do it." *Truly, O Muhammad, we have opened for you a manifest victory, so that God might show His forgiveness of all your faults, past as well as future* [48:1-2].

"Don't do it! Your sins, past and future are forgiven."
He replied, "It is the ecstasy of Love, not fear or hope."

And he continued, "By Your soul and Your head, I will do it." He remained standing so long that his foot began to swell.

The Sovereign said angrily, "Enough! I have no need of this. *Ta-ha*! *We did not bestow the Qur'an upon you from on high to make you suffer* [20:1-2]. I have seated you beside Me and speak with you, but not so that you should suffer, only as a *reminder to all who stand in awe of God: a revelation from Him who created the earth and the high heavens* [20:3-4]."

The explanation for people of this closeness is that the earth is Muhammad's body; the heavens are his enlightened faculties of perception, insight, and imagination. *The Most Gracious is established on the Throne of His Almightiness* [20:4]—I have established Myself in your heart, so much! So much!

Purified of desires, the Throne of the heart has prospered;
the Infinitely Compassionate has sat upon the Throne.

You say, "I no longer need Muhammad, having arrived at God." God himself cannot turn aside from Muhammad. How can you? He even brought him into His presence. You say, *Now, had We so willed, We could have continued as before and raised up a separate Warner in every single community* [25:53], but He has not; *If We had willed . . . .*

Muhammad, himself, said, "*If I will*—the expression '*law laka*' refers to me: *If it were not for you (law laka), I would not have created the heavens.*" It was He who gave Muhammad his name. He said, *His eye did not waver, nor yet did it stray* [53:17].

You chose me from among all;
and as for me, I desire only You.

To follow Muhammad, who rose to heaven on the night of the Ascension (*mi'raj*), is to go there yourself. Try hard to create a place of tranquility within your heart. If you seek the world, go beyond words, and find the ways to succeed; if you seek religion, don't let it be just words, but perservere in worship; if you seek God, devotedly serve true human beings.

One should look for a companion better than oneself,
so that your standing and rank might increase.

The true Muslim is one who has a heart that is broken. Those who came before us had bodies that were broken. They attained the heart and then said like Husayn bin Mansur al-Hallaj, "*An'l-haqq* (I am the Truth)!"

Others have said, "My Lord is the Highest," and even this did not satisfy them. There are people who recite the Throne verse [2:255] over a sick person, and there are others who become the Throne verse themselves. In calling to faith there is both stringency (*qahr*) and kindness (*lutf*). But in seclusion and intimate retreat all is kindness.

Those Who Are Endowed With Insight [526, VIII]

Shams also said:

If a person clutches at the branch of a tree, it will break and fall to the ground. However, if he takes hold of the trunk of the tree, all the branches become his. What does the expression, *those who are endowed with insight* [3:5], refer to, if not that he does not want that kind of reason that everyone possesses, but the reason that leads to a return towards God, but this philosopher says, "I set forth reasonable propositions" and yet knows nothing about Divine Reason (*'aql-i Rabbani*).

A Companion saw the Prophet (Peace and blessings upon him) again twelve years after his passing. He said, "O Messenger of God, the night before every Friday, you used to show yourself to me, but then you abandoned me like a fish out of water."

"I was occupied in mourning," he replied.

"Mourning for what?" the companion asked.

"During these last twelve years only seven people were turned facing the *qibla* when they have come to me; all the others were turned in another direction."

And *None but God knows its final meaning and those who are deeply rooted in knowledge . . . no one takes this to heart save those who are endowed with insight* [3:7] explains this.

Happiness is in the coming together of friends; they sit with each other, pay attention to each other, and reveal their beauty. When they become separated, selfish passion creeps in among them and their light disappears.

When you put something in honey it stays fresh and delightful, since it is protected from the air.[168] When air enters, the odor of pride mixes in, and it becomes sour.

Moses (May Peace be with him), in all his splendor, asked of Khidr (Peace be upon him) and of his companionship, to complete this quality of subtle sweetness (*lutf*) in him. So that he might obtain further grace he repented three times.[169] A dervish must repent once during his life, and experience regret, saying: "Why did this have to appear on my path?"

Prayers of the Poor [526, VIIIb]

The Prophet (Peace and blessings upon him), with all his grace, considered it a blessing to be greeted by the poor ones. He would sit down on the ground with them and listen to what they had to say.

You might not believe it,
but the Elect of God sought the prayers of the poor.

If you are in control of yourself and you encounter a man,
grasp hold of him; if you don't, you are in your own hands.

A camel was traveling in the company of an ant when they arrived at a river. The ant drew back.

---

168. This is also a play of words on the double meaning of *hawa*: "air" and "passionate desire."

169. See *Surah al-Kahf* [18:60-82] for the story of Moses and Khidr, and also section #488b of this volume.

"What's the matter?" cried the camel. "Come, it's easy, the water only comes up to the knees."

"For you, perhaps," answered the ant, "but it will be about six metres over my head!'[170]

If I had remained without a shaikh, I would not have survived.

"Whoever approaches me by a span . . ."[171]—there is a difference between one meter and another, between span and span, between knee and knee.

"Only two steps and he arrived . . . "[172] But you don't have the step of Muhammad. It is Pharoah who has appeared in you. Moses arrived and chased him away. Pharoah came back and Moses departed. See how the fickleness of color continues! Stand with Moses, so that Pharoah never returns. People of changing colors aren't capable of saying, "*Our Sustainer is God!" and then steadfastly pursuing the right way—upon those do angels often descend* [41:30]. . .

"Two steps and he arrived," means Muhammad's step, a step towards the Hereafter and a step towards God. For us, as "from knee to knee . . ," it would rather be a hundred steps, and still we would not even have reached the edge of the *suffa*. But *God is most kind to His servants* [42:19];[173] but He specified "*His servants*;" wherever you find them, devote your self.

The Light that Puts out Fire [526, IX]

Shamsuddin said:

One day, 'Omar (May God be pleased with him) struck Satan

---

170. The camel in this anecdote is a metaphor for the far-seeing spiritual guide, tall in stature in the Unseen, capable of high aspiration (*himmet*) and of carrying one across the river (*barzakh*) between worlds.

171. This is a reference to a *Hadith Qudsi* related by the Prophet Muhammad: "When someone approaches Me by a span (A span is the distance between the thumb and the smallest finger when the palm is opened), I approach him by a cubit; when he approaches Me by a cubit, I approach him by a fathom; and when he comes to Me walking, I come running to him."

172. This is a reference to the moment when during his *mi'raj*, Muhammad's journey through the heavens into the presence of God, with God's help he approached within two bow lengths or nearer [53:9]. *And thus did [God] reveal unto His servant whatever He deemed right to reveal* [*Surah an-Najm*, The Star 53:10].

173. *He provides sustenance for whomever He wills* [42:19]. *See how God grants sustenance to whom He wills, beyond all reckoning (innallaha yarzuqu man yashaa'u bi-ghayri hisaab)* [3:37].

in the face, and Satan was blinded. There is a mystery contained in this, which "they" alone understand. This idea manifests itself in all kinds of external appearances, but Satan is not a person in a body. He is spoken of this way: "Truly, Satan runs through the children of Adam like blood runs in their veins."

One day, Satan came to 'Omar saying, "Come, so I can show you some wonders."

Through a crack in the wall of a mosque, he showed him a person sleeping and another standing up in prayer. "If I were not afraid of the fire of Divine love in this sleeping man's heart, I would enter, do my work with the one who is praying, and destroy him," said Satan.

The only thing that can burn Satan is the fire of love in the heart of a man of God. All the mortifications to which ascetics submit themselves only increase his power, because he was created from the fire of lust. However, light puts out the fire, as it was said, "Your light extinguishes my fire."[174] If it were not for *One All-Knowing, All-Wise* [27:6], how would things be? Even in a thousand years, their affairs would not be set right. No matter how much effort was made, even if you joined twenty lives together, it would not happen.

That which took the other prophets a thousand years to achieve, Muhammad (Peace and blessings upon him) surpassed in just a short while, through *One All-Knowing, All-Wise* [27:6].

Let's go! Let's lower our mustaches; we are not going to war, to frighten the infidels with our mustaches. Each one of us shelters an infidel in our heart, and even if every one of the hairs of our mustache became a spear, it still would not be afraid. *But as for those who strive hard in Our cause—We shall most certainly guide them onto paths that lead to Us* [29:69].

Happy Are Those of Awakened Heart [526, IXb]

If you are going to make an extra fast, do it on a Thursday or a Monday. All of a sudden, sit on your commanding soul, saying: "I will fast until it seems hard for my soul—it's possible my soul might suddenly become a *muslim*, even though its surrender seems very far away."

Each person possesses a sin akin to his spiritual state; for one

174. Hell cries out (to the faithful), "Pass on, your light extinguishes my fire!" (*hadith*).

it might be debauchery, for someone else it might be absence from the presence of God. Happy is the one whose eyes sleep, but whose heart doesn't! Woe to the one whose eyes don't sleep, but whose heart does! *God knows best the truth*!

Sincere Alms [526, X]

He was asked about giving alms in secret. He answered:

Giving alms in secret is extreme immersion in sincerity, and in the maintenance of this sincerity, to such an extent that you are unaware of taking any pleasure in giving alms—that is to say, because one is occupied with regret that one has not been able to do better: "If it pleases God, allow me to be even better than this."

Abu Yazid (May the mercy of God be upon him) had gone on foot on pilgrimage to Mecca seventy times. One day, on the pilgrim's road, he came upon some travelers who were in great distress since there was a shortage of water, and they were about to perish. He saw that there was a dog near the well around which the pilgrims were crowded, desperately trying to get water. The dog was looking at Abu Yazid, when suddenly, the divine inspiration came to him: "Give this animal some water."

He cried out, "Who will purchase a pious pilgrimage accepted by God for one drink of water?" No one paid any attention, and so he increased his offer: five, six, seven pilgrimages on foot for a drink of water, and on it went, up to seventy pilgrimages.

Then someone cried out: "I will give the water."

Abu Yazid thought to himself, "Well done! For the sake of a dog, I sold seventy pilgrimages on foot for a drink of water." However, when he went to give the dog the water, it turned away. Abu Yazid fell prostrate on the ground and covered his face in shame.

A voice came: "You have made such a fuss about yourself, saying, 'I did this for God, I did that for God.' Even a dog will not accept your alms."

He said, "I repent. Never again will I think this way."

Immediately, the dog put his head to the water and began to drink.

I would offer a hundred intercessions and supplications
to kiss Your feet, but You will not let me.

You reproach an idolater for worshipping a stone or a painting on a wall, but your own face is turned towards a wall. This is a metaphor of Muhammad's (Peace and blessings upon him) which you have not understood: "The Kaaba is at the center of the world and when everyone turns towards it, if the Kaaba is removed, they are prostrating themselves before each other's hearts. This one is prostrated before that one's heart, and that one is prostrated before this one's heart."

There Is No Prayer without Presence [526, Xb]

The Prophet (Peace and blessings upon him) said, "An hour of true contemplation is worth more than sixty years of worship." That which we mean by contemplation is the state of tranquil presence (*huzur*) of the sincere dervish, because his worship is free of hypocrisy. Certainly, that is worth more than formal prayer without presence. One can make up for a ritual prayer that has been omitted, but concentrated presence that has been omitted cannot be replaced.

Some men of poverty have renounced formal worship because: "There is no prayer without *huzur* (concentrated presence of heart); there is no prayer without the *Fatiha*."[175] For them, the *Fatiha* is their concentrated presence of heart such that if Gabriel came, even he would be kicked out.

When [during his ascension (*mi'raj*)] the Prophet was moving towards the Presence of God, he said to Gabriel, "Come."

Gabriel answered, "No! If I came even a fingertip closer, I would burn." . . .

Pay attention with discernment, because the road has many branches. One person goes by this road, another by that. Stay on the road to the right. When you reach Konya, you no longer need to be concerned with discernment, because there is a just sultan there, and no one wrongs anyone.

The Fortress of La illaha il Allah [527]

One day, he also said:

Remember, "There is no god but God (*La illaha il Allah*) is My fortress and whoever enters My fortress is secure from My chastisement (*Hadith Qudsi*)." God says, "Whoever enters My fortress." He did not say, "Whoever pronounces its name." It is very easy to

175. See the note to section #143 of this volume.

pronounce the name of this fortress. With your tongue, you say, "I entered the fortress." Or you might say, "I went to Damascus." If it's just a matter of the tongue, in the blink of an eye you would journey to heaven or around the earth; you would rise to the Throne of God. However, He said, "One who sincerely and purely says, 'There is no god but God (*La illaha il Allah*)' enters the Garden."

Now, sit down. You say, "The brain gets dry." Who is He; who are you? You are six thousand; become one. Otherwise, what does His Oneness have to do with you? You are a hundred thousand particles and every one has been carried off with some desire of yours, some fantasy. With pure intention, and sincere action, he will enter the Garden. When he has accomplished that, there is no longer any need of the promise: "He will enter the Garden." When he has done that, he will already be the Garden itself. But *God knows best the Truth.*

The Subtlety of God's Grace [530]

One day Shamsuddin said:

In Damascus, those dogs were publicly claiming Shihab Maqtul[176] was an infidel (*kafir*).

I cried, "May God protect us! How could such a luminious being be veiled (*kafir*)?"

Yes, it is true, in the presence of the sun (Shams), a comet (*Shihab*) is veiled, but if he enters the sun's service in all sincerity, he becomes a full moon. He becomes complete.

I am very humble with those who are sincerely in need, but full of pride with others. Shihabuddin's knowledge (*'ilm*) dominated his reason (*'aql*), but reason should prevail over knowledge and dominate it. His brain, where reason resides, had become weak.

There are some who have experienced the World of Spirit (*'alam-i ruh*) and have descended and settled on earth. Then they speak about the World of the Lord (*'alam-i rabbani*), but it is the same World of the Spirit, which they imagine to be the World of

176. Shihabuddin Suhrawardi (1155-1191) was a sufi master of Iran, sometimes referred to as *Shaikh al-Ishraq* (Shaikh of Lights). One of his major works was *Hikmat al-ishraq* (*Wisdom of Illumination*) and the *Ishraqi tariqah* unfolded from his example. Opposed by the orthodoxy, he was executed (hence the name "Maqtul," "the slain") for apparent heresy due to his focus on mystic (*batini*) practice and philosophy. He taught that all of creation is an outpouring from the original Light of Lights (*Nur al-anwar*).

the Lord, unless the grace of God intervenes through one of His attractions or through a true human being who embraces the seeker and brings him from the World of Spirit to the World of the Lord, saying: "Come in obedience, for there is another subtlety. Why did you descend?"

In the World Beyond, the Spirit (*Ruh*) had not yet shown all its beauty to Husayn bin Mansur al Hallaj. Otherwise, how could he have said, "I am the Truth (*Ana'l-haqq*)"? What relationship is there between the "Truth (*Haqq*)" and "I (*ana*)"? What is this I? If he were immersed in the World of Spirit, how could there be room for these, for the letters, "a (*alif*)" and "n (*nun*)"?

How Will We Become Clean? [531]

Someone said, "One shouldn't mention the name of God when one is on the toilet; it isn't appropriate to recite the Qur'an then, even with a low voice."

But then what will I do with that within myself which I cannot get rid of by myself?[177]

Love and Intellect [531b]

Someone was describing a fish and how big it is.

Someone else said, "Be quiet! What do you know about fish!"

The man replied, "You think I don't know anything about fish—I, who have made many journeys on the sea?"

"OK, if you do know, tell us about the signs of a fish."

"A fish has two horns just like a camel."

The other man said, "I thought you didn't know anything about

---

177. See *Mathnawi* II, 1366-1367, *The Pocket Rumi Reader*, p.108 :

Water says to the dirty, "Come here."
The dirty one says, "I am so ashamed."
Water says, "How will your shame be washed away
without me?"

See, also, the reflections of Shams, from *Rumi's Sun*, "True States," p.342:

Now, the person who is connected to that state is never severed from it—neither when eating, nor when sleeping, nor in the toilet. He is sitting on the toilet and still the state is firmly established in him. It stays with him.

"What is his state like? After all, his body is on the toilet!" Some people estimate spiritual manliness by a person's beard. Say, "We'll show them the measure of the spiritual virility of the truthful *murid*." Now, since they don't make the inner work, they focus on the outer.

fish, but now I have understood something else; I realize that you don't even know the difference between an ox and a camel!"

What is needed is not someone with power, but rather someone with heart. Seek the heart, not the form. Where is the place of the heart? It is hidden. Its possessor is God; out of jealousy, they call him, "Possessor of the heart (*Sahib-i dil*)."

A Conversation with Ibn Arabi [532b]

Shaikh Muhammad Ibn Arabi said in Damascus: "Muhammad is our doorkeeper."

I said to him, "Why don't you see in Muhammad what you see in yourself? Each person is his own doorkeeper."

Ibn Arabi replied, "When there is the truth of divine knowledge (*m'arifat*), of what use is an enticing sermon, or 'Do this, don't do that'?"

Then, I said, "This knowledge was his, and his excellence (of prophethood) was even more. But this denigration of yours towards him, isn't that also another call? You are speaking such propaganda, while you say one should not."

Shaikh Muhammad was a good companion in suffering, a good friend, but he could not follow the Prophet (Peace and blessings upon him).

Someone responded, "But that is exactly what following is."

Shams replied, "No, he did not follow him. At times, Shaikh Muhammad would kneel down and prostrate himself, and say, 'I am the servant of the people of divine law,' but he did not practice that obedient service.

"His company was of great benefit to me, but not as much as our Master's which does not resemble his at all; 'There is a big difference between a pebble and a pearl.'"

Dancing with a Secret [534]

Shams said, "Most people dance without a drum (*daf*),[178] but if they heard the sound, what would they not do! Another interpretation is that within the human being, besides the external acts and pure awe and consciousness of God there are hidden acts and a hidden piety.

"That is the beauty of His Essence, because He said, 'I am pres-

178. A *daf* is a Persian style frame drum with percussive chains.

ent in My servant's good conception of Me; let him think of Me as he wishes.'[179] All his harmful acts become good in this way. The sight of sightless ones falls upon externals, but we don't look in this way. We only look at a man's interior (*batin*) and his innermost secret (*sirr*). Even though on the outside he may appear corrupt and neglectful, on the inside, by virtue of that pure substance, that pure secret, he may be honest, God-conscious, and good."

On Resurrection Day [535]

The noble Friends said that some of the generous Friends recounted:

One day, Mevlana (May God sanctify his innermost secret) was intoxicated with divine knowledge. He said, "When the Resurrection arrives, and all the ranks of prophets, Friends of God, and the faithful of the Muslim community, group after group, gather together, Shamsuddin Tabrizi and I, holding each other by the hand, well-pleased, will walk gracefully into Paradise."[180]

---

179. See also Mevlana's reflections regarding this *Hadith Qudsi* in his *Fihi ma Fihi* (Discourse #11), *The Rumi Daybook*, "I am in My servant's Conception of Me," p.58:

Jesus, upon whom be peace, laughed a lot. John the Baptist, upon whom be peace, wept a lot. John said to Jesus, "You have become mighty secure from God's subtle traps to laugh so much."

"You," replied Jesus, "have become mighty heedless of God's subtle and mysterious grace and lovingkindness to weep so much!"

One of God's saints, who was present at this moment, asked God which of the two was of the more exalted station. God answered, "The one who thinks better of me," that is, "Within my servant's conception of me, I am there. Each of my servants has an image or idea of Me. Whatever each of them imagines Me to be, that I am. I am the Servant to images within which God lives; I care nothing for any reality where God does not dwell. O My servants, cleanse your thoughts, for they are My dwelling places."

Now make a trial for yourself and see what is more beneficial to you—weeping, laughter, fasting, prayer, or retreat. Choose whichever of these states serves you best and causes you to advance further.

180. One hears here the echo of *Surah al-Fajr* 89:27-30:

To the righteous soul will be said: "O soul in complete rest and satisfaction! Return to your Sustainer well-pleased and well-pleasing! Enter then among My devoted ones! Yes, enter My Garden!"

(*Yaa 'ayyatuhan nafsul mutma'innah! 'Irji-'ii 'ilaa Rabbiki raadiyatam mardiyyah. Fadkhulii fii 'ibaadii. Wadkhulii jannatii.*)

Gifts From God [537]

Sultan Walad recounted:

Shamsuddin told my father: "When I was a child, I saw God and angels, and contemplated the mysteries of this and the world beyond. I thought that everyone could see these things but, later, realized that they could not. Shaikh Abu Bakr told me not to speak about it."

My father, also, told me, "This is Mevlana Shamsuddin's gift granted to him from eternity, not from his devotions or his mortifications. It is the same grace that God bestowed on Jesus in his cradle: *We granted him wisdom while he was yet a child* [19:12]. And so he spoke and performed miracles. It was the same for that other unique being [*Khidr*]: *Unto whom We imparted knowledge issuing from ourselves* [18:65]."

Good Manners with the Friends [538]

Sultan Walad said, "My father continually advised me not to talk about Shamsuddin in the presence of Shaikh Salahuddin and not to mention Salahuddin in Chelebi Husamuddin's presence, even though there was no difference between them. It was simply preferable and more polite not to do so.

"In the same way, the Companions never talked about another prophet when they were with Muhammad, peace and blessings upon him, unless he himself brought up that prophet's name or commented on the state of one of them."

Love from Samarkand [539]

Those who were the leaders among the companions recounted:

One day, Sultan Walad said, "My father was extremely devout, virtuous, and ascetic in his youth. He had not yet come to love the sema. The Great Kira (Kira-Bozorg), who was my grandmother, my mother's [Gevher Khatun's] mother, inspired the love of sema in him. For this reason, when he first began participating in the sema, my father would wave his hands about in the air while moving his body (*dast-afshani*). When Mevlana Shamsuddin arrived, he showed Mevlana how to whirl in a circle (*charkh zadan*)."

It was said that the Great Kira originally came from Samarkand and that her husband, the Khwaja Sharafuddin, was a rich and noble man. No one in Samarkand was wealthier, more dignified, or of a more noble lineage. When her husband died, the Great Kira gathered together her wealth and went to find our Great Master Bahauddin Walad, to become his disciple. It is said that they came to Anatolia (Rum) together, where she died when my mother [her daughter, Gevher Khatun, the first wife of Mevlana][181] was still young. It was our Great Master Bahauddin Walad who arranged for Gevher Khatun to marry my father.

The Great Kira (May God be pleased with her) was a perfect friend of God. Whenever he spoke of her, Bahauddin Walad would say of her, "My station and hers are the same; the only difference is that I possess extensive religious learning and know innumerable secrets (*asrar*)."

Finding God [541]

Sultan Walad told us this:

Shamsuddin said, "Leave that which is false to reach the Truth (*Haqq*); that is the path."

My father said, "Grasp the Truth so that you may be delivered from the false, then you will no longer need the path, the abandoning of the path, or provisions."

Now, you have a choice: if you wish, leave the false and journey toward the Truth, or if you wish, grasp the Truth and be delivered from that which is false.

I Sacrificed My Head [543]

The knowers of God among the companions reported that Mevlana told them the following:

Shamsuddin stayed fourteen months in a cell at the medresse in Aleppo, engaged in mortifications and spiritual struggle, and did not come out for a single day. Then he heard a voice: "Your

181. The daughter of Sharafuddin Lala and the Great Kira, Gevher Khatun had grown up beside Mevlana Jalaluddin listening to his father's discourses. This beautiful woman, who was known to have the heart of an angel, became the mother of Sultan Walad to whom Shams of Tabriz conveyed many mysteries. For further details, see the "Family History" section of the Introduction to this volume.

bodily soul (*nafs*) has rights over you,"[182] it said.

His bodily soul had been manifested in such a way that even minerals would not have such patience. Shamsuddin smiled and took pity on it. He ended his retreat and set out for Damascus.

*****

The old Friends, whose hearts are the ancient House of God,[183] told us that Mevlana Shamsuddin always sat outside the cell of the medresse where he had placed Mevlana in seclusion.

When someone would arrive and inquire about him, he would ask, "What have you brought? What gift did you bring in exchange for my showing him to you?"

One day, a troublesome person asked him, "And you, what did you bring, that you ask such a thing?"

"I brought myself," Shamsuddin answered. "And I have sacrificed my head for him."

And he did just that.

In the Right Moment [544]

One day, Mevlana said:

One day, Shamsuddin told me that in the past he had begged God for the intimate companionship and conversation of His Friends (*awliya*). They were shown to him in a dream, and they said, "We will make you a close friend of one Friend of God."

"It is well. And where is this Friend of God?" he asked.

---

182. This is a *hadith* of Muhammad recommending moderation: "Fast and break your fast, pray extra night prayers (*qiyyam al-layl*), and sleep, for your body has a right over you, your eyes have a right over you, your wife has a right over you, and your visitors have a right over you."

183. See Surah 22:32-35; The "Most Ancient Temple" signifies, in locality, the Kaaba and, in subtlety, the heart of the human being:

And anyone who honors the symbols set up by God—
truly, these derive their value from the God-consciousness within the heart.
In that God-consciousness you shall find benefits until a determined time is fulfilled,
and its goal and end is the Most Ancient Temple.
And always bear in mind your God is the One and Only God:
and so, surrender yourselves to Hu.
And give the glad tiding of God's acceptance to all who are humble—
all those whose hearts tremble with awe whenever God is mentioned,
and all who patiently bear whatever ill befalls them, and all who are constant in prayer
and spend on others out of the sustenance We have provided for them.

The following night, he saw them again, and they said to him, "He is in Rum (Anatolia)."

He said, "I searched for a long time and still did not find him."

Then they told him, "The time is not right: 'Everything in the proper moment.' "

His Is the Command [545]

This is an authentic story and one that came to us from Sultan Walad:

At the beginning of his spiritual journey, Mevlana Shamsuddin asked our Lord Most High, with all sorts of supplications and humility, to show him one of the beings hidden by the veil of His jealousy.

The Divine inspiration came to him: "Since you implore sincerely and with intense yearning, what gift will you give?"

He answered, "My head."

At last Divine Beauty granted him this favor, and he found happiness in this companionship, and was the object of that glance of grace.

Then one night, he was sitting with Mevlana in seclusion. Suddenly, from outside, someone whispered to him, "Come outside."

Immediately, he got up and said to Mevlana, "They have called me to the execution."

After a long pause, my father said, "*The creation and the command is His* [7:54]—God knows best."

They say that, like heretical assassins, seven miserable and envious misfits plotted an ambush. When the opportunity was right, they attacked with their daggers. Shamsuddin let out such a howl that the conspirators lost consciousness. When they regained their senses, they saw nothing but a few drops of blood. From that moment, we never again saw a sign or a trace of this Sovereign of Meaning.

That was it. No one saw him again.
He vanished from the sight of men, like a fairy.
When he disappeared from his eyes and those of others,
he became renowned like the phoenix.

When he heard of this, Mevlana said, "*God does what He wills* [3:35; 22:19] and *He ordains as He wills* [5:1].

What is there to do but agree and surrender—
you're in the grasp of a ravaging lion.

"What business is it of ours—Shamsuddin had made a promise in that place, and pledged his life, in gratitude for our secret (*sirr*). The divine command arranged the disposition; the wisdom of 'The pen of destiny has dried' became apparent. And, *All this is laid down in Our decree* [17:58; 33:6] became manifest."

If a man honors the pact he has made with destiny,
he will surpass any description you might make of him.

Then Mevlana was plunged into deep mourning, and the Friends began to weep profusely. Overcome with ecstatic love, he began the sema and recited *ghazals* of lamentation such as the one that begins:

If tears could match my sorrow, they would fall day and night
until dawn.
Shamsuddin of Tabrizi has left; who will mourn this glory
of mankind?
If this world possessed true hearing and sight,
it, too, would be weeping now.

Those miserables ones who attacked him, and who caused such discord, were themselves the captives of Destiny. Some of them were killed after a short period of time and others were struck with paralysis. One or two fell from the roofs of their houses and perished. Others were transformed by: *Their denial of this truth does but add to the deniers' loss* [35:39]. 'Alauddin who was branded by: *He was not of your family, for, truly, he was unrighteous in his conduct* [11:46][184] fell sick with a strange illness and a high fever and died within a few days. Mevlana, due to his intense sorrow, went to the gardens beyond the city and would not go to his funeral. We take refuge with God from their hatred and their wrath! The date of Shamsuddin's disappearance was a Thursday in the year 645 A.H. (1247 C.E.).

Mevlana was then extremely agitated and unable to rest day or night. He would continually walk up and down in the courtyard of the medresse and with great intensity recited these quatrains:

---

184. This verse refers to the son of Noah who could not accept his father's teaching and would not join him in the ark, and so perished, under the illusion of his self-sufficiency.

No matter where, out of love for you, I cannot sleep;
at night, the two locks of your hair spread the glow of amber.
Eternity, like an artist, paints you everywhere,
so that my heart might be tranquil.

Who says that this eternal living one is dead?
Or that the sun of hope has been extinguished?
When the enemy of the sun appeared on the roof of this house,
he closed his eyes and cried, "The sun has gone out!"

At a gathering attended by a number of distinguished people, Mevlana recited:

Who says that spirit inspiring Divine Love is dead?
Or that Gabriel the Faithful has perished,
under the thrusts of a sharp dagger!
He who, like Iblis, died arguing imagines
that the Sun of Tabriz has been extinguished.

After forty days, Mevlana set aside his white turban and put on a gray one, the color of smoke, and a cloak made of striped cloth from Yemen and India; this is what he wore until the end of his days.

Companions of the Way [546]

Sultan Walad related:

In the same way that Moses (May peace be upon him), in spite of the strength of his prophethood and the greatness of his mission, searched for Khidr (May peace be upon him), Mevlana, as well, though he possessed so many virtues, praiseworthy manners, noble qualities, spiritual stations, lights, miracles and secrets such that he was unequalled, still sought out Shamsuddin of Tabriz. And Shamsuddin, likewise, in every way was devoted to his love for Mevlana.

All the prophets and Friends of God have been ordered to seek each other and to be in each other's company like this.

Accepting His Will [549]

Mevlana Shamsuddin was on a journey when he came upon an amir, accompanied by his soldiers and his retinue. As soon as they looked upon each other, the amir dismounted, bowed, and remained standing for some time; then, weeping, he continued on his way.

Mevlana Shamsuddin cried, "Subtle is He who chastises his slaves with kindness and reserves wrath for His special friends."

The mystics who were travelling with him asked him what he meant by this.

"This amir who has the character of a dervish," he answered, "is among God's saints; he is only hiding behind this costume, this veil of riches. Through the tongue of his state, he was begging: 'I am not able to reconcile this clothing that is a symbol of the business of the world with devotion and the following of the Way of God. Ask Him if I may put on the garment of poverty and devote myself completely to His service.'

"When I prayed to God, the instruction arrived: 'The amir should continue to serve God without turning away from the signs of his command, as through that he will bring about the flourishing of the religion and the affairs of the world—within this is even greater self-mortification and polishing of the soul.' When the Amir understood this, he wept, and obediently, he left to devote himself to the difficulties of government, its affairs and the sufferings of the people."

Labors of Love [550]

Whenever Mevlana Shamsuddin became intoxicated with the frequency and intensity of divine manifestations and became immersed in ecstasy, and felt overcome by the magnificence of such beauty, he would busy himself with manual tasks. It was like the Prophet who said, "Speak to me, O dear rosy-complexioned one,[185] speak to me."

He would work in secret as a lowly day laborer and would do so until nightfall. He would find excuses not to accept wages, saying, "Save it for me, because I have a debt I must pay," and then after some time, he would slip away.

However, continually, he would pray, "Is there anyone among the intimate friends of God, in this world and the next, with the patience to bear companionship with me?"

"Among all the beings that exist, the only noble companion for you is Mevlana Rumi," said a voice, coming from the world of mystery.

---

185. See section #435 of this volume.

And that is the reason why Shamsuddin left for Anatolia [Rum].

Speaking with the Beloved [550b]

It is also reported that the second time he arrived in Konya, Shamsuddin and Mevlana spent six entire months in each other's company in the cell of Mevlana's medresse where they had nothing to eat or to drink, or any comings and goings of other people. No one except Salahuddin and Sultan Walad were allowed to enter. They ascended to such a high spiritual station that the ranks indicated by: *God will exalt by many degrees those of you who have attained to faith and above all, such as have been vouchsafed true knowledge* [58:12] remained the lowest of spiritual stations in comparison.

When at dawn, the sun shows his face in the east,
in truth, the stars cover their heads.

Endeavor on the Way [551]

At a gathering of the shaikhs of the epoch, Shamsuddin was sharing divine insights. He said:

If you are working hard, then why is nothing done?
And if you aren't, why are you so pained?

Everyone's a drum-player, and yet there is no sound;
all of them work, yet no one earns a thing.

Maybe you have followed the religious path for a long time and yet have not arrived at a village or a carvanserai; you have seen no sign, nor heard the sound of dogs or roosters—it is a strange road. Like an ox or a donkey, one can travel a long time and yet still remain in the same place.

A foolish person labors today, but says, "My pay will come tomorrow." Even if it does, shouldn't you see at least some trace of it today? You hang around the table of generous men and sovereigns, wagging your tail, but you've ended up with not even a crumb of bread nor bit of bone.

You say, "The glance of the saints is the philosopher's stone; surely he upon whom it falls is transformed, relieved of bitterness and blindness." You also say, "So and so is a great Friend of God, his miracles are such and such,"—as though you have met such people, and yet, the same bitterness and sourness absorbs you, or even worse.

You tell me, "I saw such and such a great person and drank of the Water of Life. I have polished the mirror of my self, endured spiritual struggles and fasts of forty days (*cille*), and made great efforts for many years." And yet I see that your situation is darker than ever.

Such a person appears proudly before the poor ones and, with hostility, boasts, "We possess knowledge, grandeur, position, and allowances that these people do not have."

May dust fall on their heads and on their hundred thousand bits of knowledge and notebooks!

He says, "I have students and friends."

I say, "May dust fall on his head and that of his disciples!" A chunk of ice is the friend of another chunk of ice and a piece of baggage with another bag. Try as I might I can neither see nor hear a trace or breath of life in these people. May God protect us from such a situation. They feel the challenge of their passions and are afraid. How do they expect to even find the path or ever drink from the same cup as Abu Yazid?

Flee this dervish attached to his food.
We want a true dervish, like Abu Yazid.

How beautiful this saying is: "God has created some men for battle and others for bowls of soggy bread."

Conveying the Qur'an [552]

When Shamsuddin arrived in Erzerum, he occupied himself with teaching school. In that city, there was a respected sovereign who had a son who was extremely beautiful and perfect, but very stupid. None of the scholars were able to teach him to recite the Qur'an, and the situation was such that in a whole year he was not able to recite even a thirtieth (*juz*) of the Qur'an. The king came to visit Shamsuddin and described to him the state of his son.

"With God's help, I will make him a *hafiz* in a month," replied Shams.

The king entrusted his son to him, and the boy learned a thirtieth by heart everyday, so that within a month he could recite the entire Qur'an easily. He also learned to write and to recite many pleasing and beneficial verses. The king and his wife and everyone in in his retinue, his servants, relatives, and friends, became disciples of this master. The king's son was particularly devoted in love for him. When Shamsuddin realized the extent to which his Friendship with God had become renowned, he disappeared that same day and left for Anatolia. Wherever he stayed along the way, a hundred thousand miracles and extraordinary happenings would flow forth from him; then he would set off again.

> Love has the scent of musk, and so it is covered with shame;
> that's the way it is; musk ends up covered with disgrace.[186]

Humility Elicits Grace [554]

The intimate Friends reported that one day, Mevlana called Sultan Walad to him and said:

"Go to Damascus with some of the Friends and look for Mevlana Shamsuddin. Take two thousand coins of silver and gold and pour it into the shoes of this sultan of Tabriz, and turn his shoes toward Rum. Take him my greetings as well as my prostrations of love! When with grace you arrive in Damascus, go to that well-known caravanersai on the mountain of Salihiyya. There you will find Mevlana Shamsuddin playing backgammon with a young European boy. You will see that he will win money from this Frank and that, as a result, the young boy will slap him in the face. Don't be upset by this—this boy is one of the Poles of Spirit of the Time, but he is not yet aware of himself. He must reach perfection, through association with Shamsuddin and through receiving his grace, and become his disciple."

Sultan Walad made his preparations for departure and set out with twenty gracious and worthy Friends. When they found the caravanserai that Mevlana had described, they dismounted and

186. Musk, one of the favorite fragrances of the Prophet Muhammad, has many subtle qualitites. Produced by an abdominal gland, from an area of "disgrace," and yet creative possibility, it is produced especially during the mating season. It has been renowned for centuries for both its fragrance and medicinal properties. It is known to enhance sense perception, stimulate blood circulation, and reduce inflammation and fever, and it is reputed to be more effective as an antidote for snake venom than hydrocortisone. A musk deer is extremely agile and able to turn about easily, bounding quickly from place to place.

stood respectfully at the door. The situation was exactly as Mevlana had described.

Sultan Walad and his Friends bowed, all together, and displayed such respect and submission when they greeted Shamsuddin that the young Frank paled, full of fear, and asked himself why he had behaved so rudely to such an important person.

Mevlana Shamsuddin embraced Sultan Walad, and demonstrating affection for him beyond measure, he asked about Mevlana. Sultan Walad conveyed his father's love and greetings, and then poured the gift of all the gold and silver into his blessed shoes and offered apologies. They say it was worth two thousand gold dinars.

Sultan Walad then said, "All the Friends from Rum have prostrated before you, in perfect sincerity, and ask forgiveness for their bad behavior. They beg pardon and have repented and swear that from now on they will never again be rude or allow envy to enter their hearts." He assured him that everyone was waiting for his wondrous return.

Then due to his perfect generosity and abundant kindness, Shamsuddin consented to leave for Rum. The young Frankish boy bared his head and stood in the pay-machan posture of penitence.[187] Having attained to faith, he wanted to give away his fortune.

Mevlana Shamsuddin would not let him do this and said, "Return to Europe and visit the dear Friends of God of that country. Be the Pole of their gatherings and remember us in your prayers."

When the companions were ready to leave, Sultan Walad brought his horse for Mevlana Shamsuddin to mount, and they set off at an ambling pace with Sultan Walad walking beside the saddle.

"O Bahauddin, mount, too," Shamsuddin said.

Sultan Walad bowed and said, "A King and a slave should not both be on horseback together."

Sultan Walad journeyed on foot from Damascus to Konya, out of love and in the service of this sovereign. He said:

I could travel on foot for a hundred thousand centuries,
while this celestial sphere turns, and still not find,

187. This position of *pay-machan* was the posture of penitence of the dervishes. They would stand on one foot and, crossing their arms over their chest, would hold each ear with the opposite hand, in repentance.

in the jousting-place of Time, a horseman such as you.

After an astonishing number of miracles and marvels that the Friends witnessed with him along the way, they arrived at the caravanserai at Zanjirli; from there they sent one of the dervishes ahead to announce their arrival to Mevlana. He was so overjoyed that in gratitude he gave his turban, cloaks, and other clothes he was wearing to the bearer of this good news and sent a crier to announce Shamsuddin's arrival throughout Konya, so that lowly and great, religious scholars, dervishes and amirs, and others might come to welcome him. So many people, men and women, came out that it was impossible to count them.

When Shamsuddin and Mevlana arrived in each other's presence, they cried out and fell senseless from their horses. Then they embraced, and made holy prostrations in front of each other, transported into another world. The Sultan's army unfurled the imperial banners and beat the drums. The reciters recited extraordinary poems and the Friends walked along, whirling in sema due to their joy.

The world has come to life, full of splendor!
Amazing! Today, day is really day!

Then, with great joy, Shamsuddin told Mevlana, in the presence of all the assembled distinguished people of Konya, of the kindness that Sultan Walad had shown him, of how well he had been served by him, and of their conversations.

Shams said, "God has given me the gift of two things: the first is my head (*sar*) and the second is my innermost secret (*sirr*). I have sacrificed my head in all sincerity for the Way of Mevlana, and my innermost secret I have given to Bahauddin—may Mevlana be witness to this. If Bahauddin were to live as long as Noah, spending his life in devotions and mortifications, still he could not gain that which has come to him from me during this journey. It is hoped that he also receives something from you, becomes a perfect elder (*pir*) and a great shaikh, God willing."

The Sun Rises in Damascus [555-556]

When Mevlana became completely immersed in the love of Shamsuddin of Tabriz, and his bewilderment, ecstasy, and agitation became a hundred times greater than it had before, the rebellious disciples became consumed with envy and behaved rudely.

As he said:

Once again, the foolhardy have cast aside civility
and sown the seeds of ingratitude and envy.
They have killed themselves and turned from the path.
What they have done, they have become, and disappeared.

It is reported that it was during this period that the dreadful unrighteous deed took place.[188] Our great Master was overcome with sorrow and after forty days, to calm the hatred of the envious and to stop the gloating of the faithless enemies without religion, he appointed Chelebi Husamuddin as director of the companions and decided to leave again for Syria. He went to Damascus, where he stayed for a year, more or less. All the religious scholars, the shaikhs, the king who was ruling, the lowly and the great, in all sincerity and in perfect love became his disciples and servants. On the road to Damasus he composed this blessed *ghazal*:

We, the lovers of Damascus, bewildered and crazy,
have set our heart upon seeing that city.
For the third time, we have left Rum, hastening towards Syria,
perfumed by the scents of Damascus
flowing from a lock of hair, dark like the night.
If the Master Shams al-Haqq (Sun of Truth) of Tabriz is there,
we are the servant of Damascus, and what a Master!

And in another *ghazal*, he said:

---

188. Shams disappeared twice due to the tensions in the community. The first time, after the foment grew so strong among Mevlana's disciples and friends in the community, after less than two years of being together with Mevlana (from November of 1244 to March of 1246), Shams disappeared. In his *Maqalat* (See *Rumi's Sun*, "A Cold Breath", p.230), Shams describes some of the difficulties of his journey. Mevlana was distraught to lose his friend and sent his older son Sultan Walad in search of him. He found Shams in Damascus and brought him back to Konya in May of 1247. For a while the atmosphere was better—to make Mevlana happy, his students welcomed Shams back to Konya. Shams indicates that part of the reason he had disappeared was that Mevlana also might be cooked within that separation, so that then he was even better able to receive what Shams had to give. However, it wasn't long before discontent surfaced again and Mevlana's son, Alauddin, it seems was in the midst of the conflict and among those who attacked him. On December 5, 1247 Shams disappeared, never to be seen again. It was Love that brought him back, and it was Love that took him further.

News has arrived that Shams of Tabriz is in Syria;
If this is true, it will be morning forever in Syria.[189]

The Sun Within [557]

All the inhabitants of Konya and the great ones of Anatolia were driven to despair by our Master's absence. They informed the Sultan and the amirs about the situation—they then wrote to Mevlana and beseeched him to return. All the religious scholars, shaikhs, *qadis*, amirs, and notables of the country affixed their seals to this letter and couriers were sent to summon his blessed presence home. He was called to return to his native land, to be near his dear father's tomb, and the invitation was accompanied by one hundred thousand lamentations and demonstrations of humility.

Mevlana, moved by his noble Muhammadan character, felt that it was his duty to accept the invitation; he returned to Konya and began to again call to the people.

Although he did not find Mevlana Shamsuddin in Damascus, or anywhere else in the manifest world, he found him within and more besides. He continued to overflow with love.

As he would say:

Open your hand, take hold of your own robe—
the balm that will heal the wound is this beard.

Shamsuddin of Tabriz is the beginning;
now it's our own beauty and grace that we see. It is we!

The dear Friends told us that one day Mevlana bowed before the door of Shamsuddin's cell and wrote in red ink in his own blessed handwriting: "Abode of Khidr's beloved, may peace be with him."

I Am Near [558]

Some of the companions were in agreement that when Shamsuddin disappeared, after being wounded by the conspirators, that he was buried beside our Great Master [Bahauddin Walad] (May God magnify their memory). However, our shaikh, that sultan of mystics, Chelebi 'Arif learned from his mother, Fatima Khatun [the

189. This verse includes a play of words between the meaning of *Sham* (the Arabic name for Syria) and the morning opened with *shams* ("the sun," in Arabic), highlighting the Light emanating from Shams of Tabriz.

wife of Sultan Walad] that when Shamsuddin was honored with the felicity of martyrdom, those miserable rogues threw him into a well.

At night in a dream, Sultan Walad beheld Mevlana Shamsuddin who told him, "I am lying in such and such a place." At midnight, he gathered the intimate friends together, and they pulled the saint's blessed body from the well. They perfumed him with rosewater, musk, and fragrances, and buried him in the medresse of our Master, beside Amir Badruddin who had built the medresse. This is a secret that no one knows—May God be pleased with them all.[190]

A Fortune of Blessing [559]

The scribes among the Friends related that when Shamsuddin set out for Syria the first time and remained in that region, several times Mevlana wrote him amazing letters in which he expressed his profound longing for Shamsuddin and invited him with perfect grace to return.

In the first letter, after presenting his greetings and love, Mevlana wrote:

> Come back to us, O light of my heart!
> Come, O Object of my quest and my desire—
> You know our life is in your hands;
> don't abandon us to sorrow! Come!
> O Love! O Beloved!
> Don't resist and turn away! Come!
> O Solomon! Master of hoopoes!
> Yield to our entreaties! Come!
> O You who are the first,
> who have first shown the Truth of Love! Come!
> From separation, our spirits cry out in pain;
> fulfill the promise of return and come!
> Veil faults and bestow blessing—
> that's the way of the generous. Come!
> How does one say, "Come" in Persian? "*Biya*!"
> Come then, or give us recompense. Come!

190. One may visit the *makam* of Shams at the Mosque of Shams-i Tabriz on a side street adjacent to a small park, a short walk from Mevlana's resting place in Konya. The tradition is to visit Shams first, to pray there, and then to go to visit Mevlana where he rests in what is now the "Mevlana Museum."

When you come, what fulfilled desire and felicity!
And if you don't, what desolation. Come!
O victory of Arabs and Qobad of Persians!
Your remembrance alone conquers my heart.
My heart implores you, "Come!"
O you, for whom all that has been and will be exists, come!
For you, O my moon, I have traversed many lands!
O embrace me and these lands. Come!
You are like the sun that approaches and then leaves;
O you, who are so near your servants, come!

In a third letter, he wrote:

Long life to the great chief!
May God be his guardian and protector!
All the delights others buy on credit—
may it be the ready currency of ecstasy for him.
From his warm gathering so full of sweetness
may those who are cold-natured be absent.
May the spirits that open at the door of the Unseen
be interlocked before him like the designs on a carpet.
May good fortune be on his right and his left,
to the north and south of him!
May he be the king and governor
over body and soul.
Shamsuddin of Tabriz is good fortune in ready cash—
it is enough for me!
Let someone else borrow on credit.

And a fourth letter:

I swear by God, who has existed for all eternity,
Ever-living, All-knowing, Almighty and Everlasting:
his light has lit the candles of love on fire,
so that one hundred thousand secrets have opened.
With a single command from him, the world was filled
with lovers and love, sovereigns and subjects.
Under the talismans of Shamsuddin of Tabriz
the treasure of his wonders was concealed.
From the moment you left on your journey,
we have been like wax, deprived of sweetness.
All night we burn like a candle,

joined with his fire, but without honey.
Because of separation from his beauty,
our body is ruined, and our soul, like an owl, wanders there.
Draw your reins in this direction—
cover with tar the trunk of the elephant of pleasure.
Without your presence, the sema is unlawful
and chased away with stones, like Satan.
Without you, not one *ghazal* could be written,
until the arrival of that honored letter.
Then, from the joy of hearing your letter read,
five or six *ghazals* burst forth.
May our night through you become a bright morning—
you who are the glory of Syria, Armenia, and Rum!

PART THREE

Unfolding Love

Chapter V
Salahuddin Zarkubi

The Marvels of the Sultan of Mystics, Salahuddin al-Haqq wa'l Din Feridun bin Yaghibasan of Konya, known as Zarkub (the Gold-beater) (May God sanctify his mystery).

Deepening Presence [560]

The great companions related:

When Mevlana had stopped searching for Shamsuddin of Tabrizi and had discovered the mysteries of that great saint within his own being, he brought Shaikh Salahuddin close and appointed him to be his representative and leader of the Friends, and made him his intimate companion at gatherings and on retreats. Our Master found peace in the generous presence of this Friend, and the disciples delighted in the excellence of spiritual nourishment that opened through them.

Even though some people continued to be envious and tried to drive Mevlana and Salahuddin apart, only damaging themselves, the companions profited from their presence together, without difficulties, for ten entire years. Because Mevlana had especially abundant kindness and concern for Sultan Walad (May God sanctify both their mysteries), he encouraged him to devote himself to the Friends of God and to serve Shaikh Salahuddin. He encouraged him not to deprive himself of his company but rather to attend to him attentively.

Eloquence and Ecstasy [562-563]

The noble Friends recounted:

In the ardor of his youth, before he met Mevlana and became his disciple and companion, Shaikh Salahuddin was the disciple of Sayyid Burhanuddin Mohaqqiq of Tirmidh. He was very attached to him and worked devotedly in his service. When Mevlana became the Sayyid's disciple, Salahuddin renewed his devotion and became our Master's disciple as well.

Sayyid Burhanuddin (May God be satisfied with him!) said, "Two great gifts were bestowed on me by my spiritual director, the Sultan of the Wise; the first is eloquence in words (*qal*), and the second is the beauty of spiritual states (*hal*). I gave my eloquence to Mevlana Jalaluddin, because he has ecstatic states in abundance; and I made a gift of my ecstasies to Shaikh Salahuddin, because he doesn't have the capacity for words."

There were those who criticized Salahuddin, calling him ignorant and common; but it was they who were ignorant and blind, unable to distinguish between an "*ammi* (common man)," and one who is "*ummi* (illiterate)"; they could not distinguish between a well-guarded tablet (*lawh mahfuz*) of a heart that is pure, and a recording tablet (*lawh hafiz*) of one just reciting the Quran.

For some time, Mevlana was occupied with increasing his religious knowledge and the knowledge of religious opinions, and teaching and the practice of remembrance (*dhikr*), while Shaikh Salahuddin worked in his goldsmith's shop earning his lawful sustenance and gaining the power (*quwwat*) for spiritual states.

Reunion [564]

The old Friends told us that Shaikh Salahuddin's father and mother lived in the village of Kamila, near Konya, where they fished in the nearby lake. When Sayyid Burhanuddin left Konya for Kayseri, where he died, Shaikh Salahuddin went to visit his mother and father. He stayed some time with them, and while he was there they arranged for his marriage.

One day, he returned to Konya and attended the Friday prayer gathering at the Bu'l-Fazl mosque. That day, Mevlana was giving the sermon and deep in ecstasy, he shared innumerable divine insights from Sayyid. Suddenly, the spiritual states of Sayyid came to Salahuddin through an intense light coming from Mevlana. He cried out, arose, and approached the pulpit. He uncovered his head, bowed, and kissed Mevlana's feet numerous times, prostrating before him.

Mevlana received him with kindness and asked, "Where were you?"

"I was married," answered Salahuddin. "Neglectful of your greatness, I deprived myself of your company."

"No, no," replied our Master, "You belong to us! You are our soul, our life, our own dearly beloved." He took his hand and made him his intimate Friend.

Golden Moments [567]

One day, Mevlana, who had become famous for his spiritual states and his sacred dancing, was walking in the market through the section where the goldbeaters were working. The rhythmic sound, and "tic-tac" of the goldsmiths as they worked was such a delight to his blessed ears that he began to turn.

Shaikh Salahuddin then received inspiration from the Unseen to go outside his workshop because Mevlana was dancing outside, and a considerable crowd had formed around him. The Shaikh cried out and emerging from his shop, threw himself at Mevlana's feet and fainted. Our Master then brought him into the circle of whirling, kissed his cheeks and hair, and embraced him.

The shaikh asked Mevlana for his graceful pardon, "I don't have the strength to perform the sema." Salahuddin had become weak due to extreme mortifications and spiritual stuggle.

He indicated to his apprentices to remain in the shop and to continue their work of beating the gold, and not to stop until Mevlana had finished the sema. It is customary in gold-smithery that one only strikes the sheets of gold with a certain number of blows otherwise they crumble into tiny fragments. However, the sema lasted from the noon prayer until the afternoon prayer, when the reciters arrived and began to recite this *ghazal*:

> A treasure has appeared in this goldsmith's shop!
> O form! What essence it contains!
> Beauty! Such Beauty! . . .

The Shaikh returned to the shop and saw that it was full of gold-leaf; all the gold-beating tools had turned to gold, and not a single sheet of gold had been ruined. When the Shaikh perceived the mines of the two worlds within his shop, he tore his clothes and ordered that the whole shop be given away. He then renounced any thought of the two worlds and left in the company of Mevlana. Mevlana saw the same friendship with God, and honor and glory, in Salahuddin as he had in our Master Shamsuddin, and so he treated him with the same affection and favor. Salahuddin's pure but anxious soul found tranquility. He and Mevlana spent ten years in close companionship, and Shaikh Salahuddin served as his representative (*khalifa*).

The Light of Love [568]

Sultan Walad told us:

One day, Shaikh Salahuddin said to my father, "Within my body there were sources of hidden lights, and I wasn't aware of it. You have helped open my eyes, so that I now see these lights which dance before my eyes like the sea."

One day, my father said, "Don't mention Mevlana Shamsuddin in the presence of Shaikh Salahuddin, nor Salahuddin in the presence of Chelebi Husamuddin. Although there is complete union between their lights and no differences, divine jealousy is at work, and it is not wise to excite it; to avoid doing so is the courtesy (*adab)* of the Friends."

A Part of the Whole [569]

Sultan Walad said:

My father was sharing inspired insights regarding the meaning of homogeneity and affinity. He said, "The cause of love between people is homogeneity and affinity. These are not just words." Then he recited:

What is homogeneity? Affinity
that allows us to see a path towards one another.
One destined for the Garden is harmonious with Paradise;
the worshipper of God is also like that.
It is not miracles that cause faith,
but similarity of kind that attracts the attributes.

He said, "The human being is attracted to the world of the prophets and saints, because he is a part of them and bears a similarity to them. The Prophet (Peace and blessings be upon him) said, 'O God Most Great! Guide my people!' which means 'all my parts.'

The Prophet said, 'You are a part of me;
why tear a part away from the whole?' "

Beyond Imagining [574]

One day, Sultan Walad asked Mevlana, "Our Shaikh Salahuddin used to tell us about the various mysterious lights he could see. He would say, 'Behold the sea of white light!' Or other times he would say, 'I see a sea of blue light,' or 'I see a green light,' or 'I see a yellow light!' He also spoke about light the color of smoke. And he, also, said 'I see a sea of black light tumultuous with waves!' However, he no longer mentions these lights. Could it be that they are now veiled from him?"

"God forbid!" replied our Master. "On the contrary, in the past he saw lights in small numbers in succession, and each time he saw them, he would tell us about it; now, he is so immersed in the sea of divine lights that he cannot describe them or tell us about them at all.

> How can we conceive of You, when you have no form?
> Form is just foam on the Ocean of meaning."

A Sensitive Soul [575]

The distinguished women of Konya came to find Kira Khatun, Mevlana's wife, to ask her to accompany them to the Qarata'i medresse to attend the gathering [of traveling Rifa'i dervishes displaying feats] that was taking place there. They were very insistent, and after many entreaties, even though she was not so inclined and did not have Mevlana's permission, out of embarassment, Kira Khatun agreed to go. That day, Mevlana had gone to the mosque in Meram with a few of the Friends, and when he returned home in the evening he was very upset with his wife.[1] He gave her jealous looks and staring at her with a penetrating gaze cried: "Bravo, what cold!"

---

1. There are many Rifa'i dervishes of deep heart in the Sufi lineage of Ahmad Rifa'i (d. 1181 C.E.) who are known for their healing capacities and "howling" chanted devotion. However there are also those who display their feats of maneauvers with dangerous snakes, walking on fire, and the dramatic piercing of the body with large skewers in order to impress others. It seems Mevlana may have warned Kira Khatun about such things, especially as she was such a sensitive and pure soul (clearly there was a great deal of love and respect between them, i.e., see section #457). As Aflaki mentions just prior to this passage, "To the people, these extraordinary feats seemed to be miracles. However, for perfected adepts and Masters of ecstasy to perform miracles and to reveal extraordinary things is a matter of subtlety."

Kira Khatun swooned and fainted. When she arose, trembling, she went to prostrate herself at the feet of Shaikh Salahuddin. "It was not my wish; the ladies insisted, so that I was embarrassed not to go," she wept. "For the love of God, intercede for me and rescue me from Mevlana's anger.

Forgive the weakness of our understanding,
O You who are beyond reason and imagination!
O Lord! We have erred! It is done—
be merciful, You who are so compassionate!"

Shaikh Salahuddin uncovered his head, bowed and interceded for her, as her supplicant. Mevlana responded, "The arrow has left the bow. May she be free from the miseries of the Next World and not be deprived of the Mercy that is shown towards the forgiven."

Just then, a strange illness came to the blessed body of Kira Khatun, and she suddenly became very cold. She trembled and groaned beyond description, and for the rest of her life, she could never feel warm; all the skilled doctors were powerless to cure this illness and could find no remedy. Even in the middle of July, she wore a Bartas fur and a woven veil of silk upon her head. She always had a brazier full of coals and a candle lit in her room, even in the middle of the day.

However, word spread of the miracles she could perform as a result of her state—she was able to reveal the hidden thoughts and secrets of people. The distinguished men and ladies of the city had immense faith in her and became her disciples. Until her final breath, she never left her home, unless it was at night when she would go to the bath. Many people honored and revered her. Sultan Walad and Chelebi Husamuddin (May God sanctify their innermost mysteries) respected her greatly and honored her as a mother.

Prayers for a Mother [576]

When the funeral of Shaikh Salahuddin's mother, Latifa Khatun, occurred, the reciters and mourners left after she had been buried in the sepulchral niche, but the Shaikh remained for a long time at the grave. Finally Mevlana beckoned that it was time for him to go, as well.

The Shaikh bowed and said, "I owe her a great deal. I would like to deliver her from the torment of questioning, the terrors of the grave, and the awesome presence of the angels, Monkar and Nakir; then I will go. I beg of you that in the terrible loneliness of the grave, she not be deprived of the company of the *houris*."

Finally, he smiled and agreed to leave.

Like Milk and Honey [578]

The Friends told us that when Sultan Walad reached puberty, Mevlana arranged a marriage for him with Shaikh Salahuddin's daughter, Fatima Khatun. He, himself, had taught the young girl to read and write, and he spent a great deal of time with her, since he held her in high regard.

One day, he said, "Fatima Khatun (May God be pleased with her and with her father) is my right eye and her sister, Hadiyya Khatun, is my left. All those honorable women who visit me come partially veiled, with the exception of Fatima and her sister who come completely unveiled."

Concerning Latifa Khatun, who was their mother, he said, "Latifa Khatun is the embodiment of God's subtle grace (*latif*), because she is the namesake of the Shaikh's mother (May God sanctify their subtle souls!)"

One day, Mevlana said to his companions, "When Fatima Khatun married our Bahauddin (Sultan Walad) all the archangels and *houris* in Paradise rejoiced and beat their drums congratulating each other on this marriage and joined in a sema of praise." On the wedding night, he composed this elegy of love:

> Blessed be the weddings and celebrations
>   that God has granted for us;
> our hearts have opened and kindred souls are joined.
> Care has flown thanks to the kindness of our Lord.

And on the night the bride was taken to her husband's house, he composed the following *ghazal*:

> May all the felicity of all marriages shine upon this wedding;
> May the blessings of the Night of Power,[2]

2. The "Night of Power" is the night in which the Qur'an was first revealed to Muhammad, during the month of Ramadan. One continues to watch for that Night of Power, hidden among the nights . . . See *Surah al Qadr* 97:1-5.

In the Name of God, the Infinitely Compassionate and Most Merciful

We have indeed revealed this during the Night of Power.

Ramadan, and the *'Eid* (holiday) that completes it,
and also the blessings of Adam when he met Eve,
that of the reunion of Joseph and Jacob,
and the happiness of the Garden, Paradise, be with them as well.
And a blessing beyond words—
the joyous union of the child of the Shaikh and our eldest son—
may celebration coins rain down upon this union.
May their intimacy and felicity be like milk and honey,
this intimate union and fidelity be mingled like sugar and halvah.
May the blessings of the companions and the cupbearer
be granted to the person who says "*Amin*"
for the one who offers this prayer.

Fatima performed many miracles both in the inner and in the manifest world. She constantly fasted during the day and kept vigil at night. She would only break her fast every two or three days. She gave food to the poor ones, to orphans, and to widows, and distributed clothes and gifts to the needy. She made a habit of eating little, sleeping little, and speaking little.

She could clearly see the mysterious forms that are the spiritual beings of the World Beyond and was able to show them to those of her friends who were worthy of such an experience, to Gurji Khatun, to Gumaj Khatun, and to the daughter of the Parvana of Toqat. She could clearly perceive people's secret thoughts. In her youth, when she was like the *pure milk of Paradise* [47:15], she could not bear to be separated from Mevlana for a moment and learned marvellous secrets of illumination from his blessed mouth. In achieving Friendship with God, inner discipline, and a pure, chaste soul, she was educated by this supreme teacher and was the accomplished student of his loving care.

Have We Not Expanded Your Heart? [581]

These are some of Salahuddin's reflections (May God bless his innermost secret):

And what will explain to you what the Night of Power is?

The Night of Power is better than a thousand months.
Within it the angels descend bearing divine inspiration

by God's permission upon every mission:
Peace!... This until the rise of dawn!

"The Friend of God is a mine of mercy—through his presence people find felicity, repose, and mercy, and they are brought to life through his light, which never diminishes. Someone who lacks this quality is not a Friend of God. The sema of the mystic is a presence he has with God. Someone who hears the Word of God from God—how can you say it is 'lawful' or 'unlawful' in regard to him?

"The attribute of the saint of God is that his heart has been opened, as it is said in the Holy Qur'an, *Have we not expanded your heart* [94:1]? When he looks into himself, he sees an ocean of light, and he plays lovingly (*ishq-bazi*) within it."

Then he said, "Is there anyone in this land who understands our words?"

"Yes, the poor and the unfortunate," replied Mevlana.

For everything he said was from the mysteries of an ecstastic state (*hal*) and the people of external discourse had no opening to it.

There Is No Prayer without Presence [583]

One day, Mevlana Shamsuddin of Tabriz repeated, in the presence of our Master, Shaikh Salahuddin, and the noble Friends, the *hadith* of the Prophet (Peace and blessings upon him): "There is no ritual prayer without the *Qur'an*," and also, "There is no ritual prayer without concentrated presence of the heart (*huzur*)."

Then Shamsuddin continued, "People suppose that if there is presence of heart, they no longer need the outward form of the prayer. These people say that it is shameful to continue to search for a way to meet God, after having reached the goal. Suppose it is true as they claim, that they have reached complete ecstasy, Friendship with God, and tranquility of heart. Even so, to abandon the outward practice of prayer reveals an insufficiency on their part.

"The Prophet, peace and blessings upon him, attained this state of ecstasy that they claim to have attained. If anyone says that the Prophet (Peace and blessings upon him) did not attain this state, may they die! If they say that he has, then we would reply to them, 'Why don't you follow this Noble Messenger, this Bringer of Happy News without equal, this Illuminating Lamp?'

"If there were before us two saints, one whose Friendship with God was evident and one whose Friendship with God was not outwardly manifest, if the second 'So and so'-uddin persevered and was faithful to his outward practices and the first was not, I would follow the second one, and not even greet the other."

Then Shamsuddin turned to Shaikh Salahuddin and asked him to comment on what he had said.

"The judgment is yours; we have nothing to add to your words, nor any objection to them," Salahuddin replied.

The Rain of Mercy [585]

Mevlana wrote to a great man in his own blessed handwriting:

May your exalted spirit know that when Shaikh Salahuddin talks about the arrival of the rain of mercy, he does not mean the kind of rain that make your clothes wet. He is talking about the rain that purifies your heart and makes it subtle, illuminated, and transparent.

Yesterday, a group of people arrived. There was a downpour so strong that no roof or wall could serve as a shelter. This was an illuminating and very subtle rain.

I considered, "So many thousands of turbaned shaikhs, adepts, and worthy people in the world are deprived of this divine rain of mercy. May they know that this has to do with your favor and acceptance.

He said, "This rain comes from the Beyond; it is a rain of Mercy pouring down upon the companions of deep meaning. Only those who are capable of contemplating the Beyond can see the light and the rains of this World of Mystery."

This rain does not come from the clouds of this sky;
the Unseen world has other clouds and rain.
Only the special Friends can see that—
the others are still lost *in doubt about a new creation* [50:14].

Give Something for God [586]

When they wanted to give Shaikh Salahuddin's daughter, Hadiyya Khatun (May God be satisfied with her and with her father) to be married, he did not have any provisions to offer the customary trousseau for her. The young girl continued to live in Mevlana's household.

Sultan Walad and Chelebi Husamuddin tried to organize a marriage for her with Mevlana Nizamuddin the Calligrapher (*Khattat*), that Sultan of scribes and teacher of Sultans, the second Ibn Bawwab[3] and pupil of Ibn Moqla,[4] the arraigned. The marriage plans were not proceeding, because of lack of money and trousseau, and Sultan Walad and Chelebi Husamuddin went to discuss the situation with Mevlana. He immediately called for Osta Khatun, a Friend of God, a scholar and tutor (*ostad*), who lived in Gurji Khatun's palace and taught the sultan's daughter.

He said to her, "Go to my daughter Gurji Khatun; convey our greeetings and tell her about Hadiyya Khatun's problem. Let her prepare a trousseau with the help of the amirs' wives and their daughters. If they each give Hadiyya Khatun a gift (*hadiyya*), it will please Shaikh Salahuddin, and they will receive his favor," Mevlana said, "so that his elevated thought might encompass their worldly and spiritual well-being and he might protect them."

Osta Khatun hung a begging basket around her neck and ran to the Sultan's palace, crying, "*Give something for God*!" She conveyed Mevlana's greetings to the noble ladies and recounted the situation. They all made a donation, and bowing, expressed their gratitude for Mevlana's kindness in suggesting this opportunity for generosity and encouraging them in it. Right away, the Queen of the World, Gurji Khatun, ordered her treasurer to bring two or three clothes-presses and to prepare all sorts of clothing, five sets of each.

They gathered almost twenty pairs of diamond and gold earrings, twenty valuable rings, necklaces, headpieces and hats woven out of gold thread, beautiful veils, bracelets decorated with precious stones, and other costly objects. They brought tapestries and rugs from Georgia, Shiraz, and Aksaray, wooden and copper trays, cauldrons, copper and porcelain bowls, mortars, candle holders, a complete set of kitchen utensils, and each object was of a grandeur appropriate to the donor, as is the custom with generous nobles. All of this was given to Osta Khatun who arranged for it to be transported on the royal mules to our Master's medresse. It was reported that they carried almost seventy thousand dirhems

---

3. Ibn Bawwab was a famous calligrapher from Baghdad who studied with Ibn Moqla.

4. Abu 'Ali Ibn Moqla (d. 940 C.E.) was a master calligrapher who served as vizier to several caliphs, but eventually was imprisoned on charges of conspiracy. This is a play on words between his name and the arabic meaning of "*moqla*" (pupil of the eye).

soltani in gold vessels alone, and the rest was of similar value.

Mevlana was delighted and Shaikh Salahuddin even more so, and they offered prayers to heaven for the benefactors. Mevlana ordered the trousseau to be divided in half—one half he gave to Fatima Khatun, the mother of Chelebi 'Arif, and the other to Hadiyya Khatun as her trousseau of blessing. They then gave her in marriage to Mevlana Nizamuddin the Calligrapher.

The wedding took place that same day with a great feast, and from it they distributed alms. The splendor of this marriage remained in the memory of the inhabitants of Konya for many years. Mevlana composed the following *ghazal*:

> May this wedding be blessed for us;
> may it be a happiness.
> May it remain forever like milk, and sugar,
> like wine and halvah.
> May it give shade and bear fruit,
> like the date palm, for all to enjoy . . . [5]

May the Rose-Garden of Your Face Flourish Eternally [587]

The best Companions and great Friends recounted that Shaikh Salahuddin remained in the loyal service and company of our Master for ten years. During that time, Salahuddin was his steadfast representative (*khalifa*) and his trustworthy friend. Then the era of Salahuddin's good health ended as his life was drawing to a close.

---

5. See "This Marriage," *The Pocket Rumi*, translation by Kabir Helminski, Shambhala Publications, 2001 p.34:

> May these vows and this marriage be blessed.
> May it be sweet milk,
> this marriage, like wine and halvah.
> May this marriage offer fruit and shade
> like the date palm.
> May this marriage be full of laughter,
> our every day a day in paradise.
> May this marriage be a sign of compassion,
> a seal of happiness here and hereafter.
> May this marriage have a fair face and a good name,
> an omen as welcome
> as the moon in a clear blue sky.
> I am out of words to describe
> how spirit mingles in this marriage.

Through the effect of Destiny, his complexion paled and a weakness came to his blessed body. His illness deepened more and more. Mevlana visited him continually, sitting at his blessed bedside and sharing marvellous secrets and wondrous reflections.

One day, the Shaikh, carried away by his longing and Divine coquetry, said, "Unless Muhammad, the Messenger of God (Blessings and peace be upon him) enters the grave with me, I will not leave this world."

"I will request this of him and intercede for you," Mevlana promised him. "Don't be concerned about it, your wish will be granted."

Then the Shaikh asked for permission to depart in perfect joy. Mevlana responded to his request and did not visit him for three days. Then he wrote with his own hand to Salahuddin: "I am remembering that the Master of the Heart and of the people of heart, Pole of the Two Worlds, Salahuddin (May God spread His shadow over him) protested about a certain matter which had been troubling him for some time. May God Most High forgive him, because in His forgiveness rests the forgiveness of all the truly faithful. As unique as the letter, 'alif,' if he [Muhammad], rather than I, comes to see you:

O you who are like a cypress,
may you be protected from the autumn winds.
O eye of the world, may you also be protected
from the glance of the evil ones.
O soul of heaven and earth,
may nothing come to you but mercy and repose.

I was told that he who cared for me became ill, too;
I felt worthy to be his substitute.
O my Lord, I ask that this illness be *a source of inner peace* [21:69];
may it be ease and contentment.

May the pain of the body be absent,
O you who are the repose of our souls.
And may the evil eye be far from you,
O you who are our seeing eye.
O moon! Your health is the health of our soul
and that of the world.
May your body be healthy, O moon-faced one!

May your body be blessed with well-being,
O you who whose body is the seven planets' soul!
May the protection of your grace never leave us.
May the rose-garden of your face eternally flourish,
because it is the pasture of our heart, its open country.
May your suffering be upon ourself, not your body,
so that, like reason, it might adorn our soul."

The Shaikh then knew that he was going to die, and he departed this world of manifest reality for that placeless abode of the spirits, in perfect joy, as obedient as Abraham. He had attained his soul's desire, his secret Beloved.

A spirit groans and cries; he hears a call and responds and finds himself *in a seat of truth, in the presence of the All-powerful Sovereign* [54:55]. *Truly the Friends of God have nothing to fear, and neither shall they grieve* [10:63].

Mevlana arrived weeping, uncovered his blessed head, and began to cry out in mourning. He called for the singers and the drummers as well. There was a great tumult among the people when they learned of Salahuddin's death. Eight groups of reciters led the funeral procession followed by the noble companions with the bier on their shoulders. Mevlana walked as far as the tomb of Bahauddin Walad, whirling in sema as he went. The Friends gave the reciters and the musicians so many beautiful garments and cloaks it was impossible to count them. Salahuddin was buried with magnificent ceremony near the sacred tomb of our Great Master, Bahauddin Walad, the Sultan of the Wise (May God sanctify their innermost secret and shower us with their piety). This took place on the lst of Moharrem 657A.H., (December 29, 1258 C.E.). And on the night of the funeral celebration (*Urs*), the Friends recited numerous ghazals.

May Your Faces Be Eternally Luminous [588]

One day Mevlana wrote to Sultan Walad and advised that he honor Fatima Khatun, the mother of Chelebi 'Arif, with limitless respect:

"I am writing to ask that you treat our princess with honor. She, the light of our heart and sight, as well as the entire universe, is married to our son. As it is said, *And Zachariah undertook her* [*Virgin Mary's*] *care* [11:32]. She has been put into your care, as a very great test.

"I hope that my son will burn up all excuses, and that he will never for a moment do anything to hurt her, knowingly or unknowingly. I hope that you are watchful, so that not an atom of trouble from disloyalty or boredom might disturb her spirit.

"She herself would say nothing, because of her purity and greatness of spirit, and the patience of her lineage.

Even though the duckling was only born yesterday,
the water of the sea reaches its breast.

"But one must guard against ambush and be mindful of witnesses, for she is under the eye of divine spirits, who watch over the excellent offspring: *We shall unite them in Paradise with their offspring* [52:21]. Allah! Allah! Allah! Allah! Allah! Allah! Allah! So that your faces may be eternally luminous, and that of this father, his family, and all his relations, hold her dear!

"Consider every day to be the first day, and every night to be the wedding night. In this pursuit with the net of heart and soul, do not think she has already been caught, and no longer needs to be pursued. That is the way of people who only see the outward form of things, as it is said, *they know but the outward surface of this world's life whereas of the ultimate things they are utterly unaware* [30:7]. You will not grow old like these people. Help from the Divine is abundantly available and will illuminate and perfume your abode. I swear this is true *by the fig, the olive, and Mt. Sinai* [95:1-2]. One day you will set foot at the place indicated by this *hadith*: 'O 'Ali, if you saw my heart torn upon the earth, what would you do?' He replied, 'I do not know what to say, O Messenger of God. I would shelter it within my eyelid, within the folds of my heart, and consider myself to be a neglectful sinner.' The Messenger said, 'Fatima, is a part of myself—our children are our hearts that walk upon the earth.' To cause pain to these spirits is not just a single torment, nor a hundred, nor a thousand.

It is not difficult to leave life and the world.
What is difficult is to leave one's familiar neighborhood.

This separation is not that of a lover grieving,
but that of the spirit separating from the body.

I know that you are blameless,
but lovers' hearts can be suspicious.

"Keep this advice to yourself, and don't mention it to anyone.

God knows best."

Our Souls Are One [589]

Our trustworthy Friends told us that a disturbance of heart arose between Sultan Walad and his wife Kiraga (Fatima) Khatun.

Mevlana moved by compassion, wrote a letter in his own handwriting, offering apologies and gave it to Jemaluddin Qamari to convey to her:

> "My soul and yours are mingled as one;
> anything that harms you harms me, too . . .

"As I am God's witness (May He be magnified), I swear by the pure and eternal Essence of the Supreme Truth, that anything that has wounded the spirit of this sincere girl is our concern. Anything that is your concern is our concern and ten times more so.

"We owe a debt to the Sultan of shaikhs, the East of the Lights of Truth, Salahuddin (May mercy be upon him), for his kindness and his qualities, that we cannot repay by any thanks or service. Only the treasury of God could recompense.

"I would hope that my child will not hide anything from her father and will tell me whatever it is that is troubling her. And if it pleases God, I will do my best not to fail in my duties of companionship.

"If my dear son, Bahauddin, is tormenting you, I will cast him from my heart. I will not respond to his greetings, and I will not welcome him to my funeral. I would not want him there or any other such person. I do not want you to worry, nor to be sad, as God is your helper. His servants are your helpers.

"If someone speaks against you, bear in mind that a dog's mouth cannot pollute the sea, nor can a fly ruin a sugar cake by landing upon it. Even if he declared that he had been treated unjustly and gave a hundred thousand sermons to this effect, I would still consider him the tyrant. He is not acting with love and respecting his vows, and I do not consider him as the oppressed. I do not accept his homilies and his excuses.

"I swear by the name of God, '*Wallahi*! *Billahi*! *Tallahi*!'[6] that I will not accept on the part of one who criticizes you, any excuse, homily, subterfuge, or tears. It is you who are the mistreated.

---

6. "In the name of God, through God, by God, and towards God!" is a common exclamatory oath.

"Even though they may say, 'We respect you,' and call you 'Lady and daughter of the Master' to your face or behind your back, without hypocrisy, whoever reproaches you should say to themselves, 'We are the sinners', since they are the tryants and you are the one who has been wronged. I swear by God that your rights and that of that Sultan [Salahuddin] are one hundred times greater than theirs. If I laugh at a meeting because of my high spirits, it is God Most High who has given me this radiance. May He be Praised!

"My heart will not be calm until your detractors publicly declare that their hearts and souls are in service to God and His servants. These people must throw away their tricks into the dark waters of the well and stop turning things upside down. They must become the dust under the feet, and slaves of, the servants of God, both in their presence and behind their backs.

"This father of yours will go to his grave with what he believes, if it pleases God. By God! Do not hide anything from this father, and tell him the circumstances one by one, so that, with the help of God, he can help you.

"You are the holy place of security of God in this world, for through the effect of this sultan [Salahuddin], by your blessing, from his pure soul favors shower in one hundred thousand ways from the World Beyond—may your influence remain forever with the inhabitants of earth and not be interrupted until the Day of Resurrection. May your heart and those of your children never be sad. So be it, *O Lord of all the worlds*!

May the lights of Salahuddin arise
and illuminate the souls of the mystical Lovers!
May all souls that have become subtle
    and transcendent with grace
be mingled with the dust of Salahuddin's tomb!"

Chapter VI
Husamuddin Chelebi

The deeds of Husam al-Haqq wa'l Din bin Hasan bin Muhammad bin Hasan bin Akhi-Turk, the Abu Yazid (Bastami) and Junayd of his era, Key to the Treasures of the Throne, God's saint on earth, Intercessor for the Friends on the Day of Reckoning, who associated himself with the shaikh (Mevlana) and said; "I went to bed a Kurd and woke up an Arab!" May God be pleased with him. What a beautiful ancestry! What beautiful descendents!

Every beautiful one's beauty comes from God's beauty;
it is lent to him or her, what more can I say?
That's how it is with the beauty of all beauties.

An Enlightening Conversation [591]

The dear Friends, noble and revered, guardians of the holy sanctuary of great renown, (May God have mercy on them) recounted:

When that great shaikh, possessor of perfect ecstasy and the glory of humanity, Salahuddin (May God santify his innermost mystery) left this transitory world, Mevlana appointed Chelebi Husamuddin as his successor. After Salahuddin's departure, Mevlana reserved his endearments (*ishq-bazi*) for Husamuddin. With heart and soul, he regarded him as equal to the perfection of ecstasy of Shaikh Salahuddin. For ten years without interruption they accompanied each other. "Only God knows what transpired between them."

Finding Home [592]

Sirajuddin, the reciter of the *Mathnawi* and king of discourse, recounted:

When Chelebi Husamuddin, was young, at the age of puberty, he was very handsome, the Joseph of his time. When his father died, he became an orphan pearl, and all of the distinguished men and shaikhs, as well as the masters of chivalry (*futuwwah*), invited him to be with them. They showed great affection and concern for him and offered him their protection. He considered each one in turn and then went directly to Mevlana, accompanied by all his tutors and young men (*javanan*).[7] He bowed and took this threshold as his home, settling there. He freely entered the service of this majesty and gave permission to his servants and to the young men with him to leave and earn their own living, and to take what they might need in the way of furnishings from his. Then, just as Abu Bakr the Sincere had, he issued orders for his properties and possessions to be sold, and he gave everything to Mevlana. His tutors were concerned that he now had nothing—he told them to sell his furniture, and after several days, they said, "We are all that remains."

"Glory to God, the Lord of the worlds, since he has allowed me to imitate the outer acts of the Prophet. Through love of God and a desire to please him and out of love of Mevlana, I am giving you your freedom. Let each one of you go forth to your own work."

It was then Chelebi Husamuddin's great good fortune to be accepted by Mevlana, who bestowed upon him all that came to him from the Unseen. Mevlana appointed him the leader of the Friends, the commander of God's troops, and the governor and director of the affairs of the community.

Once again, he was endowed with properties, wealth, buildings and villages. Until his last breath, he occupied himself with the affairs of the Companions. He divided the income of the pious endowments, completely and perfectly, among those who were deserving of them. The Companions were unanimous in saying that he never took a single thing for his own personal use, neither a drink of water nor a grain of wheat. Through the grace of this generosity and complete love, in the end, he became both inwardly and outwardly perfect in following the conduct (*shariah*) of the Prophet (Peace and blessings upon him), the ethical way (*tariqat*) put forward by the *Mathnawi*, grasping the Truth of Muhammad (*Haqiqat*), and cultivating Mevlevi love (*ishq-i Mawlawi*), and so became capable of perfecting others.

He received more spiritual favors from Mevlana Shamsuddin of Tabrizi and Shaikh Salahuddin than can be described in books.

---

7. *Javanan* is the word used to indicate young Akhis, adepts of chivalry (*futuwwah*), who were in his service.

The Opening of the Mathnawi [593]

Sirajuddin, the mystic traveler and chief of those endowed with the mystic glance (*nazar*), the reciter of the *Mathnawi* at our Master's tomb, told us:

The cause for the composition of the *Mathnawi*, that revealer of the mysteries of the Qur'an, was that Husamuddin, God's representative and traveler on the road of His Truth (May God sanctify his pure innermost secret) had discovered that some of the intimate Friends were reading, with complete longing and great love, the *Ilahi-nama* . . . and the *Mantiq al-tair* and *Mosibat-nama* of Fariduddin 'Attar and were deriving great pleasure from their secrets.

Watching for the appropriate opportunity, for they pass by as quickly as the clouds, one day, Husamuddin found Mevlana alone, bowed, and said: "Your collection (*diwan*) of *ghazals* and the lights of these mysteries are spreading east and west, to the ends of the earth and sea, praise and thanks be to God. The speech of others cannot compare to the majesty of your poetry. If a book were to be written, in the same style as the *Ilahi-nama* but with the meter of the *Mantiq al-tair (Conference of the Birds)*, it would remain forever in man's memory and would become the companion of mystical lovers and the afflicted. That would be a great and generous mercy. Your servant desires that the noble Friends might turn towards and contemplate your noble face and not become occupied with anything else, but of course this depends upon your wish and capacity."

Just then, Mevlana pulled out from under his blessed turban a manuscript and gave it to Chelebi Husamuddin—it contained a description of the mysteries of the particular and universal in the form of eighteen couplets. This was the beginning of the *Mathnawi*:

"Listen to the *ney* (reed flute),
how it complains of separation . . . "

Up to the line that says:

"The raw cannot understand the state of the ripe,
so my words will be brief; *Salaam*."

These verses were composed in the *ramat* meter of six beats, with the modifications of *mahdhuf* and *maqsur*:

Fa'ilatun fa'ilatun fa'ilat
Jahl-i zolmat-astu 'ilm ab-i hayat

Ignorance is darkness;
knowledge is the water of life.

Mevlana said, "Even before this idea emanated from your blessed spirit, and nature requested it, a thought appeared in my heart, from both the visible and invisible worlds, an order came from the Compassionate, the Merciful who cast this thought into my heart—to write a book of this kind in which pearls of meaning might be threaded.

"Now, come, follow the high-flying bird (*huma*) of your aspiration (*himmet*) and fly toward the ascension (*mi'raj*) of Truth in the way of Muhammad. Open yourself to the revelation of truths like Muhammad (Peace and blessings upon him), so that your intention might be stirred with the wisdom in my heart to bring these spiritual meanings to verse."

As Mevlana makes clear in the fourth book of the *Mathnawi*:

O Light of Truth, Husamuddin,
through your light, the *Mathnawi* surpasses the moon. . . .

Through the attracting force of this sovereign among men, Mevlana was overcome with restlessness and continually recited couplets (*mathnawiyat*) whether during the sema or at the bathhouse, sitting or standing, walking or at rest. At times it would pour forth from him from dusk to dawn, without interruption.

Chelebi Husamuddin would quickly write down the subtle words Mevlana had spoken and then reread them, out loud, in a beautiful voice in Mevlana's presence. When the first volume was finished, Chelebi occupied himself reciting it again and correcting certain words and grammer mistakes, and then he read it out a second time.

Suddenly, Chelebi's wife died, and all work on the *Mathnawi* came to a halt. He was no longer drawn to this spiritual work that nourished the spirit and gave strength to the soul; his spirits rose and fell and he was completely preoccupied with his grief, unable to do anything else. Mevlana continued to be absorbed in the world of ecstasy, in the explanation of the Truth and the unfolding of subtle thought, and said nothing to Chelebi.

Two years passed. Chelebi began to think of getting married

again and busied himself with this. Suddenly, he became aware of the child of his soul and saw how it was weeping and sad, yearning to drink the milk of God's lions. At every moment the call of the heart came to the ear of his intelligence. He recited:

> Give milk to your soul-child and deliver us from these tears,
> O You who every moment comfort a hundred helpless ones
> like me.

The next morning, he went to find Mevlana, prostrated himself in all humility and in complete certainty and longing, and without tongue for interpreter or any lengthy explanations begged him to continue with the composition of the *Mathnawi*.

Mevlana, moved by his great generosity and universal compassion, true to the adage: "There is no kindness unless it is completed," began to spread out the cloth on the table of meaning. He dictated the preface to the second volume . . .

> This book that is the polisher of souls—
> his return signaled the opening of the door.
> Six hundred and sixty-two (A.H.) is the date
> of the opening of this effort and success.
> A nightingale left us and returned a falcon
> to continue the hunt in pursuit of meanings.
> May the king's arm be the perch for the falcon,
> that this door might be forever open for his creatures.
> So be it, *O Lord of all the worlds*!

There were no other interruptions, and Mevlana continued to recite without a break. Chelebi would recite back to him what had been written as it unfolded, until the very end of the work.

Breathing the Fragrance of Love, the Scent of Certainty [595]

Sultan Walad (May God sanctify us through His eternal light) told us:

I went with a group of Companions to Chelebi Husamuddin's garden. He was chatting with the people there about mundane matters, about gardens and orchards. As I listened to the thoughts coming from his blessed mouth, I heard such subtleties and secrets; I praised this power and was in ecstasy with the beauty of the situation. Transformed from state to state, I was completely bewildered—then the meaning of these verses that my father wrote in the *Mathnawi* became clear to me:

> In this street of love, everything the lover says
> carries the fragrance of love.
> If he speaks of jurisprudence (*fiqh*), the fragrance of poverty (*faqr*)
> flows from this sweet breath;
> if he speaks of denial, it is the perfume of faith one receives;
> though he speaks of doubt, one catches the scent of certainty.

Honey in Abundance [597]

One day, with immense courtesy, Sultan Walad honored Chelebi Husamuddin by a visit to his garden. The noble Friends gathered there didn't voice their wish aloud, but they were yearning to taste some of the Chelebi's fine honey.

"Bring some new honey from such-and-such hive," Chelebi said to his gardener, who then opened a hive and brought out several pieces of white honeycomb.

"Take some more from the same hive and bring it for us," Chelebi asked again. The gardener brought five more pieces, but the Chelebi requested still more.

"That's all there is," said the gardener.

"What!" cried the Chelebi, "It flows from the limitless sea for our great Master's son—though you continued to bring it until Resurrection Day, it would not come to an end!"

The astonished gardener brought seventy more combs of pure honey from the same hive, but the hive still remained full.

"All this is a result of the blessings attached to Mevlana Bahauddin's footsteps," said Chelebi Husamuddin.

The Friends continued to eat the honey, two hundred of them, and took some with them for the journey, but still the plate was full.

When Sultan Walad got up to go, the Chelebi gave him the hive, and they carried it to his home. This hive produced many other hives, and the Friends delighted in it for a long time. If someone was ill and was given a remedy prepared from this honey, *in it is a remedy for people* [16:69],[8] they were immediately cured.

---

8. See *Surah an-Nahl* (the Bee) 16:68-69:
And consider how your Sustainer has inspired the bee:
"Prepare for yourself dwellings in mountains and in trees, and in various abodes;

Purity of the Inside [601]

Sirajuddin, the King of the brethren and reciter of the *Mathnawi*, (May the mercy of God be upon him) told us that Chelebi Husamuddin had a strange way of being and an unusual practice of praising in extravagant terms, even in the presence of strangers, certain people known for their evident debauchery and immorality.

"These are advanced ascetics, outstanding in their fear of God and their piety," he would say.

And he would criticize other people who were known for their ascetism, piety, and observance of the religious laws, saying that they were immoral and debauched. The Friends were mystified by this and some went to ask Mevlana what Chelebi Husamuddin could possibly mean by this.

"It is the truth," Mevlana said. "The group he praises may seem debauched and ill-behaved, but that is just on the surface of things. Inwardly they are pure and refined. Those ascetics whom he criticizes inwardly are hypocritical and perverse.

"God Most High glances with favor at the innermost secret of his servants, not their exterior. It has been said: 'God does not pay any attention to the monk's cowl, nor to those who know the Book by heart, but He looks toward the heart that is turned towards the Eternally Compassionate One.'

"Another explanation is that, in addition to his exterior acts and piety, there are in a man hidden acts and a hidden piety which constitute the beauty of his essence—this causes his bad deeds to become beautiful and his doubt to become faith. God has said, 'O my servants, you look only upon the exterior, while We look at the interior and the innermost secret of a person.'

We, who can see everything everywhere,
We look at the heart, not the outward display.

Though outwardly he might be sinful and imperfect, because of this pure essence, his interior is pious and virtuous. *Those who ascribe divinity to anything beside God are nothing but impure* [9:28]—this

---

and then eat of all that the earth produces, and follow humbly the paths ordained for you by your Sustainer."

There issues from within their bodies a fluid of varied hues, within which there is healing for mankind.

Truly, in all this, is a sign for those who reflect!

refers to the impurity of the heart, not the body, and *this is sufficient for one of understanding*."

Seeing What Is on the Way [602]

The best of the brethren told us that, one day, Chelebi (may the Mercy of God be upon him) was sitting in a circle of Friends and sharing divine insights. Suddenly, he asked one of the Friends to go to Gurji Khatun, that Queen of the world, First Lady of the Hereafter.

"Give her my greetings and tell her to leave the palace where she is and to go to another palace quickly to avoid disaster; the command has occurred for the roof to fall in," the Chelebi said.

As soon as she received this message, Gurji Khatun immediately left that palace and went to another. Her entourage left as well, carrying the furniture out with them, and no sooner had they done this than the roof fell in, and the house was demolished.

Gurji Khatun's devotion and faith increased a thousand-fold. She gave alms to the needy, offered sacrifices, and sent five hundred dinars *yusufi* and ten thousand dirhems *soltani* to Chelebi Husamuddin as a token of her gratitude, and she sent her best wishes and bestowed beautiful robes of honor on each of the Companions.

Love Beyond the Law [605]

The Chelebi (God's *khalifa*) was a follower of Ormawi,[9] of the Shafi'i school (*madhab*). One day he came to see Mevlana, bowed respectfully, and said, "From now on I would like to follow the teachings of the great Imam Abu-Hanifa (May God be satisfied with him), since Mevlana is of the Hanifi school (*madhab*)."

"No, no," replied our Master, "it is better if you stay within your *madhab* and observe it, but journey on our path (*tariqat*) and guide people on our way of love."

Happy is the Soul Enfolded in His Mystery [606]

Sirajuddin, the reciter of the *Mathnawi* (May mercy be upon him) related:

9. Abu Bakr Muhammad al-Ormawi (from Ormawi in Afghanistan) was a student of Abu Ishaq ash-Shirazi (d. 537A.H./1142 C.E.), of the Shafi'i school of Islamic jurisprudence (*madhab*). Traditionally a disciple would follow in discipline the same school of Islamic law as his spritiual teacher, in full obedience to his way of being.

It was Mevlana's custom to go to the thermal baths once a year and to stay there forty or fifty days. The Friends would go, too, reciting *ghazals* by the thousand as they walked along, whirling with joy all along the way.

One year, as usual, he went to the hot springs, but he stayed longer than usual. All of a sudden, messengers from the Unseen announced to Chelebi that Mevlana would arrive the next day. Chelebi distributed thanks offerings, and in the morning, the inhabitants of Konya, young and old, went out to meet him.

The travellers landed in the plain near the caravanserai of Rouzbeh near Konya. They prepared food and dried fruits, and erected a large tent for Mevlana. That day, Mevlana had put a great deal of collyrium around his two blessed eyes.

As soon as Chelebi saw our Master's tent, he cried out, got down from his horse, and prostrated before it. Mevlana came out in bare feet, and took Chelebi in his arms, embracing him for a long time. Then holding his hand, he brought him into his tent.

Chelebi (May God be pleased with him) told the fortunate Friends:

"I sat down facing Mevlana in complete tranquility (*huzur*). Not a word was exchanged, but I heard clearly with the ear of my intelligence, the bird of my soul, in the cage of my breast, sighing like a dove in response to the cooing of Mevlana's soul. The sweetness of the voice of Mevlana's soul came to my soul's ear and captured my spirit. It was not possible to say anything."

As he said in the *Mathnawi*:

Every moment, the melodious voice of this pure body
is traveling to the ear of his hearing
by a way unknown to humankind,
because it is without form or substance.
His companions do not hear this song; he hears it.
Happy is the soul enfolded in his mystery.

After that, Mevlana, his companions and the distinguished people of the city, continuing their sema and chanting sacred songs, went to our Great Master Bahauddin Walad's tomb (May God sanctify his innermost mystery). That day, what Divine favor, mercy, and joy rained down on the heads of the Friends! *This is of God's bounty unto us and unto all humankind* [12:38]! *God singles out for*

His grace whom He wills [2:105].

Love Swallows Illusion [607]

Sirajuddin, the reciter of the *Mathnawi* and knower of exalted meaning, recounted:

When Mevlana left the world of deluded self-importance (*ghorur*) for the world of joy (*sorur*), distinguished scholars, the proud and full of error, out of envy and denial held a great assembly at the lawcourt of Qadi Sirajuddin (May the Mercy of God be upon him).

They summoned Chelebi Husamuddin, to whom they declared, "The *rebab* is *haram* (unlawful) and to perform the sema is not permitted."

The chief judge (*qadi*) Sirajuddin agreed with the great imams and scholars of Islam.

"What do you have to say about it?" they asked Chelebi.

He answered, "When you look at Moses's rod do you see wood or a serpent?" They said not a word.

"Just like Moses' rod, our *rebab* was just a piece of wood, to which no one paid attention," the Chelebi continued. "Mevlana, who manifests the reality of our Prophet, the Moses of his time, with the order of God chose this piece of wood—he looked upon it with love, and it became a serpent in his hand capable of swallowing all the snakes of man's illusions. It is not wise to act boldly and impudently in the presence of such a terrible serpent. May it not suddenly roar and, as punishment, in the blink of an eye swallow all your rulings and authority without pardon for anyone, destroying you all.

And he recited:

"It may seem like a rod, but inside it's a dragon;
since you're not a Moses, don't approach such a serpent. . . .

"Through the elixir of his glance, its unlawful character was transformed into that which is lawful, and it became accepted by all those who have been accepted by God."

Whatever the sick man grasps takes on that illness;
If the perfect man grasps denial, it becomes surrender.

Those present were deeply moved and applauded and congratulated Chelebi. Those who had started the controversy, who had been so ready for dispute, asked forgiveness and surrendered. Before long, not one among them remained; there was not a trace or any mention of them. Meanwhile, this higher meaning increased in strength and spread throughout the world.

An Intercession [608]

From the time of Mevlana, Chelebi Husamuddin always visited, every day without fail, the tomb of the Sultan of the Wise, Bahauddin Walad, as well as that of Shaikh Salahuddin (May God be pleased with both of them).

One day, he made his visit as usual and completed offering his litany (*wird*) and prayers of the moment. As he was leaving, he turned to look again towards the blessed tombs. Suddenly, he cried out, "No, no, that is not right, it is not right to take him away!"

After a few moments, he smiled and left. The Friends bowed and asked what this meant.

He answered, "I saw that the avenging angels from the World Beyond had put heavy chains on 'Alauddin's feet and hands and were about to take him away. He saw me and pleaded for help, and my heart was touched. I felt ashamed before Mevlana and his infinite compassion. I cried out and interceded for him. The intercession was accepted and right away the angels released him and left him where he was."

'Alauddin was Mevlana's son, Sultan Walad's brother. According to divine destiny, he was rebellious, with no regard for his obligations, and warring against Mevlana Shamsuddin of Tabriz (May God refresh his soul), he aligned with other rebellious ones who led him into this trouble. Afterwards, Mevlana rejected him from his blessed heart and withdrew his glance of fatherly favor from him. When 'Alauddin died, Mevlana refused to go to the funeral or to say the prayers over his body. *Only God knows its final meaning* [3:7]!

On the tablet of the heart, guarded by you and I,
you wrote words we can read, you and I.
You said, "I will tell you when it's just you and I;
it is one of those things we know, you and I."

The Qur'an Is Like a Shy Bride [609]

The great companions and distinguished nobles recounted:

Chelebi Husamuddin told Mevlana (May God magnify the remembrance of both of them):

"Last night, in a dream of good news, I saw Bilal[10] the Abyssinian (May God be pleased with him) who carried the text of God's Words upon his head while the Lord of the First and the Last, Muhammad, the Faithful Guardian (Peace and blessings upon him), was holding the *Mathnawi* close to his breast. He was reading it and praised it very highly to his noble companions."

"Yes, by God," cried our Master. "Your blessed eye saw truly. God forbid your eye would ever claim to have seen things that it has not seen. May all those whose sight is entrusted to people of sight also become seeing, able to discern the truths of the Invisible.

An eye which can see the Unseen is a quide, like the Unseen.
May this perfect vision never be lacking from this world.
The faces of those who cannot see will be black,
but those with sight are the mirror for the moon.
Who will see you except the mirror of sight—
may that sight keep increasing in this world.

"The Qur'an is like a bride, with a beautiful face and gracious brow; she is adorned with beautiful jewelery and clothes, free of all faults and blemishes, sanctified, far from idle talk, but still hidden behind the veil of jealousy.

As the poet said:

The Quran is like a shy bride who only removes her veil
when she sees the palace of faith free of tumult.

"Our *Mathnawi* is also a spiritual beloved unequalled in beauty and perfection. It is a cultivated garden and wholesome nourishment for men of enlightened hearts, people of clear sight, and lovers whose hearts are on fire. Happy is the soul who contemplates

10. The first *muezzin* (one who loudly chants the call to prayer to gather people for the ritual prayer, *salaah*, five times a day) and devoted follower of the Prophet Muhammad. He had been a slave, terribly tortured for declaring his faith in the Oneness of God, until Abu Bakr as-Siddiq purchased him in order to set him free.

this mysterious beauty, enjoying the favorable glances of the men of God so that it comes to be inscribed in the record of: *How excellent a servant [of Ours], who, behold, would always turn unto Us* [38:29]."

Mevlana continued, "A deep faith, a persevering love, truthful sincerity and a sound heart are necessary in order to penetrate the mysterious lights of the *Mathnawi*, and all the embrace of *hadith* and Qur'anic verses, the parables, tales, proofs of the secrets of the treasures, and the details of the Reality it contains. One must also have great insight and intelligence to be able to grasp the different branches of knowledge shared within it and to contemplate its exterior and reach its innermost secrets.

"However, even without all of this, if the seeker is sincere, the mystical love in his heart will serve as a guide, and he will attain a certain station. It is God who grants success and gives guidance—He is the ultimate helper and the One who shows the right way.

Love is a flame that consumes everything
until God alone remains.
Draw from this love and light a fire in your soul!
Burn thought and speech completely away."

This Hand Is Used to Giving, not Taking [610]

The Parvana Mo'inuddin (May the mercy of God be upon him) held a large gathering and invited all the great scholars and distinguished people. That day, Mevlana was silent and not sharing divine insights. Chelebi Husamuddin hadn't yet been invited, and the Parvana realized that it would be good thing to do so. He asked Mevlana for permission to summon him from his garden.

"It would be appropriate," answered Mevlana, "because he is the one who draws forth the milk of divine insights from the breast of Reality.

These words are milk from the breast of the Soul;
they don't flow if there is no one to draw them forth."

When Chelebi arrived with his companions and friends, the Parvana ran to meet him, kissed his hand numerous times, bowed his head to it, and then held out a torch to guide them in.

Mevlana quickly arose from his place and greeted him, "Welcome my soul, my faith, my Junayd, my light, my master, my friend, beloved of God and the beloved of saints and prophets."

Chelebi lowered his head, while the Friends expressed their appreciation. At this moment, the thought passed through the Parvana's mind: "Can all this truly be said of Husamuddin, or is our Master exaggerating?"

Immediately, Chelebi grasped the Parvana's hand tightly and said, "O Mo'inuddin, even if it were not so, when our Master says it it becomes true, and one hundred times more so—he has the power, right away, to bring the nonexistent into existence and to grant life and increase to his disciple's soul. With one glance of favor, he brings him to perfection."

As Mevlana has said:

O son, it may be only a glance from the man of poverty,
but this glance can take you to the Highest Heaven, O my son!

Chelebi continued, "Consider that in the past, these palaces and shops did not exist. This tranquil and joyful society came into being through the goodwill you have shown and orders you have given. The just saints possess a similar power and absolute authority. If they give, they give absolutely. Those whom they favor with compassion come to possess the best of religion and of the world. They are distinguished with nearness and intimacy and reach a station that is the envy of perfect and generous men."

Overwhelmed by these words, immediately, the Parvana bowed his head to Chelebi's feet and rubbed them with his beard and mustache. Chelebi was sitting in the center of the salon of the house. Mevlana came down from a high seat and sat beside him, and so, the middle court became the place of honor and the other seats were left empty.

Some envious people whispered, "Why would an important person take a lesser place and disturb the gathering? The seats were apportioned already!"

Mevlana became upset and cried, "What difference does it make whether they sit in a high place or lower one? They are lamps! If a lamp seeks a higher place, it is not for itself, but for another's benefit, so that another might profit from its light. Whether high or low, it is still a lamp. The saints are eternal suns! If they seek high places in this world, rather than seeking the recognition of the world, their intention is to hide their greatness—they want to catch people in the net of this world, take them to the other spiritual dimension, and drop them into the net of the Life Beyond.

"Similarly, the Prophet (Peace and blessings upon him) did not conquer Mecca and the other territories for himself, since he had no need of them, but only to give them new life, clarity and vision: 'This hand is accustomed to giving, not taking.' The saints attract people in order to give them something, not to take something from them."

Suddenly, the sema began, and they remained immersed until midday the next day. Then Mevlana, still whirling, returned to the medresse barefoot and continued to whirl for three more days and nights.

Tending the Garden of the Soul [612]

Chelebi Husamuddin had a close friend called Haji Mubarak Hayderi who, out of devotion and love, became Chelebi's gardener. He was quite adept at gardening. He recounted:

One day, I was angry at Chelebi. I left the garden and went to another garden with the intention of never going back again. Suddenly, I saw Mevlana approaching in the distance. He was accompanied by another person carrying an axe. I was so terrified by this sight that I lost consciousness.

"Cut this man's head off, since Chelebi Husamuddin is angry with him," our Master ordered the person.

I was seeing this plainly with the eyes of my head. This person struck me with the axe, without any regard, and my head flew off—I was annihilated. After a few moments, Mevlana picked up my head in his blessed hands and put it back on my neck saying, "In the name of God, through God, by God, and towards God!"

I was immediately restored to life, and in a state of great joy I jumped up and bowed. When I arose from the prostration, there was no one there. I saw evidence of the blood I had lost, but felt no ill effects from the blow. I ran back to the orchard and resumed my work with great enthusiasm.

"Well, here we are, Shaikh Muhammad!" Chelebi said gently, "If our Master had not yanked your ears and cut off your head, you would never have become a perfect *muslim* nor been freed of your rebellious nature. And if I had not interceded for you, you would have died and been lost for all eternity."

I apologized a hundred thousand times, took on the robe, and declared myself a sincere student of Chelebi.

This incident took place four years after Mevlana's death (May God sanctify his innermost secret).

He who gives life also has the right to take it.
He is His khalifa—his hand is the hand of God.
It is God's hand that deals death and brings to life.
To life? Rather, life eternal!

Witnessing the Lights of Revelation [614]

Chelebi (May God increase his mention) asked Mevlana:

"Why was Muhammad the last of the prophets? Why did he say, 'I am the Seal," and *but the Messenger of God and the Seal of the prophets* [33:40]?"

"It was God's wish that Muhammad should be the last of the prophets," Mevlana replied. "If prophethood ends with him, even so, what difference does it make to God? God is unchanging, and he who possesses His attributes is also unchanging."

If the eye of certainty opens within your soul,
you find a guide under every stone.

"There are times when God's infinite gifts manifest themselves to people through the prophets and other times when they manifest directly without an intermediary.

At times, He reveals Himself directly to the heart,
 clothing the poor.
An intermediary acts as a guide, but only hinders
 one who sees directly.

"Those who see God directly do not need intermediaries or guides. They have been honored and illumined by the Lights of divine revelations within the heart. Blessed are they: keep company with them in sincerity and certainty (May God be pleased with all of them)."

To Him We Shall Return [616]

For a long time after Mevlana's death, Chelebi fulfilled the conditions of his khalifhood to perfection. He made an immense effort to look after the companions and to protect the descendents of the spiritual Poles (*aqtab*), and rendered innumerable services. He distributed the pious endowments to everyone, each according to their rank and virtue. . . .

After the Friday prayer he would preside over the sema, the reading from the glorious Qur'an and recitation of the *Mathnawi*. He welcomed and served any travelers who arrived and conveyed greetings when they left.

There were five hundred wealthy Friends who wore the dervish cloak and three hundred who were deeply versed in mystical knowledge in service to him. Also among his followers were many prolific scribes and skilful teachers. They were immersed in spiritual ecstasies and the passionate flashes of Divine manifestation that came to them.

One day, Chelebi Husamuddin went with the Friends to Homam's garden where a large gathering was being held. Suddenly, a dervish arrived with the news that the crescent on top of the turquoise dome of the holy tomb had fallen, leaving a large hole.

The Chelebi sighed deeply and fell into a profound reverie. After a while, he slapped his knee several times and began to weep. The Friends joined him with a deluge of tears, and the entire group began lamenting.

"Consider the date of our Shaikh's death," Chelebi said.

Everyone then realized that ten whole years had passed since Mevlana's death and that this was the eleventh year since his passing. Immediately, a change took place in Chelebi's blessed body and he began to shiver. He said, "Take me home; the cup of my life is almost full, and the hour of departure is near. I have no choice. When the Beloved brings the good news of union, it is time to go, running—drawn by my head and not my feet."

Then he added:

"Tell this illusory body it is time to go.
Who am I, anyway?
The painting diminishes, for I am Eternal.
God has said, *Wish for death! If you are sincere* [2:94].
I am sincere, and for this, I sacrifice my life."

The Friends led Chelebi, mounted on his horse, back to his house, where he then remained bedridden for several days. He transferred to the Mercy of God and His gentleness on a Friday, the 22nd of Sha'ban 683 A.H. (November 3, 1284 C.E.) just as the crescent was being replaced on the turquoise dome. He passed into the Paradise of His Magnificent Presence—*Truly unto God do we belong and truly, unto Him we shall return* [2:156]. It is due to separation from Him that we feel sorrow.

The son has returned to the city of his birth.
After the flowing of time, he has returned to unity.
God said, "Return!" and the return occurs,
like the herd leaving the fields for home.

Healing Hearts [617]

The old Friends, confidants of the women in Mevlana's household, told us that after he died, Kira Khatun, that Lady of the World to Come and a Friend of God on earth (May God have mercy on her and on her husband), also passed from this world [in 1288 C.E.].

All the distinguished of Konya carried her coffin. All the Friends, following Sultan Walad's example, removed their turbans. When the funeral procession arrived at the *Chashnagir* gate, it suddenly stopped facing the tomb and would not budge. They remained stopped there for half an hour, while everyone wept bitterly in a state of bewilderment. Then Sultan Walad led the Friends in a sema and a tumult arose from the people's hearts. As the Friends rejoined the procession, it was suddenly able to begin moving again.

When this lady's honored body was placed in the tomb, a blinding white light filled the entire enclosure and many people fainted. That night, an intimate friend and possessor of insight beheld Kira Khatun in Mevlana's holy presence and asked her why the funeral procession had stopped at the *Chashnagir* gate.

She replied, "That day, a man and a woman had been stoned for adultery under that same gate. Overcome with compassion, I delivered them from their wounds and commended them to the mercy of the Infinitely Compassionate One. That is the reason we stopped."

God's servants are fully merciful and patient.
They have a divine capacity to set things right.

In the morning, this esteemed one went to relate the story to Sultan Walad. The Friends were filled with joy and held an immense sema that continued until nightfall.

Serving God's Servants [619]

One day, Mevlana saw a servant who with complete love was carrying a heavy wicker basket with provisions on his shoulders enroute to Chelebi's home. He said, "Would that I might be in your place and you in mine, that I might earn the distinction of such service." Quickly, he gave the servant his blessed cloak and asked his forgiveness, "This is so that you might know the extent of the services that one must render to the servant of a Friend of God. The splendor of these saints goes beyond any strict calculation or limits.

> Among all the great and lowly,
> nothing is higher than to be a servant.
> For one who finds true life in Love,
> to be anything other than a servant would be infidelity."

The Belt of Sincerity [620]

Chelebi Husamuddin, having wound the belt of sincerity around the waist of his soul, served our Master's family with perfect loyalty all his life, from childhood until old age. Due to the immense favor Mevlana bestowed upon him, having rendered service toward everyone, he was served by and became Master of the Masters of the world. O Lord, may our lives end well!

Chapter VII
Sultan Walad

The Deeds of Mevlana Bahauddin Walad, Sultan of Mystics, Manifestation of the secrets of Certainty (May God illuminate us with His eternal, comforting light).

The Guardian of Humility *[622]*

This was recounted by the great companions:

On the seventh day after Mevlana (May God magnify his mention and allow us to praise him) had left this world of appearances for that of eternal life, Chelebi Husamuddin and the Friends came to find Sultan Walad.

Chelebi offered consoling words and bowed before him, saying, "From now on, I would like you to take your father's place and give guidance to the disciples. Be our true shaikh and pour the mysteries of the Way over mankind. I will walk faithfully at your stirrup and carry your horse's blanket. I will be your servant and your tutor."

He then bowed and recited this verse:

O my soul, who is that standing within the mansion of the heart?
Who can occupy the throne but the king, or his princely son?

Bowing, Sultan Walad wept, and full of joy, he replied, "It is the sufi who most deserves to wear his cloak, the orphan more suited to carry his torch. During my father's time, you were our *khalifa* (leading representative) and the greatest among the Companions and Friends; now, too, you are our *khalifa* and the great one among us, and a remembrance of such a Master. The khalifhood and throne are yours, according to our late Sovereign's wishes, which he would often make clear to me." He bowed and, weeping, kissed Chelebi Husamuddin's hand, due to the perfect faith and sense of union he felt with him.

Sultan Walad showed greater respect and humility for his father's officers than any other son of a shaikh. It was the same as when he walked beside the stirrup of Shamsuddin as he rode from

Damascus to Konya, [when he had declined to ride,] saying, "The king on horseback, and the slave on horseback, too?" It is impossible to describe the extent of the humility and enduring dedication with which this sultan of horsemen served Shaikh Salahuddin, his father-in-law. Having made Sayyid Burhanuddin Mohaqqiq the *qibla* of his heart and soul, he rendered him limitless service and innumerable kindnesses.

For eleven entire years, Sultan Walad regarded Chelebi Husamuddin (May God sanctify their spirits) as the one fulfilling his father's place; he looked upon him as a loving father and the *khalifa* who was his spiritual director. He acted as Chelebi Husamuddin's servant and disciple in perfect truth and sincerity.

For seventy years without interruption he conveyed and commented upon his father's teachings, with eloquence and a freshness of interpretation. His skill in interpreting the mysteries of the mystical path and the traditions was miraculous. He sent his noble representatives into all of Asia Minor (Rum), teaching humankind the secrets of the family of Abu Bakr the Sincere.

His cherished son, Jalaluddin Amir 'Arif, the descendent of saints, pearl of the sea of divine knowledge, the light of the eye of the people of certainty, sovereign of *abdals* and *autad*, he made Chelebi's close disciple.

Sultan Walad's Adab [623]

One day, Chelebi invited Kira Khatun, Mevlana's wife, to his home and by chance Sultan Walad suddenly arrived to pay a visit as well. The blessing of such a companionship was as beautiful as the lights of the mysteries of the holy names of God.

They shared secrets of meaning, divine insights and grace. Then, Kira Khatun said, "Last night, I saw Mevlana in a dream. He came like an *anqa*[11] from a place beyond the east and the west and stretched his wings over Bahauddin to protect him as he accompanied him everywhere he went."

When he heard this, Chelebi thought to himself, "Why didn't she see me?" His jealous admiration showed on his face, as jealousy

11. The *anqa*, or *simurgh*, is a mythical huge bird (sometimes described as being part mammal, part eagle, and similar to the phoenix in its immortality) said to be as large as thirty birds, and so long-lived that it possesses the knowledge of all Ages. See Attar's *Conference of the Birds.*

does among the manly men.

If you feel envious, allow it to show on your face,
because even the prophets experienced such jealousy.

So it is said, "Beware of the vision of the truly faithful one, because he sees with the light of God Most High."

For someone who *sees with the Light of God*,
there is an open way through the skin.
The shaikh who *sees with the Light of God*,
can see the beginning and the end.

Sultan Walad, with his great discernment, was aware of what Chelebi was feeling.

He said, "This is the meaning of the dream: when a bird wishes to raise (*tarbiyat*) her egg, she keeps it under the warmth of her wing and cares for it very attentively. She stays close until the chick hatches, protecting it, and then teaches it how to gather seeds, so that then when his wings are strong enough, he can leave the nest and fly through the open air on his own. When the young chick has grown and can fly on its own, the mother bird no longer hovers over him.

"Our Chelebi is the perfect falcon raised by a royal falcon; he flies with his own wings. We are still feeble chicks, enclosed in the shell of our body. Mevlana is still teaching us, and protects our souls on the road to perfection and the ultimate station."

By the blessing of the light which accompanied these inspired words, the constriction of Chelebi's heart eased. He arose, embraced Sultan Walad abundantly, and praised him. It is said that he presented him with a gift of three pieces of silk from Egypt and a fine turban wrapping and rendered him much devoted service.

You are My Action [626]

One day, Mevlana embraced Sultan Walad and said, "My coming into this world was for the sake of your arrival. Because all these words that I speak are mine, but you are my action."

The Secrets of Retreat [628]

The enlightened Friends, those guides on the road to certainty, recounted:

When Sultan Walad was twenty years old, he asked for our Master's permission to perform a forty day retreat in seclusion.

"O Bahauddin," his father answered, "for Muslims, there are no seclusions and forty day retreats. In our religion, these are considered to be innovations. These practices existed in the religions of Moses and Jesus (May peace be with them). All the spiritual effort we make is to ensure the well-being of our children and our friends. No seclusion is necessary. Don't subject yourself to this hardship, don't cause harm to your body."

However, Sultan Walad persisted, "Truly, I sincerely wish to be in seclusion for forty days, but I ask our Master's blessings and help."

Mevlana finally gave his permission and ordered that the retreat cell be prepared. Sultan Walad entered and the door was sealed. Mevlana and Shaikh Salahuddin went to the cell every three days to support him and to make sure all was well. After forty days, all the Friends, accompanied by the reciters, arrived and opened the cell with great respect and honor.

Mevlana saw that his son was bathed in light and had been transformed in an astonishing way. When he saw his father, Sultan Walad fell to his knees in prostration and kissed his feet, and that day many infinite favors rained down upon them. Due to their extreme happiness, the Friends began a sema and many robes were bestowed on those who participated.

After the sema, when only the close Friends remained in the intimate chambers, Mevlana said, "O Bahauddin, in our Shaikh Salahuddin's presence, tell us some of the secrets revealed to you during your retreat, because those who go on retreat must always manifest their ecstasy."

Sultan Walad bowed and answered, "After thirty days, I saw lights of different colors like high mountains pass before my eyes. And in the midst of these lights, I heard a voice that said clearly, '*Behold, God forgives all sins* [39:54].' As if through the eye of a needle, this voice came to the ear of my intelligence. I fainted at its sound and then saw various red, green, and white tablets on which the words, *All sins will be forgiven you, except for turning away from Me*, were written."

Mevlana cried out and began to whirl, and a great clamor arose from the excitement of the Friends.

"O Bahauddin," Mevlana cried, "It is just as you saw and heard and a hundred thousand times more so. However, in respect for the religious law and to follow the Conveyor of the Law, keep these secrets and don't tell anyone. Wicked people with donkey tails exist who dance without the sound of a drum (*daf*). If these people were told such secrets of the truth, disasters would result. The weak-hearted members of the religious community are unable to support the secrets of God's decree. They know nothing of Divine wisdom."

Step Down from Your High Horse [632]

Sultan Walad told us that one day he went with his father to Chelebi Husamuddin's garden: "The Friends had put me on a horse, and I rode slowly at the rear of the group, gazing at the beautiful countryside. That day, through his divine grandeur, my father seemed to be a like an ocean of grace flowing over the earth, among the people. The thought occurred to me that I would like to cut into pieces with a sharp sword one who would deny the power of such a sovereign, and throw him to the dogs saying, 'Why did you turn away from such an ocean of mercy; why do you oppose him?' "

Suddenly, my father said to me, "O Bahauddin, this self (*nafs*) presumption of yours is the result of the challenge of high position—you are on horseback while the Friends are walking on foot. This elevated position is unfortunate—you are finding fault with the lowly. What business do you have with deniers and the proud?"

And he recited these verses:

What does this story matter to us:
    the ox arrived, the donkey left?
Come on! The moment is subtle grace! Stop arguing!

Immediately, I got down from the horse, prostrated myself at Mevlana's feet, and asked for forgiveness.

Mevlana concluded, "It doesn't please me that you speak ill of the deniers, because everyone is constrained by the Divine Will. One must hope that they will be delivered from this fault and that they will become as you wish them to be, through Divine Grace."

The Springtime of Souls [633]

The great Friends related:

Sultan Walad said, "One day, I walked with Mevlana to the mosque at Meram where there was an immense sema. That day Mevlana composed seven odes regarding Spring with the refrain:

Come! The king is calling the falcon of the soul.
Come! The shepherd is leading his flock to the fields. . . .

"I joined in with, 'How amazing God is (*Subhanallah*)! This countryside of Konya is so beautiful! Mercy shines like divine lights from her fertile fields.'

" 'Yes, by God,' answered Mevlana, 'Our Konya is a great city, flourishing and blessed. With the Friends as our witness, I bestow it upon you.'

"I prostrated myself at his blessed feet, and he continued, 'O Bahauddin! As long as the blessed tomb and the bones of our Great Master Bahauddin Walad, and of his children, descendents, our friends and companions, are here in this city, this country will not fall into decline. The shoes of foreign horses will not trample it, nor will the enemy's sword be raised against its people. No blood will be shed, it will not be ruined nor completely destroyed, nor emptied; its inhabitants will continue to flourish in safety. Within the protective embrace of the blessed tomb, they will be sheltered from the vicissitudes of time, if it pleases God Most High!' "

The Speech of Paradise [635]

Sultan Walad told us:

One day, a group of distinguished men came to visit my father. That day he became quite passionate as he explained certain aspects of mysticism:

"O Bahauddin, if you wish to be in Paradise forever, be a friend to everyone and never hold malice towards anyone in your heart."

Then he recited:

Don't ask for more; don't be superior to others;
be like balm and candle, not a stinging needle.
If you don't want evil to come to you from anyone,
don't speak evil, teach evil, or even think evil of anyone.

When you speak with goodwill about others,
you will always be happy, and this happiness is Paradise itself.

If you speak with bitterness about someone,
you harbor anger, and this anger is Hell itself.
When you remember your friends,
the garden of your heart blooms with happiness,
filling with roses and basil.
If you speak of enemies,
thorns and snakes enter the garden of your heart,
and you grow tired and wither.
All the prophets and saints (May peace be with them)
have realized this and acted accordingly.
Their fellow human beings,
overwhelmed by their beautiful character,
are drawn to their kindness and willingly,
happily, follow their path."

Just a Glimpse of His Beauty [636]

All bounty is in God's hands alone; He grants it to whomever He wills [3:73], so that the lovers might clearly discern the right path of the person with divine favor.

As the poet said,

I would give my heart to one who is worth a soul.
A glimpse of his beauty is worth a whole world.
I don't give my heart to just anyone,
but for useful profit that is worth a loss.

There is a great difference between a pebble and a pearl, between a stick and Moses' rod; this should suffice for people who have the capacity for understanding.

Be Mindful of Your Trustworthiness [637]

[One day, Mevlana said to Sultan Walad:]

Always observe good manners and do not scratch sincerity's face with the nails of denial. For even though through the intercession of a prominent man they may free a thief from the gallows, they will not make him the chief steward or vizier of the sultan.

Search for Us in Joy [638]

Sultan Walad said:

One day, my father said to me:

"O Bahauddin! One day, my light shone in the world of power and encompassed all the horizons to such an extent that the great luminary, the sun, in the middle of this light, vanished like a particle of dust.

Before Your face, the sun vanishes like a mote;
this is as clear to all the world as the sun is.

"As this was unfolding, I said to God Most High, 'I should show myself to Bahauddin.' A response from the Most Glorious came to me: 'This is not the time.' Now, whenever you truly see yourself, and in a moment you are filled with joy, know that I am that grace and joy that descends upon you.

Search for us in joy,
because we inhabit that delightful land of bliss."

A Friend Must Know How to Cry [639]

The trustworthy Friends, guardians of the treasure of certainty (May God be pleased with them all) recounted:

When Chelebi Husamuddin was in the throes of his final illness (May God illuminate us with the pure light of his grave), Sultan Walad went to visit him.

"After your departure, what will become of me?" Sultan Walad cried, weeping, beside himself with grief. "Who will be my soul's companion? Who will I have for company? To whom shall I turn for the nourishment of my soul? To whom will I whisper the secrets of my heart? From now on, who will keep me company? Who will console me in this terrible separation that could set the world on fire?"

Tears of blood flowed from his blessed eyes, and he was overcome with such an intense compassion, that all the companions present at the bedside, also, became flooded with tears.

One must know how to weep for others.

Chelebi sat up for a moment and leaned against Sultan Walad.

"My soul, my light," he said, "don't be sad, and banish worry from your heart. After my death, in every important endeavor, in every difficulty, in every situation for which you don't have a solution, I will appear to you in a different form; I will find you. I will assume a luminous body and manifest myself in rays of light so that you might untie the knot of your difficulties. You will not need anyone else. In just that way, at the edge of a river in Khorasan a green light appeared to our Great Master Bahauddin Walad and helped him resolve his dilemma. Know that any form which might appear to you to guide you, know that in reality it will be me, and no other, nor does it belong to anyone else. I will appear in your dreams to share my ecstasies with you, and through me you will attain your worldly and spiritual goals."

At the beginning of his *Mathnawi*, *Ibtida-i Waladi*, Sultan Walad speaks about the dream. If you look for it, you will find it, but *God knows best*!

Listening to the Beloved [640]

The Friends told us that one day an important person asked Sultan Walad:

"Does God Most High ever speak to his servant?" This person had been wondering: "In what way should I honor Sultan Walad? Should I give him gold or perhaps a turban of Indian cloth?" And he remained unable to decide.

"Yes, by God," Sultan Walad immediately answered, "He does speak to him."

"How?" he asked.

Walad said to him, "There was a preacher in Balkh, a noble saint and one of the intimate friends of God, surrounded by many friends and mystic lovers. Often during his sermons he would say, 'So often the Lord speaks to you, but you do not listen. This is strange for an obedient servant.' Then he would recite these verses:

> You disobey God, while showing love for Him.
> This is ridiculous! What a strange way to act!
> If your love were sincere, you would obey Him.
> A lover always does what his beloved asks.

"And he repeated, 'Allah! Allah! One must listen to the word of God and obey Him.'

"Suddenly a dervish got up and asked for a turban. A noble khwaja was seated in a corner of the mosque. The inspiration to give the dervish his turban came to him three times, but each time something prevented him. As all this was going on, the khwaja stood up and asked, 'O our Master (May God have mercy on you) how does God speak? Please explain it clearly.'

"The preacher answered, 'He will not speak more than three times for a turban.'

"The man let out a shout and fell at the preacher's feet. He then gave that dervish all the clothes that he was wearing and declared himself to be the preacher's servant and disciple in perfect sincerity.

"Now, O great ones of Islam, listen to the word of God. Give away your turbans, and give away your gold! When you listen to what God says, He also will listen to what you say—He will give you all that you desire, and you will find with Him all that you are seeking."

At this moment, this distinguished person became a servant and disciple in all sincerity.

It is certain that the miracles of Sultan Walad are infinite and a drop of water from this roaring sea is sufficient as a sign, just as it is said, "A little is an indication of the lot, and a handful is indicative of the whole granary." Even if one were to try to describe all his virtues and stations, it could never be contained in words.

A Rose May Have Its Thorns [641]

In a gathering one night, Sultan Walad told the Friends the following:

One day, when I was still a child just learning to write, my father and I were walking in the Meydan cemetery.

"O Bahauddin," he said, "Most of these people died from blows of the evil eye because they were full of self-importance and were stubborn and preoccupied with themselves. They died from repeated blows of the evil eye and rapidly faded away. There is no evil eye like self-importance when it comes to the destruction of a man."

As the poet said:

Don't contemplate your peacock feathers,
but rather keep your eyes on your feet.
Then the evil eye won't capture you in ambush.

"How can a mountain crumble simply from the looks of the

wicked? Read about this in the Qur'an: *They who are bent on denying the truth would all but kill you with their eyes* [68:51]."

Mevlana continued, "In a similar way, a wound, a pain affected the Messenger (Peace and blessings be upon him) as a result of the evil eye of the Qurayshi chiefs and the accursed Ahabish;[12] his grandeur and miracles surpassed all known limits—he had attained the summit of perfection and was victorious. These envious men with darkened hearts and dim eyes could not bear to behold that face, nor could they take pleasure in his sweet words. I also have undergone the effects of the evil eye.

A blow from the evil eye is like a drink of poison—
I, too, have received wounds that exhaust the spirit."

Then I began to weep and asked, "Will I also be struck by the evil eye?"

"No," my father replied. "They've planted foolish ideas in the garden of your mind! You will live happily and die in happiness.

"A rose bush is not cut down just because it has thorns. One may encounter great Friends of God with thorny characters, but one does not strike a blow against such a head—this thorn is the wish of the domes of His rose garden and it is hidden under those domes of God.[13]

We are the thorn of the rose, O my brother,
witness that this kind of thorn is a glory, not a shame.

"Similarly, a rough stem provides nourishment and life and is equal in importance to the fineness of the flowers.

A single fault among a hundred life-giving ones
is like the woody stem of the sugar cane.
They are weighed together in the scale,
because both are pleasing—
like the body and the soul."

The Provision of Spirit [642]

[At the dedication of a medresse in Kayseri] Sultan Walad was asked to speak. With hesitation, he finally agreed. He turned his

---

12. The Ahabish were allies of the Quraysh.

13. Remember the *Hadith Qudsi*: "My saints are sheltered within my domes, and no one knows them but Me." See selection #138 of this volume.

turban sideways and gave a very eloquent sermon and offered a prayer. Then he began the following speech:

"I learned from my shaikh, my imam, my qibla, my strength, my Lord, my support, my confidence, the dwelling place of spirit in my body, the provision of my today and my tomorrow, the perfect one among the seekers of truth, my Master, my refuge, my father, the Splendor of the Truth and of Religion (*Jalal al-Haqq wal Din*) . . . ."[14]

As he spoke these words, there was a great tumult and everyone in the mosque cried out and uncovered their heads. The cries of the mystics calmed the disturbance in the assembly of angels of Heaven.

The Parvana tore his clothes, and Qotbuddin Shirazi untied his turban and threw it aside. Men and women wept out loud, and a torrent of burning tears poured from their eyes. The clamor was such that it was not possible to hear the sermon, and the gathering became a sema.

Sultan Walad then straightened his turban, offered a prayer, and descended from the pulpit. . . .

When, earlier, he turned his turban to the side, a tumult arose as people turned their glance to the other world in lamentation. When he straightened his turban, the whole assembly was calmed.

As Spirit Flows . . . [643]

Fakhruddin recounted:

"When I was young," said Sultan Walad, "there was a time when I did not see my father for a few days, and I was overcome with longing for him. Suddenly, he called me to him, and I went to his room and bowed in greeting. From within a deep spiritual immersion, he gazed at me so intensely with such an awesome look, that I was overcome and my father also fainted.

"When he came back to himself, he looked at me in an intense way a second time, and lost consciousness again. A third time, he

14. This remembrance is included in the Mevlevi litany of prayers recited daily by Mevlevi dervishes: *The Mevlevi Wird*, (*Awrad-i Sharif*), Translated by Camille Adams Helminski with assistance from Cuneyt Eroglu, Mahmoud Mostafa, and Amer Latif, The Threshold Society, 2000, p. 67.

looked at me with such compassion that I saw myself as completely effaced and non-existent.

"When I came back to consciousness, he said, 'The first time that I looked at Bahauddin, I saw an unsurpassed beauty and spiritual presence. The second time that I studied him, I saw an extraordinarily lovely crown on his head similar to Solomon's; the third time, I saw a very handsome earring hanging from his ear.'

Sultan Walad continued, "The interpretation of these three important visions has become known to me: the beauty and perfection he saw in me represents the knowledge of mysteries that he himself has bestowed upon me. The royal tiara is the shadow of his favor which protects me, and the pearl earring—the innermost secret of our Jalaluddin 'Arif who came into being through me. Praise and thanks be to God!

"My father has favored me so that within me is the sea of gnosis and upon my head, the crown of grandeur. I have been given a beloved son, 'Arif. All the exoteric and esoteric knowledge that I possess comes from the blessings of this sovereign of religion."

As Walad said:

A child (*walad*) does not have any wisdom or holiness
except that which his parent has given to him.

Carrying the Fragrance [648]

A tradition tells us this story about one of God's Friends, Sultan Walad's nurse, Keramana (May God be pleased with her).[15] Keramana had become famous throughout the world for her extraordinary miracles. One day she was sitting in her retreat cell. Some time before, Mevlana had sent his sons, Sultan Walad and 'Alauddin, to Damascus to study.

As Keramana cleaned the carrots and the turnips she was preparing for a meal, she bemoaned the absence of Bahauddin Walad and 'Alaeddin. She was listing their good qualities to herself when suddenly two angels arrived to take her to God.

"I have business here, and cannot follow you," she told them. "I am lamenting Bahauddin's absence."

The angels left and then returned, saying, "You must come;

15. This was his grandmother, the Great Kira. Another version of this same story appears earlier in the *Menaqib*, within the chapter of Shams of Tabriz where she is mentioned: see section #539 of this volume.

God Most High is calling you."

When they insisted, that sincere poor lady (*faqira*) said, "O my eyes, cry. O my tongue, continue your song. O my hands, don't stop your work! Continue to work while I go to be near God; keep busy until I return."

This transpired just as Keramana had requested. Her soul went to be near God and then returned; she returned to find her physical self just as she had left it. Delighted, she took her body in her arms and said,

> "If at every moment I can discover the scent of the Beloved,
> why would I not want to embrace myself continually in my arms?"

Enduring Light [649]

When Sultan Walad left for the world beyond, he recited these verses while the Friends wept with grief:

> There are dangerous streams which you should not try to cross;
> take care and pay attention. Don't enter every stream.

He continued:

> I said, "Two pomegranates on one breast!"
> She answered, "Yes, my fruit!"
> I said, "O my idol, you are a pine-tree!"
> She answered, "Yes, take me!"
> I said, "Will you take me with you wherever you go?"
> She answered, "Yes, I will take you."
> I said, "What are you putting on my breast?"
> She answered, "My heart, too!"

The night he died, he recited this:

> I will be full of joy tonight,
> since I'll be free of self!

Then Sultan Walad gave up his soul. For seven days, an intense light rose from the dome of the holy tomb up to the heavens and the height of Simak.[16] Everyone, both exalted and lowly, were able to see it, and the faith of the mystic lovers increased a thousand-fold.

The Friends who were clear seeing (*basirat*), members of the

---

16. *Al-simak* is one of the brightest stars in the night sky, either Arcturus or Spica, both of which are sometimes referred to *as al-simak* ("the uplifted one").

brotherhood of mystery (*sarirat*), told us that this light was Chelebi 'Arif who adopted this form when he was sitting on the blessed throne, illuminating the world, because his light was that of seven Friends of God.[17]

Sultan Walad passed from the world during the night, just before the Saturday of the 10th of Rajab 712 A.H. (November 11, 1312 C.E.). May God bless his spirit and pour his graciousness upon the lovers.

Celebrating Souls [650]

In Sultan Walad's time, the son of a prominent person died. His parents expressed their wish that the Friends recite *ghazals* during his funeral procession. Akhi Ahmad, otherwise known as 'Anud (the stubbornly opiniated), was against this and wouldn't allow the reciters to recite a word, claiming that it was an innovation, forbidden by religious law.

Just then, Sultan Walad arrived and asked, "Why are the reciters not reciting? Why are they not expressing their joy at the soul's meeting with Ridwan[18] in Paradise?"

He seized Akhi Ahmad's hand and held it tightly, saying, "O Akhi Ahmad, a very great person established the foundations for this practice and deemed it lawful. It would take one greater than he to change it; this custom will not disappear from among the lovers until Resurrection Day. Why are you torturing yourself, causing yourself difficulty, throwing yourself against the sword of the saints?"

The unfortunate Akhi Ahmad could not answer and remained silent. The masters of sufism who were present reported what had been said to Shaikh-al-Islam Sadruddin (May the mercy of God be upon him).

---

17. Mevlana had said that 'Arif carried within him the light of the Great Master Bahauddin Walad, Sayyid Burhanuddin, Mevlana Shamsuddin Tabrizi, Shaikh Salahuddin, Chelebi Husamuddin, Mevlana, and his own father, Sultan Walad. It was Mevlana who chose, in addition to the name 'Arif, the name Feridun for him, the name of his mother Fatima's father, Mevlana's beloved friend, Salahuddin Zarkub.

18. "Ridwan ("pleased," as in *nafs al-radiyah*)" is the name of the angel who is the guardian of Paradise. See *Surah* 89:27-30:

To the righteous soul will be said:
"O soul in complete rest and satisfaction!
Return to your Sustainer well-pleased and well-pleasing!
Enter then among my devoted ones!
Yes, enter my Garden!"

"Mevlana Bahauddin is right," said Sadruddin. "It is as he says. This is similar to when a caliph asked a lover who was greater, Junayd or Abu Yazid (Bastami). The mystic replied, 'It would take one greater than both of them to know.' The beautiful innovations of the saints are like the customs (*sunnah*) of the prophets. One cannot suppress them."

When the young man's funeral procession arrived, Sultan Walad said, "There are only seven days of life left to Akhi Ahmad before his tumult calms!"

Everything happened as Sultan Walad said it would, but *God best knows the truth*!

Chapter VIII
‘Arif Chelebi and the Unfolding Lineage

(Highlights of Aflaki’s Chapters VIII through X)

The deeds of ‘Amir ‘Arif, the Sovereign of the Lovers, Proof of those with insight, Pole of the *abdal* and the *autad*, Sultan of the sovereigns of ecstacy, Jalaluddin Feridun, ibn Muhammad ibn Muhammad ibn Muhammad al-‘Arif al-Balkhi (May God assist us and make us eternal through the light of his effort and that of his grandfather), and those that followed him.

The Coming of ‘Arif [651]

The Friends told us that when Sultan Walad was a young man, he and Fatima Khatun, Shaikh Salahuddin’s daughter (May God comfort their spirits) had many children together, but most of these children died at six months, or ten months, or a year more or less, and Sultan Walad’s blessed heart had been painfully wounded by this sorrow.

Sultan Walad had still been unmarried when our Master had honored his spirit and placed an earring from the Unseen into his blessed ear. He had been gifted with such vision that the delightful essence of the eye would manifest in support of his spiritual states.

Sultan Walad (May God magnify his remembrance) recounted:

One night, my father, as usual, was performing the night vigil of: *One who devoutly worships God throughout the night, prostrating himself or standing in prayer* [39:12]. I was sleeping with the future mother of ‘Arif, when, suddenly, I had the desire to make love to her.

In the morning, my father said to me, “O Bahauddin, what have you lost there? What are you looking for? Perhaps it is Amir ‘Arif that you seek? I hope that your hope has been renewed.”

I bowed, and my father left. It was on this night that Fatima Khatun conceived ‘Arif (May God be pleased with her).

A Fruitful Tree [652]

Fatima Khatun had had twelve or thirteen children by Sultan Walad, but they had all died in infancy and joined their ancestors. Their compassionate mother was overcome with the grief of not having a righteous descendent and was lamenting in great pain.

In an effort to end another hopeless pregnancy, she had been taking all sorts of remedies, and making violent movements in order to detach this fetus, but without result.

However, when Sirajuddin conveyed to her Mevlana's good tidings about 'Arif's arrival, she was so happy to know that the tree might yield fruit that she began to care for the child growing within her. She avoided heavy meals, offered sacrifices, and distributed alms to the needy.

Under a felicitous ascendent, in a favorable moment, 'Arif arrived from the World of Eternity and set foot on the plain of this existence on a Sunday, the 8th of Dhu'l-Qa'da 670 A.H. (June 6, 1272 C.E.), just before the afternoon prayer. Even before they rubbed salt on that ocean of beauty, Mevlana arrived in haste like a brilliant full moon and poured a handful of gold coins over Fatima Khatun's head. He asked for the new-born and the mother handed the infant to him. He swaddled the newborn child in his blessed shirt, placed him in his sleeve, and left.

After he had breathed the necessary qualities of light (*nur*), joy (*sorur*), and tranquility (*huzur*) into 'Arif and expanded his heart, he returned him to the women in the early evening. It is said he placed 'Arif into the special care of Latifa Khatun, Kiraga's (Fatima's) mother.

Mevlana had tied a few pieces of gold into a corner of his shirt. The money-changers of the city had never seen dinars of this kind. Kiraga kept all of it for many years, as a blessing. These thirty dinars and two *mithqal* were used for the trousseau of Mutahhara Khatun and Sharaf Khatun.[19]

> What am I saying! The value of these golden coins
> minted in the Divine workshop never diminishes—
>   it is everlasting.

Right away, Sultan Walad came to greet Mevlana and bowed;

19. Mutahhara Khatun and Sharaf Khatun were the daughters of Sultan Walad and Fatima Khatun.

the Companions were bursting with joy. That day, Mevlana overflowed with delight and began a sema that lasted three days and three nights. It was then that he composed the *ghazal* beginning:

> If the garden had known of his arrival,
> blood would be bursting from the branches;
> if reason had been told of him,
> the Oxus would flow from their eyes.

The sultan, his vizirs, and the distinguished of the time offered such kindness, and sent so many gifts of gratitude, and rendered such service that it is impossible to describe.

Light Openings [655]

Fatima (May God be pleased with her) told us:

When our Khodavandgar left this rough world to set foot in the Unseen, because of this separation, my heart was on fire, blazing like a furnace. I wept night and day and had no tranquility or rest. From my childhood until my maturity, Mevlana had bestowed abundant favors and been a sultan and a father to me. I was afraid of losing my mind from grief. For three nights and three days, I was unable to nurse Amir 'Arif, and, like Moses, he would not accept milk from any other wet nurse nor take any food.

Then one night, I saw Mevlana in a dream standing on the fortress walls of the angelic assembly (*mala'-i a'la*), "O Fatima Khatun, why are you crying so? If this is for me, know that I am still present. Look for me in 'Arif's cradle, because I am there. The rays of my light fall upon him, and my secret is contained within him."

Startled, I awoke, and the milk of love began to flow from my breasts, drenching my clothes. My heart stirred, and it was as though Mevlana had pulled me from the world of contraction into the world of expansion. I felt new life emerging in the secret of my being and went to 'Arif in his cradle.

He opened hs blessed eyes and smiled at me; his eyes were filled with the light of Mevlana's splendor. When he looked at me, and this heavenly light shone into my soul. I let out a cry and fainted. When I came to myself, I beheld the ocean of Mevlana's light flowing in 'Arif's eyes and, within the luminous waves, thousands of hidden pearls of divine meaning revealed themselves. In all sincerity, I bowed down at the foot of 'Arif's cradle and became his disciple.

I consecrated my life, heart and soul, to the service of 'Arif, whether he was on a journey or at home. In this way, my soul, which had been so anxious, found peace.

He Who Has a Child Should Become Like a Child for Him [656]

Mevlana Sirajuddin, the reciter of the *Mathnawi* (May the Mercy of God be upon him) related the following:

One day, in the company of the representative of God, Husamuddin (May God magnify his remembrance), I had gone to the medresse to visit our Master. Suddenly, I saw the door of the garden open and we beheld Chelebi Amir 'Arif on a little cart that was being pulled by his tutor. Just then, Mevlana got up and took the rope of the wagon onto his own blessed shoulder and began to pull it himself, saying, "I have become 'Arif's little ox."

Then Chelebi Husamuddin, accompanying our Master, also took an end of the rope, and together they pulled the cart around the courtyard of the medresse. Chelebi 'Arif smiled sweetly and playfully swung about.

"To embrace little children," said Mevlana, "is for the people of Islam a heritage from our prophet, King of the Religious Law and Moon of the Truth (May God's peace and blessings be upon him). As he said, 'One who has a child, may he become like a child for him.'

To each new child, the father says, 'ti, ti,'
even though his mind comprehends the world's geometry.
Since I am playing with a child,
I must use their language."

To illustrate this, he told the following story:

"One day, his two grandchildren, Hasan and Husayn, were playing outside the retreat cell of the Messenger of God. A Bedouin on a camel passed by; he cropped his camel, and it brayed. The children laughed, very amused by this, and went to tell the Prophet about it.

"The Prophet (peace and blessings upon him), with his perfect generosity, got up and wound the end of his turban around his neck and bent down; Hasan and Husayn (May God be pleased with them) climbed onto his blessed back, laughing, and our Prophet carried them on his hands and knees around the courtyard of the house. He turned sharply to the right and to the left, braying, and the children screamed with laughter. Then he recited this *hadith*, 'What a beautiful camel your grandfather is, and what fine riders you are!'

"We are also saying and doing the same with our 'Arif," Mevlana concluded.

Sevenfold Healing [659c]

Sultan Walad recounted:

When Amir 'Arif was seven months old, a large tumor appeared in his throat, and for seven days and nights he refused to eat or drink and cried all night. All desire for life disappeared from his mother's soul, and the Friends were all plunged into despair. Night and day, I was anxious and upset, from the pain of the situation. The doctors were powerless to cure his illness.

Finally, I took 'Arif in my arms and brought him to the roof of the medresse. There I found my father walking about like an intoxicated lion. I put 'Arif at his feet, and without my willing it, with tears pouring, a terrible cry arose from my heart as I said, "Surely, my 'Arif is leaving us."

"No, no," replied my father, "O Bahauddin, let your heart be eased. 'Arif did not come into this world in order to leave so quickly, because marvellous deeds will open through him; he will be a remembrance from us in this world."

He called for a pen and inkwell and drew seven long lines down 'Arif's neck, and seven others across, and then, finally, he wrote: "An indication is enough for the wise."

Immediately, the tumor burst and poured from his throat. 'Arif opened his eyes and nursed at his mother's breast. The Friends were overjoyed, and his mother offered sacrifices and distributed alms to the poor and needy. In gratitude, Sultan Walad arranged a sema for the Friends.

Some of them imagined that this meant that 'Arif would live seven years, and others thought that it would be seventy years, thinking that each line was indicative of ten years. When 'Arif died at forty-nine years old, the wise Friends recognized that the crossing of the lines in length and width meant seven times seven (forty-nine). Even so, the life of this sovereign was governed by the number seven.

In the Way of Mevlana [660]

That King of Men of letters, Salahuddin Malati (May God's mercy be upon him) recounted:

When Jalaluddin 'Arif (May God sanctify his innermost secret) was six years old, he was studying the Qur'an with me. Whenever he entered the door of the medresse, Sultan Walad would show him great respect; he would stand up and make a place for him in his prayer-niche (*mihrab*).

One day, overcome with boldness, I said, "Really, 'Arif is your son; it's not necessary to pay such honors to a little boy. The great saints did not do it. Have they begun to do it now?"

"No, no, don't say that," replied Sultan Walad. "What you're saying is actually the opposite of how things are, so stop rebuking people. I swear by God, when 'Arif comes through the door, it's as though my father were coming. His graceful step, his gathered movements and gracious demeanor are exactly the way my father walked, in the manner so familiar to me in my youth, and 'Arif's movements in the sema are exactly those of Mevlana.

"'Arif was still nursing at the breast when his grandfather was alive. If he had been older, I would have explained it by saying that he acquired this manner through observing it, as graceful people may naturally copy another's movements. However, in 'Arif's case, it's not due to a rational process, because he was still too young; it is a gift, not something acquired.

This is a royal extravagance without corruption,
a pure gift from Divine Compassion—
God's bestowal, his gift to the true.
It is the reflection of His graciousness
within the realm of five senses and six directions."

With the Blessing of Fakhrunnisa [662]

That sovereign of the knowers of God, Chelebi 'Arif (May God sanctify his innermost secret) one day recounted:

My father, Sultan Walad, wanted me to marry, so that I would have a house and household of my own, but I liked being a bachelor and my freedom and would not consent. One day, at the beginning of autumn, I had gone for a walk in the gardens with some friends.

The grapes were very ripe, and grape molasses (*pekmez*) was being prepared.

Returning that night, I spurred my horse on ahead of the others. I was passing along the middle of the road through the gardens, near the abode of Fakhrunnisa, when, suddenly, I saw two beautiful children with shining faces, belonging to the world of the spirit run towards me. Then one from the right and the other from the left, they each placed a bouquet of roses in my hands. When I looked again, they had disappeared, but the bouquets remained in my hands—I put them under my arm. I was utterly astounded and bewildered by this extraordinary event, and beside myself, I made my horse gallop as fast as it could. When I arrived at the blessed tomb, I told my mother and the noble companions what I had seen and showed them what I had been given. Everyone was overcome with joy.

The next morning, when the good news reached my father, he called me to him and said, "This is good news for you—the World of Mystery has sent a sign that you will have two fine children. You must listen to me now and consent to marriage."

And so, having arranged to take a wife, I was married. Through the favor of our Khodavandgar and the blessings of my illustrious father, God Most High blessed me with two children. My father gave the elder the name "Amir 'Alim" and named the younger "Amir 'Adil" (May God support them with the light of certainty and grant them life until the Day of Reckoning). He gave the eldest the surname of "Bahauddin" and called the younger, "Muzaffaruddin."

For many years, Kiraga[20] kept these bouquets of roses and distributed the petals one by one to the worthy ladies. The freshness and color of the flowers never diminished, and the fragrance of the whole world was perfumed by the scent of these roses.

It Is the Wise Who Recognize the Wise [667]

Chelebi said, "The revelations of the angels belong to the prophets, and those of the heart to the saints. However, the average man cannot make a distinction between the true and the false, truth or a lie.

> For the ignorant in doubt, whose sight stops short,
> the false dawn and true dawn seem the same.

20. Kiraga is another name for Lady Fatima, the wife of Sultan Walad and mother of 'Arif.

O young man, the false dawn has been the windy cause
of the destruction of thousands of caravans.
For every true coin there is also a counterfeiter.
Alas for the soul who lacks scissors and touchstone.

[*Mathnawi* IV: 1692-1694]

"The truth is this: the Friend of God knows the friend of God, it is the Pole (*qutb*) who knows the Pole, the wise one who knows the wise, and the mystic who knows the mystic. It is only people of worth who can recognize people of worth.

The saint alone can know a saint;
if he desires, he can help another know this.

"The rest of insect-like people are at the stage indicated by: *No, they are like cattle—no, they are even less conscious of the right way* [7:179]. They have become the imitators of the prophets and saints, and they have neither clear insight nor an illuminated heart, so they believe in false people, in the hope that they might be true. They allow themselves to be seduced by external miracles and do not realize that the people who perform these miracles are tied to rebellious demons. They have no knowledge of the World of the Spirits (*arvah*) and the mystery of the Tablets (*alvah*) and have strayed far from the straight path of Muhammad.

"The reason they have manifested themselves and appeared in this way is that it is their destiny to lead astray the reprobates. 'It is by means of their opposites that things are made clear.' The pure manifestation of the Friends of God is for the sake of giving guidance to the spirits of the God-conscious people: *They cannot attain to anything of His knowledge except that which He wills* [2:255].

To the best of your ability, O excellent in geometry,
don't confuse revelation with diabolic whisperings.
The possessor of revelation has a hundred worlds within;
the other is a man, but just a man alone."

Those Who See You, See Me [674]

It is clear to the people of Certainty and the Brotherhood of the Way, that sometimes God Most High reveals His immense power through the saints and the prophets (Greetings of peace be upon them), so that people might realize that these saints and prophets are the beloveds of God and that everything He has created is for their sake, because He has said, "I have created creation for you, and I have created you for Me"; everything that He does, is to make known their grandeur: "But for you, I would not have created the heavens." God said, "Go with My attributes towards My creatures; those who see you, see Me; those who go towards you, also go towards Me . . ."[21]

And as the poet said:

He is holy, and Glory is His attribute,
so He has no need of anything, whether kernel or rind.
Every prize and every gift of grace that exists
is for the sake of His servants.
The King has no desire—
He has made this whole dominion for His creatures.
Happy is the one who knows this!
Of what use is the possession of any realm,
to the Creator of all realms and both worlds?
[*Mathnawi* I: 3140-3143]

One should recognize their words and actions as being those of God. The friends of these people are also God's friends, and those who consider them their enemies are enemies of God.

And as the poet has said:

God joined His secret to a body,
so that they would challenge it and be put to the test.
They don't know that to challenge it, is to challenge Him;
the water in this jug is connected to the water of the river.
He connected the two,
so that the saint might be the refuge of the world.
[*Mathnawi*: I: 2519-2521]

Kings on the Chessboard of Blame [675]

It is well-known and often repeated in the circles of the great ones, that the Sultan of the knowers of God, Chelebi 'Arif (May God water his grave and perfume his soul) was one of the great *abdal* and a perfect man of ecstatic states. He was one of the distinguished rascals of the world of the spirit, accomplished in the destruction

21. These are three *hadith qudsi,* sayings of God conveyed through the Prophet Muhammad, outside the Qur'an.

of the world of external appearances and the rules of the rational. He continually strove to break the constrained behavior of those who were imprisoned by dogma and formality—for those who can see, this was true manners.

From the uninitiated, Chelebi 'Arif always hid the beloved of his higher meaning behind the cloak of gathering (*jam*) and the veil of the goblet and wine of spiritual intoxication. He would block the seeing of even seeing men's eyes, hiding himself within the bridal chamber of Divine splendor, far from the view of men.

And as the poet has said:

If you come across deniers on your path,
let the wine cup be a veil for you.

He did not want his perfect beauty to become the target of the arrows of profane glances, rather he sought peace far from the tumult and chaos of the crowd and self-important strangers. Those who were intimate friends and allowed to enter his hidden sanctuary—as far as they were able, and through the grace of the One who sees—could witness him, and through his mercy, see what he wished to reveal. Those capable of seeing understood his meaning.

Excessive jealousy became a veil for the friend,
hiding you from his sight.

Most of his life was spent traveling and reading books of secrets. One day, the noble Friends, as well as Kiraga and Khvosh-liqa of Tokat,[22] that devoted *faqira*, arrived in the City of Glory, Amasia. At that time, the king of *khalifas*, the accepted of the saints, the unifier of realms of excellence, 'Alauddin Amasiyyavi, the son of Bayram (May the Mercy of God be upon Him) was still alive. He was renowned for his spirituality and had sent representatives throughout the region, spreading his magnificence. Capable and perfect disciples, learned companions, and devoted ascetics were in his service and kept company with him. Angels of the heavens were jealous of the purity of their innermost secrets, and, in sincere devotion, became disciples and rendered limitless service and respect.

Due to a change of atmosphere, the Chelebi suddenly became

22. In section #711, Aflaki notes that Khvosh-Liqa of Konya, that Lady of the Hereafter, wise mystic and Friend of God on earth (May God shower mercy on her) was Mevlana's representative in Tokat. Many of the noble ladies of this region were her disciples.

ill, and the doctors advised him to drink wine diluted with water as a remedy. However, Mevlana 'Alauddin wanted him to fast and observe the details of external religious form, as well as preach to the people. As 'Alauddin was against what Chelebi was doing, several of his disciples followed his lead, manifesting their hypocrisy. There was a group of aware Friends and poor dervishes whose hearts were illumined by the light of clear inner seeing (*basirah*) who were able to see the pure spirit of this knower of God and were not distracted by his external conduct.

When the news of all this reached Chelebi, he became upset, and went into the cell of seclusion (*halvathane*) where he fasted for almost fifteen days, neither eating nor drinking a drop of water. Kiraga and the Friends tried to convince him to take at least a mouthful, but without success.

He said, "Our friends imagine that our sustenance consists of this drink and roast meat—that this sustains our life. They are unaware of the nourishment of: 'I spend the night with my Lord.'[23] They do not realize that we are intoxicated with a different wine; they judge by their own circumstance. If they do not set aside their hypocrisy and pretentiousness, the day will come when they will not be given their daily bread, no one will greet them, and their shaikhhood will vanish. If they don't eat for five days, they're afraid they might die."

The sixteenth day was a Friday, and a large group of the distinguished had gathered on the divan of the *zawiya*. When the sema began and Mevlana 'Alauddin was passionately absorbed in the sema, Chelebi suddenly emerged from his retreat cell and let out such a loud cry that everyone lost their senses. Having turned the sema inside out, overwhelmed with ecstasy, he recited this quatrain:

> Those who reveal the heaven of happiness,
> are also the kings on the chessboard of blame (*malamat*).[24]

---

23. This is the beginning of a *hadith* of the Prophet Muhammad. As it was with Muhammad, and with Abraham, and Mary and all the Prophets and Friends of God:

The Sustainer and Cherisher of the Worlds, Who created me,
it is He Who guides me, Who gives me food and drink,
and when I am ill it is He Who restores me to health [26:77-80].

24. The Path of Blame (*malamatiyya*) is an approach within Sufism the practice of which includes appearing less than one is, rather than attempting to appear as better or more pious. Melamatis make an effort to hide their inner purity and not

Those who understand the secrets hidden in the words
may appear lost, but really are on the straight Way.

Keep Seeking God's Support [677]

One day, at a gathering of the Friends, Sirajuddin, the reciter of the *Mathnawi* and divine knower of God, recounted:

In his youth, 'Alauddin of Amasia served Chelebi Husamuddin, making every effort to accomplish the fine details of service. When the moment opened, he would practice the sema and recite the *Mathnawi* with great care; he would even ask me to assist in the recitation. After a while, he felt the desire to depart and to return to his home in Amasia.

"This is not the time to leave," Chelebi Husamuddin said. "Stay in the company of the Friends for a few more years, and then you will know what you should do."

But 'Alauddin asked again to depart. So Chelebi wrote out a diploma of dervishhood (*ijazet*) in his own blessed hand, and giving him the title of *khalifa*, he put a *khirka* on his shoulders and sent him off on the road to Amasia.

After his departure, Chelebi said, "Alas! This man's grapes have taken on color but are not yet sweet. Now, he has gone into the shade, far from the sun. I am afraid he may become the prey of a jealous mystic."

The end of this unique person came about as he said.

Having slain the lovers, he washed them in blood,
and then offered prayers over their bier.

Such is the custom of lions and their offspring; this reveals the secret of their power.

O Love! Lion-like, you are not to blame for spilling blood—
who reproaches a lion for drinking blood?
Souls always tell you: "Let our blood be lawful for you!"
When you drink someone's blood, you grant him eternal life.

The moral of this is that one must not oppose, mock, nor act in a presumptuous way towards people of God. On the mystical path, there is no blasphemy more dreadful than disdain and pride. One

---

to be attached to people's opinions of them, which might tend to feed the ego or distract them from their devotions.

must always be considering the outcome of things and the end of one's life. Ask God at every moment for help and support, so that, with the good guidance of those of right guidance, one might have provisions for the life to come. One must constantly seek God's support and know that this support and help comes as a gracious gift through our guides.

May no one make efforts here without Your help!
For God best knows that which is right.
Because the efforts of Pharoah lacked His help,
everything he sewed ripped apart.

In truth, without the protection of the people of God, no one is safe from the dangers of his or her own faults; without their protection and their faith, no traveler on the mystic path can rely on wellbeing. Our shaikh (May God elevate his rank) said:

Blessing without religious obedience is beneficial,
but obedience without blessing is of no use.

If through the shaikh's blessing, the two exist together, then it is truly blessing upon blessing, *light upon light* [24:35] as Mevlana has said (May God sanctify his innermost secret):

Without the favors of God and His special friends,
the seeker's page will be black, though he may be an angel.
O amir, set aside your careful cunning
in the face of such Divine favor, and die happily!
What can I say! Even death is not deprived of this blessing,
but pay attention—without this blessing we are in loss.

The Earth, Wind, Water, and Fire Are His Servants [678]

The old Friends (May they be happy and delighted in Paradise) recounted:

One day, Chelebi was walking in western Persia (*'Iraq-i 'Ajam*), along the river Korr. Overcome with passionate emotion, he suddenly threw himself into the fast-flowing water. He seemed to be a column gliding over the surface of the water. Now this river was so powerful that huge camels and elephants would have seemed like flies or ants within it. God had offered his protection and made for him a throne supported by the water, like the throne of Solomon that through Divine favor was carried by the air, and the way that the sea became a ship for the Messiah (May peace be upon him) and likewise out of the seventh atmosphere, Buraq served as a mount for Mustafa (Peace and blessings upon him). The miracles of the prophets and the saints (May peace be upon them all) have surpassed all limits of understanding. We have faith in what is said about them, as well as in their deeds. "Someone who loves a people, becomes one of them."

> If you cannot find the intoxication of the heart,
> ask the intoxicated eye.
> And if you have strayed far from God,
> let the prophet of miracles show you the way.
> From a guide of pure conscience,
> secret miracles can touch the heart.
> Miracles, coming from a perfect soul,
> impress the seeker's soul, bestowing life.
> Such a heart contains the currency of a hundred resurrections;
> the least of these is shared intoxication.
> The fortunate one becomes God's companion
> by pitching his tent near someone of real felicity.

Chelebi went along the distance of several miles, while the Friends ran along the bank of the river, crying out and beating their breasts. Outside the water, they poured dust on their heads. Burning with the fire of passion and love for him, they called out to their Master, invoking Mevlana's intercession to convince him to leave the water. That generous being, the son of generous beings, granted their request through his infinite graciousness and stepping onto the surface of the water, came out of the river. Embracing the Friends, he brought them new life.

"How can it be that such a great river does not drown men, who are so small in comparison?" he said jokingly. "But the Nile, itself, what could it do but obey Moses? The fire prepared by Nimrod could be nothing but a bouquet of roses for Abraham, God's illustrious friend. The cold wind, Sarsar, had to submit to the Prophet Hud, and the air had to obey Solomon, that dissolver of the atmosphere, out of love for him. And so my grandfather said:

> The earth, wind, water, and fire are His servants;
> to you and me they may seem dead, but with God, they are living."

These miracles and these states illustrate the stations (*makams*) reached by the noble Poles (*aqtab*), the great people of Oneness who are the *abdals* of God and the Pillars (*autad*) of the earth. Perfection of this kind is not available to every perfect man. *God chooses for Himself whom He wills* [42:13].

It is one of Mevlana's qualities, that he is the inheritor of the secrets of the Messenger of God. Chelebi's fearlessness has come to him through this pure lineage. May God sanctify his innermost secret and bestow His sanctity upon his followers—*So be it, O Lord of all the worlds.*

The Game of Graciousness [681]

The Chelebi Pulad-beg recounted:

Once, when I was in the service of Chelebi, we were enjoying ourselves at a gathering with the Sahib's children atop the fortress of Qara Hisari Daula, in the palace of the Sultan 'Alauddin Kay-qubad (May the Mercy of God be upon him). A third of the night had passed when suddenly, Chelebi got up and went out, saying, "No one should follow me or bring a candle for me." It was very dark and gloomy. We waited an hour, but he did not return, and we became quite concerned at his absence.

Finally, beside myself, I took a candle in hand, and went out to look for him. I stopped at all the villas and asked the guards but was unable to find out what had happened. I told the amirs that Chelebi had vanished. Crying out, they ran outside the palace, to see if by chance he had fallen off the battlements and was lying on the ground.

By that time, at least twenty or thirty people, with candles and torches in their hands, were looking for Chelebi, when, all of a sudden, I heard his voice: "Hey! Pulad, what are you looking for?" he cried.

It seemed his voice was coming from the roof of the palace below us. We opened the gate of the citadel and ran down. Chelebi was sitting quietly on the roof of the palace.

"Were you afraid that I had fallen and killed myself?" he asked, smiling.

Everyone bowed. I said, "This power and strength is beyond human capacity. How wonderful the son of such a father, who can accomplish such things."

Then Chelebi said, "Most of the circumstances in which a real man finds himself are impossible. The miracle is that the powerlessness of the people is revealed in the face of his strength, so that by recognizing both the greatness of the man of power and his own helplessness, a person becomes the object of Divine favor and mercy. These ecstasies, these miracles are nothing but a game of graciousness for a mystic. The smallest bird can fly from one mountain to another, and a sliver of wood can be carried in a stream of water. The strength of pure men is that they can lead their disciples to God without their realizing it, in such a way that their spiritual and earthly desires are met and that on the Day of Reckoning, these pure men become compassionate intercessors for their disciples."

As the poet has said:

Night and day, our spiritual guides (*pirs*) have labored
to deliver us from corruption and chastisement.
They accomplish our work, knowing only God,
the Generous, the Beneficent.

A Breeze from Eternity [683]

One day, Kiraga (May God be pleased with her) was with Chelebi in Tokat. She bowed in front of him, displaying her limitless respect and admiration for him. The noble women, sultaness Gumaj Khatun, the Parvana Mo'inuddin's daughter, Khavandzada, and the daughter of the Keeper of the Wine (*sharab salar*), and the Controller (*Mostawfi*) and others criticised her, saying, "It's not appropriate for a mother to bow before her son and to honor him to such an extent; rather, a good son should honor his mother, bow before her, and kiss her hand."

Kiraga replied, "*Your Sustainer knows best as to who strays from his path, and best knows He as to who are rightly guided* [6:117]. When I look at 'Arif, I see Mevlana, himself. This radiance burns within my soul, and I can hardly bear it. This is the reason that I bow before him—I do not consider him as a son, but rather as my shaikh. Khodavandgar has entrusted him to me."

That Friday, all the ladies gathered for the sema, and Chelebi, filled with mystical love, recited this quatrain:

We are a subtle soul, hidden from sight.
We appear in a place, but we are placeless.
If we were to lift the veil from our face,

we would ravish spirit, heart, and reason.

Then, while whirling in sema, he recited:

The essence of love is in the world of spirits;
love's nurse is a subtle breeze in pre-eternity.
If the shadow of love falls upon a seeker's head,
he becomes life itself, like the sun.

All the ladies, bewildered and ashamed, bowed and asked forgiveness. They rendered all sorts of service to Chelebi and bestowed rare gifts upon him.

Awakened Dreams *[688]*

The compiler of this book (*May he be happy and enjoy a happy return* [13:29]) recounts:

"On the day of Arafat, the eve of the Feast of Sacrifice (*'Eid al-Adha*), in the year 717 A.H. (1317 C.E.), we were seated, Friends and the distinguished, in Sultaniyya, at the lodge (*zawiya*) of Shaikh Sohrab-i Mevlevi, in the service of Chelebi (May God refresh his spirit). We were all occupied reading books or working, and Chelebi was quietly dozing. He suddenly let out such a cry we were totally petrified with fear and bewildered. Then he went back to sleep again.

When Chelebi awoke, I, his humble servant, bowed and asked him what had happened.

He answered, "I was on my way to visit the blessed tomb, when Nasiruddin Qattani, the Mevlevi, and Shojauddin Hannaqi, both illustrious Friends, grabbed each other by the collar and began to fight. I shouted at them to stop, and as they did, I noticed that two men and one virtuous woman were watching."

Immediately, devoted servant that I am, I made a note of the date of this incident. When we arrived with good fortune in Rum, in Ladiq, by chance we met our dear friend Nasiruddin Qattani.

Chelebi asked him, "So what was the dispute with Shojauddin all about?"

Nasiruddin Qattani bowed and gave this explanation: "The day of Arafat, I was standing at the head of the blessed tomb. Shojauddin arrived suddenly and began to behave strangely, acting inappropriately.

I told him, "Behavior like this isn't allowed," whereupon he attacked me, and we began to fight. Then all of a sudden, from the foot of Bahauddin Walad's tomb, we heard Chelebi shout at us. Bewildered and in awe, we embraced each other and lowered our heads. More than that, I don't know."

Then turning towards me (Aflaki), Chelebi said, "Tell this story to the friends, so that they might catch the scent of our poverty."

Aflaki said, "When I had described these miracles in writing exactly as they happened as well as the dates, the Friends cried out with joy, and a feeling of infinite well-being, coming from the Unseen World, entered their hearts."

Then Chelebi said, "By the sanctified soul of Mevlana, this manifestation of miracles and the way they draw attention to us does not please me, but at times, a small thing that happens serves to attract the Friends towards the Unseen World. Our Shaikh Aflaki, on the other hand, loves our miracles and records them faithfully. The shaikhs of unveiling call these sorts of miracles, 'assimilation (*tamaththol*)' and 'dissolution (*enselakh*)' and there are many kinds."

> Even without sleep, a mystic is like this.
> God has said: *While they are asleep . . .* [18:17];
> don't concern yourself about this.
> Night and day, he is asleep in regard to the world—
> like a pen moved by the hand of God.
> One who while awake sees happy dreams
> is a lover of God—rub his dust on your eyes.
> He has awakened dreams
> and opens wide the gates of Heaven.

When we all arrived safely in Konya, Shaikh Mahmoud, who was Najjar's son, my Master Nizamuddin Erzinjani (May God have mercy on them), and Karima Khatun, the daughter of Shaikh Muhammad Khadem (May God be pleased with her) acknowledged: "On the day of Arafat, the eve of the 'Eid al-Adha, we suddenly saw Chelebi standing at the foot of Bahauddin Walad's tomb, and heard him cry out loudly."

From the Hand of Beauty [690]

That dear friend, Shaikh Karimuddin (May the mercy of God be upon him) who was one of the intimates of Amir Najmuddin Dizdar (the Commander of the Fortress) (May God have mercy on him), recounted:

One year, Amir Najmuddin had arranged his beautiful garden and just planted it afresh. Suddenly, Chelebi honored him with a visit; Amir Najmuddin and the other amirs ran to the foot of the fortress at Gavala to welcome him.

After conversing together, Chelebi said, "O Karimuddin, it would be a blessing if you brought me some cucumbers from this new garden for the Friends."

"O Khodavandgar," I replied, "I would do anything I could to serve you, but we only just planted yesterday—they might be ready in a month."

"Don't talk so much, just go and bring them," he said.

I quietly left and went into the garden. I saw that on one single plant there were four delicate, thin cucumbers. I lowered my head, picked all four, and brought them to Chelebi. The distinguished people present were overcome with astonishment.

Chelebi said, "These are only little cucumbers. Bring me the large yellow ones with seeds, because there is something I would like to do with the seeds."

Once again I left and looked among the beds. I found two enormous cucumbers filled with seeds and brought them to Chelebi.

He smiled and said, "These cucumbers have grown thanks to our Karimuddin's aspiration (*himmet*). Otherwise, how could we find them? God Most High can produce, from the World of the Beyond and from Non-existence, hundreds of thousands of pomegranates and cucumbers for His excellent servants. However, it is Divine law that His servants must ask for them, and show complete devotion and present their requests with supplications (*niyaz*) at His court where there is no need (*niyaz*), so that their desire and aim might be attained."

As the poet said:

It was Mary's painful need and supplication (*niyaz*),
that caused the infant Jesus to speak in his cradle.

O my heart, voice your desire!
The gift is in cash, and the King is here.
This moon-faced one will not say,
"Go and wait until next year."

He asked that the cucumbers be distributed among all the friends and the inhabitants of the fortress. On that day, all the amir's sons became servants and disciples, except Najmuddin Dizdar who continued to doubt: "How can these cucumbers have grown so quickly before their season? What is this strength and power that God has given Chelebi 'Arif?"

Then Chelebi said, "O Amir Najmuddin, haven't you read the *surah* about Mary that says: *Shake the trunk of the palm tree towards you; it will shower fresh, ripe dates upon you* [19:25]. If God can bring fresh dates from a dry tree for Mary, a virgin, pure of all contact with a man, then there should be nothing astonishing or strange about a few cucumbers being brought forth for someone with the breath of Jesus."

Everyone bowed and asked for forgiveness. After Chelebi left, they saw that the plants had not yet even flowered, and it wasn't until a month later that the first fruits began to appear.

What the Friends of God wish for happens;
everything submits to their commands.

Rejoicing in the Friend [691]

The late Amir Najmuddin, governor of the fortress of Gavala (May God have mercy on him), recounted:

One day, Chelebi went to the monastery of Plato the Philosopher. With a group of about fifty people, we went to join him, and, for three days and nights, celebrated with the monks. I had the thought that it was odd that Chelebi would spend the holy days of Dhul-Hijja[25] that precede the Feast of Sacrifice[26] this way. Immediately, Chelebi read my mind, shouted at me, and recited:

In the Way of God, don't hold power as a partner—
don't use your eyes for blaming someone else.
God knows the secret of every servant's heart.
Pay attention to your self, and don't meddle with others.

---

25. Dhul-Hijja is the Islamic month named for the Hajj, the holy pilgrimage to Mecca, which takes place during the first ten days of the month.

26. The 'Eid al-Adha (Feast of Sacrifice) is one of the two most sacred times of the Islamic year: the first ten days of Dhul Hijja are followed by this time of celebration in remembrance of Abraham offering a sheep for sacrifice after the Angel Gabriel stayed his hand, when God did not allow him to sacrifice his son.

The Hospitality of God [692]

[One day, when a fountain that had been taken from the *khanaqa* in Konya was restored, Chelebi said,] "A basin, a piece of stone without ability, a bit of mineral, which doesn't have the capacity to serve our family, has not kept it company in spiritual conversation (*sohbet*), or profited from gnosis—this pool which is not able to take pleasure at the sight of our face, secrets, or words, has however spent a great deal of time in this place under the gaze of men of God. The Supreme Being did not consider it right that it remain among people with hearts of stone, in exile far from this resting place. He found a graceful way to restore it to its original place.

"Now, consider the Friends, who have for so long served our blessed family and kept company with saints with their heart and soul, in perfect trust and certainty, rendering service to us, as in: *Strive hard in God's cause with your possessions and your lives* [9:41]. How could God abandon those Friends to the company of wayward people without any religion and deniers without faith? How could He deprive them of sight of Him? May He who is such a generous and gentle Lord never withhold His immense Grace and Beneficence from His servants."

And he added:

God forbid that a being such as You
should throw one who has placed his hope in You into despair.
Your forgiveness is immense and Your gifts are ample.

O You who give Your kingdom and the angels their sustenance,
O Pole around which Heaven turns,
may this goodness and hospitality forever refresh Your guests.

The Friends rejoiced and bestowed gifts in gratitude. That day, they held a great sema at Mevlana's tomb, and Chelebi recited this quatrain:

All the doors are closed except Yours
where the stranger must enter.
O Door of generosity, glory, and illumination,
the sun, moon, and stars are Your servants.

A Shared Fragrance [695]

It is also said that the great Kira (May God be satisfied with her) loved the Chelebi 'Arif very much. She would put him on her lap to feed him the nourishing food she had prepared for him.

"How wonderful! What a great sweet soul this child has," she would say, giving him many kisses and rocking him to sleep in her arms.

Meleke Khatun, Mevlana's daughter (May God sanctify their innermost secrets) would embrace Chelebi and placing her face close to his would say, "Arif carries Mevlana's fragrance. If God (May He be exalted) removed the veil of jealousy from his face, the lights of his soul would shine from one end of the world to another (from Mt. Qaf to Mt. Qaf) and illuminate the whole world."

A Watchful Heart [696]

Fakhruddin Lala (May God have mercy on him) would carry Chelebi on his shoulders to Husamuddin's, who would then take the child into the house, kissing his head, cheeks, and hands. When he kissed his hand, Chelebi 'Arif would kiss his, returning the affection, and Husamuddin would give him sorbets and sweets to delight him. When he would leave, Husamuddin would dress the child in costly clothing of all kinds and Egyptian turbans.

Husamuddin would say, "I wish that Sultan Walad would entrust 'Arif to me. With all my heart and all my soul, I would have liked to be his guardian. I would have liked to take charge of his education, but in order to avoid the attacks from the envious, I have filled this office as tutor from a distance and tried to oversee his spiritual state in secret. I am hopeful that Spiritual beings will turn to him and that the lights of his soul will envelop the universe. Since he possesses the lights of seven Friends of God, he will become the guide of the Poles (*aqtab*)."

When Secrets Are Told [700]

Gurji Khatun (Queen of the world) had a daughter named 'Ayn al-Hayat (May God illuminate her proof) who was a beloved friend of the dervishes and Chelebi. One day, 'Ayn al-Hayat invited Chelebi to come to her palace in Erzerum. He arrived with Salahuddin Adib and the Friends.

This lady began to ask the Chelebi about Sultan Walad and the meetings of the Friends of the tomb and those at the medresse.

She asked questions about them, one by one, and Salahuddin, as intermediary, did his best to answer.

'Ayn al-Hayat commented, "What this devoted Mevlevi says is true, and a hundred times more, but can't the young man speak for himself? I would like to hear from the mouth of the Master."

Immediately Chelebi responded, "It is in the retreat cell (*khalvat*) that a mystic speaks, and God willing, this will happen."

This inspiration caused a spring of life (*'Ayn al-hayat*) to open in 'Ayn al-Hayat's heart, and the fire of mystical love was kindled. She became enraptured, heart and soul with Chelebi 'Arif's words. For many years she pursued it, and said:

> Love is agreeable in the head of the mad,
> on the condition that that love is for You.

She performed so many services that it was impossible to enumerate them.

Letting Go [703]

One of the distinguished men of the era could not understand Chelebi and would raise objections, opposing him, motivated by evil intentions: "Such rascally behavior and careless permissiveness are not good. To stretch out one's legs on this carpet for anything other than rest is inappropriate," he said.

By chance, at a gathering he found himself face to face with Chelebi who, in the middle of the conversation, told this story:

"A dervish was lying down in all tranquility, with his feet stretched out, in the middle of the bazaar. A mystic passed by and said, 'What sort of dervish are you to stretch your feet out this way and to fall into such a careless sleep?'

"'It is because I have drawn in my hands so as not to touch things which don't concern me, and because I have rid myself of the arrogance of this deceitful world and have abandoned bodily desires,' the mystic responded." Then Chelebi recited:

> Since I drew in my hands and heart from the affairs of this world,
> I now stretch out my feet as I wish, with happy heart,
> O blessed one.

This critical man then asked forgiveness of Chelebi and became a completely sincere disciple.

Let Me Be Your Prey [713]

The humble author of these pages recounts:

In the company of Chelebi (May God magnify his remembrance), we left Kayseri to go to Siwas. Imaduddin, the qadi of Amasia, Sa'duddin, Khatib of Siwas, his brother Majduddin al-Hafiz (the Qur'an reciter), and others accompanied us. Chelebi was asleep on his horse when a messenger arrived to tell me that my father had died in the palace of Uzbek-Khan. He had been an influential man of high stature and had a great many properties. They were waiting for me to arrive to distribute the goods.

I was very upset by this and grief-stricken, thought, "When we arrive in Siwas, I won't ask permission. I'll simply go and claim my inheritance as well as my father's library. Then I'll hurry back to our Master."

Suddenly, Chelebi awoke and cried out, "We don't need this money and possessions, and if you go without permission, you'll perish in the sea."

Poor one that I am, I cried out and fell off my horse. I lay my head upon the hoof of Chelebi's horse, weeping. The other dervishes were bewildered and did not know what to make of this.

Chelebi then raised his blessed head and showed me great affection, saying, "As long as I am alive don't go in pursuit of such game. Let me be your prey. When we are gone, do what you wish."

Then he fell asleep again, but first, the *qadis*, Imaduddin and Sa'duddin, asked what he meant.

"Shaikh Aflaki's father has passed from this world in the Saray, and he wanted to leave without our permission to claim the goods left by his father. Separation did not please us, and I warned him that he should not trade the reality of his relationship with us for a phantom of useless wealth, that he should not abandon the company of the Friends of God, since he might regret it later and lose on the whole transaction."

Immediately, Imaduddin and Sa'duddin al-Khatib became disciples. This poor one asked forgiveness and willingly gave up my plans, no longer concerned with it.

The Fools of God [714]

One day, I [Aflaki] left Tabriz, on my way to Sultaniyya. Shihabuddin Maqbul of Qirshahri (May the mercy of God be upon him) a worthy, noble man of Tabriz, who was a Qur'an tutor at the Qubba (Dome) of Ghazan, accompanied me, and we chatted as we rode along. Suddenly, the groom of the horses did something to irritate Chelebi and Chelebi chastised him severely and rode off.

"It does not seem right that such a great person should act so foolishly, but then the fools of Asia Minor are renowned," observed Shihabuddin.

"It is not permitted to slander the saints when one knows nothing, and to speak such nonsense," I said, objecting. I succeeded in quieting him, and he said no more.

However, just then, Shihabuddin's horse reared and threw him into some black mud, so that his head was plunged in black peat and his feet were in the air. I was afraid he would suffocate.

Chelebi galloped over and said, "O Shihabuddin, don't fight with the 'fools of Rum.' "

Shihabuddin cried out, got up out of the mud, and bowed. He changed his clothes and vowed to change his behavior towards Chelebi, declaring himself his servant and sincere disciple. He gave Chelebi a commentary on the Qur'an by Najmuddin Daya,[27] one of the foremost, and rendered him infinite services.

Chelebi then gave the manuscript to that king of hearers of *dhikr*, 'Alauddin of Kastamonu (May God have mercy on him). Until then there had not been any copies of this commentary in all of Asia Minor. It spread throughout these regions thanks to this sovereign's blessings.

Qitmir [720]

One day, a sufi had a heated argument with Shaikh Nasihuddin, the *khalifa* of Nakida (Nigde) (May God have mercy on him).

"Why are you so attached to this dog you call 'Qitmir'?"[28] he asked, and promptly began to list the dog's faults.

"I love him, because he is a Friend of God and knows how to distinguish a friend from an enemy, the lovers from the deniers,"

27. Najmuddin Daya (d. 1256 C.E.) was a renowned sufi author who was a disciple of Najmuddin Kubra (one of Mevlana's ancestors) in Khwarazm. He also wrote the *Mirsad al-ibad ala'l mabda' wa'l ma'ad*, translated by Hamid Algar as *The Path of God's Bondsmen from Origin to Return*, New York, 1982.

28. Qitmir was the name of the dog of the Companions of the Cave. See *Surah al-Kahf*, 18:9-26, and note to section #126 of this volume.

said the Shaikh.

"It's not true," the sufi cried. "Impossible!"

Nasihuddin answered, "He is the same dog as the dog of the Companions of the Cave (*ashab al-kahf*). He is of the same vein and exactly the same color.

If a dog doesn't have the vein of love,
how can it be that the dog of the Seven Sleepers sought a heart?[29]
The lion, wolf, and bear all know what love is.
One empty of love is less than a dog."

"Can you prove this to me?" asked the sufi.

"If you give him a lovely almond cake, he will refuse it, but he'll take a crust of dry bread from me."

The sufi offered two dirhems to buy a cake, and he put it in front of Qitmir. Through the power of God, Qitmir sniffed it once and paid no more attention, however when Shaikh Nasihuddin brought out some dry bread, he gobbled it up. The poor sufi, renounced his pride and disdain, and demonstrated his simple devotion. Shaikh Nasihuddin put his own cloak around his shoulders, and later he became a disciple of Chelebi 'Arif, who had said, "Our dogs are also spiritual teachers. So consider what our lions are like!" As the poet said:

O you, whose dogs the lions serve!
He said, "It's not possible!" Silence and *salaam*!

It is said that Shaikh Nasihuddin gave Qitmir to the Chelebi as a gift, and when they were parting from each other, the Chelebi beckoned to the dog to come with him. When the animal had gone a few feet, he turned back and looked at Nasihuddin, who said to him, "What are you looking at? If it pleased God, I would like to be in your place and become the guard dog at such a palace."

Qitmir rolled on the ground, yelped, and ran off with Chelebi. When Chelebi reached Ladiq, and a sema began, Qitmir entered the circle and began to whirl together with the Friends.

Another miracle was that whether in the country or the city, no other dog dared attack or even bark at him. When the other dogs saw him, they would form a circle around him and lie down. When the Chelebi sent off a messenger on a journey, he would send

29. Through his devotion, the dog (*kalb*) of the seven sleepers gained a heart (*qalb*).

Qitmir along. Whether they were on the road ten days or a month, the dog would accompany him to his destination and then return.

To cure a fever, they would trim a little bit of Qitmir's fur and burn it, and the invalid would be healed by the smoke. . . .

The Chelebi always fed him with his own hands and would often pet him. He said:

Since we bestow such favors on a dog,
consider what happiness we will bestow upon men.

By Intention [721]

One day, an important person came to see Chelebi and apologized:

"I regret that I cannot visit His Majesty often to pay my respects and honor him."

The Chelebi replied, "That which we ask of the Friends is sincerity of intention, purity of faith, and friendship of the soul. They might have difficulty in fulfilling their commitment to service and be unable to come because of their occupations or their relationships. Even so, their desired goal both in general and particular will be attained under our guidance and they will surely succeed. We respect the lives of our sincere Friends immensely and like to bestow favors upon them."

Then he told a related parable: "An amir's son was studying literature and *adab* in a private religious school. Every day he gave his master two dirhems. One day, the young man was not able to go to school, and he sent his daily fee with a servant. The master took the two dirhems, without inquiring about the reason for his student's absence. To test his master, the student sent the money on several other occasions without returning to school. Still the master did not inquire about him.

"The amir's son became angry: 'How can you take the money, and not be bothered to find out about me?'

"The master replied, 'What I want is the dirhems. If you wish, come, or if you wish, don't come.'

"Now, a true shaikh desires the currency of the disciple's love. Whether the student comes or not, the shaikh tries to assist him, and night and day works to bring him to perfection."

Then he recited:

They are the philospher's stone of happiness—

through their actions they bring felicity to all.
They even save the jealous from jealousy
and make everyone into seekers and disciples.

Your Compassion Is Boundless [728]

Aflaki, that writer of the secrets, and sincere servant of enlightened men (May God grant him peace) recounts:

One day, on a trip to Ladiq, I did something foolish, poor miserable soul that I am. The Chelebi looked at me, and my whole state (*hal*) changed. I trembled and was overcome with a burning fever. I became like a phantom, and it seemed as though my very life was in danger. I could see myself clearly, suspended with my head over the fires of Hell and then removed. However, I continued to burn with love for the Chelebi and separation from him. I could see the Angel of Death hovering over me. I lamented loudly and showed my distress, but Chelebi paid no attention and did not come to visit me.

For forty long days, I remained in this dreadful and hopeless state. Then on the eve of the Feast of Sacrifice, we arrived in Kutahya, where my illness became even worse. I retired to a corner of the *zawiya*. My fever was so high, I was unable to speak, and I feared for my life and wept.

Suddenly, Chelebi appeared, smiling and looking at me kindly: "Get up out of bed and grasp your ears with your hands.[30] Leap three times and say:

'*Lord, we have wronged our souls* [7:22]; error is done.
Be merciful, You whose compassion is boundless.' "

He then gave this half-dead servant a pomegranate and said, "Recite the *Mathnawi* and do sema."

As he spoke, I felt the illness disappear, and it was as though I had never been sick; I was once again a living and active human being. As long as I live, I will be drawn towards this court in service.

Gratitude is a hunt for abundance, an obligation for God's servant,
but whatever happens is as God wills.

Whatever He commands, say, "*We hear, and we pay heed* [2:285]."

---

30. This is the position of *pay-machan*, when a dervish stands on one foot, acknowledging fault, repentent, seeking forgiveness.

For all that you fear, know that He is the Protector. It is He![31]

There were many thousands of miracles of this kind and proofs of his Friendship with God unfolding from him. At times, he hid these manifestations from ordinary men and strangers, while revealing them to those who were intimate with secrets.

Intellect Ties Us in Knots, but Love Dissolves Those Tangles [729]

That guide of chivalrous young men, that witty and noble companion, Shaikh Begi (May the Mercy of God be upon him), sincere supporter of Chelebi, recounted:

A disagreement arose between Sultan Walad and Chelebi 'Arif and they were not speaking to each other. However, longing for 'Arif, Sultan Walad was very anxious to repair the rift. He called me to him and with much graciousness asked me to intercede: "Go to meet 'Arif outside the sacred tomb and bring him here. I will prepare a feast to welcome him, because one must always mend quarrels."

I bowed and informed Chelebi, and we left with a group of Friends to visit his father. When we entered the dergah, Chelebi bowed. Sultan Walad came forward, placed his cheek upon Chelebi's cheek and kissed his face and hair and forehead, then took him in his arms and held him in a warm embrace for a long time. The Friends cried out in joy and threw coins of blessing upon them. Then Sultan Walad

---

31. This is a reference to a beloved passage of the Qur'an, from *Surah Baqara*, 2:285-286:

The messenger, and the faithful with him, have faith
in what has been revealed to him by his Sustainer:
they all have faith in God, and His angels, and His revelations, and His messengers,
making no distinction between any of His messengers; and they say:
"We have heard, and we pay heed.
Grant us Your forgiveness, O our Sustainer, for with You is all journeys' end!"
God does not burden any human being with more than he can bear:
in his favor shall be whatever good he does, and against him whatever harm he does.
"O our Sustainer! Do not take us to task if we forget or unknowingly do wrong!
O our Sustainer! Do not lay upon us a burden
like that which You placed on those who lived before us!
O our Sustainer! Do not make us bear burdens which we have no strength to bear!
And efface our sins, and grant us forgiveness, and bestow Your mercy on us!
You are our Supreme Lord: help us when we face those who stand against truth."

recited this quatrain:

> Those whose feet are firmly planted on the path
> have rejoined the way of conversation
> and haven't washed their hands of the friend
> just because a little dust has fallen.
> No one has ever arisen from the realm of water and earth
> without a fault dusting his face.

The Chelebi answered his father:

> The arrow of your guidance never misses its mark,
> and if one of us makes a mistake, it is you who pardons.

Sultan Walad ordered that a wholesome meal be brought, but the Chelebi lowered his head and, with extreme courtesy, was too embarassed to eat in front of his father. Sultan Walad withdrew from the group and went up into the upper balcony and sat down there. He suggested that everyone enjoy their meal in tranquility and not pay any attention to him.

After the table covering was removed and *ghazals* had been recited, he said, "Akhi Begi, I have heard that our 'Arif sings beautifully and is as excellent in music as he is an accomplished horseman in the fields of other kinds of knowledge. I would like him to sing a *pishrau*, a *nawbat* and a *basit* (prelude)."

The Chelebi 'Arif continued to bow his head in shame. His father insisted two or three times more that he sing a *naubat* for his sake.

Then Chelebi answered, "It is not possible to give a concert without an instrument; there is no ecstasy."

However, Sultan Walad was in an ecstatic state and his joy only continued to increase. He said, "I am very weak, and I cannot join you, but I will provide the instrument, you make the ecstasy. I'll sit in a corner while you continue in all tranquility and enjoyment. From time to time, recite, so that I can hear and share your joy."

That night, with Sultan Walad present, a gathering was held until the morning, of such intensity that it can only be described as: *The Night of Power is better than a thousand months* [97:3].

The Cherubim of the Heavenly Assembly were biting their lips in awe of the cherubim that surrounded this sultan, and seeing the holy nature of this assembly, the Holy Spirit (Gabriel) said, "*Oh, would that I had been among them* [4:73]!"

And He Is With You Wherever You May Be [731]

One day, some of the masters of Sufism in the city of Aqshehir took great pains to arrange a great gathering in honor of the Chelebi. After he left, he and his companions went to the Mevlevi *zawiya*. On the way, the king of *khalifas*, Akhi Musa, (May the Mercy of God be upon him) bowed and asked, "What kind of group are those dervishes? What is their state?"

Chelebi answered, "They are agreeable and distinguished people who guard externals, but they come together without God. One who is ignorant of the secret of his innermost secret is equally ignorant of God and is deprived of the truth of: *And He is with you wherever you may be* [57:4]. Among the knowers of God, one who has knowledge of God is one who sees Him, not just one who calls upon Him.

> The soul of one who simply calls upon God is dead;
> the soul of one who knows God has attained.

The spirits (*ruh*) of our Friends are knowers of God. On our spiritual path, the knower is the one who knows God (*khoda-dan*), not one who just calls upon Him (*khoda-khvan*).

> A person without reason cannot know with certainty
> what reason is.
> From this, understand who is the one who knows God.

There are signs to indicate the proximity of God and companionship with Him. Although God's companionship includes everything, His companionship with the perfected one who conveys perfection is something else; this special closeness is one of the characteristics of the prophets and the saints. As my grandfather said:

> You imagine that the proximity of God
> means that the maker of the platter is not far from the plate.
> Don't you see that the proximity of the saints
> has a hundred miracles and celebrations?
> In David's hands iron became wax;
> wax, in your hands, hardens like iron.
> Nearness in regard to creation and nourishment
> are for everyone,
> but these generous ones enjoy the proximity of love's inspiration.
> O father, closeness comes in many different ways.
> The sun shines on gold and the mountains

but gold shares a closeness with the sun
of which the willow knows nothing.
The sun shines near the dry and moist branches—
how can the sun veil itself in front of them?
But what closeness the moist branch,
which gives us ripe fruit to eat, enjoys!
While for the dry branch, closeness to the sun
only causes it to dry more quickly.
See how God has given nearness to everything;
seek that which He has given to those who are aware."

[*Mathnawi* III: 701-709]

Blessings for the Mothers *[732]*

The lively Friends and drinking companions recounted:

One day, a religious scholar, an enlightened poor one (*faqira*), came to pay a visit on Chelebi, bearing unusual gifts and clothes. After a long conversation, she asked:

"What will happen to the unfortunate like myself, on the day of Resurrection? What destiny is reserved for us mothers?"

The Chelebi answered, "God Most High, having bestowed His grace, you will enter the highest Paradise and the *houris* of the celestial garden will be your servants."

She cried, "*Praise to God who, out of His bounty, has made us alight in this abode of eternal life*! [35:35]. What else will there be?"

"You will be clothed in all kinds of beautiful clothing and will drink precious drinks and live in contentment."

"And after that?" she asked.

"Every day the truly faithful and the dervishes will visit with the prophets, the Friends of God, the contented, the martyrs, and the dear ones. They will partake of all the delights of: *There will be found all that the souls might desire, and all that the eyes might delight in* [43:71]. Rising to the pavilions of light, they will devote themselves to contemplation."

"And what else will there be?" asked the *faqira*.

"At last they will gaze upon the Face of God, as the pure wine spoken of in the Qur'an: *God Most High has prepared a wine for his Friends,*[32] and they will be intoxicated for years beyond count,

---

32. *Truly, the record of the truly virtuous is [set down] in a mode most lofty! (19) And what could make you conceive what that mode most lofty will be? (20) A record [indelibly]*

transported beyond themselves in eternal delight."

"And what else will there be?" asked the woman.

"They will know joy and tranquility so great it is beyond description in accordance with: *And with Us there is yet more* [50:35][33] . . . What more could there be than this?"

The *faqira* bowed in all sincerity. She gave all her clothes to the reciters and left full of joy.

I Am Not Flesh, but Light [736]

The great companions recounted:

On his last journey, the Chelebi (May God magnify his remembrance) went from the city of Laranda to the region of Aksaray. In the city of Aksaray, the nobles and shaikhs of the region showed him great respect and held many sema concerts for him. After he had spent about ten days there, one night, after laying his blessed head upon the pillow, he began to groan and cry out and wept while he was sleeping. In the morning the Friends of Certainty (*yaqin*) asked him about these cries.

Chelebi answered, "I had a strange dream in which I heard beautiful voices. I saw myself sitting in a high building overlooking a garden; I could see it through the windows. It was such a garden as *unseen by any eye, in which are sounds that no ear has ever heard.* Paradise itself would be jealous of this garden.

"All kinds of trees and fruits, sweet-smelling herbs and flowers were growing on the banks of the streams that watered this garden. The leaves on the trees were so thick that the rays of the sun did

---

inscribed, (21) witnessed by all who have [ever] been drawn close unto God. (22) Behold, [in the life to come] the truly virtuous will indeed be in bliss: (23) [resting] on couches, they will look up [to God]: (24) upon their faces you will see the brightness of bliss. (25) They will be given a drink of pure wine whereon the seal [of God] will have been set, (26) pouring forth with a fragrance of musk. To that [wine of paradise], then, let all such aspire as [are willing to] aspire to things of high account: (27) for it is composed of all that is most exalting - (28) a source [of bliss] whereof those who are drawn close unto God shall drink. [83:18-28]

33. *And [on that Day] paradise will be brought within the sight of the God-conscious, and will no longer be far away; [and they will be told:] (32) "This is what you were promised - [promised] unto everyone who was wont to turn unto God and to keep Him always in mind - (33) [everyone] who stood in awe of the Most Gracious although He is beyond the reach of human perception, and who has come [unto Him] with a heart full of contrition. (34) Enter this [paradise] in peace; this is the Day on which life abiding begins!" In that [paradise] they shall have whatever they may desire - but there is yet more with Us.* [50:31-35]

not reach the ground of this garden, and in the dense shade, wondrous spiritual beings and beautiful *houris* were strolling about. At the edge of a stream that ran through this rose garden, I saw Mevlana. In a state of ecstasy and bewilderment, I wondered what our Master was doing in this place.

"He made a sign towards me with his blessed hand, saying, ''Arif, what are you doing there? The period of sojourn in the world has come to an end; now, you see the regions where I dwell—come and see what spiritual beauties and worlds you will behold.'

"I wept with delight and cried out upon hearing this invitation and due to the grace of this garden. Now the moment had come to depart for the heavens and to sip from that celebrated cup of perfect well-being."

Then Chelebi recited:

The moment has come to abandon my body and go, naked,
to be nothing but spirit.
Tell this outer form to disappear! Who am I?
The painting may fade, but I am eternal.

The next day, he left for Konya. When he arrived in that city, a slight change in his blessed constitution began; his illness grew worse day by day. One morning, he left his house and went to the blessed tomb, where he stood for a long time without saying anything. All the Friends lined up in rows in front of him. That day was the last Friday in the month of Dhu'l-Qa'da of the year 719 A.H. (January 4, 1320 C.E.). Suddenly, that great luminary, the sun, rose in the east to the height of a spear in the sky and began to turn, like a ball of gold thrown by Divine Power in the arena of Heaven. . . .

Chelebi 'Arif smiled and said:

The saints are the sun of the sun!
From their light, the sun gains its brilliance.

A little later, he continued, "I am weary of this miserable world. How long must I stay under this sun amid this dust and sorrow? The time has come to place my feet on the head of the stars of Farqadan,[34] to rise above the sun and sing above the princes of heaven, and to be delivered from all the changing

34. The Farqadan are two stars near the Ursa Minor (Little Bear) constellation. If the pole star were not visible, as in the southern latitudes, a navigator would use these stars from which to site and chart his course.

colors of existence."

He then recited:

At every moment, the voice of love surrounds us.
We are departing for the heavens! Who yearns to see this sight?
We have been in heaven; we were friends with angels.
Let us all return again, for that is our Homeland . . .

He recited this *ghazal* until the end and walked a bit. The Friends were by his side, ready to be of service, and contemplating his grandeur, began to moan and weep.

"Death is the only remedy," he told them. "While alive, I have seen many wonders and made many journeys, both in the outer world and within. Unoccupied spirits enter the world of form to contemplate the marvels of countries and the wonders of souls, for the acquisition of gnosis, and the peace of Certainty. Now, due to the heaviness of this body, I am powerless to move and cannot continue the journey.

"Let's journey to the future life. In this world, no friend, companion, or anyone remains to share my suffering. The ones who shared my pain were Mevlana and my father. In their absence, how long will I remain concerned with making the best of things in this unhappy world of trials? I burn with longing to see the face of our Master; I am going to find him." Just then, he cried out and gesturing, went into his house and began quietly weeping.

In spite of his state, he offered the Friday prayers. He then honored the noble and sacred tomb with his presence and was clothed in the lights of the secrets of that Majesty.

He then honored the sema with his presence. That day, he experienced troubles of such perfect magnificence that it is impossible to describe it in words. During the sema, he recited this quatrain:

I must travel to the end of the Beloved's road
and leave behind my own existence.
Don't approach this moon boldly!
Come with pale face and moist eyes.

He left the sema and lay down within the area of the tomb where he now rests. Then he said, "The dust of a man is the place where he is buried. Bury the treasure of my being in this place."

That day was like the twin of the Day of Resurrection. A great clamor arose, and the inhabitants of the world above and the world below were immersed in lamentation. On Saturday, Chelebi's blessed face began to show the ravages of illness, and he began the struggle for his life. What remained of his health returned to accompany him and his struggle continued for twenty-five days.

On the night of the 22nd of Dhu'l Hijja, there was a powerful earthquake that lasted for three days, with one tremor after another. Many walls and chimneys of houses collapsed.

The *abdal* of Konya, who was Khwaja Faqih Ahmad's successor and one of the Companions, had remained sitting in the same spot, winter and summer, for forty years. He was called Danishmand (Jurist), because he had begun as a scholar of religion. He was well known for his ability to predict earthly events, and he cried out, "Alas! They are taking the Lamp of Konya! The world will be in disorder; I also am leaving, following after this sovereign."

As the earthquake continued, Chelebi cried, "It is time to depart. Don't you see how the earth leaps in anticipation of devouring the mouthful of our existence? She wants a plump morsel."

Then he recited this verse:

When the earthly grave swallows the morsel of this body
my soul will fly beyond the sky,
because I am not a body; I am light.

He continued, "Glory to God! What marvelous birds have arrived."

He closed his blessed eyes and contemplated the birds of the souls. At every moment it seemed as though he was going to fly away as he made astonishing movements and gestures. The Friends, and all the men and women present, young and old, wept and moaned in sorrow.

"Don't be upset," said Chelebi. "Just as the purpose of our descent into this world was for your benefit, so, too, is our death. We are with you in all circumstances; we are never separate from you, and we will also be with you in the Other World.

"In this world, it is not possible to avoid separation. In the Other World, there shall be union without separation, coming together without dissolution. Let me go in peace. Although this departure appears to be an absence, in reality (*haqiqat*), we are not absent; this is not an absence. A sword cannot cut when it is in its scabbard. When it is unsheathed, then you shall see. From this day on, I will rend the veil of mystery in such a way that the Friends will hear the uproar."

As he was speaking, his dear and illustrious sons, the descendants of the Friends of God, and inheritors of the light of the prophets, the noble Shahzada and the Chelebi Amir 'Adil[35] (May God lengthen both of their lives) came in and sat beside him . . .

Passing into the Ocean [736b]

Then this poor servant, Aflaki, weeping, bowed his head and said, "The Chelebi is leaving on his blessed journey and with the tongue of his state will be saying, 'O God Most Great, bless me in death and in that which follows death.' To whom will he entrust these Friends and what advice does he leave?"

The Chelebi answered, "They belong to Khodavandgar[36] and have nothing to do with me. It is he who will console them."

Aflaki replied, "Unfortunate stranger that I am, I will soon be a sad orphan. What will I do and where will I go?"

"Be in service of the Tomb," he said. "And take care with this service, so that they may take care of you. Don't go anywhere else. And as I suggested, work to gather the stories of our fathers and ancestors, and commit them to paper. Continue until you have completed it, and do not neglect it, so that you might have a shining face in the presence of our Master, and the Friends of God might be content with you as well."

All the Friends wept and were overcome. They trembled at what might come to them from the world beyond and this world of manifestation. Chelebi opened his blessed eyes, recited the following quatrain, and then slept again. The outward appearance disappeared and the reality of meaning was hidden.

O You whose lovely Face is desired by the beauties of the world,
whose two eyebrows are the direction of prayer for lovers,
I have stripped myself of all my attributes,
so that I might dive naked into Your stream.

Then he called out, "Allah, Allah, Allah!" let out a great sigh, and recited this verse:

---

35. Chelebi Amir 'Arif, the son of Sultan Walad, married Daulet Khatun, the daughter of the Amir Qaicar of Tabriz. Together they had two sons and a daughter. The eldest was Shahzada (also known as Amir 'Alim); the younger son was Amir 'Adil, and the daughter was Melika Khatun (also known as Despina).

36. *Khodavandgar*, in other words, indicates Mevlana.

The moment the Sea of God's essence becomes my all,
the beauty of atoms will become bright for me.
I will burn like a candle, so that, in the way of love,
all the "moments" of my life will become one.

Between the noon and afternoon prayers, after the surahs of "Afternoon" [*'Asr*, 103] and "Help" [*Nasr*, 110] had been recited, on Tuesday the 24th of Dhu'l Hijja, 719 A.H. (February 5, 1320 C.E.) he departed with blessing and in complete joy, drawn towards the eternal, primordial, luminous, and Divine center. *Limitless, then, in His glory is He in whose hand rests the mighty dominion over all things; and unto Him will you all be brought back* [36:83], and *Truly, unto God do we belong and, truly, unto Him we shall return* [2:156].

His sanctified soul, wise, and brilliant as a pearl, plunged into the sea of the Light of the Divine Essence.

In that moment, he lay down and gave up his soul,
unfolding like a rose, smiling and joyous.
The light of the sun heard the call to the soul: "*Return* [89:28]!"
She returned promptly to her origin.
He saw the light, and the light of his eyes returned;
the countryside and plains remain yearning for him.

Chelebi Shamsuddin Amir 'Abid

[Aflaki's Chapter IX: 737]

In the same way that Chelebi (May God sanctify his subtle mystery) bestowed abundant favors and innumerable kindnesses upon Chelebi 'Abid while he was alive, at the end of his life, he bestowed upon him his "throne." When 'Arif was leaving the visible world for the world of Unseen Mystery, he conferred upon him the totality of the affairs of his children and his disciples, not by a verbal conveyance of the tongue or speech, but by way of the soul and the light of the heart. All the brethren and children of our Shaikh ('Arif) held him in special regard and served him as the faithful slaves of a king. And due to the perfection of his generosity and innate justice, he abandoned everything other than God.

Calls to Love *[Aflaki's Chapter IX: 742]*

. . . They cannot attain to any of His knowledge except that which He wills them to attain [2:255].

Abu Bakr, the Sincere, throughout his blessed existence, followed the enlightened Prophet (Peace and blessings upon him) and was guided by him in all ways, and the right guidance he received was from the Messenger. The miracles of his descendants, created of heaven and earth, are the result of the Prophet's miracles, peace and blessings upon him.

This is true of the sovereign of mystics, the beloved of the lovers, our Master Jalaluddin (May God sanctify his precious innermost secret). There are calls to love in this *hadith* of the Prophet (Peace and blessings upon him): "O how I long to meet my brothers and my helpers in the Way," and it refers also to Mevlana's blessed existence. In the *Mathnawi*, he describes the grandeur of the approach of this love:

If you have an ear, listen. If you have an eye, see!

The real beloved is that one who is unique,
who is your beginning and your end.
When you find that one,
you'll no longer expect anything else:
that one is both the manifest and the mystery.
He is the master of states and dependent on none.
Month and year are slaves of that beautiful moon.
When he bids the "state," it does his bidding.
when that one wills, bodies become spirit.
He conveys consolation or joy;
unwaveringly present, he is infinite.
He awaits a favorable state;
his hand is the philosopher's stone of states—
if he shakes it, copper becomes intoxicated.
He causes death itself to become sweet—
thorn and lance become narcissus and wild rose.
Man is dependent on circumstances—
sometimes they are favorable, sometimes not.
The Sufi is "the child of the moment,"
yet that pure one (*safi*) is free of moments and states.
States of being depend on his judgment and counsel,
quickened into life by his Messiah-like breath. . . .
One who is sometimes perfect, sometimes not,
isn't worthy of worship,
as Abraham said of the star that disappeared over the horizon—
that which sets and is sometimes this and sometimes that

cannot be the Beloved: *I love not that which sets* [6:76],
nor that which is sometimes pleasant, sometimes not,
one moment water and the next moment fire.
He is the constellation where the moon resides,
not the moon herself.
He is the painting of an idol,
knowing nothing of that idol.
A sufi seeking purity is the child of the moment
and holds it as close as though it were his father.
The pure one is immersed in love of the Glorious.
He is nobody's child and is not concerned with moment or state.
He is immersed in a light described by:
He begets not, nor is He begotten [112:3],
and this belongs to God—
If you are alive, go and seek such a love.
If you are not, you're just a slave of circumstance.

[*Mathnawi* III, 1418-1436]

The special beloved of the Messenger of God in this end of times is the blessed person of Mevlana. The Prophet, Messenger and beloved of God, became manifest from the glorious light of Abraham's prayer, as he said: "I was a prophet on a mission at the request of your father Abraham (Greetings upon him) when he said: '*O our Sustainer! Send them a messenger from among themselves who will recite to them your signs, teach them the Book and wisdom, and cause them to grow in purity*' [2:129]." Likewise, Mevlana appeared because of the prayer of God's Messenger.

The Prophet said, "There is a man among my community
whose substance and thought is like mine.
His spirit sees me by means of the same light
as the light by means of which I see him."

The Lights of the Essence of the Creator

[Aflaki's Chapter IX: 745]

The Lights of the Essence of the Creator (Exalted are His Power and His Word) will shine forever on all beings, in general and in particular. In all times and moments, miracles and extraordinary happenings appear from the outpouring of this Light through the deeds of the prophets and Friends of God (Greetings upon them all). The generous fruits that these miracles produce and which grow, until the end of time, on the blessed tree of their being are confirmed in the truth of this passage: *It is like a good tree, firmly rooted, its branches reaching to the sky, yielding its fruit at all times by its Sustainer's leave* [14:24-25].

If one were to begin to list the virtues and ranks of each one separately, the commentary could never be finished, nor the recording ever completed.

I would need many lives as long as Noah's
to describe this opening and these blessings.

Keep Mentioning God's Name *[Aflaki's Chapter X: i]*

Our Book concludes with remembrance of the chain of transmission of the *dhikr* of *La illaha il Allah, Muhammada Rasulallah* (There is no God but God, and Muhammad is the Messenger of God).

The worthy guardians of the traditions told us the following:

One day, 'Ali, the son of Abu Talib, the Commander of the Faithful, victorious Lion of God (May God ennoble his countenance) asked, "O Messenger of God, show us the best and easiest road to God for God's servant."

The Prophet (God's blessings and peace be upon him) answered, "O 'Ali, make use of that which I have practiced and through which I attained the blessings of prophethood."

"O Prophet, what is it?" 'Ali asked.

Muhammad answered, "It is to persevere in mentioning God's name[37] in seclusion."

'Ali asked, "Is the excellence of the *dhikr* such that all people will practice remembrance of God?"

The Prophet cried, "Hush, O 'Ali, the Resurrection will not take place as long as there is one person left on earth reciting the remembrance of God."

Then the Prophet taught him the way of the *dhikr*, *La illaha il Allah* (There is no God but God). He recited it for him and then said,

37. Resonance with several verses from the Qur'an arises here, e.g.:
He guides to Himself all who turn to Him—
those who have faith and whose hearts find satisfaction in the remembrance of God—
for, truly in the remembrance of God hearts find rest (*ala bi-dhikrillahi tatmainnul qulub*). [13:28]
And truly remembrance of God is the greatest (*wa la dhikr-llahi akbar*) [29:45].

"Be silent and listen, while I remember God three times, then you repeat it, so that I might listen to you."

The Commander of the Faithful, Imam 'Ali, taught this *dhikr* to Hasan of Basri, and he taught it to Habib-i 'Ajami who then taught it to Daoud Ta'i, who taught it to Ma'ruf Karkhi, who taught it to Sari Saqati, who taught it to Junayd of Baghdad.

Junayd conveyed it to Shibli, who taught it to Muhammad Zajjaj who taught it to Abu Bakr Nassaj. The transmission of the *dhikr* then went from Abu Bakr Nassaj to Ahmad Ghazali, then to Ahmad Khatibi of Balkh who taught it to Shams al-A'imma of Sarakhs from whom it passed to our Mevlana Bahauddin Muhammad, known as Bahauddin Walad. Bahauddin Walad taught it to Burhanuddin Mohaqqiq of Tirmidh who transmitted it to our master Jalaluddin Muhammad, may God sanctify their innermost secret. . . .

> So be it, O Lord of All the Worlds, Most Generous and Merciful! Through Your compassion and through the rights of Muhammad, his family and all his companions! Praise be to God alone!

Index of Prophets and Friends of God

Beyond the immediate circle of Mevlana,
his family, and Friends who appear frequently